THE PROGRESSIVE UNDERGROUND

KEV ROWLAND

Vol 5

Edited and scanned by Kevin Rowland
Typeset by Jonathan Downes
Cover by Martin Springett.

Photo on P9 by Steve Shyu
Photo on P320 by Mark Derricutt

First edition by Gonzo Multimedia 2023

c/o Brooks City,
6th Floor New Baltic House,
65 Fenchurch Street,
London EC3M 4BE
Fax: +44 (0)191 5121104
Tel: +44 (0) 191 5849144
International Numbers:
Germany: Freephone 08000 825 699
USA: Freepho*ne* 18666 747 289

© Gonzo Multimedia MMXXIII

All rights reserved. Without limiting the rights under copyright reserved above, no part of this publication may be reproduced, stored in or introduced into a retrieval system, or transmitted, in any form of by any means (electronic, mechanical, photocopying, recording or otherwise), without the prior written permission of both the copyright owners and the publishers of this book.

ISBN: 978-1-908728-19-7

Dedicated to my incredible wife Sara: without her continued love and support, I would never be able to spend so many hours on music.

To my amazing daughters Nicola, Elizabeth, Hannah and Amanda, who make me so very proud every day with everything they achieve.

Finally, to my grandchildren Katherine and Evan, who are a constant source of joy.

Foreword

I am humbled and honoured to be given the opportunity to write a little something for my friend, author, and musical colleague Kev Rowland. Music tells a story and Kev knows how to present that story while adhering to great journalistic principles.

I have been in the music business in one form or another for the past 40 years. Starting out in music retail as a teenager back in the late '70s, to owning and operating a few brick and mortar music retail stores over the years in California, Florida and New York.

Nearly two decades ago I was fortunate enough to move to a small village in upstate New York for a few years and create a music experience for the residents which included a weekend All Genre Music Festival called Summer Breeze and a Community Art and Music Festival that is now in its 17th year. Starting out as a small CD store (Melodic Revolution) we quickly realized that the town needed more cultural events, adding an art gallery by day and live music venue (Live at the Revolution) at night. Initially, acoustic music only showcasing the wonderful local talent. Very quickly this would evolve into nightly shows with numerous bands not only from around the country but from Europe, Canada and South America.

Like the music itself, my musical journey has always had its twists and turns and my retail store would become a progressive rock music label as I found myself relocating from the winters of NY to the land of perpetual warmth of sunny Florida, taking its name from the store, Melodic Revolution Records (MRR) was launched. My intent had always been to focus on melodic rock, but my progressive roots kept finding new music and MRR has become a progressive label with an impressive list of artists. Three years ago PeacockSunrise Records (PSR) sub-label of MRR emerged to support our growing list of genre-bending artists.

Always loving music, and trying to reach new audiences for my artists, I spent about a decade broadcasting on AiirRadio and House of Prog, starting out playing all styles of digital music to doing vinyl only shows on the latter. I also publish two music news and reviews blogs; ReZonatZ and Power of Prog.

I was first introduced to **The Progressive Underground** series of books by Kev Rowland some years ago. The books focus on progressive rock album reviews he has been writing for over 30 years. While there are many books about Progressive Rock and Progressive Rock bands, none of them focus on album reviews. It was natural that Kev and I would strike up a friendship through an introduction by a mutual friend.

It was 5 years ago almost to the day that I had my first conversation with Kev Rowland based in New Zealand, I had sent him a Facebook request and followed up with a message. I was recommended to Kev by my good friend, Olav Martin Bjørnsen, I had met Olav at RoSFest in Gettysburg, PA back in 2012. At the time Olav wrote the press releases for the festival as well as being a DJ and music journalist for Progressor, Prog Archives and AiiRadio and later at House of Prog, an Internet Radio station that we both volunteered our time at. Coincidentally Kev had just written me to tell me that he had just reviewed an album by Nth Ascension, a UK Prog Rock band, and another album by their keyboardist Darrel Treece Birch who had released a solo project, both were artists of mine at Melodic Revolution Records.

Kev told me that he had also written previous reviews for Peter Matuchniak another MRR artist, and as we wrote one another back and forth I learned that he had already reviewed 338 albums to date, that year, that's like 2 albums a day 7 days a week! He divulged that he was pretty much a prolific writer that enjoyed writing music reviews when he wasn't holding down his regular job. At this point I asked Kev if he would mind if I published his reviews on Power of Prog my music news blog as he was already contributing to Prog Archives, Progressor, as well as Amplified whom he had been writing for since 1988. Kev was more than happy to have another source of readers for his reviews, now he had an even larger audience with Power of Prog publishing his work. In fact, over the last 5 years Power of Prog has published hundreds of album reviews.

In January of 2021 I reached out to Kev and asked if he would like to contribute to

ReZonatZ a second music news publication that I had just launched: this site is dedicated to all genres of music unlike Power of Prog which is a site dedicated solely to all things Prog. Kev was all in, as he also wrote reviews for anyone that had music and wanted an ear and a review. By mid 2022 Kev started sending me interviews that he was conducting as well as concert reviews.

I have been reading album reviews about my favorite bands since the 1970s. There are many reviewers over the years that I have come to trust in various publications. Simply said, I love Kev's writing; it is his relentless passion for painting a picture of any given release much like a musician does with their music.

This is Kev's fifth book in the series and is just as relevant as all the books that came before. Kev refuses to hold back, as he's written thousands of reviews not just focused on Progressive Rock, but many other genres: jazz, blues, punk, pop, metal, etc., he feels his audience deserves the unvarnished truth from his ears and heart.

Kev doesn't just tell you what he likes or doesn't about an album, he also does his homework and researches the band he is reviewing. He will not only give you the history of the band but also the backstory of the album he is reviewing.

Over the years Kev has become a good friend and a major contributor to ReZonatZ and Power of Prog. Additionally, he has always been happy to provide honest heartfelt album reviews for artist releases on both Melodic Revolution and PeacockSunrise Records: we are so grateful for his support.

The Progressive Underground is one of the most important books on Progressive Rock and an essential part of any proper music literary collection. Kev has introduced the world to great music and is helping preserve its legacy through the pages of **The Progressive Undergroun**d, now it's time to crack open the book and discover "music you didn't know you would love".

Nick Katona, Melodic Revolution Records, PeacockSunrise Records

Introduction

To misquote a phrase from Richard Adams, we have now a trilogy in five parts. When I first started thinking about compiling my progressive rock reviews and interviews into a book, it was always planned that it would contain my writings from the years 1991-2006. I had been inspired by the excellent 'Strawberry Bricks Guide to Progressive Rock' which finished its coverage in 1982, and was annoyed there was nothing which included "my" scene (and apart from some specific band histories that is still the case today). That period was when the mass media's contempt for the genre was at its height, and included the days when the internet was either non-existent or in its infancy, while personally it neatly encompassed the years when I was running Feedback fanzine in the UK.

I was involved with Feedback from its earliest beginnings as a newsletter for Mensa's Rock Music Special Interest Group in 1988, before becoming secretary myself in 1990 and running it until we emigrated to New Zealand in 2006. The concept was always to compile a single book, which soon became an issue when the text amounted to more than half a million words. The original concept no longer worked as it was too large, so it was suggested that instead it should be broken into smaller sections and include all the album artwork. This resulted in The Progressive Underground Volumes 1-3, which really is just one large book, divided into more easily digestible chunks.

The positive reaction was more than I could ever have imagined, and it was wonderful to feel I had shone a light on a dark period for progressive rock music. I got back to normality (whatever that is), knowing I had accomplished something special, but was soon being asked questions by many artists, namely "when are you going to print my

The Progressive Underground Vol 5

reviews?" or "why isn't my album in the book?". My response always was that TPU Vols 1-3 were over a specific period, from 1991-2006, and the reason they were not included was because that particular piece of writing had been later. However, it did start me thinking. The older writings were hard to pull together as I only had that in hard copy fanzines, but all my more recent scribblings were in electronic form, so just how difficult would it be to compile another one?

The result was Volume 4, which covered my writings from 2008-2013, and yet again it was well received but I soon started getting the same questions as before, except now there was expectation that of course there would be another collection and when would I get it out?

Well, here it is, just two years after Volume 4, we now have the next in the series, this time covering my writings from 2014 into 2018. As with Volume 4, this is complete, in that it has the full alphabet of A-Z, plus the interviews I undertook at the time and even a few live reviews.

This volume sees an introduction from Nick Katona, one of the most important promoters of progressive rock there is, running labels, putting on gigs, supporting artists and running his own radio shows. On the rear cover there are comments from Peter Matuchniak and Steve Bonino, who have both released multiple albums on Nick's label, and I am pleased that through my musical journey I have become friends with all of them. While all those who have contributed this way to the series so far have all been from Europe, this time we have three from America showing how truly global this genre is, although it should be mentioned that Peter is actually British and first came to fame in the UK underground prog scene of the Eighties.

I truly hope you enjoy discovering yet more bands and albums which are new to you. Use this and the other books as a guide, a way of seeking out wonderful music which has been overlooked for no other reason than being the "wrong" genre. Prog never died, it just went underground.

Read on, I hope you enjoy it.

Kev Rowland, New Zealand
December 2023

Album Reviews

25 YARD SCREAMER
KEEP SENDING SIGNALS

I was more than a little surprised to discover this is the sixth studio album from 25YS, a Welsh progressive rock outfit who formed in 2002 after Donal Owen (drums) and Matt Clarke (bass) augmented Nick James (guitar, vocals) at a showcase gig in Bracknell, for his then solo project. This 2016 album features four brand new pieces of music and four reworkings of very early material, again featuring the collaboration of Tom Bennett (keyboards, orchestrations) who had assisted with the recording of 2013's 'Something That Serves To Warn Or Remind' (the band is still a trio when playing live).

Apparently, the band have been quite heavy in the past, but here they are showing a more restrained side to the music, having very much a classic neo-prog sound . The guitars are doing some interesting things, but there is no doubt there are troubles with the mix. The drums are too far to the front, and don't sound nearly powerful enough (which is a real shame, as Donal is putting his heart and soul into this), while Nick doesn't really have the Steve Hogarth vocal quality that he is going for, so possibly they should also have been pulled back a little. As it stands there is the impression that they do have some things doing for them, and I am sure that in the live environment they would be well worth watching. But six albums down the road the recording quality should be better than this.
Feb 2018

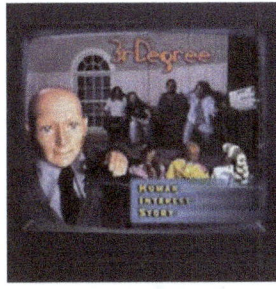

3RDEGREE
HUMAN INTEREST STORY
When I heard the 2012 album 'The Long Division" I was blown away, and somewhat alarmed that here was yet another band that had been going for some years which I had not previously come across. Robert Pashman then kindly sent me a copy of their 2008 album, which I also loved, but I hadn't heard any of their material that was released prior to their split. That has now been corrected as 10t Records have issued a remastered version of their 1996 album 'Human Interest Story'. Now, I can't compare the sonic quality to the original self-released edition as I haven't heard it, but I do know that the sound quality on this is extremely good indeed. It also comes with a bonus song, but the track sequence has been amended and it appears the band have taken the opportunity to revisit this without re-recording anything.

The first thing that strikes the listener is that this doesn't sound as if it is the best part of 20 years old, but rather is fresh and striking, almost as if it is a follow-up to the last album as opposed to one that preceded it by many years. As with all their albums, this comes across as melodic and immediate with strong vocals, good harmonies, great piano and keyboards, strong guitar (with a nice use of both acoustic and electric) and a rhythm section that gets it just right. The band always strikes me as being heavily influenced by City Boy, along with Steely Dan, Alan Parsons Project, and Peter Gabriel among others. They know a hook when they hear one, yet also understand when to throw in a hard edge to create impact. Listen to "Top Secret" and you will see what I mean, as the guitar is quite abrasive with strong keyboards and the whole band punching hard while George's vocals are clear and rising above it all. This could easily have found its way on City Boy's 'The Day The Earth Caught Fire': and given that album is one of my all-time favourites, this isn't something I say lightly.

This is the third of their four albums I have heard, and it is three for three as again I find myself unable to give this anything but 5 *'s. The more I play it the more I love it, and each time I find something else to enjoy and concentrate on. Superb.
Mar 2014

LEE ABRAHAM
DISTANT DAYS
Although Lee first came to prominence with the release of his second solo album 'View From The Bridge' in 2004, he is probably best known by many as being bassist with Galahad between 2005 and 2009, playing on 'Empires Never Last' and the live 'Resonance' DVD as well as numerous gigs. He released 'Idle Noise' with Steve Kingman in 2008, then followed that with 'Black and White' in 2009, since when he has been performing live as well as working with other artists. But after a gap of five years, he is now back with his fourth solo release, 'Distant Days'. On this he is joined by Gerald Mulligan (Credo) on drums, and other members of his core

live band Chris Harrison on guitars, Alistair Begg on bass/Chapman Stick and Rob Arnold on keyboards. Jon Barry and Simon Nixon added their guitar talents and Lee was delighted to welcome Robin Armstrong (Cosmograf) on acoustic guitar and Dave Phillips on backing vocals while he also had numerous other guests including Karl Groom (Threshold/Shadowland), Dec Burke (Darwin's Radio/Frost*/Brave New Sky/Solo), Marc Atkinson (Riversea/Nine Stones Close/Mandalaband/Solo), John Young (The John Young Band/Lifesigns) and Steve Thorne (Solo)

This is one of those albums where the writer wants the listener to really pay attention to the lyrics, which here deal with topics such as childhood, the oppression of Government authority and the cause of the recent global recession. As Lee says, "Some of the lyrics may sound heavy going, but I wanted to cover subjects that everyone could relate to, especially here in the UK. Recently, we have had a lot of scrutiny of our government's behaviour and how it goes about governing us. It also looks at the financial institutions that are also largely to blame for the recession we're just trying to sort out. But rest assured, there's happy stuff in there too!"

It kicks off with a mighty bang with the commercial prog metal of "Closing The Door", which mixes tempos and moods with plenty of strong guitars and swirling keyboards. In many ways this is a great opener as not only does it set a mood and a level of expectation, but it also showcases many of Lee's ideas as although it is prog metal, there are times when it is strongly Neo, while there is also room for a much more reflective element even though that can be tempered by a kick ass guitar solo. The use of different singers works well, and isn't the distraction that it can sometimes be, just because they all fit in so strongly together and there is always very much a band feel and direction as opposed to 'just' a project.

One band I kept being reminded of at different times when playing this was Asia, as not only are the harmonies spot on but there are loads of great hooks and the production is second to none. This just doesn't feel like an underground release on the artist's own label, but rather something that has had some serious money and time put into it. Closing number "Tomorrow Will Be Yesterday" is one of the two epics, and is the longest at fifteen minutes, starting with some beautifully reflective and delicate piano, but it soon becomes something that is far more bombastic and with real presence, although the piano is never too far away. Overall, this is a real delight, and I only hope it isn't five years until the next one.
Jun 2014

LEE ABRAHAM/STEVE KINGMAN
IDLE NOISE
Somehow, at some point in time (could be any time in the last eight years), I ended up with a copy of this album by Lee Abraham (vocals, guitars, keyboards, bass) and Steve Kingman (vocals, guitars, keyboards, drums). Now, Lee was bassist with Galahad for a period, and I have reviewed one of his solo albums and have heard bits and pieces of others, so thought I'd drop over to his website and get some more information. But it's not listed among his solo albums, and there is no mention of it in his biography. So, a trip

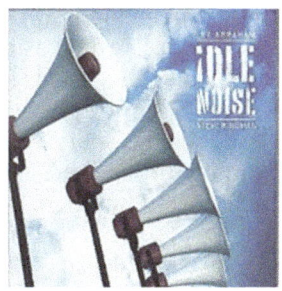
over to the amazing ProgArchives and the same thing there – although Lee is listed, and I mention this album in my review of one of his solo works, this is just non-existent. This piqued my curiosity, as well as getting me to start doubting my sanity, so I did a search of the web to see if there have been any reviews anywhere or if this was just a figment of my imagination and I had mis-catalogued it somehow. Thankfully I did come across a nice review of this, in Polish, which reaffirmed all I thought about it, but why has this seemingly disappeared from existence?

I have no answer to that, apart from thinking that it's a real shame, as although there is nothing here that will set the world on fire, it is an album that in many ways is quite beautiful. Engineered by none other than Karl Groom, who also worked with Lee on some of his other releases, this album is solid, mature, and packed full of harmonies and great songs. It is quite keyboard led in many ways, but the focus here is always on producing a solid song, full of melodies and hooks, as opposed to being flash and over the top. No-one could ever accuse this of being bombastic, yet at the same time it is much more than just simple easy listening. It is music to drift into, something that can be enjoyed at first hearing. It is delicate and restrained and moves along at its own pace as opposed to being driven frenetically. There is nothing to prove here, it is all about the songs and performing them to the best of the players' ability. A little bit of Jadis here, a dollop of John Wetton there, this music creates a world that I want to inhabit. It's just a mystery to me there is so little written about it anywhere.
Jan 2017

ABWH
LIVE AT THE NEC
Like many Yes fans, I wasn't too sure what was happening with the band with all the line-up changes they went through. I was surprised at just how good 'Drama' was, but after that I felt that the rest of their releases either didn't sound like Yes to me, or were patchy (and to be honest, the next really good album after 'Drama' was 'Fly From Here'). So, when back in the late Eighties I heard that Jon Anderson, Bill Bruford, Rick Wakeman, and Steve Howe were joining forces to record a new album I was incredibly excited, and I wasn't disappointed with the results. But as we all know by now, that project only lasted the one album and there have been few official live albums available by that line-up, but here we have a double CD of their performance at the NEC on 24th October 1989. As well as the four they were of course joined by Tony Levin on bass/stick, with Julian Colbeck on additional keyboards and Milton McDonald on additional guitar.

Musically it is interesting to hear how the songs from the album fit in so easily with the Yes numbers, and it really does sound as if the classic Yes line-up has just expanded slightly and is well at home with all the music and does everything justice. Bill was of course playing is electronic kit at the time, so it does sound a little different, but given his

mastery and control it all makes sense. The booklet is a little strange in that while it talks about how the decision was made to get back together, it is almost as if it was written as a press release for the 'new' album, and that shows had yet to be performed. Given this is a booklet for a live album that seems unusual to say the least, and there are no group photos of the band performing, which is what one might expect, instead of solo studio shots. It's great to have a Pete Frame family tree detailing where they came from but fitting the Yes/ABWH story on one page of a CD booklet is not ideal – I have 20/20 vision but there is no way of reading the detail comfortably. But that really is nit-picking, as this is all about the music, and that is just wonderful. The production is very clear indeed, and kudos to whoever was behind the controls, but again there is no information about who engineered, produced, and mixed this. Simply put, if you are a Yes fan then this album shows what could have been, with songs such as "And You And I" just superb. Sure, the lack of details is annoying, but for anyone interested at all in the music of Yes (and there can't be many progheads who aren't) then this is essential.
Jan 2014

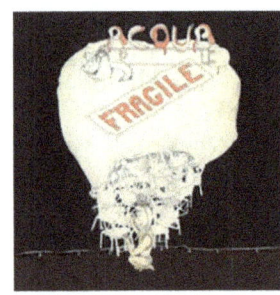

ACQUA FRAGILE
A NEW CHANT
When I was asked if I would review this album, I obviously said yes, partly because I knew I already had at least one other of theirs in my collection. Now, when you've been writing about music for as long as I have and have the odd album or two in one format or another, sometimes things don't connect as quickly as they should. Yes, I do have another Acqua Fragile album in my collection, 'Mass-Media Stars', which was released back in 1974!! Unlike many other Italian bands at the time, they decided to perform in English, with songs that weren't always quite as symphonic as the rest of the Italian progressive scene, and these two factors really put them up against it. But the real nail in the coffin for the band was the departure of Bernardo Lanzetti to PFM, and although the band did keep going for a while, they never recorded again.

Over the years Bernardo has appeared in different places (I remember interviewing him when he joined Mangala Vallis), but now, more than 40 years since his departure the group have reformed around him, drummer Piero Canavera and bassist Franz Dondi along with multiple guests. 'Chocolate Kings' is probably my favourite PFM album, the one where Bernardo made his debut for the band, but arguably he is singing better than ever, with a band that are bringing together styles that have as much in common with neo-prog, Gabriel-era Genesis, and IQ as they do with the Italian scene. This is glorious prog, soaring and symphonic when it needs to be, layered, and structured at times, but simple and reflective at others. If ever an album oozed class from every pore, then this must be it. There are ballads, there is an Italian march, there is intensity but throughout there is also always beauty. Bernardo's Chapman-style vocals have weathered and become more rounded, as happened with the Family man, but still have the stridency when it is required. The only real question now, is do we have to wait 43 years for the next one? Superb.
Feb 2018

The Progressive Underground Vol 5

AFENGINN
LUX

When I went over onto their Bandcamp site to see how they described their music themselves, I see that Danish group Afenginn call themselves "world", "ambient", "contemporary", "classical", "folk" and "Nordic" while PA list them as RIO/avant-prog. I think that there is a great deal of jazz in what they are doing and if I had to force them into a musical pigeonhole that is where I would put them. But, as you can see, there is a lot going on and they don't really fit anywhere. The band themselves comprise Rasmus Kr'yer (clarinet, bass clarinet, contra bass clarinet), Niels Skovmand (violin), Kim Rafael Nyberg (mandolin), Erik Olevik (contrabass) and Rune Kofoed (drums, percussion) while they also have guests in Bent Clausen (marimba, vibraphone, waterphone, percussion), Mads Hyhne (trombone) and Nikolaj Busk who provides grand piano on "Autumnus Elegia". Kim Rafael Nyberg composed all the music, which to my ears is somewhat strange as the mandolin rarely takes centre stage. I am also a little surprised that Bent is just a guest, as his marimba playing is key to the overall sound.

In many ways these guys come across as a highly orchestrated jazz group, with everyone knowing their part and playing it to the full. It is an album that is incredibly hard to describe as in many ways it is quite different to anything I have heard before, although Robin Taylor and possibly Frank Zappa did come to mind as potential influences (and give that Robin is also Danish and has been prolific over quite a long period I would think that this could be quite possible). Certainly, if you enjoy the more structured Robin Taylor's Universe then this could well be for you. This is something that one should hear before listening, but luckily it is possible to do just that at their Bandcamp site. I found it polished and intriguing and am certainly pleased it came my way.
Mar 2014

ALGABAS
ANGELS AND DEMONS

Sergey Milyaev (bass, vocals) first formed Algabas in 2007 in the Northern Russian city of Vladimir, with the band name meaning "thinking ahead" in Kazakh. He was already a locally well-known musician and writer, but it was only during the recording of their debut album in 2012 that the line-up crystallised as he was joined by Ilya Frolov (keyboards, guitar), Vladimir Mikhailov (guitar) and Albert Pogosian (drums). The album was originally released through Bandcamp as a digital only release, but it has now been made available by Mals who also translated the album title into English, but that is the only real change as the album itself is performed in Russian.

If ever there was an album out of time, then this is it. Realistically this should have come out twenty years ago, as it is to the early Nineties that these guys look for their inspiration. It took me a while to work out who they sounded like on the opening title cut, but eventually I twigged that it was very much like Winter performing the classic "Toybox". But they have taken their cue from more than just the Irish lads and have brought together elements of IQ and Marillion with Pallas and Citizen Cain and have also then thrown in some traditional Russian folk elements, which gives the album quite a twist.

Vocally Sergey is not as sweet and pleasant as many prog singers, but I don't have an issue with it and like the additional edge. The keyboards are for the most part basic, but the guitars and bass are strong, as are the drums, and while the result may be slightly off-balance for some, I found I really enjoyed it. I have been playing this album far more than I normally would to review, as there is something here that appeals to me, although I find it hard to put my finger on it. Possibly it is just hearkening back to the early Nineties when the neo scene was so buoyant, as these guys would have fitted right in back then.
Jun 2014

ALSO EDEN
[REDACTED]
This is the fourth studio album from South-Western neo-preggers Also Eden, but although I am sure I heard the debut when it came out in 2006, I have somehow missed these guys through the years, and I can see that based on this I am going to have to undertake some searching as this is superb from start to finish. I know they have been through some line-up changes but as I am treating this as basically a new band, I can't comment on what impact that may have had on their overall sound, all I know is that I like this. A lot. Rich Harding's vocals remind me of a lower version of Galahad's Stu Nicholson, with the same quality and melody yet with the edge at times of Credo's Mark Colton. Certainly, on a musical front there are similarities with the aforementioned Credo as well as IQ, but although I mention these just to give some sort of idea of the sound these guys are very much their own band.

I have often thought that some progheads look down on the 'neo-prog' genre, and some of the bands themselves hate being called that, but to me this album epitomizes all the best from the Nineties when I and many others (but not enough, let's be honest) traipsed around from Walthamstow to Whitchurch and all points in between as we tried to support the progressive underground. It brings back the memories of hearing Winter for the first time when I was the only person in the audience (Red Lion Brentford – sadly missed, but never forgotten), or jumping around to the madness of Grace or the metallic monsters that were Mentaur and Freewill. Harmony vocals, great riffs and hooks, keyboards and a rhythm section all joined together, who could wish for more? This is progressive rock that brings a smile to the face of the listener and the desire to get up and move, as they remember that the second word of the genre is indeed "rock", something that often gets overlooked. Sheer fun from start to end, here is a band I need to hear more of.
Mar 2014

ALTAVIA
KREOSOTE
AltaVia are a new band to me, but apparently, they formed in 2008 in a small town in northern Italy, when after leaving his former band, Andrea Stagni (keyboards and vocals) started searching for new musicians. A friend introduced him to Marcello Bellina (drums, vocals), Mauro Monti (guitars, vocals) and Giuliano Vandelli (bass), who coincidentally were looking for a keyboard player for a new project, so it suited everyone. Although they were from different musical backgrounds, they were keen to all move in a new direction, even if that direction was taking them solidly back into the Nineties. The line-up was finalised when they brought in a backing singer, Betty Copeta, to assist with the harmonies.

This is the second album, released in 2016, of which I have only just become aware, and the initial reaction is that the guys have been listening to classic It Bites, have brought in some serious doses of IQ and have tempered it all with some modern Yes. They are a long way removed from the classically based Italian progressive scene, but instead are more melodic and modern in their approach, with some great rock guitar. This is fresh and invigorating, laid back but also with some strident riffs and attack, combined with lush vocals and harmonies. There are times when they almost fall into Camel territory, but although they can happily sit within that relaxed form of music, they normally pull themselves out and create some very special sounds indeed. It is an incredibly enjoyable album, from the first note to the last, and is immediate and powerful. I can only hope that my delay in hearing this album means that there is a new one to come soon!
Dec 2017

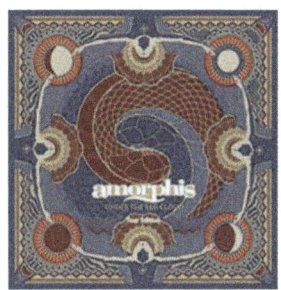
AMORPHIS
UNDER THE RED CLOUD (TOUR EDITION)
Formed in Helsinki in 1990, Amorphis have moved from being a death metal act to one that has incorporated many different styles and textures. A song could be "straight" death metal, but also containing flute, or a rock song could be based around a piano and acoustic guitar, with a low baritone vocal instead of a gruff death growl. So, they have become a band that are masters of many sounds, and in 2015, they kicked off the celebrations for the 20th anniversary of 'Tales From The Thousand Lakes'. Although they were touring hard, they kept returning to the studio to write and record their twelfth album with famed producer Jens Bogren (Soilwork, Kreator etc.) at his Fascination Street Studio in Örebro. The result of this two-month recording session was once again a heavy, melodic statement, called 'Under The Red Cloud.' During the recordings, the sextet was joined by some famous guest musicians: Chrigel Glanzmann (Eluveitie) played flutes on "The Four Wise Ones", "Death Of A King" and "Tree Of Ages", Martin Lopez (ex-Opeth) provided percussion on "Death Of A King" while Aleah Stanbridge (Trees of Eternity) sang guest vocals on "The Four Wise Ones", "Sacrifice" and "White Night".

The result of a band prepared to experiment, a producer who knows how to capture the best of guys prepared to play loud and hard, plus additional guest musicians, resulted in an album that is very special indeed. It is no surprise to see they consequently toured with Nightwish and Arch Enemy on the same bill, as they are the perfect link between the two. They always maintain a high level of melody and move between different genres (often within the same song), so they can drop from folk metal into melodic death into metal and then even move into something softer if that is where the music takes them.

Released in September 2015, the album was viewed as a great success, with their first ever chart entry in United Kingdom and Australia, as well as their highest ever entries in Germany, Switzerland, Austria, Belgium, the Netherlands, and France. In August 2016, at 'An Evening With Friends' at the Helsinki Festival in Huvila, the band performed a very special set list with guest musicians and friends "We were honoured to take part in the Helsinki Festival in Huvila, so therefore we wanted to do something special for that particular night," states guitarist Tomi Koivusaari. "The gig itself happened in a large tent in the very centre of Helsinki on a late summer evening. The Huvila-tent has quite long history, so there was already some excitement in the air beforehand. We wanted to invite some guests to be featured on that show - musicians we already had worked with during these years and musicians we have a huge respect for, so Sakari Kukko, Pekko Käppi and Anneke van Giersbergen joined us on that evening with friends. Originally, Aleah Starbridge was supposed to join as well, as she sang on the 'Under The Red Cloud' album, but sadly she passed away before that. It was surely a night to remember!". These shows are now part of the new tour edition, as the original album now has two additional bonus songs, as well as the live tracks from Helsinki.

The live set starts with acoustic guitar, violin, saxophone, and piano, and one really does have to stop and realise that this is/was a death metal act. The vocals are certainly not one would expect from a band of that genre. This was a special night, and any time I can listen to Anneke van Giersbergen perform is going to be alright with me!

This was already an excellent album, and the additional CD has ensured that those who haven't already purchased this need to rush out and get it now, if not sooner.
Mar 2017

APOGEE
THE ART OF MIND
Apogee is a side project of Versus X singer, guitarist and composer, Arne Schäfer, and here he provides everything except for drums, which are provided by Eberhard Graef. According to the press release this 2015 album revives the typical characteristics of the golden age of prog, and references Jethro Tull, Yes, Genesis, Gentle Giant, Rush, Zappa, and UK. Hmm, I guess that means that the album I'm listening to isn't that one at all, as this is the type of album that gives prog a bad name. Normally, when I come across an album where the opening song is twenty minutes long, and the others are all eight minutes plus then I am singing the praises right off the bat.

Here, not so much.

There are bits here and there that are quite pleasant, but just when I think it's just me there is another dire passage, or melody switch that doesn't make sense. It is almost as if he has taken those classic bands and has tried to pull together bits and pieces into a coherent whole, but if he was given a jigsaw puzzle there are pieces missing and he's lost the picture he is supposed to be recreating. I find it incredible this is his eighth album, as in many this is reminiscent of so many tapes I was being sent more than twenty-five years ago, although in fairness the production is a lot better (and easily the best part).

My last review of an Apogee album had me feeling rather the same way, that this is likely never to darken my player again.
Feb 2017

ARGOS
A SEASONAL AFFAIR
Argos are a German quartet, who released their debut back in 2009 and this is the fourth. They have also brought in a few guest musicians, including Andy Tillison (PO90, The Tangent and others), so they have three different keyboard players involved, but strangely this isn't an overtly keyboard based album. What this is, is something that is looking back into the Canterbury scene, but with an Eighties twist to it, as opposed to going back into Seventies or Sixties, which can create some almost jarring counterpoints at times. "Divergence" reminds me of Thomas Dolby every time I play it, and I'm sure that's not the intention, as the latter part of the song is nothing like the former and when Thomas Klarmann repeatedly sings line "How did it come to this?" I found myself agreeing with him and asking myself the same question.

This isn't a bad album though, far from it, but I did find it somewhat disjointed, and it is when they let the music naturally flow in a more relaxed manner that they come into their own. It is almost as if they were trying too hard, and the result is something which is forced and therefore not as easy and interesting to listen to as it could be. The use of saxophone is inspired (care of guest Marek Arnold (Toxic Smile, United Progressive Fraternity), as is the flute from Thomas, yet while there are some wonderful moments on here, there isn't enough for me to keep revisiting it.
Mar 2017

ARKAIK
NEMETHIA
I can remember the old days when we used to discuss is something was hard rock or heavy metal, but now the music we all love has become so diverse that even sub genres have sub genres to describe what it is that we listen to. One of my personal favourites is progressive technical death metal, and there can be few who do it as well as Arkaik. This is their fourth full length for Unique Leader and is probably their most ambitious studio

album to date. It was produced, engineered, and mixed by Zack Ohren (Immolation, Fallujah, Suffocation, Decrepit Birth et al.), and features guest appearances by Joe Haley of Psycroptic, Arde Ostowari formerly of Burning The Masses, Stephen Paulson of the San Francisco Symphony Orchestra, and former Arkaik guitarist Craig Peters, as well as Gabe Seeber from The Kennedy Veil and Decrepit Birth (live) performing drums for the entire album. The cover art and booklet were designed by visionary artist Tyler Space, who worked with the band on their previous release, 'Lucid Dawn'.

They created a series of wildly psychedelic concept albums revolving around a protagonist named Cyrix, a disillusioned character in a dystopian society. Cyrix' latest journey introduces new characters and brings you into a world of dark occultists, magical allies, and hidden forces. From resurrecting ancient goddesses to cracking the codes of reality and activating hyper dimensional stargates, the chronicle of Cyrix continues.

Said founding vocalist Jared Christianson of the record's concept, "This album fully sets the stage and builds on the story we started developing two albums ago with Cyrix and 'Metamorphignition'. We've begun weaving together our own mythos of synchronicity and symbolism to encapsulate and distil the journey of the alchemist through the gnostic dream. It attempts to reveal through storytelling and allegory that we can experience real freedom and discover the inner treasures that guide us to who, what, and where we want to be, if we are willing to pull back the veil of lies blinding us from the truth of our nature. If I could sum up everything we've done so far, my personal journey and our message as a band in three words it would be the lyric 'pain to power' from the song "Telegnosis". To me, it's about transmuting your struggles into strengths and refining your personal power and will. I really enjoyed making this album and hope people dig it!"

Massively over the top in every sense, this is essential to anyone into this sub-genre as it rarely gets any better than this.
Sep 2017

ART ROCK CIRCUS
VARIATIONS ON A DREAM
I am as much a fan of strange time signatures and music moving in weird directions as the next proghead, but with this album it seems that I am somewhat missing the point. This just doesn't feel like a full-blown release to me, as if there is something not fully formed. Part of that must be down to the production, the quality of which seems to vary greatly throughout the album, as well as the music itself. There are passages, and indeed songs, where this is truly striking. There is a great deal going on, and it all makes musical sense. Who needs vocals when the music is as complex and dynamic as this? But there are other times when it just doesn't seem to gel, and to my ears

"Variation 7" would have sounded even better without the bass, as the drums and vibraphone do enough to more than carry it through. Overall, it is an album that to me contains a lot of promise, with Zappa and ELP being just two of the many influences on display, and the use of disharmony and repeated melodic structures are mostly well done, but overall, this is an album that I just couldn't warm to.
Mar 2014

ART ZOYD
44 ½: LIVE + UNRELEASED WORKS
Over the years my musical tastes have broadened, which is probably both a good and a bad thing when one is as much of a musical addict as I am. A quick check on the Mac tells me I have more than 11,000 albums, a terabyte of music, stored there, and that doesn't include all the CDs and vinyl in the study. Over the years I have taken advice from both critics and friends and have investigated music I should have known much earlier in life. I don't know how or where, but at some point, I became aware of Art Zoyd, and their 1976 album 'Symphonie Pour Le Jour Où Brûleront Les Cités', and from then on, I have been a keen investigator of their works as they are like nothing else I have come across, although they are often cited within the RIO movement. So, when I heard that Cuneiform (one of my favourite labels) was going to release a set containing 12 CDs, 2 DVDs, 2 books and 2 posters I knew I just had to have it. This was a huge undertaking for the label, as the set was going to be the largest and most artistically lavish project they had ever been part of, and consequently they checked with fans to see if they would purchase it before they went ahead with the deal, and luckily enough there are enough people with discerning taste to make this a reality in November.

The tale told by '44½' incorporates everything from decades-old demos for brilliant but abandoned pieces to live recordings of multimedia extravaganzas involving film, theatre, and more. It encompasses intimate trio performances as well as full orchestral assaults featuring dozens of musicians in full flight. It offers explosive industrial soundscapes and sweeping symphonic surges, quiet dread and monumental wallop, delicate acoustic chamber pieces and bustling electronic outbursts. Art Zoyd has always been a band in flux, not only stylistically but in terms of personnel as well. Countless musicians have come and gone through the band's ranks over the years, but most of them can be heard here, with core players like bassist/cellist Thierry Zaboitzeff, trumpeter Jean-Pierre Soarez, keyboardist Patricia Dallio, and violinist/keyboardist Gérard Hourbette providing the through-line. On recordings that go all the way back to 1975, this sprawling set—you can't capture the gist of an ensemble like this without going heroically deep—spotlights the multitude of ways in which Art Zoyd blazed a trail unquestionably their own. Their constantly shifting sound was even a million miles from their RIO comrades, let alone anything even minutely more conventional. They've always been left field of the left field, the maverick's mavericks, and if anything, this set underlines just how diligently they've pursued that grand idiosyncrasy decade after decade, offering new views of their evolution in the bargain.

The packaging is amazing, the music incredible, the production spot on. This is simply indispensable for anyone who have ever wanted their music to be real and not plastic. If ever there was an example of a label showing that they are there for the fans, for those who love what they do and are proud of it, as opposed to searching for the next big thing, then Cuneiform is it. I am proud to say that I have been involved with the label for more than twenty years, and the guys never cease to amaze me with their search for the very best in music, but this time they have outdone themselves. It may take months to get through everything in the box, to read the books, and truly understand what this band means in terms of the history of modern music and the impact they have had, but it is time very well spent indeed. It simply doesn't get any better, or any more complete, than this.

It is impossible to imagine what else Cuneiform could have done to make this release any more essential than it already is.
Dec 2017

ARTEMIY ARTEMIEV & KARDA ESTRA
EQUILIBRIUM
I was having a conversation one day with Richard Wileman and had been looking through his back catalogue and noticed that I hadn't heard everything he had released. So, this how I have come about to be listening to this 2002 album which was a collaboration between Russian composer Artemiy Artemiev (synthesiser, sampler, electronics, percussion) and Richard Wileman (guitar, bass, electronic and acoustic percussion, loops, vocal and woodwind arrangements), along with Ileesha Bailey (vocals, breathing loop) and Caron Hansford (oboe, cor anglais). Apparently, this was one of four collaborative albums released by Artemiev in 2002, and he has certainly had a major impact on the overall sound as there are significant parts where I wouldn't have said that this was a Karda Estra release at all.

It is the songs where Richard has the upper hand, such as "Open Window", where the album comes to life. The background stays where it belongs, and Richard's guitar provides a repetitive motif that works well, but there are many others where this is an ambient electronic album where Richard is not able to make the impact that he would if it was all under his control. That the artists recorded separately, Karda Estra in England and Artemiev in Russia, probably says a lot about the album itself. That Artemiev's name comes first on the cover probably says even more.

I have been a huge fan of Richard for more than twenty years, long before Karda Estra back when he was working as Lives & Times, but although there are elements that I really enjoyed, overall, this is just too ambient electronic for me.
Apr 2017

ASIA
GRAVITAS
Probably best to start this review with a couple of admissions. Firstly, when the first Asia album came out it was purchased immediately and I very nearly wore the needle out playing it (yes it was vinyl, yes, I really am that old). But, to me it was a state of diminishing returns as each album wasn't quite as good as the last and I soon lost interest. It was only later that I listened to some material and realized that there were still some good songs, but it wasn't really working for me. But, when I heard the original line-up was going to get back together then of course I was excited, but while 'Phoenix' and 'Omega' did have some good bits here and there, 'XXX' had little in the way to save it. So, when I was offered this album, I was quite in two minds, especially when I saw that Steve was no longer involved and instead, they now had Sam Coulson (who has worked with Paul Gilbert and Walter Trout).

After I had played the album a few times I found myself questioning how to review it. If one is looking for ground breaking music then this isn't it, but if one wants an album filled with anthems that just beg the listener to sing along then maybe it is. Although this has Asia on the sleeve and is filled with Asia-style harmonies and songs, there is a real feeling that this is a Downes-Wetton album. Carl always played a more subdued role with Asia than ELP due to the style of music, and Sam seems to be content to provide backing riffs and has little to do with the way of lead roles (although they do throw him the occasional solo and he does a great job) and this makes the album somewhat one-sided. But did I enjoy listening to it? The answer to that must be a resounding yes, and I know that if they deigned to tour down here then I would be delighted to go and see them. So, for pure listening pleasure (and I know that this is weighted with sentiment) it must be 4/5, but I wouldn't be surprised to see others rate it much lower than that. But it is a million miles better than 'XXX', although that wasn't too hard to be fair.
May 2014

ATOMIC ROOSTER
THE DEVIL HITS BACK
In 1989 organist Vincent Crane committed suicide aged 45, and John Du Cann put together this compilation with Vincent's widow, Jean, as a tribute. This is at least the fourth reissue of the album since then, and reverts to the original 12-track, although the Gonzo website does state that it includes three rare early live tracks which although available on some editions of this album are not on the Gonzo release. Atomic Rooster was one of those bands that never really gained the acclaim they deserved, and these days are probably best known for "Devils Answer" and "Tomorrow Night" (both on here) and for having Carl Palmer as their first drummer. That is incredibly unfair, as through the Seventies they released a series of significant albums with various line-ups. When I saw them in concert in the early Eighties, they were back to the same trio that worked together in 70/71, namely John Du Cann, Vincent Crane, and Paul Hammond. By

now they were firmly part of the NWOBHM, and this album reflects that period of the band.

The insert provides a very potted history of the band and seems to suggest that this album includes songs from many of the different line-ups. Given that there appear to have been 22 versions through the years, and there are only 12 songs, that somehow seems unlikely. I would much rather have had some information as to exactly who was playing on the songs (my guess, and it is only a guess, is that they are all by the trio above) and where and when the live versions were recorded. As a sampler for the early Eighties period of the band it is well worth hearing, especially as it also includes "Play It Again" which was a minor hit on the rock charts at the time (I've still got the 12" vinyl version). Whether it is the perfect introduction as is stated on the insert I'm not so sure, but it certainly is a good way to find out about one of our most maligned and ignored bands.
Oct 2017

SOPHYA BACCINI'S ARADIA
BIG RED DRAGON

Sophya Baccini has built a reputation in the Italian scene for her vocal prowess, recording with various bands (most notably Presence) and performing in multiple languages. The daughter of a tenor singer, she has been immersed in music since a very young age and released her debut solo album 'Aradia' in 2009 then took it as the name of her next project, 'Big Red Dragon (William Blake's Visions)'. As is suggested by the title, this album is based on the work of Blake (although somewhat sadly there isn't a song called 'The Tiger', which is probably one of his best-known works). Sophya decided that this would best be undertaken as a symphonic progressive rock album, but there are passages where it is just her and a piano, although at others it is more full-blown. Not all the album is in English, and she has also brought in a host of guests to augment her own band, including Christian Decamps (Ange) Sonja Kristina (Curved Air) Elisa Montaldo (Il Tempio Delle Clessidre) Steve Sylvester (Death SS), Lino Vairetti (Osanna), Irwin Vairetti (Osanna), Enrico Iglio (Presence) and Roberto Tiranti (Mangala Vallis).

Somewhat unfairly I found myself comparing this with Clive Nolan's 'Alchemy', and while there is no doubt at all that this is an incredibly clever album, I found that it was something that I enjoyed only in bits and pieces as opposed to throughout with not enough hooks. It feels much more like a classical piece of music than a progressive rock album, and I am sure that this is deliberate intent, but not really what I want to hear. The vocals are wonderful, and when the album really gets going, as it does on the much more upbeat "The Number" then it shows just what is missing.

I would have much preferred for this to be less clever, and less pure classical/operatic, but I am fully aware that this is just down to personal choice and there will be many who will feel this is an incredible piece of work, which it undoubtedly is, just not something I want to play a great deal. It closes of course with Blake's most famous poem, which was put to

music by Sir Hubert Parry many years after his death. "Jerusalem" has been recorded in many different styles and is seen by many as one of the most quintessential English songs of all time. ELP's version is one of the most well-known, and to her credit Sophya has created an arrangement that is very different to many, with multi-layered female vocals and a sparse musical backing, but somehow it doesn't gel right with me. I knew the song as a hymn long before I came across ELP's version and love the majesty and power that this demands and the emotion it always invokes, but somehow here it seems somewhat sterile and devoid of passion. A very clever album, but just not for me.
Jan 2014

BAND OF RAIN
THE DUST OF STARS
It has been six years since the last Band of Rain album, but Chris Gill is finally back with another release. As has been the case with his other albums, he continues to mix it up, and this time he has provided guitar, programming etc. and has been joined by Micha Steinbacher (bass, flute, sax, multi-instruments, programming, vocals). Most of the album is instrumental, but on two of the songs he has again engaged the vocal talents of Ria Parfitt, which takes the music into quite a different direction from the rest. This is hypnotic, almost trance-like music, treading a line where progressive rock and psychedelic music meet, reminiscent of Hawkwind, Pink Floyd and very early Porcupine Tree.

It is complex and complicated, and for all the times where it feels that it is driving and forceful there are others where the music just washes over the listener and allows them to relax into it. My favourite is "Indian Summer", where the combination of flute and synthesisers provides an introduction that makes one think it is going to be in the style of Native Americans, before it goes into traditional Indian, and then something quite different altogether. This really shows the experimental aspect of the music, as the band bring together music from different cultures to create something that is both different and enjoyable. I know that Chris is often busy working on albums by others, but I do hope we don't have to wait quite so long for the next one.
Dec 2017

BAROCK PROJECT
DETACHMENT
Many years ago, long before the days of progressive rock being back in fashion and discussed in the mainstream, I had been at a gig in London. Afterwards the normal band of hardcore progheads had gathered, and there was only one topic that everyone wanted to talk about, "Had anyone else heard this amazing debut album that had been released in the States?". The album was 'The Light', and the band was of course Spock's Beard, and it amazed me firstly that everyone knew about it

when it was yet to be made available properly in the UK but also we all felt the same way. Fast forward to 2017 and I was in conversation with Artur at MLWZ in Poland asking him he thought of the new Cast album, and while he loved it, he wanted to know what I thought of the new Barock Project release as it was amazing. The following week I asked Olav up in Norway the same question, and received the same response, which got me thinking that if two of my greatest progressive friends both thought the same thing I really ought to get onto it.

A short time later and I had this, their fifth release, playing and I immediately knew exactly what all the fuss is about: this is incredible. It is music like this which first got me into progressive rock – it is complex, it is magical, it keeps jumping into unexpected musical places, all with a sense of joy and happiness. I'm not going to bother trying to pick out all the musical clues and keys to their influences as they are many and diverse, but they have put them together in a way that is new and different, yet also incredibly melodic and the whole album is immediately accessible the very first time it is played.

The four-piece band of Luca Zabbini (lead vocals, keyboards, guitars (electric, acoustic & 12-string), mixing & mastering), Marco Mazzuoccolo (electric guitar), Francesco Caliendo (bass) and Eric Ombelli (drums, percussion) have been joined by three additional singers in Alex Mari, Ludovica Zanasi and Peter Jones and the vocals are wonderful, but it is the diversity of the music and how it is performed that keeps the listener glued to the speakers. I can't pick a favourite song, as whatever is playing is always the one I want to listen to most, whether it is with vocals and just a simple piano, or harpsichord, or something that is way more bombastic and over the top. These guys are masters of all the styles, and I am having a hard time understanding that they have been around for years, yet it is the first time I have ever come across them.

That is something I am going to have to get on top of it, as if the rest of their output is even half as good as this then they are all essential. There have already been some incredible albums released this year, and this one may just be the best of the lot. This is indispensable. When it comes to progressive rock, it just doesn't get any better than this.
Apr 2017

BAROCK PROJECT
SKYLINE
I may have only just come across this Italian outfit with their latest album, 'Detachment', but I am determined to make up for lost time so am now listening to their last studio album, which was their fourth. Released in 2015, this is very much the forerunner to the most recent, and although it isn't quite in the same league is still an incredibly impressive piece of work. The flute only appears on a couple of songs this time, although there is also some cello and viola at times. From the acapella opening, through to the very last note, this is an incredibly polished and controlled album: one that takes the listener on a journey that they are sure to enjoy.

I'm not quite sure why, but there does appear to be a much heavier Jethro Tull feeling to parts of this album, and this has nothing to do with the use of flute, but rather the way that some of the acoustic numbers seem to flow and sweep. I have seen them likened to Echolyn in some places, and I can see why, but to be honest although I always enjoyed Echolyn I don't think they were quite in the same league as these guys. This the second studio album I have heard and am still getting to grips with the fact that up to a few months ago I had never heard of them! Still, like finding a good author after he has been going a while (I first read Stephen Donaldson as he was about to release the sixth volume of "Thomas Covenant" novels), it does give one the opportunity to go back and see what else they have been doing over time, and that is something I fully intend to do.

Barock Project are easily one of the most impressive bands currently operating within the progressive scene and I heartily recommend this to anyone who enjoys the more melodic and less challenging forms.
Apr 2017

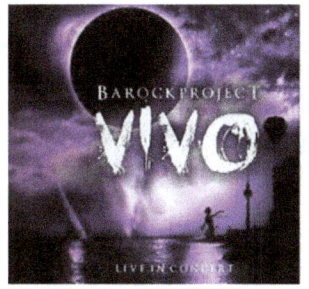

BAROCK PROJECT
VIVO: LIVE IN CONCERT
After the release in 2015 of 'Skyline', the Italians returned the following year with a live double CD. The first of these features songs from the band's first three albums, 'Misteriose Voci' (2006), 'Rebus' (2009) and 'Coffee in Neukolln' (2012), plus a version of "Los Endos". The second contains six live versions from 'Skyline' (2015) with a bonus studio song, "My Silent Sea", which was written and recorded in 2015 as a 'Skyline' follow-up. Unlike the two studio albums I have heard there aren't any additional guests, so no woodwind or strings, just five guys showing what they can do onstage (although as keyboard player Luca Zabbini does also play acoustic guitar, they can provide different inflections at times).

I was amazed when I looked in ProgArchives, the bible and most important guide to progressive rock on the web, to discover that this album was yet to be reviewed! But it has been rated thirty times and is subsequently the fourth highest ranked live album of 2016. I do hope that this is a true reflection of how the guys are live in concert, and that there hasn't been too much work carried out in the studio, as this is awesome from start to finish. That these guys are masters at this musical form is never in doubt, nor is their ability to provide complex interweaving songs that keep the listener enthralled throughout. At times, there is an American style to what they are producing, but they temper it with good old-fashioned English neo-prog when the moment requires it. Given they have also worked with some of the finest musicians in the Italian progressive scene, it is somewhat surprising there aren't more influences from that genre within their music, but it is only occasional keyboard passages that allude to where they are from.

Complex, melodic, structured, progressive, brilliant. To say I am a fan of this band is something of a massive understatement. I just can't wait to hear more of their music.
Apr 2017

BARROWS
OBSIDION

This is the third album by Los Angeles-based Barrows and depicts the experience of a man who is abducted from earth and brought to Obsidion, a place where dimension is indefinable, and the boundaries of human consciousness cease to exist. The band claim their cinematic, instrumental rock organically and seamlessly blends elements of prog, space, kraut, and psych, citing influences of early King Crimson and Pink Floyd to John Carpenter and Goblin, and they may just be right. Formed in Syracuse by Jim Leonard and Richy Epolito, before the two relocated to Los Angeles, where they recruited guitarist Ryo Higuchi and bassist Brock Haltiwanger to flesh out the live line-up. But this album, as with the others, was recorded by just the original duo.

Musically this is all over the place, as they take influences from wherever seems most suitable and then blend it together. That they should be called "progressive" is never in doubt, but here in the truest sense of the word as opposed to sitting within one sub-genre or another. This is music that does need to be sat and listened to intently, as otherwise there is a real risk that it can just fall into the background and not be fully appreciated, and that would be quite the wrong thing to do, as this is quite an impressive piece of work. Cinematic, yet also touching on ambient, it really does feel like an organic beast as it gently moves through different passages, somehow bringing together quite different styles of music. There are many times when the guitar is notable by its absence, and then others when it sounds very Gilmour-like and has a major impact.

The only way to fully appreciate this is by hearing it, and as well as being released on vinyl by Tonzonen the band have also made it available on Bandcamp.
May 2017

JOHN BASSETT
UNEARTH

I have known John for some years now, back when KingBathmat was just John providing all the instruments, vocals, songs etc. instead of the band they are now. So, when I discovered he would be releasing a solo album I was somewhat intrigued to hear it as would this be a continuation of the KB material or something quite different? I should have known really that the result is something which is of course both and neither at the same time. Primarily an acoustic album, this has allowed John to create a new world that to me feels like a reflective melancholic walk through the countryside. Every time I play this I "see" a landscape in my mind, but something more akin to rolling English countryside than what I see every day when I look out of my window here in NZ.

Somehow there is incredible depth and restraint, all in an album where there are often very few instruments playing. John has of course provided everything himself (although he has allowed Nathan Summers to share the drum seat), from all instrumentation and vocals through writing the material, recording, mixing, and mastering it. I do also have to make mention of the stunning photography one can see in the booklet (and there are full versions on his website) as they are pieces of art in their own right – strangely the photographer isn't credited, but they have captured the passion and force of the sea against the stillness of the musician, a depth and power in its' own right that has been carried through to the album.

If I had to describe the music as a genre then I would go for progressive folk, but this is music that is transcending sheer description and pointedly refuses to be pigeonholed. The only thing people need to know is that this is a stunning piece of work that displays singer song writing at its' very best. In the words of the press release, "The emotive songs of 'Unearth' encompass and depict the dark substratum of modern life. Social engineering, existential contemplation, survivalism, childhood trauma, love & despair and everything in between are covered and flow out through lyrics that are fused with an uncanny knack for melody".

Classic song writing, classic performance, classic album. Indispensable.
Jun 2014

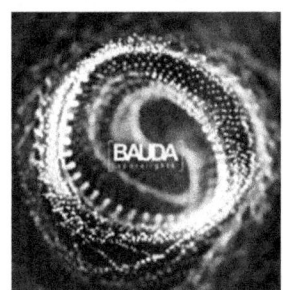

BAUDA
SPORELIGHTS

César Márquez started using the name Bauda in his native Chile in 2006, and with the assistance of session musicians he released an EP, 'Del Mar Al Aire' in 2006, and followed that up with a full-length album, 'Oniirica' in 2009. It wasn't until 2012 that the solo effort became more of a band approach with the addition of Nikolas Recabarren on drums and Juan Díaz on bass guitar, and it was this line-up that released the second full-length album 'Euphoria… Of Flesh, Men and the Great Escape' which saw them compared with the likes of Porcupine Tree and Opeth. Prior to starting on the next album, Edgardo González joined on keyboards, and they then invited René Rutten from The Gathering to work with them as producer. It took a full two years to complete the work, which was eventually released in October 2015.

It was only after researching the band that I came across comments pertaining to Porcupine Tree, which I found interesting as it was the band I also thought they had most in common with, but I certainly didn't pick up on any Opeth tendencies – possibly they had dropped those for this album. But I'm getting ahead of myself, as when the album started, I was convinced that here was a band that was heading into an Ozric influenced Hawkwind styled type of space rock. The opening song, "Aurora", is one of two instrumentals on the album, and is incredibly powerful and vibrant, and I was immediately impressed and was looking forward to hearing the rest, and certainly wasn't expecting the shift in style that was to come. After that bright opening, it all slowed down; the Porcupine Tree influences were there, but there was also quite a lot of Manchester scene indie rock such as Blur and even Oasis.

The power that was so prevalent in the opener was lost in a layering of sound that was dreamy, with power in the background that was being suffocated by mountains of cotton wool. The strange thing is that the production of the drums is crisp and punchy throughout, so that often I found myself concentrating more on the wonderful work of Nikolas, who is a revelation with his differing styles, touches, and nuances, than on the song itself. Per their own statement, the music is "fused with landscapes, textures, surfaces of Chile in different shades and styles of music, either post rock, folk, ambient, dark, finally alternative rock." There is certainly a great deal going on, but to me it is too alternative/post rock for me, and not nearly enough progressive. I can see what they're trying to do, but it's not for me.
Dec 2016

BIG BIG TRAIN
GRIMSPOUND
Over the last few years Big Big Train have been making a real name for themselves in the prog world, but I have missed out on the last few albums, so haven't really been fully aware of what has been going on. To me they will always be special, the first band ever to send me something to review, and I still have that 1991 demo tape, 'From The River To The Sea', and am looking at it now. My brain has real issues in understanding that this small independently recorded and released cassette is the same band who are now playing this incredibly complex and professional music that is coming out of my speakers. True, there have been one or two line-up changes over the years, and they have gone from a five-piece to an octet, but Andy Poole and Greg Spawton were there at the very beginning, and they are still there now.

It is interesting to note not only the people in the band, but the instruments being played, as it does give an insight into the complex and layered nature of the music. These days it is David Longdon (lead and backing vocals, flute, acoustic guitar, mandolin, percussion), Dave Gregory (guitars), Andy Poole (acoustic guitar, mandolin, keyboards, backing vocals), Rikard Sjöblom (keyboards, guitars, accordion, backing vocals), Danny Manners (keyboards, double bass), Rachel Hall (violin, viola, cello, lead and backing vocals, string arrangements), Greg Spawton (bass, bass pedals, acoustic guitar, backing vocals) and Nick D'Virgilio (drums, percussion, lead and backing vocals). If that wasn't enough, they have the one and only Judy Dyble guesting on vocals on one number as well.

I will never forget Greg making a beeline for me when he saw me in a pub in Winchester as he wanted to know what I thought about their new album, and I had to admit that I didn't like it as I felt they had moved too far away from their sound and it was nothing like I expected to hear from BBT (I later changed my mind after I had played it some more, honest). But this is not a release that I would ever have expected to hear from the Dorset boys, as this is something of incredible depth and layers. I think one of the things that really makes this album work so much for me is that it is obvious that everyone involved is a master of their craft, but they are all incredibly restrained and working together to provide what is right for the music. I have been lucky to see Nick play live with Spock's Beard numerous times, and have many albums on which he has performed, but this must be the most laid-back I have ever heard him. In many ways, the lead instrument is that of Rachel, but it only works as it does due to the backdrop that is provided, which can be a 'simple' acoustic guitar, or something far more powerful.

David Longdon has a wonderful voice, and it is his vocals, combined with the melodies and instrumentation that makes this a very special album indeed. According to ProgArchives they released the best live album of 2016, and I would have thought the chances of this being the top 2017 studio album are very high indeed. I was one of the very first reviewers of their music, and back in December 1991 I said, "If you like Genesis (prog not pop), Galahad or Marillion, then this is the band for you". More than twenty-five years on, I am pleased to amend that, and just say that here is a band for lovers of all great music, whatever the genre. Superb.
Apr 2017

BIG BIG TRAIN
THE SECOND BRIGHTEST STAR
Having been blown away by the sheer beauty of 'Grimspound' earlier this year, I certainly wasn't expecting another album just yet, so when I received an email telling me about this, I was incredibly excited. The album features forty minutes of new songs and instrumentals which explore landscapes, rivers and meeting places and take the listener on voyages of discovery across the world and to the stars. Alongside the new tracks, there is a bonus selection of thirty minutes of music where songs from the last two albums are presented in extended format. Nick D'Virgilio is probably my favourite drummer in modern progressive music, and I have always loved watching him play, yet with BBT one doesn't notice the complexity of what he is doing unless one listens for it, as he is so much at one with the rest of the band.

The use of so many different instruments within an octet allows them to layer sounds that would be beyond many others, but the pastoral progressive sound they create never overpowers David Longdon's rich vocals. They are a very English band in so many ways, and not just when they are singing about London, as they evoke a feeling not of the current age, but of times gone past when the world was a simpler place, but there is nothing simple about the music they are performing, but it never feels heavy handed or over the top. It is fresh and bright, never leaden or conspiring to show what everyone can do just because they're proggers, but rather the music always seems perfect and on point, with all the musicians doing exactly what is required. This can mean they sometimes provide accompaniment to others as opposed to demanding a lead role or may even sit out sections of songs if that is what is right for the music.

Big Big Train will feature at the top of many music critic's albums of the year, and that there may be a doubt only about whether it is this or 'Grimspound' shows just how important the band has become. Truly wonderful, in so many ways.
Jul 2017

A BIG GOODBYE
HISTORY IN REWIND
So, the guys are now back with the difficult second album, and I have to say that I think they've nailed it well. Although PA have them listed as Heavy Prog, there is a lot on this album that would find them more happily suited to Crossover, with a very strong sense of melody. Whereas the first album impressed due to the complex heaviness of much of the music, on this one I have found that it is the 'simpler' songs that hit home. This feels very much like an album of restraint, where the band have taken their time to craft something that builds on the first and takes it in a slightly different direction, without ever straying too far from the path they set out in the debut. There are times when they are reminiscent of Vangough, or possibly Pain of Salvation, but with a more melodic almost AOR feel to the vocals. The guitars are kept (mostly) under control on this album, but the bass is allowed to run riot with some incredibly complex lines.

The piano sound is just superb, and that combined with strong harmony or double-tracked vocals and wonderfully beguiling atmospherics and hooks makes this a delight. "Breathe" is a full-on duet with Elise Walker guesting, and the gentle percussion and rhythmic accompaniment allows the listener to drift away on a sea of vocals that have a wonderful pop feel, without every straying too much into that area. In many ways this feels like a very mature album, by a band who really know what they want to achieve. The result is something that is very easy to listen to and enjoy on first hearing, and the more it is played then the more the listener discovers.
Jun 2014

BIONATOPS
VOICES
The only way to really describe this album is by saying it is weird, and has obviously been influenced by Mike Patton in some of his more way-out outfits. Oh, and it has been influenced by Throbbing Gristle, and noise, and prog, um and tech metal and loads of other stuff. Did I say it was weird? Bionatops is the brainchild of Joseph Spiller (ex-System Divide, Caricature, The Binary Code, Too Late The Hero), the band serving to keep himself free of having writer's block, and to break the tension of writing 'serious' music within his other groups. While the music is designed to be thematically light-hearted and fun, the songs are still crafted with serious musicianship that doesn't rely on editing tricks. Spiller, who records all guitars, bass, vocals, and other instrumentation, is joined by Jeff Willet (ex-Black Crown Initiate) who adds the drums and percussion to the attack. It may be designed to be fun, but mostly it comes across as, you guessed it, weird.

This is their debut album, and the PR Company describes it as "an incredibly unique sound, with progressive and technical metal elements merging with spastic alternative rock". They missed out "weird". Apparently, this is a family friendly album about a

lovable schizophrenic southerner that tells tales of his life that may or may not be true while interacting with other voices in his head that might not even be in his head. Spiller worked on this while simultaneously writing the new album for his other band, Caricature, which took five years to complete and will also see release this year. I found the album incredibly compelling, and something I have been drawn back to time and again, even though I can't explain why with any confidence at all. Did I say it was weird?
Oct 2017

BIRZER BANDANA
BECOMING ONE
Birzer Bandana are a new band, formed by Progarchy's Brad Birzer (lyrics) and Salander's Dave Bandana (music and performance). Dave provides vocals, bass, guitars, drums, drum programming, synths, piano, organ, and mellotron, with Olga Kent assisting with violin on two songs and Mick Bennett guitar on one. This is quite a mixed bag of an album, with quite a slow starter in "Awash" which doesn't set the scene as well as it could, and it would have been better to have the second song "The Dance" as the initial cut, as this more upbeat number is a great song with good vocals and melodies brought to life with some great violin. For some reason this is one of the numbers that definitely reminds me of late Seventies Barclay James Harvest, which can only be a good thing in my book.

From here on in the listener is taken on a pleasant journey through crossover prog, mixing pop influences with prog rock. Different ideas have been tried here and there, such as the choral introduction to "3 To 1", and the result is a pleasant varied album that has quite a lot to offer. I like the way each track segues into the next, providing an excellent transition through the album. I do think the next step for these guys is to move away from a project and more into a full band, as having a human drummer will make a real difference to the overall sound, and I would like Olga to become far more involved as she provides an edge that cuts through the Floydian styles to good effect. This is a promising debut album, and is probable the first one I have ever heard from Lanzarote (Dave moved there a few years ago) – not normally an area thought of as a hotbed for progressive rock.
Mar 2017

THE BLACK NOODLE PROJECT
GHOSTS & MEMORIES
So here is the latest album from French group The Black Noodle Project, one that sees them stay firmly in the realm of Pink Floyd, yet becoming more atmospheric, and at times darker and heavier, than previously. I have been in contact with these guys since the very first release, and the more I listen to them the more I enjoy what they are doing. Some may argue that when one is so heavily influenced by another

group then that questions the very validity of what they are doing themselves, but there are many within the genre that have a similar approach, and if the band are attempting their own style within the field of influence, then I don't have a major issue with it. Yes, there are passages within "Ghosts" that could have come from 'Dark Side', and these do seem a little close to the mark, but generally this is another fine album from a band who are consistently releasing strong albums.

The vocals have taken more of a back seat this time, with an emphasis on the atmosphere and overall feel and the vocals become part of that as opposed to being an important presence: they are just another instrument to be used. In many ways this is a hard album to judge, as if I was not aware of anything that had been released by Pink Floyd then I would be hailing this as a masterpiece, particularly with songs such as the brooding and oppressive "A Purple Memory". But, given that I, like many progheads, own all of Pink Floyd's releases I must gauge this in relation to those. Conversely, I also need to factor in just how much I have enjoyed playing this as opposed to who may have been an important influence on what they are doing. Simply put, if you enjoy the style of mid-Seventies Pink Floyd and you don't worry that it isn't being performed by the boys themselves then this is essential. Nothing less.
Mar 2014

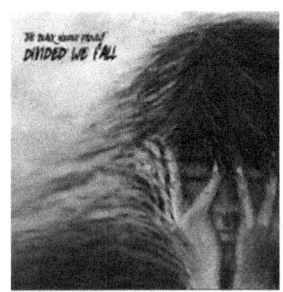

THE BLACK NOODLE PROJECT
DIVIDED WE FALL
Four years on from their last album and Jérémie Grima (guitars, voice, programming) and Sébastien Bourdeix (guitars) are back with the sixth studio album. They are the only survivors from the line-up that recorded 'Ghosts & Memories', and here they are joined by Tommy Rizzitelli (drums) and Frédéric Motte (bass). The band was originally a solo outing by Jérémie, and we were first in contact at about the time of the debut album back in 2004.

I have always enjoyed their music, but this time they appear to have taken it to another level. They have always been heavily influenced by the likes of Pink Floyd and Porcupine Tree, but this time I believe we need to add Muse to the mix plus a real feeling of self-awareness and control. Heavily instrumental, this is an emotional album with the guitar often at the forefront, with just a few notes plucked from the ether to create something that is very special indeed.

From the very first sounds of "Isolation" I felt that I was onto something very special indeed and decided to not listen to the album until I could sit and give it the sole attention it deserved. I decided against headphones, but instead sat quietly in the middle of a room and let the sound wash over me (accompanied just by a rather large glass of rum, just to keep me company). There is a presence and self-control in this album that other bands need to pay attention to: there is no need to play five thousand notes to the bar when every note is placed with such perfection. There is a deep melancholy within this, with emotions let rampant, and a crying guitar that David Gilmour would be proud of. I have found it hard to write the review as I keep stopping just to bask in the splendour of this release.

It may have come out right at the end of the year, but possibly that makes it the perfect Christmas present for the discerning proghead who doesn't know what he/she is missing out on? They riff when they need to, and there is so much space within the layers that the proverbial truck could waltz right through, while the rhythm section not only knows when to crunch into life, but also when to sit quietly drinking their café au lait and let the two guys at the front create some real magic. Album of the year? There have been some great releases and I would have to go back and play them all to be sure. But, easily in my Top Ten and I have reviewed nearly 600 in 2017. Wonderful, amazing, indispensable, and if you enjoy any of the bands listed above then you simply must get this.
Dec 2017

BLOW UP HOLLYWOOD
BLUE SKY BLOND
This is the first album I have heard from BUH since 2004's 'Fake', although it has only been three years since 'Collections', and there have been some other albums in between as well. Their website gives little in the way of who is involved, although singer/guitarist Steve Messina obviously is as it is his band, but interestingly they say that this album is "ambient pop/rock" whereas they originally came to prominence through the prog scene. Well, there are some prog influences here, but the prominent sound is that of a laid-back Coldplay, with some slight touches at times of Muse and Porcupine Tree. The result is something that is, well, pleasant. "Shine" wouldn't sound out of place on radio and is easily the standout song on the album. Piano led, with hooks aplenty, gentle orchestration and some good female harmony vocals against Steven's voice make this song a delight. But, for the most part this is an album that drifts along with little in the way to really capture my attention. It's not that it is bad, as it is well recorded and well performed, but rather this style of music is not one that I would generally listen to. If you enjoy music that drifts along without being obtrusive then this may well be for you, and although it would appeal to fans of the likes of Coldplay, I somehow doubt it will sell in the same quantities.
May 2014

THE BOB LAZAR STORY
GHOST OF FOODSTOOL
Looking at their Bandcamp page, I can see that Matt Deacon describes his band as "Purveyor of tritonal wankery, The Bob Lazar Story hail from Christchurch, NZ and offer you an oasis of ProgMathsFusion to soothe your weary earholes". I've been lucky enough to hear both their albums, and their first EP, with this one following in 2014. Seven songs, with a total playing length of fourteen minutes, this is even more eclectic and brilliant than normal! One could argue that this is a close relative to Zappa, while I have also seen someone describe their music as "a tasty cake of dribbly madness". Chris Jago has an incredibly important part to play behind the drums, making

them much more of an in-your-face instrument, very much in keeping with jazz, than one may expect from a rock act. Mike Fudakowski has a similar role with the bass, and they both try to keep up with the manic Matt on guitar.

They are all obviously off their rockers, as this music is hard to describe, yet also always makes total perfect sense. It is melodic, controlled, easy to listen to, yet takes King Crimson to a whole new level. Why these guys aren't huge I will never understand, but until the world sits up and takes notice, us in the minority will smile and nod knowingly that these guys are musical geniuses.
Feb 2017

THE BOB LAZAR STORY
SELF-LOATHING JOE
Released in 2015, Matt said this EP "sounds like two small bands having a fight on some stairs.". I guess one of those bands plays acoustic guitars, while the other is into harder rock, and somehow, they share a drummer. And they all like Zappa, and Fripp, and jazz, and being able to make musical sense out of intricate melodies where nothing should gel but does. Somewhere along the line Chris and Matt managed to misplace Mike, so they were down to a duo. There are even quite a few "vocals" here, but they are mostly spoken word, so it doesn't detract too much from the instrumental insanity that is going on for the rest of the piece. One of the songs is nearly nine minutes long, but another is only sixteen seconds, with the seven songs getting just past the twenty-minute mark.

All their albums/EPs stretch musical boundaries without ever seeming to do so, as this music is just so easy to listen to yet shouldn't be. I was playing this at work the other day, and I was asked what on earth it was, as it was so compelling. When I told him they were a local band (I now work in the city these guys are from) he was amazed and immediately went off to find out more. Which is exactly what you should be doing right now. Music as adventurous and wonderful as this needs full support. They have signed to Bad Elephant for their next album, which should be out in a few months' time. Until then get over to Bandcamp and listen to some music that will blow your mind.
Feb 2017

THE BOB LAZAR STORY
BARITONIA
According to their Bandcamp site, these guys are purveyors of tritonal wankery, and offer an oasis of ProgMathsFusion to soothe your weary earholes. The guys behind the band are Matt Deacon (guitar, synth, mouse, jews harp) and Chris Jago (drums, finger cymbal). Although they originally met at a music college in Liverpool, they are now living rather separate lives with Matt in New Zealand and Chris in Los Angeles. So how they manage

to produce music quite like this says a lot about tenacity and perseverance, as well as something about the internet. This is the first new album in five years, and back then they were a four-piece, but they have released a couple of EP's during the intervening period, and this is more of a follow on from 'Self-Loathing Joe' than 'Space Roots' (the cover of the EP was of a coffee mug, the cover of this album is of a stain left on a table when said coffee cup is removed). The other big change of course, is that even though Matt is on the other side of the world from the UK, he managed to convince David of BEM to release this album, which will undoubtedly assist in it getting far more awareness than previously.

Complex and interweaving, this never comes across as a duo, and certainly not one that is split on different continents. When Matt and I met up recently we had some long discussions on the impact on music of guitarists such as Allan Holdsworth and Frank Zappa, and it is possible to hear the influences of both within his own style. This is music that sometimes contains elements of Hawkwind, but these are just in the background, allowing Matt to move away and create something quite different. Some of the keyboard sounds are very dated, very Eighties, but within the music they definitely work. Matt isn't afraid to use an acoustic guitar when he wants to either, it is all about using the right tool for the job, and sometimes he slows down what he is doing and lets Chris pick up the pace. This is not a solo artist with a drum machine, this is a duo working and bouncing ideas off each other.

I have long been a fan of these guys, and I can only hope that by signing with BEM their music will be become more widely known and appreciated, as it deserves it.
Apr 2017

THE STEVE BONINO PROJECT
STARGAZER
Although I have previously heard some albums in which Steve has been involved, most notably the awesome Bomber Goggles and their incredible album 'Gyreland' (if you haven't already bought it then you need to), this is the first time I have come across one of his solo albums. Steve provides guitar, bass, keyboards, drums, and vocals, and is joined by Böhn (acoustic and electric guitars and backing vocals) and Bingo Brown (drums, percussion and backing vocals). 'Stargazer' is a concept album, and is the nickname given to the hero of our story born into a dystopian future in which man's neglect has made Earth no longer habitable. This is a similar theme to 'Gyreland' and the impact of humanity's impact on the earth, and at this point it is not possible to save the planet, so people must leave.

Steve has a knack of bringing together multiple musical themes and styles and bringing them together in a fashion that is best thought of as crossover progressive rock, with large elements of power pop styles. The songs are all short, with only a couple daring to break the five-minute barrier and are incredibly infectious. In fact, one can imagine quite a number of these being played on radio to great effect. Take "Phoenix Rising" for example, here we find Steve channelling Weezer while with "In The Darkness" it is much more like Nik Kershaw! The music is fluid, sonorous, and always with stacks of melody and hooks.

It is an incredibly accessible album, one I knew I was going to enjoy from the very first note, as the title cut opens proceedings with layered harmony vocals. This is a poppy funky rocking number that shows inspiration from Utopia, and I defy anyone not to sing along with the chorus when it returns. Straight away I was smiling, grooving in my chair, knowing that this was yet another to add to my list of albums of the year – and given that 'Gyreland' is also in the Top Ten, Steve's not doing bad. He has a real knack of producing catchy songs, giving them enough depth so that they have real presence, but also showing restraint. There is the impression that 'Stargazer' could have been a lot heavier, it wouldn't have taken much in the mix, but it works great as it is. There are also little touches, like the bass slide up and down the frets in the chorus, which add to the overall piece, and from that we go into the far more jagged "The Celestial Show" which has a very different attack both in terms of arrangement and vocals yet is also another great number. This is quite some album, highly recommended.
Oct 2018

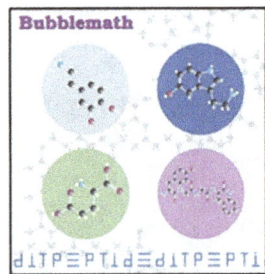

BUBBLEMATH
EDIT PEPTIDE
According to the label, Bubblemath are an Eclectic Prog/Avant-Pop/ Technical Metal Quintet, while Prog Archives simply call them "eclectic". In my humble opinion, they're both correct, and wrong. When I put this on the player, I knew immediately what this style of music was, namely "pronk". Yes, boy and girls, at long last we have a band that is determined to keep the name "Cardiacs" alive and kicking. A mere short fifteen years since the debut, the line-up (who got together in 1998) is still the same, they just had a small issue getting this finished. I'm sure they haven't been recording full-time for the last fifteen years, but there are times when the listener wonders how on earth they managed to move from point A to point B in a song, as this is complex, tight, and completely off the wall.

Don't try to work out what time signature a certain piece of a song may be in, or what chord structure they are using, and instead just relish the total insanity and musical chaos of what is going on. They have a (fairly) straightforward musical line-up, just use the instruments in somewhat unusual manners. The quintet is Blake Albinson (electric guitar, acoustic guitar, nylon string guitar, keyboards, tenor sax, vocals), Jay Burritt (electric bass, fretless synth bass, fretless electric bass, upright electric bass, vocals), Kai Esbensen (keyboards, vocals), James Flagg (drums, percussion, vocals) and Jonathan G. Smith (vocals, electric guitar, acoustic guitar, flute, clarinet, chimes, gong, glockenspiel, xylophone, mountain dulcimer, mandolin, banjo). Yes, they all sing.

I love this album, it's just plain awesome, although I can pretty much guarantee you won't be singing any of the songs, although they somehow manage to be melodic as well as, well, weird. Zappa would love these guys, who also have a hint of Specimen 37 in

what they are doing, and if you want something so far out of both normal and the progressive mainstream, then this is going to be worth discovering.
May 2017

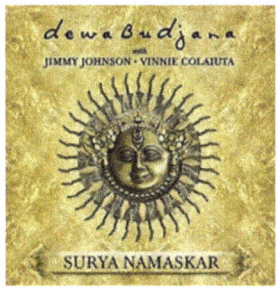

DEWA BUDJANA
SURYA NAMASKAR

Budjana is certainly making the most of being involved with a label boss who allows his bands to release material as often as they like, as he is already back with his third album, recorded with Jimmy Johnson and Vinnie Colaiuta. This time around Dewa is showing his harder more frenetic side, with loads of distortion and the use of fuzz. This provides a real edge to the music, but as always, he is aware of the need for light and shade to provide the contrast and he often takes the back seat and lets Jimmy provide some well-placed fretless bass before continuing back into the melody. There are also plenty of times when he and Jimmy are being very restrained, but the driving force that is renowned session drummer Vinnie Colaiuta can't keep still for long and provides plenty of force and angst.

Apparently, most of the songs on the album are first takes, and although they were mostly charted it appears that Vinnie often didn't follow the charts but stayed with Dewa and Jimmy, while the longest song on the album, "Kalingga" (just over nine minutes) was improvised. The title of the album means "Salute To Sun", which is fitting as many of the songs are homages to various of Budjana's guitar heroes, so "Campuhan Hill" was inspired by Ralph Towner and uses open strings, while "Capistrano Road" relates to his meeting with Allan Holdsworth. Musically this is just stunning, a fusion masterpiece, and it is all credit to Leo Pavkovic that the packaging stands up to close investigation as the fold out digipak contains an essay by John Kelman about the recording of the album which I would have loved to have copied out and used as the review as it is so well-written. Budjana is making lots of friends in the Western world with his incredible techniques and love of the genre, and I'm sure that it won't be long until he is back with another winner, but until then, if you enjoy fusion, then you will love this.
Jun 2014

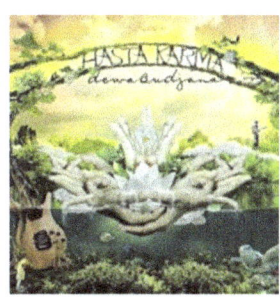

DEWA BUDJANA
HASTA KARMA

One of the real joys of following the Moonjune career of Indonesian guitarist Dewa Budjana, is that one is never sure quite what to expect with each release, as he often changes the musicians he is playing with, which has a direct impact on each album. This time he has brought in NYC vibraphonist, Joe Locke, and Pat Metheny Unity Group's bassist, Ben Williams, with drummer Antonio Sanchez, and Indonesian keyboardist, Indra Lesmana. There are so many wonders and delights contained within this 2014 album that it is hard to know where to begin. In many ways

Dewa has taken something of a back seat with this release, and it has a much stronger band feel than the others, as he shares the melody lead with Joe. I used to regularly see Poli Palmer (ex-Family) play and his touch on vibraphones was great, but he never sounded like this! Gentle touches, or blistering speed, Joe can do it all, and consequently is incredibly relaxed as there is nothing left for him to prove. This has allowed Dewa also to relax and go with the flow, not always having to be at the centre. With Ben and Antonio playing their part to perfection, the result is fusion that is mind-blowing in just so many ways.

From the cover artwork of the digipak, through the sleeve notes of John Kelman, and then into the fifty-two minutes of the album itself, this is the complete package. If I had to pick one track to showcase the beauty of this majestic album, then it would have to be "Desember" where Dewa provides some stunningly quick runs, and then leaves the song for bars at a time to allow the rest of the guys to build new rhythms and melodies, returning when the moment is right. When it comes to modern instrumental jazz fusion then it doesn't get any better than this. Faultless.
Feb 2017

DEWA BUDJANA
ZENTUARY
For his tenth solo album Dewa signed with Steve Vai's label and brought together a stellar group of musicians to realise his vision. Although this album was only a year after 'Hasta Karma' he has again completely switched things around, and none of those who were involved in the last album are on this one. His core band this time was Tony Levin (King Crimson, Peter Gabriel, Stick Men), Gary Husband (John McLaughlin, Allan Holdsworth, Jack Bruce, and others) and the incomparable Jack DeJonette (Keith Jarrett, Miles Davis). If that wasn't enough, he then added some further guests in Guthrie Govan (The Aristocrats, Steve Wilson, GPS), Tim Garland (Chick Corea, Bill Bruford), Danny Markovich (Marbin) as well as some cameos from the Czech Symphony Orchestra as well as Indonesian musicians Saat Syah, Ubiet and Risa Saraswati. Given that amount of talent is it any surprise that they have combined to produce yet another stunning piece of work?

Dewa has a wonderfully fluid style that always reminds me of John McLaughlin, and although there are huge amounts of fusion within this album, it is also quite experimental, bringing in progressive sounds that wouldn't be out of place with keyboard pioneers like Vangelis as well as local sounds and styles from Indonesia: it is fusion and progressive music in its truest sense. Some numbers, such as "Lake Tangengon" wear me out just by listening to them – there is an amazing amount of work and styles being displayed in the melody lines, and then at the back of them all Jack is killing the kit. How he keeps it up throughout the whole song is beyond me. Just twelve songs on this double CD set, but the 100 minutes' pass by quickly, and one must jerk oneself back into the real world at the end.

This is music that covers a great deal of musical areas, with multiple layers and threads, but it all combines into an incredible majestic whole. Yet again he has produced an album that is totally indispensable, essential, complex, and challenging yet easy to listen to, and a sheer delight from the first note to the very last.
Feb 2017

DEWA BUDJANA
POSTCARDS FROM BALI
Dewa started his solo career in the late Nineties, having already been at the forefront of the music scene in his native Indonesia for some twenty years by that point, but it was only when New York's Moonjune Records started working with him more than ten years later that he started to make an impression on the worldwide jazz and fusion scene. Dewa is an incredibly fluid guitarist, often likened to the mighty John McLaughlin, but he mixes jazz and fusion with the sounds of Indonesia to create music that is quite different from anyone else around. "The Little Master" has an innate sense of knowing what is musically right, and his arrangements are both complex and yet simple to understand and he brings together top musicians of all styles to help him to achieve his goals.

This release is unlike his others in that it is a compilation of music taken from albums as far back as 2003, is only available as a download, and best of all is totally free! This has been released to hopefully spread the word a little wider beyond the critics and reviewers and help those who enjoy the very finest fusion to discover some of the best that the genre offers, at no cost whatsoever. Of course, once you have downloaded and enjoyed this then the only thing to work out is which of his albums to explore next. Given I firmly believe that everyone I have heard is a masterpiece I don't have anything to offer on that score. All lovers of music that breaks boundaries, yet is both compelling and interesting on first hearing, just must give this a try. Did I say that it is free, available at absolutely no charge whatsoever? (*KR – at least it was when I originally wrote the review*)
Oct 2017

BUGENHAGEN
BU:GEN'HEIGEN
This is the debut mini album from Cumbria-based progressive/melodic rock band Bugenhagen. Fronted by multi-instrumentalist and vocalist John Turpin, the trio (the line-up is completed by Paul Fligg on drums and bassist Daneo Duran) initially came together as a Pink Floyd tribute act, but began to work original material into their set, here represented on this thirty-minute CD. The PR company likens their music to Pink Floyd and David Gilmour along with echoes of No Man/Tim Bowness, Muse and Hogarth-era Marillion, but for me one of the main standouts must be Mr So & So. As soon as I started playing opener "Without You By My Side", I could see

where the band was coming from, and it reminded me the So & So's need to get a new album out!

These guys crossover the progressive and melodic rock genres, bringing in pop sensibilities that could also seeing them being likened to It Bites and possibly Porcupine Tree. It is mostly a laid-back affair, with my biggest criticism being it is too short, and I would have liked to have heard a much fuller version. In many ways, it does remind me of the early Nineties progressive scene, and I can see this being picked up by those into either the crossover or neo-prog sub genres. John's vocals are often the highlight, although he has a deft touch on keyboards and his Gilmour-style guitar noodlings are also interesting, while the rhythm section keeps it all nicely pinned down. Overall, this is worth further investigation, and it will be interesting to see where the band goes from here.
Jan 2018

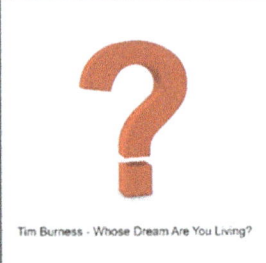

TIM BURNESS
WHOSE DREAM ARE YOU LIVING?
Originally released digitally towards the end of 2015, Tim has now slightly remixed and extended (three new tracks) and made this album available on CD through the Expanding Consciousness label. As with his 2007 album 'Vision On', the core of the band was Monty Oxymoron (keyboards, vocals, Theremin, and percussion), Fudge Smith (drums) and Keith Hastings (bass), while there were contributions from guests such as Gregg McKella (synthesisers and effects), Lee Abraham (sub-bass guitar), and Andrew Bradstreet (bodhran). Tim of course made his name with Burnessence in the Eighties and had been around the progressive scene for some thirty-five years or more, but doesn't release albums that often, so this was the first since 2007.

That is a real shame, as he has a very English approach to progressive and neo-progressive rock and hits many, many musical bases. He is a bit like a musical magpie, picking up the shiny things and hoarding them, and while they are all valuable, they certainly don't all sound the same. The first number, "These Are The Days" could have come from Fudge's previous band Pendragon in the very early Nineties, while "And Set Your Spirit Free' has so much energy that one can imagine it being played in the clubs in Ibiza. Some songs are full on and over the top, while others (such as "Hold Me") are incredibly delicate and restrained. This is what makes this such an incredibly solid album, there is huge variety and depth in what he does.

Tim feels it is his best work, and even his cynical bass player (his words, not mine), agrees with that. I believe Tim and the band recorded far more tracks than they used on this album, so hopefully the next album will be here much quicker!
May 2017

CAIRO
SAY

One of my roles on ProgArchives is being a member of the Crossover sub-genre team. We are asked to listen to bands and gauge whether we believe that they should firstly be listed on PA, and secondly if they should be classified as "Crossover Prog" or sent to another team for them to see what they think. It certainly leads to interesting discussions, and I get to hear a lot of music I wouldn't otherwise. But I rarely read any information we are also provided with (which can be as much as full history or as a little as a name), as I just want to listen to the music. One of the bands we recently assessed was Cairo, who we quickly and duly passed, and I then contacted the band to see if they could provide me with a biography. So, I was quite surprised to get a response from Rob Cottingham, who I have known since Touchstone first started, as I thought he was still with that band and hadn't realised that he had formed a new one.

Listening to an album to determine style is quite different to listening to it for review purposes, and I was glad to have the opportunity and go back and play it a few more times with a different set of ears. What immediately strikes the listener right from the introductory beginnings, is that this is an incredibly mature piece of work, and the production from John Mitchell (It Bites, Frost*, Arena, and others) is simply spot on. With Rob being joined on lead vocals by Rachel Hill, the use of both harmony and different lead vocals adds to what is a sumptuous and incredibly deep music soundscape. Some albums feel light, as if something is missing, while others are complex and want to tie the listeners in knots while they try to follow one overly intricate musical thread after another. Not so with Cairo, this is a band confident in their abilities, whether it is the few fretless bass notes to draw the music in with a warmth, or the delicate piano, or those simple guitar lines, percussion, or unaccompanied vocals. Each time I play this I get something more from it, and fall in love with it all over again, and the more I play it the more I realise just how special it is. This isn't something that is going to hit the listener in the face, but rather is an arm around the shoulders gently guiding them to the best seat in the house, by the fire, and enwrapping them with a blanket that is majestic yet never over the top. This is something very special indeed and must be treated as such: if you enjoy melodic prog then you will love this.
Mar 2017

GADI CAPLAN
MORNING SUN

Continuing my odyssey of discovering albums I should have heard long below, here is Gadi Caplan's third studio album, which was released in the middle of 2016. Originally trained on piano as a child, Caplan switched to guitar in his teens and developed a passion for rock and blues which took him on many journeys. He lived in India for two years studying traditional Indian music and sitar, before moving to New York City in 2006 where he joined various rock bands, then to Boston in 2007 to study jazz, fusion, and funk along with composition at the Berklee College of Music. Now based in Brooklyn, in 2014 he joined The Weeping Willards on lead guitar, forming a strong relationship with singer/composer Danny Abowd. They soon started writing songs together which form the backbone of this album.

On this album Gadi provides guitar, bass, and synth while Danny provides vocals and trombone. There are some songs when it is just the two of them, but they also know what is needed to take the music to the next level, and have brought in some guests as well, who all play a major part in how the album sounds. Bruno Esrubilsky is on drums and percussion, Duncan Wickel on violin, viola and cello, Jesse Gottlieb background vocals and trumpet, Jonathan Greenstein on tenor sax, Christian Li on keyboards and Jay Gandhi on bansuri flute. At times, I am reminded of the music of Anthony Phillips, turned into songs with wonderful vocals, at others it is more like world music with so many different influences all combining into something that is Western but being taken to a new level. Although it is laid-back and never forceful, there is a sense of real purpose and direction in this album, so much so that it cannot ever drift into the background as the listener keeps wanting to understand where the next musical twist will take them. Reminiscent at times of Gilmour or Chandler, Gadi's solos are always part of the piece, and his skill is in never really taking centre stage, but letting the vocals do their job while he layers on both acoustic and electric guitars. This is a truly glorious album.
Jan 2018

CAPTAIN OF THE LOST WAVES
HIDDEN GEMS (CHAPTER 1)
One of the joys of being in contact with other underground writers, is that every so often they will send something along they feel might be of interest to me. One of the very top reviewers around, in my humble opinion, is Olav Bjørnsen from Norway. I sent him a copy of the wonderful 'Sand' by Miss Peach & The Travellin' Bones, and when I explained to him what it was like, he immediately sent me a link to a video by Captain of the Lost Waves. I was blown away, and the album followed swiftly afterwards. On first hearing I was immediately entranced, as here is the much-missed Bond Street Bridge combined with Mumford & Sons, Fairport Convention, Edith Piaf, and possibly even a little Captain Beefheart.

I wasn't surprised to see that he has performed at Steampunk festivals, as this music would fit perfectly within that scene. It is folk, alt-folk, acoustic yet poppy, melodic, and easy to listen to yet also full of thought and passion. Once you get inside his world it is hard to get back to reality, as here is a place where acoustic instruments are the order of the day, and the piano accordion is once again a key musical component. As with much music these days, I listened this to the first time in the car, and here is my only complaint about the whole piece. I noticed that the final song on the album, "Mr. Many Men", was more than twenty-eight minutes and I braced myself for a folk epic extravaganza like I had never heard before. So, imagine my disappointment when it faded out after about six minutes, to which I thought "Great, a hidden track, I thought they had gone out in the

Eighties". There was nearly nine minutes of silence before the album started up again, and then there was a series of songs that continued through to the end – but, they can't be separately selected, and these are worth hearing so why not list them as such and get rid of the silence? It's not clever, not wanted, and I don't want to drive in silence for so long, so why bother? The reason it annoyed me so much is apart from this, the album is a masterpiece and a delight from start to end.

I can't pick a favourite, so won't bother, but will heartily recommend this to anyone who wants music that has been carefully crafted from the finest wood, polished, and honed to perfection, as opposed to yet another piece of throwaway plastic that will only last a few minutes before the bright colours fade: another disposable commodity. This music may have found a strange way to get down from the UK to me at the other side of the world, but I am so very happy that it did as this is a 'must have'.
Feb 2017

ALEX CARPANI
4 DESTINIES
It appears that fate has had quite a part to play in Carpani's career, as being in the same class as Aaron Emerson, and having the opportunity to meet his father Keith at the tender age of 7 started his interest in progressive rock and keyboards from a young age. Later, when recovering from an accident he took the opportunity to compose and record what ended up being his debut album, 'Waterline', which was released in 2006. Since that time, he has formed a full band and has toured much of the world (although not this area I note). The second album followed in 2010, and now he is back with the third. This album features all the Alex Carpani Band with Alex providing keyboards and lead vocals, Ettore Salati on guitars, GB Giorgi on bass, Alessandro Di Caprio on drums and Joe Sal on additional vocals. In addition, David Jackson (VDGG) adds various saxophones and flutes as special guest, while it has been produced by Cristiano Roversi (Moongarden, John Wetton Band, Submarine Silence, CCLR).

'4 Destinies' is a progressive rock concept based on four eventual destinies that a man can find on the path of his life. Alex states there are four destinies that irradiate, moving from the same point, in four different directions of life... and this is depicted in four songs, all of which are thirteen minutes or more in length. If one was asked what country Alex hails from, I think many progheads would fathom a guess at Italy as although his style may be more symphonic at times, there is no doubt the Italian scene has had a major impact on his music. The use of Jackson is interesting, as although there are times when he is very much in step with the rest of the music there are also others such as on "Sky and Sea", where there are passages where he is producing a melody that is almost as odds with the rest of the band. There is a fine line here between creating chaos and providing emphasis and he just stays on the right side of that line, but it is a close call at times. From ballads to more powerful numbers, this is an album that is quite atmospheric, and while never getting to the same dizzy heights as Goblin also has nods in the same direction.

There are times when the contrast between the instruments, and the arrangements being deployed, makes one think here is something that is going to veer off into avant-garde jazz territory, but it always comes back safely to the prog side. Overall, an intriguing and interesting album, while never being truly essential, but worth hearing all the same,
Jun 2014

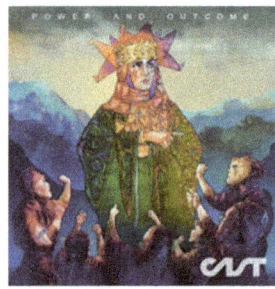

CAST
THE POWER & THE GLORY
The last album I reviewed from the Mexican prog masters was 'Beyond Reality', more than twenty years ago, so when I saw this pop out of the envelope, I had a huge smile on my face. I have lost touch with the guys and the many albums they have released in the intervening period, but I know I used to like them and was sure I would enjoy this. It wasn't too long afterwards, that I was telling everyone who would listen that this was a masterpiece, and I found that those who had already heard it were saying the same thing. The comment I had back from one reviewer I value very highly was that as soon as he first started playing it, the only decision he had to make was whether it was a 4* album or a 5* album. I knew exactly what he meant, except that it was only halfway through the first listen that I was convinced that here was an album that not only deserved a 5* rating, but I knew I was going to fall in love with it even more every time I played it, which has turned out to be just the case.

This release is a "review killer" in the sense that it prevents me from listening to all the other albums I should be playing as it is just so good in every single aspect. Much of this is instrumental, as there is just no room for vocals, but the two singers (Bobby Vidales and Lupita Ancuna) make their presence felt when they have the opportunity. It's just that when there are maestros such as those on display, then there just isn't always the place or time for that element. They even start with an instrumental that is nearly twelve minutes long, I mean, is this prog or what? With three lead melody instruments in guitar, violin and keyboards, there is an incredible amount going on, but they rarely really show off. One of the exceptions to that is guitarist Claudio Cudero who tears his instrument to pieces and shreds like a lunatic in "Ilusions and Tribulations"; yet this is also a thoughtful number with some great emotive vocals and beautiful repetitive piano motifs.

This is an album that has made me incredibly excited, wanting to shout to the rooftops that the band I knew and loved in the Nineties have released a stunning album, yet it is tinged with disappointment that I lost contact for so long, and what are the albums like that I have missed out on! This is going to be a contender for my personal album of the year as for me this majestically sums up just about everything I love about prog music. It is powerful yet melodic, full of instrumental brilliance and simplicity, layered and complex yet also is full of space and plenty of room for everyone to breathe and show just what they can do.

This is a stunning album, and to my ears is essential. Nothing more, nothing less.
Apr 2017

IL CASTELLO DI ATLANTE
ARX ATLANTIS
When a band has been around for forty years, with a fairly unchanged line-up for more than thirty, it perhaps isn't unsurprising that they know what they are doing. Aldo Bergamini (guitar, vocals), Andrea Bertino (violin), Davide Cristofoli (keyboards), Paolo Ferrarotti (keyboards, vocals, drums), Dino Fiore (bass) and Mattia Garimanno (drums) follow a classic RPI path, with strong symphonic elements, all lyrics in Italian, and plenty of bombast to combine with the different styles they are bringing together. The arrangements are lush, and while the vocals may not be as strong as some may wish, to me they are perfectly matched to the music. Unusually for RPI the drums are quite high in the mix, but this has been done quite deliberately as Mattia has a deft touch, and his various rhythms make the album stand out, along with complex keyboards and wonderful violin.

Hugely structured and complex, yet also incredibly enjoyable and listenable, this is a wonderful album for any lovers of this style of progressive rock.
Feb 2018

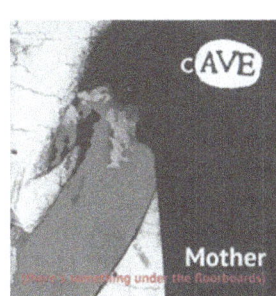

CAVE
MOTHER
So, I was sent some CDs recently by my good friend Thierry Sportouche from Acid Dragon in France, and included within the envelope were two CD-R's with photocopied inserts by the band Cave. Having played them I asked Thierry what he knew about the band so that I could have some information for the review, and he told me that he knew absolutely nothing. Not to be deterred I searched the web, only to quickly discover that "cave" is a very common word. Instead, I then searched for the name of this five-song forty-minute-long album and discovered that they had both a Soundcloud account and a Facebook page. I have tried contacting them through both but have met with no response. So, all I know for certain is that the line-up (according to FB) is Julian Walker, Dave Spowage, Mark Flood and David Littler (although I don't know who plays what, or who was on this), and they come from Knaresborough. Oh, and their FB page hasn't been updated in 2017 so they may not even exist anymore for all I know, which could be why they aren't responding to emails.

Recorded at Orb (which I think is Orb Community Arts in Knaresborough) last year, I think this might be a live recording, although there isn't any audience sound. They describe their music as "electronic sonic goodness" and that's as good a description as any, although early Tangerine Dream or Kraftwerk could also be included. And there is the most frustrating aspect of the whole affair: this is very good indeed and I can't even tell you where to get it from! Some all-keyboard albums can be quite sterile, but this has a warmth and depth, and instead of meaningless meanderings there is a feeling of purpose, as if they are building something together that is quite special. This is one of the

reasons I believe it has been recorded live, as there is the impression that the different players are improvising based on the sounds being put out by the others. I've played this quite a few times now, and each time it comes across as both simplistic and intriguing, something quite hard to achieve.
May 2017

CAVE
REAL TIME
This was again recorded at Orb, this time in 2015 and 2016 (both are marked as 2017 releases, but I don't know which one was released first): it is very like 'Mother', except this often feels darker and even more like early Tangerine dream. This time we have fourteen songs (of course, all instrumental), many of which are quite shorter than on the other album, and a running time that has extended to fifty-two minutes. At times this makes me think of Hawkwind, especially during "Are We Ready", even though the only instruments are different synthesisers and electronic sounds and effects. White noise is often utilised and there is something quite compelling about the album that keeps me coming back for more, even though I can't really say why.

I have the feeling they will probably sink without trace if it is this hard to get hold of them, and that is a shame as both these albums are worth hearing if you enjoy listening to electronic music that has nothing at all to do with dance.
May 2017

CAVE
GENERIC
After my recent reviews of Cave, I heard back from David Littler who apologised for being so difficult to get hold of, he has moved to the highlands of Scotland with no internet or phone signal, hence the silence. Apparently, Cave are in the process of recording a new album, but until then would I be interested in 'Generic', a CD of demos and ideas they released earlier this year. They will also soon be starting a page on Bandcamp, so it will be easier to both get hold of them and listen to their recordings. As to how they make them, "You're correct in your guesswork about us creating work in real time, improvising, and responding to each other - we're composing as we go, and all recordings are in a single take. We aim to create sonically primitive music evoking secret worlds of insect and subterranean life, geological time, and the lost elements of the English landscape." Dave Spowage plays the Notron (a sequencer he invented), David Littler is responsible for field recordings and live sampling, Mark Flood plays air synths and toys, and Julian Walker plays various Korgs and guitar.

As with the earlier CDs, I am incredibly impressed with this album, as it is electronic music that in many ways hearkens back to the very beginning of that genre, and while

Tangerine Dream are obviously an influence, so are Can, while it isn't too hard to imagine Art Zoyd also having a role to play. This is nothing like the style of electronic music that seems to be the favourite these days, as it is dark, atmospheric, and rewards being listened to closely instead of being just another form of annoying muzak that is best left in the background where it belongs.

All of 58 people have liked their Facebook page (and I'm one of them), but these guys deserve support and a few more "likes" wouldn't go amiss, I'm sure. They may not be as visible as many bands, but this is music which is compelling and needs support.
Oct 2017

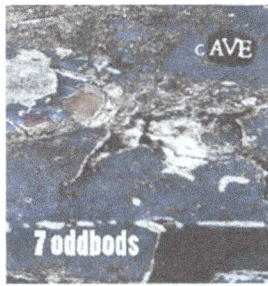

CAVE
7 ODDBODS
The band were sorry that it took so long for me to be able to contact them, so they also sent me another of their releases with comedy titles, '7 Oddbods'. All their releases are CD-R's, with a home printed inlay, but don't let the DIY ethos let anyone judge their music in the same way. Okay, this one is in a much lighter vein than the other three and isn't necessarily the one I would suggest starting with, but is still something I found intriguing and interesting, even though I wouldn't call it indispensable. Mark (air synths and toys) told me "This is the first time I have been able to regularly contribute instrumentally to the creation of something that appears to have a life and soul of its own. Being in tune and carefully listening to each other and hopefully knowing when not to contribute to the mix to give space is some of the key criteria for the pieces to work."

They have released at least four albums so far, all instrumental, all electronic, and all composed and performed in real time without overdubs or corrections. I would probably look to 'Generic' first to discover this band and come to this one at the end of the trip, and while that will be long and strange it will ultimately be incredibly rewarding for those that take the journey.
Oct 2017

CHARLIE CAWOOD
THE DIVINE ABSTRACT
Charlie has been a veteran of the London music scene for more than a decade now and is best known as bassist of critically acclaimed psychedelic octet Knifeworld, and instrumentalist/co-arranger for Emmy-nominated Classical choir Mediaeval Baebes. He also plays stringed instruments in Bad Elephant Music stable mates My Tricksy Spirit. 'The Divine Abstract' is Charlie's first album of solo compositions, and it was conceived and written over a 7-year period, centred around themes of change, transformation, and transcendence. In many ways, it is hard to know exactly where to

start with this album, but the band that springs to mind when first hearing this is Karda Estra, but one where Richard Wileman has been taken on a pilgrimage through the likes of India, China and Indonesia and has also brought those elements into his modern classical progressive style.

Charlie provides acoustic, electric & classical guitars, Fender VI, acoustic & electric bass guitars, sitar, and pipa (a four-stringed Chinese musical instrument, belonging to the plucked category of instruments, sometimes called the Chinese lute). But if that isn't enough variety, how about the guests who have worked with him and the instruments they brought to the party? Katharine Blake (treble & sopranino recorders), Lucy Brown (French horn), Flora Curzon (violin), Hannah Davis (vibraphone, glockenspiel), Julie Groves (flute), Chlöe Herington (bassoon), Steve Holmes (piano, celeste, Minimoog, bass synth), James Larcombe (piano, dulcitone), Dennis Kwong Thye Lee (xiao), Nicki Maher (clarinet), Ben Marshall (oboe, cor anglais), Elizabeth Nott (darbouka, riq, frame drum), Josh Perl (clarinet & bass clarinet), Alexandra Petropoulos (flute), Oliver Sellwood (baritone saxophone), Diego Tejeida (piano), Francesca Ter-Berg (cello), Lucie Treacher (kendang, ceng ceng, gong, kempur, kenang, klentong, kempli, genterak), Wang Xiao (erhu) and Ben Woollacott (drums, percussion & cymbals) all have a part to play.

Somehow, this album doesn't sound contrived and over-arranged, but simply flows unimpeded, mixing different instruments and musical styles to create a journey which shows just how much Charlie understands musical form, arrangements, and how instruments from different parts of the world can come together to create something both unique and beautiful at the same time. It is the perfect album to play on the deck on a warm summer's evening, and let it combine with the birdsong and become something that feels a part of the natural environment very much. Too much music these days is disposable and plastic, created without a thought for the end results, apart from sounding like every other pop hit out there and hopefully gaining the performer some airtime and possibly a part on the next Celebrity Look At What They've Got Me Doing Now (but you're watching it while I'm being paid, so who is the real idiot?) programme.

This has been created because it was the right thing to do, and there are times when I am glad that I spend so many hours sat behind a keyboard writing about music, as every so often a real diamond comes my way that otherwise I would never have discovered. This is incredible, majestic, visionary, and essential, nothing less.
Nov 2017

ALAN CHARLES
ELETRIA
In the early Nineties Canadian band Existence started making their name performing a rock opera of original songs, and over the next few years released a couple of albums, including 'Small People, Short Story, Little Crime'. I was incredibly impressed with the album as not only did I enjoy the music, but it came with a 56-page booklet, not bad for an independent release. I must confess that for one reason or another I lost touch with the band

until 2017, when they released a double CD featuring the two acts of the original show, originally performed some 25 years earlier. The band was basically on hiatus between 2002 and 2010, but that didn't stop the guys working, and in 2007 bandleader, songwriter and pianist Alan Charles released another album, 'Eletria'. Again, this is an opera, and four members of Existence were involved in the album and the stage play, which Alan also released as a book.

The story is about a young 16-year-old girl who follows the wrong guy to Toronto (from Montreal) and ends up captive, forced into prostitution. After almost three years of this life, she manages to escape to Vancouver with a "client" but finds out she is pregnant – from who knows who. She decides to keep the child so her "saviour" gives her money to go back to Montreal where she cleans-up (she had become a junkie) and gives birth to a healthy boy she names Gabriel. But at aged eight, the child is diagnosed with leukaemia and finally dies in her arms. Before he died, he made her promise to survive him and tell her real story. Alan told me that it is based on a real-life story he was told in a club after an Existence gig in 2002. He changed many things but it's essentially it: the girl had told him then that Existence's music kept her alive.

Musically it is very much based around the piano, sometimes with a full band and at others with just one or two choice instruments such as a violin. The vocals are by Catherine Boulanger, and they are incredibly passionate and evocative – it's just a shame that she sings the album in French, and I have no idea what is going on! The arrangements allow the passion to come through the instruments, and the fretless bass is incredibly warm and delicate, providing a strong counterpoint to the more staccato approach of Alan's piano. I am somewhat surprised not to have come across this album before, as this is music of real quality and delicacy, but I am sure this can be explained by the fact that it is really a musical captured on CD, and the lyrics are obviously incredibly important, and by being in French will bypass most of the prospective audience.

Given that the new recording by Existence has put them more into the public progressive eye, I can only hope that people will try and discover more about this band, who I firmly believe have never received the attention they deserve. Along the musical journey people may well then come across this album, which even to a non-French speaker such as me is incredibly enjoyable. To discover this lost gem, plus other releases by Existence then visit the website (which thankfully is in both English and French).
Feb 2018

CHEER-ACCIDENT
PUTTING OFF DEATH
Six years after their last album, 'No Ifs, Ands or Dogs', Cheer-Accident are back with their eighteenth studio album. During the last thirty years they have had something of a fluid line-up (including members who don't actually perform with the band, or do normally but don't play on this album), and there are fourteen musicians credited here, but at the heart of it there has always been Jeff Libersher (guitar, trumpet, vocals, keyboards) and

Thymme Jones (drums, vocals, piano, trumpet, keyboards, acoustic and electric guitars, Moog, noise). I think the politest way to describe their music to a newcomer would be "eclectic", with some RIO thrown in for good measure. They've conjured up a unique collage of intricate prog, lush pop, and experimental noise, drawing on the disparate influences of Pere Ubu, King Crimson, Can, Art Bears, Wire, early Genesis and Yes, and the more Baroque leaps of the Beatles and the Beach Boys without ever settling on a sound that could be definitively traced to any of them in isolation.

Take opening number "Language Is" for example, which starts off as a piano and vocal number, but just when the listener feels they know what is going on and settles back in their comfy chair, all sorts of weird stuff starts, so by the end of the eleven-minute-long epic they end up scratching their head asking "what on earth just happened?". This is progressive rock that really is, refusing to conform to any ideal of what the sound should be like, but organically playing and experimenting with the music until the band themselves understand what they have before them. However, unlike many others operating within this musical sphere there is often a great deal of melody, and the music makes logical sense. But don't relax too much, as there are also plenty of times when it doesn't, but does, if you get what I mean.

Yet again Cuneiform is working with a band (this is their third album on the label) that the mainstream music industry wouldn't touch with a barge pole, and all of us who hear this are much the richer for the experience.
May 2017

CHRISTINA
THE LIGHT

For progheads in the know, mention just the single word 'Christina', and everyone is aware that the person under discussion is Christina Booth, frontwoman of Magenta since their inception in 2001. This was her second solo album, released nearly three years ago now, but I have only just come across it. Joining her on this musical odyssey was Rob Reed on keyboards, guitar and bass (with whom she has worked with for many years, all the way back to Cyan), Andy Edwards (Magenta, drums) and Chris Fry (guitar) along with Fran Murphy (backing vocals), Dan Nelsen (fretless bass), John Mitchell (It Bites/Arena, guitar, vocals), Andy Tillison (PO90/The Tangent etc., organ) and Theo Travis (saxophone, flute).

Although she has surrounded herself with musicians she knows and trusts, this album isn't an out and out prog album, although it does contain progressive elements and could, just, be considered as crossover, but rather is an album that is based around her voice and reflective songs that show her restraint and control to best effect. Although I have known her through band albums, I haven't heard her other solo work, but can see that I am now going to have to search it out as this is delicate and beautiful. There are times when it is just her and a piano, and the use of a fretless bass is a great touch as the warmth given by that instrument works perfectly with the feel. Most singers feel the need to be forceful and overtly in the listener's ears and face, but here Christina is singing wonderfully, with emotional songs which fit her voice perfectly, while the arrangements are also doing all they can not to take away from the, at times, waif-like quality of her voice.

That it has taken me three years to come across this is very much my loss, and I hope to hear more from this wonderful singer soon.
Jan 2018

CIRCLE
TERMINAL

This Finnish band released their debut as long as 1991, and if RYM are to be believed (and I generally find the site infallible), they have released north of thirty studio albums since then, of which this is the latest. I had the misfortune to be sent a photo of the band, and it has been a while since I have seen people of a certain age wearing that much bright pink spandex, and once that vision has been put in front of your eyes you can't unsee it, more's the pity. So, it would be incredibly easy to discount Circle as being a comic band, but while there is obviously a large part of that within their makeup, there is also something quite unusual and serious happening within the music.

Here we have a band that explore sonic soundscapes, venturing curiously into terrains of Stooges-esque swagger, trance-inducing kraut rock mantras, beautiful electronic ambience, psychedelic rock noodling, arena storming AOR weirdness, Seventies prog rock extravagance, glam pop pomp, and of course their core sound, heavy metal, not to mention other peculiar and daring sounds that simply cannot be pigeonholed. Intrigued? Well, you should be. This is music that somehow sounds fuzzed out and distorted from the Seventies, with all these different musical styles and fashions coming together, but the result is an album that is incredibly impressive. The more I play it, the more I like it, and if you enjoy experiencing something that is out of left field yet also somehow being quite mainstream, then this could well be of interest.
Jun 2017

CIRCU5
CIRCU5

Before I get started on the music, let's talk about the presentation of the CD itself. What I have in my hands is a CD-sized hardback book, with the disc inside the front cover (and interestingly space for another at the back – what's that for Steve?), and 28 glossy pages of photos with the lyrics and details of musicians etc. Let's bear in mind that Steve Tilling, the man behind Circu5, is not an incredibly well-known musician signed to a major label, but instead has put his hand in his pocket to deliver something that in today's market stands out like a flashing neon sign. Not for him just relying on streaming or digital downloads, but something the listener will enjoy looking at while playing the album, just like in the old days. Some bands do make the effort (Galahad, stand up and take an immense bow) by releasing vinyl themselves, but it is indeed rare to come across an "unknown" putting this much care into it. So, of course even before playing it I was intrigued. It is a concept album, detailing the life of a child raised as a psychopath in a secret government organisation, which aims to cure the condition, while harnessing positive traits for certain roles. The character discovers the truth as a dysfunctional adult– with catastrophic consequences. Steve Tilling is a multi-instrumentalist and vocalist, and he spent five years getting this right. It also features guest performances from Dave Gregory (XTC, Big Big Train), Phil Spalding (Mike Oldfield), Matt Backer (Julian Lennon), Alan van Kleef (Rachel Stamp), Johnny Warman (Peter Gabriel) and Andy Neve (Steve Hackett). Dave is riding high with major kudos in the prog scene currently, so by now I guess that everyone is assuming that this is a prog album, and you would be right, but you would also be wrong.

There is very much a progressive feel to the album, and the acoustic opener "Coming Home" has a Tull-ish feel, although the vocals are far lighter and double-tracked, and the electric guitar that comes in is very American indeed. But it took a while for my head to get around the second song "My Degenerate Mind", and it was ages before I realised that I was listening to the best Foo Fighters song Dave Grohl never recorded. It was at this point that I realised that this album was going to be something a little different to what I was expecting. Given that Steve had been put onto me by Mark Colton of Credo I had automatically assumed that Steve was part of the prog scene, but rather he is part of the "I don't give a shit what genre you think I should be playing, I'm just going to deliver bloody good songs that you will love: I refuse to be pigeon-holed because music isn't a pigeon" scene.

The only way to play this album is loud, proud, and with a massive smile on your face. The press release mentions bands such as Foo Fighters, Queens of the Stone Age, King Crimson, Rush, Yes, Cardiacs, Jethro Tull, Radiohead, Jellyfish, Nick Drake, Hawkwind and King's X depending on what section of what song you are listening to, and they're probably correct. This is a fun and enjoyable album from the beginning to the very end, and if you don't believe me then listen to the anthem that is "Stars" and join in on the chorus. My only concern is that this album took Steve five years to make, and I really don't want to wait that long for the next one!
Feb 2018

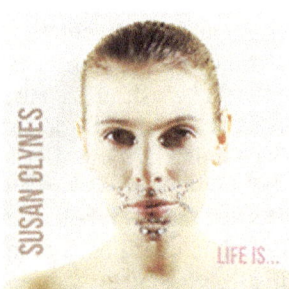

SUSAN CLYNES
LIFE IS…
Susan Clynes is a Belgian singer, pianist and songwriter who is forging her own path in music. After taking classical and jazz piano lessons and attending jazz workshops while in high school, Susan chose to follow her heart: shunning a more traditional course of university studies and career path to study music composition and earning a master's degree at the Ghent Conservatory. Her debut album was released in 2005, 'Sugar For A Dream', but this is her first full album since then. She is

married to keyboardist Antoine Guenet (The Wrong Object, Sh.t.gn and Universe Zero) and Antoine encouraged her to perform as a guest vocalist on The Wrong Object's 'After The Exhibition' and then suggested casually to Leonardo that Susan should join the label in her own right.

Leo also thought it was a good idea, and this is the result. Unusually, this is a live album in the sense that these songs are taken from three different concerts, and while she is joined by Pierre Mottet (bass) and Nico Chifki (drums) on two songs, there are another five where she is accompanied by cellist Simon Lenski (from RIO band Daau), and they obviously have a real connection. There are times when I am reminded of early Suzanne Vega or Tori Amos, but at others we are treated to RIO or avant-garde jazz, or torch, or any number of jazz styles. She has a wonderfully clear voice, combined with incredibly effective piano, and there is just the slight use of reverb on her microphone that assists in giving additional presence and the result is something that is immensely powerful. It really demonstrates that it doesn't need crashing guitars or over-the-top dynamics to come across with something that grabs the listener and holds them enthralled to the very end. It is a stunning piece of work, and I for one would certainly be interested in hearing the debut now, I wonder if Leo is thinking of releasing that as well? (hint). Sheer beauty from the beginning to the very end
Jun 2014

COBURG
THE ENCHANTRESS
A little while back I heard from Dean Baker, keyboard player with Galahad, who asked if I would be interested in hearing a new project he and Mark Spencer were involved with. Mark filled in with Galahad for a while, and of course he and Dean were both part of the reformed Twelfth Night, so I was intrigued to say the least, as although Galahad have been around for more than thirty years, it was only during the Twelfth Night period that band members were active in another outfit. Coburg came together in July 2017 after Anastasia Coburg (Jet Noir, Naked Lunch – lead vocals and lead guitar) approached several musicians she had either worked with in the past or were on her professional 'Wishlist', including her brother Pietro (Jet Noir, drums). The line-up is completed by Dean (synths, programming and backing vocals) and Mark (bass guitar and backing vocals) with Sarah Sanford (Jet Noir, rhythm guitar and backing vocals) and Tony Mayo (Naked Lunch, vocals, and percussion). Now, to be honest, I haven't come across Jet Noir or Naked Lunch before, but I may have to do some digging to find out some more, as this debut album is one that I have enjoyed immensely.

Over the years, Galahad have been through a few different musicians, but to my ears the one who has made the largest single impact to the sound of the band is Dean, and anyone coming across 'Battle Scars' would have some problem realising that it was the same band who released 'Nothing Is Written' (apart from Stu's vocals of course), as not only has the music become far heavier, it is driven far more by the keyboards than it was previously. I don't know how much impact Dean had on the actual song writing on this album, but he obviously had a major role to play in the arrangements as his style is very much to the fore.

Anastasia has a great voice, and a strong sense of melody, able to power through in the manner of Doro when she needs to, but it is when she is at her most reflective such as at the beginning of "Requiem" that her class really shines. The album itself is straddling many styles, from progressive rock, prog metal, melodic rock, and symphonic metal through to elements from Rammstein. One of the joys is the way the music has been structured so that often it is just Dean and Pietro supporting Anastasia, and this allows the band to provide tremendous contrast when they all come back in together. "Requiem" is musically all over the place, with poppy synths that easily give way to a lead guitar at just the right moment. Opener "A Cold Day In Hell" is riff heavy, with bass and drums playing a basic pattern, and it is the vocals that lift the song as it moves to the bridge, and straightaway the listener is entranced. Anastasia's voice has a slight catch to it, which provides far more depth and allows her to portray emotion in many ways, and it took me a long time to work out who she reminded me of. That person was Candia of Incubus Succubus, and Anastasia has a very similar gothic approach, with her vocals high and proud in the mix.

This is a superb debut, which I have really enjoyed, and if they have produced this after only a short time together, what on earth are they going to bring us in the years to come? Go to the website and discover more, your ears demand it.
Oct 2017

CORMORANT
DIASPORA
Even before I started playing the debut full-length release from Californian progressive black/death metal band Cormorant, I had fallen in love with the artwork by Jeff Christensen. Apparently, there are four separate panels, which were created as sixteen-inch square oil paintings, quite an undertaking for a self-release. Formed in 2007, the group consists of bassist/vocalist Marcus Luscombe, guitarist Nick Cohon, guitarist/vocalist Matt Solis, and drummer Brennan Kunkel. In addition to performing numerous shows throughout the Bay Area with notable acts like At The Gates, Wolves In The Throne Room, Ne Obliviscaris, and Pallbearer, they have completed full US tours with Primordial, While Heaven Wept, YOB, Norska, and others. For this release the band were also joined by cellist Jackie Perez Gratz (Grayceon, Giant Squid, ex-Amber Asylum).

Cormorant are bringing together black, death, prog, and folk metal, while there are also pronounced psychedelic, dark ambient and funeral doom influences. This album is a respectable length at sixty-one minutes, but there are only four songs. Closer "Migration" is more than twenty-six minutes in length, which is epic by any standards, certainly for a band playing music like this. But they never seem too long, as it allows all the styles to mix, and the listener finds themselves deep inside the music, not even realising that the

real world has been passing them by. As well as releasing this as a double vinyl album and CD, the band have also made this available digitally, so if this sounds intriguing why not give them a listen. What have you to lose?
Jun 2017

COSHISH
FIRDOUS
In these days of the world getting ever smaller I suppose I shouldn't be surprised when I get sent an album from an Indian progressive rock band, but when I saw the complete package, I was just blown away. I know they obviously have some backing from Universal, but the amount of work that has been put into the debut album from an unknown band is considerable and must have cost a packet. The first thing one notices is the cover of the digipak itself, which features a man in a yoga position. When looking closely one can see that one of his tattoos is the Star of David, he is wearing a hat with the all-seeing eye, there are fish, and by his feet is Ouroboros! And take it from me there is a lot more symbolism than just these. Apparently, the artwork is collaboration between Bernard Dumaine from France, Daeve Fellows from Canada and Bharath Chandrasekhar as well as Imran Ladak from India.

'Firdous' is a concept album that documents a young man's journey towards attaining Mukti (salvation). To aid this story telling, the packaging contains photographs that help in recreating the strife and emotional turmoil that ultimately guide him towards self-realization. There are two separate visual stories to assist in understanding lyrically what is going on here, with the first being the photos inside the digipak itself. When it is opened, on the left side there is a boy looking at an old, abandoned house, while in the middle he has obviously entered and is now walking up the stairs. The last shows him in the attic looking inside an old trunk and staring at some photos. When he looks at the photographs, he realises they tell the story of the man who lived in that house. These ten photos are included with the album, with each showing a different image and the date when it was taken (while on the rear are the 'handwritten' lyrics for the song it relates to).

So, the main story and concept is that the man in the photographs was a boy from a village who has dreams of moving to the city and making it big. One day, a soothsayer tells him that he is meant for greater things, but he doesn't understand what that means. When he is about to leave for the city, his family is killed in riots, and he feels his plans and his life are destroyed, and he goes into depression. After a few months, he decides to put his past behind him and still follow his dreams, so he moves to the city, finds a job, and thinks he is living his dream. A few months later, he realizes his dream is an illusion and that trying to become rich and successful is not really making him happy, so he becomes more spiritual and realizes that the entire world is stuck in this illusion of material wealth. He gathers enough courage to look beyond the illusion by giving up all his worldly belongings tries and attain salvation or "Mukti". Now, if all that wasn't enough, the sequence of the album is not actually correct! The only way to get the music in the order in which it is supposed to be played is by listening to the songs in the date order of the photographs. When you do this the album becomes one giant track in which all the sound samples are connected, and the story flows.

Given that I don't know the language (typical lazy pom) I have ascertained all this by going through the various documents sent to me by the band, but it is more than worth retelling here as it adds depth to what is already sonically a very interesting release. Ah yes, the music. I have already spent a few hundred words talking about the album but haven't mentioned the music at all! They say their collective influences range from Tool, Porcupine Tree, A Perfect Circle, Opeth, Isis, Karnivool and Meshuggah to AR Rehman, Pandit Bhimsen Joshi, and Lucky Ali. I don't know the final ones in this list, and Meshuggah are a little hard to detect, but the rest are there in abundance, with Porcupine Tree probably taking the lead. It was recorded, produced, and mixed by Zorran Mendonsa from New Zealand and mastered by Jens Bogren in Sweden, and they have managed to capture an incredible band in all their glory. The music is often extremely complex and layered, yet every instrument is clear and distinct, and there is a feeling of space at times, while at others it is heavily compressed, but it is all about what the music needs. Mangesh Gandhi has a wonderful voice, clear and pure yet with depth, and the way he brings in both Western influences and Indian into the way that he sings adds to the whole effect. It is probably these vocals more than anything else that really showcases the Indian element of the band.

The one thing that really concerns me more than anything else is that given that this is a debut what on earth do they come up with for a follow-up? Musically this is accessible on first play, and the more I listen to it the more I enjoy it. Yes, there are elements that some will say are way more commercial than a prog band should be doing, but at the end of the day I rate this on whether I enjoyed it and that I did, a lot! I have no idea what he is singing, and can't read the lyrics, but I recognise that this is a hell of an album and something that has been hitting my player regularly and there is no doubt this will continue in the future.
Apr 2014

COZHE
PRESSURE FRACTURES
This Finnish band can trace its' beginning back to more than twelve years ago, when singer and keyboard player Janne Nevalainen first came across drummer Harri Kokkonen. They started playing together in 2002 and over the years other musicians have come and gone, but they stuck it out and the result is this their debut album which was released in 2012. At the time the line-up was completed by Joni Seppälä (guitars) and Sami Järvinen (bass), although Joni moved to Sweden not long after the album was completed. In many ways this is an album of the Seventies, as it has been heavily influenced by the likes of Family from that era and more recently by Discipline, and while crossover prog is obviously the correct genre, that is because it hits so many different musical areas including that of hard rock.

This isn't a gentle melodic prog album, but something that has rough angular edges which contrast strongly with the fluidity of Joni's wonderful guitars. Although the keyboards are an important part, the use of piano is more direct and powerful, while special mention should also be made of Harri's drumming as there are times when he is working incredibly hard, with a far more rock bent than the rest of the band which also provides wonderful dynamics. It is the fractured nature of the music that makes this such a compelling album, although it does also have its weaknesses, most notably in that the lyrics don't always work as well in English as they should, and Janne's vocals do sometimes go off key. But these are small issues that I am sure will be resolved with the next release, which apparently, they are planning at present. Personally, I would not have included the final song on the album, as joke pieces only really work once and although I found this fairly amusing the first time I played it, the novelty soon wore off. An enjoyable album, quite at odds with most of the current scene, and I look forward with interest to the next one.
Jun 2014

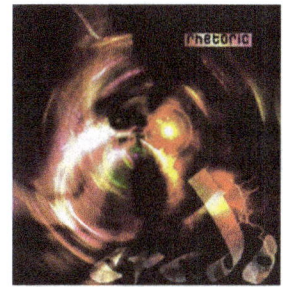

CREDO
RHETORIC
Just to let you all know the score between me and this band, at one time in their career I was getting gigs for them and assisting them with promotion etc. I was there the night when the contract with Cyclops Records was signed for 'Field Of Vision', and this album followed only eleven years later in 2005. Originally released by F2 Music, it was then reissued by then band themselves in 2013 as a digipak with an additional track, namely a demo mix of "Skintrade". Singer Mark Colton and I first got in touch with each other when he was with Casual Affair: when that band broke up, I then wrote the newsletter for his next band Freewill, and when he joined Chequered Past (later renamed Credo) I started following them around as well. When I got married only two people knew in advance as they were the witnesses, and one of these was Mark. Many years later I was asked by Mark and his wife Elaine to be godfather to their younger son, and I even traipsed out to see him one night front a folk-rock band called Phyre!

Eleven years is a long time for any band to produce their second album, during which time more than a few things have happened. Musically they brought in Shadowland (and now Landmarq) keyboard wizard Mike Varty which changed their sound, as it meant that Tim Birrell finally had someone to play against (poor old Mik Stovold was never in the same league), while drummer Paul Clarke announced one night after a blinding gig that he was also off, and was replaced by Martin Meads from the aforementioned folk group! The line-up is completed of course by the one and only Jim Murdoch who as well as playing bass also assists Mike with the backing vocals. And then there is Mark, who got married, had two children, and was at one point only thirty minutes from dying. Luckily there were some very clever consultants around that managed to keep him in this world, but there were many who thought this album would never be completed. Even now, in 2017, he still has health issues and is a long way from being fully fit, but he is singing and very much full of enthusiasm for the band.

It seems many years since I was in the studio listening to Martin lay down the drums with Karl Groom et al, but there again it was. Looking at the track listing I recognised many from those heady days playing in Staines and other toilets but putting it on the player I know it never sounded like this! This is polished neo-prog we never hear these days, songs with a meaning, a singer who can turn on the vitriol when he needs and somehow is also singing better than ever - given what Mark was going through during this process the result is nothing short of incredible, as they produced an album that rated as one of the best of the year, when it came out. But you're biased I hear you cry, and maybe I am, but hopefully those who know me would realise that if I felt that this was under par then I would say so. It just isn't possible to fault this in any way - Mike is an incredible keyboard player as anyone who has seen him will agree. There aren't many who have been chosen by Clive Nolan to fill his own shoes, while Tim Birrell managed to shrug off an approach from Fish who wanted him for his own band, and who is I firmly believe one of the best guitarists around and is Credo's secret weapon as no-one outside of those who follow the band know who he is! Martin and Jim have a real understanding, nailing the rhythm to the floor either slowly or flying with a passion, and then there is Mark. Mark is probably more of a frontman than just a singer, as he throws himself into every performance with passion, but here he has proved what a bloody good singer he is as well.

Nine songs plus the bonus, with two of them over eleven minutes in length, but the one I feel must be singled out appears halfway through the album and is just under eight minutes long. I was there at The Compasses the night "The Letter" had its first public airing, the night when the person it was directed at fled to the toilets in tears. Back then it was full of passion and incredible guitar, but somehow it has now become so much more. If ever a song builds to a climax, then this is it, with Mike much more to the fore - giving the song balance, while Jim also changes his bass approach during the song which gives it further depth. There is a polish and togetherness which wasn't there before, with the vocals flowing and providing the background for Mark to vent his passion, his anger. I could rave about these songs - the wonderful intro to "The Game" or the closing masterpiece that is "Seems Like Yesterday", but all the numbers have benefited from a new approach and cleaner, sharper, but also very layered, arrangements.

"Skintrade" was originally a very different song, written and recorded by Freewill, but when Mark was presented with some music one day, he knew he had already written lyrics that would fit perfectly, so plagiarised himself!

If somehow this album passed you by when it was originally released, then now is the time to correct that one. They are now working on their fourth album, and I was listening to some demo tracks when I was over with Mark recently and am sure that yet again, they will surprise a lot of people with their depth and passion. But for now, get this, get the last album 'Against Reason', and prepare yourself for the next one.
Sep 2017

DAMANEK
ON TRACK

Damanek is a new project from Guy Manning, where he has been joined by Dan Mash (bass), Marek Arnold (sax, clarinet, keyboards) and Sean Timms (keyboards, banjo, backing vocals) and then on top of that there are quite a few guests including Nick Magnus and Phideaux. Guy had disbanded Manning and was then invited to join a new band called United Progressive Fraternity to which he also then brought in Dan and Marek. After the release of the debut album Guy started writing for the second, only for the band to fold, so he decided to start a new one to use the songs, and asked Dan and Marek to be involved, hence the name (DAn, MANning and MarEK), with Sean joining later.

I have long been a fan of Guy's music and spent a very pleasant evening with him in his studio some dozen years or so ago and have enjoyed all albums he has been involved with from PO90 through Manning and The Tangent, so I knew I was going to enjoy this, and that was indeed immediately the case. Guy has an innate sense of melody, and his songs are always enjoyable on first hearing, with strong arrangements and a feeling that every note is in exactly the right place, played on the right instrument. This is commercial symphonic pop influenced classic crossover progressive rock that oozes class and confidence in equal measures. I can't pick a favourite as all eight songs are simply superb. This may be a debut release, but all the guys involved have been around the scene for some time and it shows. Let's hope it's not long until the next one.
Oct 2017

THE DEAD CENTURIES
RACE AGAINST TIME

Apparently, these guys started off with a standard line-up, with a female singer, but over time various people left and the band evolved so this recording features just two people, namely Adam Tremblett (guitar, bass, programming) and Bryant McNamara (drums) although second guitarist Jacob McSheffrey joins them for live shows. What we now have is an instrumental progressive metal act, who as well as the usual culprits have also been inspired by fellow Canadians Protest The Hero (who finally came to NZ last year and were just as awesome as I expected them to be) and the likes of Animal As Leaders. They bring in plenty of mathcore into the mix, as well as djent when the need arises, but there is always the feeling that everything is being undertaken for a reason, that there is a destination in mind how matter how intricate and complex the path being taken to get there. There are a couple of very good reasons for not having vocals, the first being that there really isn't any room for them, and the second that there definitely isn't any need. The guys have managed to keep the music interesting and intriguing, so the listener is compelled to keep paying very close attention. The shredding is there when needed, incredibly quick, or just that tad slower to provide variety and it never becomes a wall of noise or "aren't I clever". The result is a complex and diverse

album, which should appeal to a wide variety of those who appreciate their metal to be far more than crunching down and seeing who can get to the end of the song first.
Feb 2018

DELUGE GRANDER
OCEANARIUM
This is the fourth album from Deluge Grander, but it is the first time I have come across them. To be honest, if it wasn't for bandleader Dan Britton (keyboards, guitars, other instruments) contacting me through both ProgArchives and LastFM, I still wouldn't have! But I personally think it is great when musicians push themselves out there to people who may be interested, so I was intrigued to hear this. Joining him on this album is Brett d'Anon (bass, guitar) and Patrick Gaffney on drums along with assorted guests, and by having certain instruments only involved with certain songs it gives the music an incredibly varied feel.

I have seen some people liken this to Mike Oldfield, but that isn't at all fair on either artist, and doesn't represent what the music is like, as for me this is what would have happened if Frank Zappa had moved more into the symphonic progressive field as opposed to the avant garde. There are times when the music becomes almost oriental, and I found myself thinking of Dennis Rea and his incredible 'Views From Chicheng Precipice', but again brought more into mainstream progressive music. Dan's keyboards are always at the very heart of this instrumental album, and here the music really does live up to the album title as when playing this I can envisage myself underwater following fish near the seabed. Due to the variety of sounds and instruments, one doesn't always know what to expect around the next coral reef or valley in the sea floor, which makes the album consistently interesting and enjoyable. I did warn Dan that if he sent me the album, he had to understand that it would be reviewed honestly, and I would say exactly what I thought, which may not be what he wanted. But he accepted that, and from the moment I put this on I knew that it was never going to be an issue, as this is one that I have enjoyed throughout. Well worth further investigation.
Jan 2018

DESCEND
WITHER
Descend is a progressive death metal band from Stockholm, Sweden who formed in 2003, with the current line-up dating back to 2008. After three demos, the debut album 'Through the Eyes of the Burdened' was released through Supernova Records in May 2011. The album was well received and supported through numerous live performances including festivals in Germany, Canada as well as the renowned Metaltown festival in Gothenburg in the summer of 2012. Now they are back with their second album, released at the beginning of 2014, and it is certainly an interesting

proposition as they are moving in a vast array of styles, far more than one might expect from how they describe themselves. There are complete passages where no-one in their right mind could call themselves death, whereas there are others where they fit right in.

But, for me the production doesn't really provide enough punch to this. Drummer Jonathan Persson is doing a lot behind the kit, and is a real asset to the band, but he isn't as much in your face as I would like. There is a feeling that they have been ever so slightly muted, and this has a detrimental impact to the harsher elements of the album, while gentler passages such as the title cut do come across really well. I get the impression that these guys are far more in your face in the live arena, and while this is overall an interesting and enjoyable album, I can't help but wonder what would have happened if Colin Richardson had been at the controls. It certainly is a grower though, and the more I played it the more I enjoyed it, just not quite as much I should have.
Mar 2014

DWIKI DHARMAWAN
SO FAR SO CLOSE
Dwiki Dharmwan is one of Indonesia's most prominent musicians – a cultural icon in his homeland. Dwiki is an accomplished pianist, keyboardist, composer, arranger, performer, peace activist, and a true cultural ambassador of his beloved country. He has forged a very successful career (one that already spans more than 30 years), performing in over 60 countries with both solo and collective projects. (Dwiki's band, Krakatoa, remains one of Indonesia's most famous bands ever.) This 2015 release was his first on a major Western label, Moonjune, and he has found a home that really suits him. Not only has this given Dwiki the opportunity to have his work heard by a far wider audience but has allowed him access to some incredible musicians. So, while he contents himself by providing Fender Rhodes Electric Piano, Mini Moog, Hohner Clavinet, Hammond Organ, Korg Synth, acoustic piano, and vocals (the album is mostly instrumental), he is joined by Jimmy Haslip (bass), Chad Wackerman (drums), Dewa Budjana and Tohpati share guitar duties (although not on the same songs) plus Jerry Goodman provides electric violin on one. It is often a very Western sounding album, but I Nyoman Windha (Gamelan Jegog, Balinese Kendang, Suling vocals) also has an important part to play. This just doesn't sound like an album that has been released in the last few years but sounds as if it is a lost gem from the Seventies, bringing forth influences and touches of bands such as Weather Report and John McLaughlin. While some of the songs sound highly rehearsed and tight, there are others such as "Jembrana's Fantasy" that are far freer and more improvisational in style, and it is here where the guys move away from classic fusion into an area far more Gamelan influenced. The sound is warm throughout, aided by the incredible warmth of Jimmy's bass, and his partnership with Chad cannot be understated, as they seem to always know exactly where each need to be, to provide the support for what is happening above. Highly recommended for anyone who loves classic fusion.
Mar 2017

DWIKI DHARMAWAN
PASAR KLEWER

Just a year on from his debut, Dwiki returned with an album that featured not only a totally different group of musicians, but a quite different approach. Instead of a whole series of keyboards, here Dwiki used just a piano. On bass, he brought in Yaron Stavi, who used an upright throughout the album (apart from one song on the second CD), while on drums he used Asaf Sirkis, so the rhythm section has a very different approach, style, and sound. He didn't bring back fellow Indonesians Tohpati and Dewa Budjana on guitars, instead using Mark Wingfield and Nicolas Meier. Add to that some Gamelan instruments plus clarinet and sax, and from the outset this is very different indeed. It is not surprising therefore, as to just how different this album is from the previous. It is also a double CD, which gives the guys the chance to expand on their ideas (and amazingly was recorded in just two days). With this release Dharmawan wanted to try something different. "Indonesia is the place of 'ultimate diversity,'" the pianist says. "Here, the urban cultures accelerate the 'acculturation' process, which generates changes in cultural patterns and creates new forms of musical expression. 'Pasar Klewer' is the answer to my search for 'the difference,' and a valuable answer to our modern crises and urban uprooting. The album's distinctive sound originates from an ancient Gamelan tonal system called Salendro, known in the Karawitan traditional music of the Sundanese, Javanese, and Balinese. Based on the Gamelan tonal system, I also adapted, as my inspiration, other musical elements from all over the Indonesian archipelago, as well as the western diatonic system."

I have to take his word for it, as all I know is that I haven't heard anything quite like this before. This is world fusion on an epic scale, bringing jazz together with progressive tendencies, and then wrapping it up on a musical form that is quite different to western ears as he mixes it all up with styles from his home. There is a freedom and space within the music, that makes it feel live a living breathing entity, and very quickly the listener is immersed in a brand-new world. It is full of energy, full of life, and is an amazing musical experience.
Mar 2017

DIABLO SWING ORCHESTRA
PACIFISTICUFFS

There are times when just the name of the band is enough to make the casual critic to become quite intrigued, and that is the case with this Swedish octet. Eight musicians? Yep, and it isn't the line-up that one might expect from a rock band: Daniel Håkansson (guitars and vocals), Pontus Mantefors (guitars, FX, and vocals), Kristin Evegård (vocals and piano), Anders Johansson (bass), Johannes Bergion (cello and vocals), Martin Isaksson (trumpet and vocals), Daniel Hedin (trombone) and Johan Norbäck (drums). In many ways, this doesn't come across as a band, but something far more eclectic, as if it was a group of musicians performing a score for a Tim Burton movie. As a family we watched 'The Nightmare before Christmas', and some of the songs on here (especially "Superhero Jagganath") could have been dropped into it and would have fitted incredibly well!

Since the start back in 2003 the band has defused the seriousness of everyday life with a humorous twist where everything is allowed. The musical framework is wide to say the least and DSO strive to constantly surprise and challenge their listeners: it is eclectic and rule-breaking, but somehow always makes total musical sense. The arrangements and melodies are unusual to say the least, but this is not out about being "out there" just for the hell of it, this is music that is both compelling and always interesting. Since 2012's 'Pandora's Piñata' the band have taken the opportunity to reinvent themselves and approach their task with fresh eyes and ears. Annlouice Lögdlund left the band in 2014 to pursue her opera career, but new singer Kristin Evegård has brought some serious new writing skills to the mix, both in the lyric departments as well as composing. It is also the first studio album for Johan Norbäck, who joined the fold in 2012 for the touring of 'Pandora's Piñata': not many drummers have to wait five years to make their recording debut with a band, but he really has started with a bang.

Although it is possible to call these guys progressive metal, the first word of that term in their case covers a huge number of genres from swing to prog, incorporating some RIO and plenty of avant combining with musical theatre and soundtracks. At the beginning of "Jigsaw Puzzle" the strings are so delicate that they could have been used in a James Stewart movie, before it morphs into disco ELO, yet all in a way that just works. This is not a band who are content to sit within a genre and treat music as it is a living free thinking animal that is going to go its own way in the jungle. There may be times when it will follow a path that has already been created, if it happens to be going in the same direction, but it never stays on it for very long as there is way more fun to be had in the wilderness. It is seriously like nothing else I have heard in the last year, during which time I have reviewed more than 600 albums of different genres, and that is a statement in itself. Superb.
Jan 2018

DIALETO
BARTÓK IN ROCK
What we have here is the latest release from Brazilian trio Dialeto, whose last album 'The Last Tribe' was excellent. I was a little surprised it has taken four years for them to come back with the follow-up, but that may have something to do with the fact that only guitarist Nelson Coelho was in the band last time around. He has now been joined by drummer Fred Barley and bassist Gabriel Costa, which makes them more how they used to sound, as for the last album the bassist had been replaced by touch guitar. This album is an attempt by Dialeto to take compositions by Béla Bartók and then move them into their own genre, with lots of improvisation. Bartók is considered to be one of the most important Hungarian composers of the last century, and through his collection and analytical study of folk music, he was one of the founders of

comparative musicology, which later became ethnomusicology.

With six of the ten songs named Roumanian Folk Dances it isn't hard to see where the music originally stemmed from, but here it has been taken to new levels as jazz fusion takes this as a base and then moves it into quite new areas. The whole album is fresh, exciting, and interesting, taking the listener through many twists and turns, and by the end I found myself thinking that I loved this so much that I really ought to discover the originals and see just what Dialeto had done to them to transform them into this modern style of music. David Cross makes an appearance on the first number, and my only wish was that he had could have stayed for the complete album as he had so much impact, but as it is this really is an album to savour.
Jul 2017

DISCIPLINE
THIS ONE'S FOR ENGLAND

There is no doubt in my mind that one of the most important bands to come out of America in the last 25 years is Discipline, and when they reformed and released 'To Shatter All Accord' it was certainly no surprise to see it rated so highly: according to ProgArchives it is still the #1 album of that year. They were then invited to appear at the mighty RosFest in 2012, and this double CD is the recording of that performance. So, just eight songs, but that equates to nearly 100 minutes of music. Some of these songs have appeared on live albums before but given they haven't released that many albums that really isn't surprising. And to be honest, a live album without a performance of "Canto IV (Limbo)" would be both unthinkable and unforgiveable.

Singer and keyboard player Matthew Parmenter also provides all the material, but this is much more than just a one-man show and the rest of the guys were all there when 'Push & Profit' was released in 1994. This is a group that have been influenced by the likes of early Genesis and Anekdoten but have created a path very much of their own making. One would never guess that these guys are from North America, as they have much more in common with the European progressive rock movement. Their approach is sometimes restrained, harmonic and almost lulling, but there are plenty of times when they are jagged and abrasive, Jon's guitar a strident noise against Matthew's organ while Matthew K and Paul provide the backdrop to let the music grow and move. I have been a fan of the band for many years, and the only thing wrong with this album is that it makes me realize just how much I am missing out by not being able to see them in concert. This is an essential purchase.
May 2014

DISEN GAGE
SNAPSHOTS

There are a lot of great bands coming out of Russia these days, and thanks to both the internet and people wanting to promote them, it is getting easier to understand some of

what is going on. This is the fourth album from the band, and to say it is intriguing is somewhat of an understatement. It is an instrumental album, much of which I would imagine was recorded live, as the interaction between the four (plus guests) couldn't have happened any other way. According to the band themselves, the album "is whimsically balancing on a weird edge between psychedelic trance and romantic mood, between a krautrock improv and a soundtrack to a western. To us, the aftertaste of the album feels like what one feels after casting an accidental glance at a pile of randomly scattered photos. They may be a part of someone's, or your own life, or they could be snapshots of Nature - but then we are all part of Nature."

Whimsical and weird is probably one of the best ways of describing this album, as I've been playing it a great deal and I still have no idea at all of what is going on. There's RIO, there's King Crimson, Radiohead, fusion, art-rock, avant-garde jazz, plus loads more, all mixed together so that in some ways none of this makes musical sense at all, although at the same time it is in perfect harmony with each other. It builds, it moves, and never with a standard verse/chorus structure, and often not in 4/4 time, but none of that matters as Disen Gage are presenting us with music as a fluid living beast, something that is making its own path. Having heard this I am now intrigued to what the other albums sound like, as when music refuses to conform yet also is as compelling and interesting as this, then it is something very special indeed.
Jul 2017

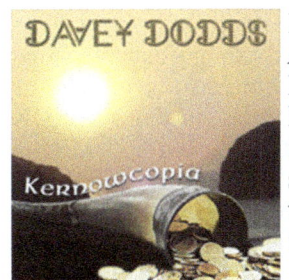
DAVEY DODDS
KERNOWCOPIA
Missing from the latest Red Jasper albums was original frontman Davey Dodds, so when I heard he had a new album coming out in 2017 I was intrigued, so asked him a few questions to get some background. When he sent me his response it was so good that I knew I just had to reprint it in its totality, so before we get into the review itself, just what had been happening with Davey?

When I stopped playing music in 1994, I didn't suffer from withdrawal symptoms! I moved to a different planet and buried myself in an interesting, entertaining, and absorbing life. I worked as a fly-fishing guide. It took me to some fabulous places. Wielding my fly rod in the pristine wilderness of Northern Manitoba was good for the soul. My need to be creative and innovative was satisfied – I wrote a book – I wrote articles – I gave fly-casting demonstrations at game fairs – I developed new techniques, fly fishing for pike and more recently sharks.

A couple of years ago, my wife Jeannie retired. We moved back to the far west where I had started my adult life and looked forward to a pleasant easy-going lifestyle. Life had other ideas! A neighbour (who had no idea I was a former musician) dragooned me into going to an open mic night at a local pub. The people there were hospitable and very much part of the local community. I was surprised and delighted that a couple of bands recorded old songs of mine (The Unthanks – The Magpie and Mawkin – I Can Hew) Jeannie bought me a mandolin as a late birthday present last year. I could remember which way round it went and enjoyed learning how to play again. With Jeannie's agreement, I sold it and put the pennies towards a better instrument that I could plug in to a PA.

I played at some local sessions and ended up getting a couple of low-key gigs. These led to some better gigs. Local musicians played with me and were so supportive. Getting my playing back to a decent standard had to happen before I had space in my head to write new songs. Since the muse has revisited me, I can't shake her off! Life here in Darkest Kernow provides plenty of inspiration for song writing.

Derek Aunger (a fellow fly-fishing guide) who runs Salty Dog Studio in Looe in Cornwall, invited me to record a couple of old songs and things spiralled from there. I wanted to work with a violin player and had a couple of attempts working with people. The first of these fizzled out because the people simply couldn't commit the time. I knew that Martin Solomon would be the perfect musician to work with but had assumed that he would be too busy, too important, and not really interested in collaborating with an old weirdo who hadn't played a note for 22 years. I was wonderfully wrong! Playing with Martin has been hugely enjoyable and working with the Jaspers – Robin Harrison and David Clifford has been fabulous. I'm looking forward to playing live gigs to help promote the new album. Life is sparkling, and I'm getting younger by the day!

So, onto the album. The first thing to note is that Davey has finally given into his inner Folkie and has released an album that concentrates on his vocals accompanied by mandolin. Martin Solomon is present on most of the songs, providing fiddle as well as Celtic harp, and while there is the occasional bodhran, only two songs feature actual drums. As with the Red Jasper albums, Davey's also has some wonderful symmetry as not only does he perform an a cappela version of "The Magpie", which originally appeared on 'Sting In The Tale' and the live 'Action Replay', but he also invited both D.C. and Robin Harrison to perform on "Merlin's Isle of Gramarye". In many ways, this was the most exciting song on the album for me, with Robin providing some glorious riffs and D.C. driving it from the back, as back again were the Jaspers playing together. But both Davey and the boys have moved on from those days, it's a long time indeed since 'Anagramary', so although I enjoyed it immensely it did seem somewhat out of sorts with the rest of the album, and I am sure it is quite deliberate that the next song is an instrumental with delicate haunting tin whistle and Celtic harp.

I have always enjoyed Davey's vocals, and the album certainly doesn't give the impression that he has been away from the scene for so long, nor that he had to get himself a mandolin, as he is in full control, and it really was only yesterday that he was treading the boards (I commented that he didn't seem to have changed much, and the response was "I have a painting in the attic"). This is a truly beautiful album, and credit must be given to Derek Aunger who has worked with Davey to capture an incredible sound. The only real issue with it is that I have been playing it so much that it stopped me from listening to other material I should have been getting on with!

As to the album title, if you didn't know, 'Kernow' is the Cornish name for Cornwall, so it is a play on that and "cornucopia" (an abundant supply of good things). Even though I'm from Devon, I must admit it's not just pasties and the A38 that are the only decent things coming out from Cornwall: I'll add this album to that incredibly small list.
June 2017

DRIFTING SUN
TWILIGHT
Back in a different life, when I was still working the night shift in a supermarket and living in an ex-council house in the UK, I used to run a fanzine called Feedback. These were the days before the internet, and as I was one of the few outlets for prog reviews, I used to receive a lot of material from different bands and labels. One of these labels was Musea, and one day they sent me the debut album by Drifting Sun. I said some nice things about them, and I was sent the sophomore release at the end of the Nineties, and then, nothing. Keyboard player Pat Sanders had always been the main man in Drifting Sun, and after some years away he eventually decided to return to the music industry and to resurrect the band name with a brand-new line-up. The third album was released in 2015 (what's sixteen years between friends?), the fourth followed just a year later, and now we are here with the fifth. I haven't heard the intervening albums, but one day out of the blue Pat contacted me again (one advantage of keeping the same email address forever) and asked if I would be interested in hearing what they sounded like today, and now here I am playing Drifting Sun more than 20 years after our paths first crossed.

I deliberately haven't gone back and played the first two albums, although they are still here on my shelves, as I felt that would probably be unfair and I should treat them as a new act. Immediately, what did surprise me were the harmonies and sheer professionalism that pervades this release. It certainly doesn't remind me of what they used to be like, as there is a lot more thought and attention to detail in the arrangements, which are full of space and room for everyone to move and breathe. Although they are different in many ways to Big Big Train, they are the band that they remind me of the most, both in terms of musical construct and how they have moved such a very long way from their roots. ProgArchives list these guys as neo-prog, and at one time that would have been the case, but they have moved far more into the Crossover sub-genre and if they were put forward for inclusion now, I am sure that is where they would be placed.

They have been heavily influenced by Hogarth-era Marillion but have managed to stay away from the twee and contribute something that is both interesting and easy to listen to. This is prog that invites the listener in. True, it could never be played just in the background as it might disappear, but when wanting to play music in the evening to sit and relax to then this is almost perfect in many ways. With three albums in three years, it is safe to say that Drifting Sun are very much back, and I for one am very glad they are.
Oct 2017

DRIFTING SUN
ETERNAL CYCLE
The band have made this two-track EP available free of charge from their website, so that progheads can see what the band sound like in 2017. The title song isn't available elsewhere, while the second, 'Soldiers" is taken from the latest album. This is a great way to find out about a band that will certainly not be on many people's radars, and yet with the string arrangements and vocals, they would be if people just heard them, so this a great idea. I have known about them for more than 20 years now and am just annoyed that I have been missing out on them for the last few years, but now I know they are back I am going to be watching for future releases with interest. If you enjoy strong thoughtful crossover progressive rock with powerful influences from recent Marillion (except more enjoyable to my ears) why not visit their website, go to the Music tab, and download this yourself.
Oct 2017

ECHOES
BAREFOOT TO THE MOON
Over the years I have heard many tribute acts and cover versions, as have we all, but generally I find them poorly constructed and rather pointless. But there are some exceptions to the rule, as with the excellent 'Genesis For Two Grand Pianos' albums by Roger T Matte and Yngve Guddal. So, I must confess, I wasn't looking forward to playing this album, as I know all the songs incredibly well, and was rather concerned as to what they were going to do with it. Echoes have built a reputation as being one of the premier Pink Floyd tribute bands around, but I have never understood the concept of buying an album of a tribute band – why not just listen to the original instead? However, this was promising to be slightly different as they had the idea of approaching the music in an acoustic fashion, yet not losing any of the power and emotion that makes Floyd such an amazing entity. Could it be done? The line-up for this was Oliver Hartmann (acoustic guitar, vocals); Martin Hofmann (vocals, acoustic bass, guitar); Paul Kunkel (piano, vocals); Steffen Maier (drums and percussion); Michael Unger (woodwinds and vocals); Carolin Riehemann (vocals); Irena Morisáková (cello); Terezie Fadrná (cello); Milena Kolárovà (violin) and Alice Vasilová (violin). Oliver is the most well-known of them all, as he is singer with Avantasia as well, but while he has incredible presence on songs like "high Hopes", it is the complete band presence that makes this such a success.

From the first few notes of "Shine On You Crazy Diamond" through to the final "Run Like Hell" this is a masterpiece. The music is still very much that of Floyd, but it has been treated with great respect and the arrangements maximise the space and atmosphere from the originals but in a very new setting indeed. I can't imagine any Floyd fan not falling in love with this the very first time they hear it – in some ways it feels like the old painting has been carefully restored and new life provided. Some songs feel closer to the originals than others, but all have gained a great deal from this treatment. Sit down, relax,

and fall into the world of songs that are all familiar yet here are revitalised and refreshed. This is an album that comes highly recommended indeed.
Dec 2016

ECLIPSE SOL-AIR
BARTÓK'S CRISIS
Released in 2011, 'Bartók's Crisis' was the second album by this German French outfit, following on from their debut some four years earlier. At this time the band were a six-piece, although there are numerous guests to boot, but they were the brainchild of Philippe Marie-Arnauld des Lions (vocals, keyboards, rhythm guitar) who always saw this as a project with a revolving line-up. With male and female vocals and songs in three languages this is a band that obviously wants to be different, yet these are probably the simplest to understand as when it comes to music it is way more complex. Imagine as a base a band that is bringing together strong elements of both Horslips and Red Jasper, and then mixing in a little Renaissance. From there all bets are off as this is an incredibly varied album and there are times when they are pure Symphonic and at others they are obviously Neo. The first time I played "Waiting For You" I was amazed to notice at the end that it was more than fifteen minutes long as it just flies by, with some wonderful hooks and loads of different phases.

But that is just the first of the four longer songs found in the middle of the album, with "Benedictus" closing in at 11:06, "Phantome" at 13:03 and "Die Rumanen" at 21:25. It is true to say there are places here where it does sound as if the long song has been artificially created by putting in some sections that have little connection with the rest (such as the drum solo), but we're progheads so does it really matter? By the end of the album, I was totally confused as to what I had been listening to, yet knew I enjoyed it. This feels much more like a theatrical production than 'just' an album, as the songs are often very visual. I must confess to doing a double take on the last song of the album though, as it is the old sing in a round "Frère Jacques" I was taught as a young child, it never sounded like this though. This is one of the longest single discs I have come across, at 82 minutes, and it is certainly never boring and well worth investigating further.
May 2014

ECLIPSE SOL-AIR
SCHIZOPHILIA
Although it is a different cover artist for their third album, there is certainly a feeling this is going to carry on where the last one left off, and in a way it does. Of course, Philippe Marie-Arnauld des Lions is back, but only co-singer Mireille Vicogne and guitarist Fritzh Hoffmeister return from the previous work. There aren't any guests this time either and consequently there is a different sound as the multiple strings previously made quite an impact. The next thing I noticed is this album is a great deal

shorter than 'Bartók's Crisis' at just over 51 minutes in length, quite different to the 82 minutes last time around. The last album really worked due to its' sheer diversity and the listener never really knowing what was coming around the corner next whereas this one works, as it is so direct and focused. In many ways this is a much heavier album, but Horslips and Red Jasper are still influences, although possibly different eras of both. There is plenty of guitar, and still a lot to take in lyrically with songs in multiple languages, sometimes within the same song! No songs more than ten minutes long this time, and the complexity has been somewhat simplified, but this has been replaced with a stronger pop sensibility and there are plenty of hooks to be interested in. This is the more immediate of the two albums and one that can be more easily enjoyed on the first play, but I have to confess to missing the sheer wildness and strangeness of the last one. But this is still a fine album and anything short of 4 *'s would be just wrong. Another album well worth investigating.
May 2014

EDEN SHADOW
MELODIES FOR MALADIES
This is the second album from neo-prog/prog metal outfit Eden Shadow, released in 2016, who are a trio based around Ryan Elliott (vocals, guitar, keyboards) with Alex Broben (bass) and Aled Lloyd (drums). Although the three of them are the sole musicians on four of the six songs, they are joined by some others for the other two, most notably the famed Theo Travis on flute and saxophone. What really works on this nearly sixty-minute-long album is the syncopation, and the way that the three musicians tie it in so tightly, almost moving into mathcore territory. The arrangements are solid, and the production quite superb, but that just isn't enough. From the off I found I was struggling with Ryan's vocals. It is not that he is a poor singer, but just that he doesn't seem quite right for the style of music being played, and I found it quite jarring. Added to that the songs are nothing more than okay, and I found myself wishing there was an outside influence in the studio to push the ideas that really worked and give guidance. But, as always, views on music are subjective as opposed to objective and there are plenty of people who seems to say that this is the best thing since sliced bread, so all I can say is it doesn't work for me.
Jan 2018

EDISON'S CHILDREN
THE FINAL BREATH BEFORE NOVEMBER
When I was playing this for the first time, I could already imagine what had been written about it, and when I checked I found that I wasn't disappointed. Yes, many seem to be saying that this is one of the finest albums that one is likely to find anywhere on the planet, so it looks like I am in the minority again. This isn't a bad album, but neither is it a particularly good one. Unlike the debut, which featured the rest of Marillion as

guests, here we are down to the core duo of Pete Trewavas (Marillion, Transatlantic) on bass, vocals, guitar, synth and programming and Eric Blackwood on vocals, guitar, synth, and bass with Henry Rogers (DeeExpus, Touchstone) on drums and Wendy Farrell-Pastore on backing vocals.

I was supplied with this as a download to review, so I am not sure if this is the case with the CD, but there are only three songs, with "Silhouette' coming in at 67 minutes long, and it isn't possible to play just parts of this as it hasn't been broken up (although the track listing does denote 12 sections). Now, I'm a proghead, and have no issue with long songs per se, but I don't believe it is a long song. To me this is several songs which have been put together in such a way that they can have an 'epic', but there isn't enough inter-relation or repetition of refrains or key musical hooks to make one think that this is indeed one piece of music. And what's worse, is for the most part just plain boring.

There are some truly magnificent sections on the album, which had me doubting my own comments, but there are others where I just wanted to turn the whole thing off and play something that was far more interesting. I kept thinking back to The Flower Kings, who have produced some albums where they really need an outside set of ears to cull the material and provide some judicious editing, and the same is very much the case here. Looking at the chart for 2013 on PA, before I post this, I see this is ranked at #13 so there are a great deal of people who think this is incredible. I'm just not one of them.
May 2014

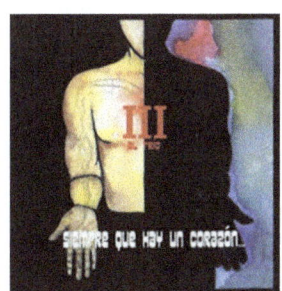

EL TRIO
SIEMPRE QUE HAY UM CORAZÓN...
El Trio is a jazz rock fusion trio from Dominican Republic, formed in 2003 by Jonatan Piña Duluc (vocals, guitar, keyboard, saxophone, producer), Kilvin Peña (bass, backing vocals) and Pablo Peña (drums, backing vocals). 'Siempre Que Hay Un Corazón...' (Whenever there is a heart) was their debut album, originally released in 2007 and now digitally reissued in 2017 by Progshine Records. As far as I'm aware, this is the first band I have heard from the Dominican Republic, but music really doesn't have any boundaries, and in Jonatan they have a quite outstanding guitarist, who can shred with the best of them. It is obvious that Kilvin is playing a fretless bass, which allows for some real warmth and depth, while his relationship with Pablo is incredibly strong. For me the songs that really work are those without such a high South American feel to them, as these move more to the mainstream. Also, Jonatan is an okay singer, but nothing more than that and I personally would have liked to have heard more passages where he is leading proceedings with his sterling guitarwork. Given this was a self-release the production is strong, and I can see why Progshine Records have decided to make this available once again.
Oct 2017

EL TRIO
LA BLANCA Y LA GRIS
Two years on from the debut, and El Trio were back with their second album 'La Blanca Y La Gris' (The white and the grey). I tend to play albums initially through iTunes, and this was the first one of theirs I heard as it was the first one to appear in the playlist due to where the title appeared in the alphabet. What this meant was that I managed to treat myself to possibly the worst introduction to the band, as while the jazz rock is forceful with a huge input of blues, along with South American influences, it is also the one where the vocals jar most for me. Jonatan has a vocal style that seems to either work very well and is totally in keeping with the music or isn't working at all, and when it is the latter, it is quite painful.

But he more than makes up for it with some great guitarwork again. There was a line-up change between the two albums, as drummer Pablo Peña had departed to be replaced by Johandy Ureña. They also brought in an additional percussionist, as well as a guest guitarist on one number and a guest trombonist on another. The music is more forceful than the debut and is a real progression as they have expanded but to my ears it would have been better either as an instrumental release or with a different vocalist. Again, digitally reissued in 2017 by Progshine Records.
Oct 2017

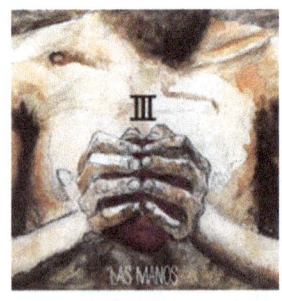

EL TRIO
LAS MANOS
This 2013 release saw the same line-up as the last one, but an even more extended list of guest musicians as the band continued to expand their musical styles. This is easily the most powerful album of the three, as the band mix jazz with hard rock, fusion, progressive styles, blues, and Caribbean stylings to create something that really works. To my ears, it is also the first time where Jonatan's vocals play a positive role as he seems to have a far better idea of what will work best with the instrumentation, moving between a rough hard-edged gruff style and falsetto where it is the right place to do it.

There is a palpable confidence on the album, perhaps due in some part to reaching their tenth anniversary as a band and for making it through to their third album. I know very little (okay, nothing) about the music scene in the Dominican Republic, but I would guess that by the time of this release El Trio was very well known indeed. The album was still recorded in their home country but was mixed in the States, and the sound quality is spot on. If you are intrigued to understand what El Trio is doing, then this is the album to start with, as it is well worth it. Digitally reissued in 2017 by Progshine.
Oct 2017

EL TRIO
LEÑA!!! EN VIVO
This is the band's first live album, and it was originally self-released by the band as a DVD in September 2014 and has now been released as a digital album by Progshine. Away from the studio, with no additional musicians, here we find El Trio acting far more in the style associated with bands such as Cream. The guitar is right at the front of the mix, Jonatan's vocals are packed with emotion, while Johandy and Kilvin Peña keep it all locked down. What is interesting for me is that Kilvin is still playing a fretless bass in the live environment, but what he lacks in attack he more than makes up for in emotion.

This is obviously where El Trio really comes to life, far more than in the studio, and this music has a far rougher edge with less of the Caribbean and South American influences and far more straight-ahead hard rock with jazz and blues elements combined with psychedelia. They somehow manage to channel Blue Cheer during this performance, it is that fuzzed, distorted and aggressive. Recorded in Santiago, it would be good for the band to be able to break out of their geographical territory as music as strong and vibrant as this deserves to be heard everywhere. I may have no idea what they are singing about, but I do know I enjoyed this immensely and that many others would as well if they heard it. Hopefully these reissues from Progshine will find the band gaining interest from new territories, and it will be interesting to hear where they go to from here.
Oct 2017

ELEGANT SIMPLICITY
UNFORGIVING MIRROR
It has been way too long since Steven McCabe's last album, 2007's 'Too Many Goodbyes', and I wasn't sure if there would be another, but at long last he is back with his 16th studio album to date. I'm not saying I have known him for a long time, but I have the early albums on pre-recorded cassette tapes, so I guess you can say that I am familiar with the music. As has been the case on many of his albums he has been joined by Christopher Knight on drums and percussion, while Ken Senior (isn't it about time we had another Evolution album?) provides vocals on one track. Everything else is by Mr. McCabe, and as ever he shows himself to be a dab hand at both guitar and keyboards as he creates music that is sometimes evocative of Gong and Camel as well as bringing in some Neo and even fusion influences as well. The use both of 'live' drums and moving between keyboards and guitar means that this generally sounds like a band as opposed to a multi-instrumentalist project.

Melody as opposed to repeated mindless meandering is the order of the day and this is very much an album of six songs, even though five don't contain any words. 'Un-Apology' is one of my favourites, very much in your face with clever interplay between the lead instruments and quite a funky Seventies feel throughout with some dated

keyboard sounds and a real groove to the whole thing. It fairly belts along and is a joy throughout. But, a very special mention needs to go to the title track, which is one of Steven's most epic numbers to date. At more than eighteen minutes long there is plenty of room for the music to move in many ways (and it even contains some great sax work!), and each time I play it I find it draws me in, taking me to a world that contains complex arrangements and layers yet also has a simple elegance, as one might well expect. Let's hope that we don't have to wait so long for the next one.
Jan 2014

ELEGANT SIMPLICITY
ENRAPTURED
Steven McCabe has been pursuing his musical path as Elegant Simplicity for more than twenty years now, sometimes solo, and sometimes with some guest musicians. This three track EP was released in 2014, and he brought in two different drummers to assist, but apart from that this short instrumental release is all Steven. Immediately before playing this for the first time I had been playing the 2014 remaster of his 2002 album 'Architect Of Light', and they are completely different entities altogether, with this being far more reflective and almost gentle in manner. Two of the pieces are just over four minutes in length, while opener "Enraptured I" just gets to ninety seconds. For fans of classic Camel, this release is a taster of the delights of what is now a comprehensive canon. I have known Steven since the days of his cassette releases (which I still have!), and I have yet to hear something of his that I don't like. His beautiful guitar solos, against perfectly balanced keyboards and piano, make this EP a delight.
Jan 2017

ELEGANT SIMPLICITY
ALL LIFE IS ONE
The first thing one notices when studying this 2015 release is the large number of performers taking part, and the second thing is that neither of Steven's long-time collaborators, Ken Senior, and Christopher Knight, have a part to play on this album (although apparently, they were involved with the original demos). It is also quite a short album, in that it is only just over forty minutes in length, although originally it was destined to be more than an hour. But although it is shorter, it is easily one of the most diverse that multi-instrumentalist Steven McCabe has released so far. Sometimes it is just him, sometimes he may have a drummer and a singer, but this time we have a whole host of guests: he hasn't even provided bass on this album, but instead has used three different bassists in Jair-Rohm Parker Wells, Damjan Kapor and Justin Bassman. Nathaniel Graham provides the drums, with David Lipari Jr on vocals, but the biggest difference to the overall sound is the use of other musicians who have been invited to take part. With William Stewart (violin), Nathan Madsen (saxophone), Allen Bruce Ray (native American flutes) and Hendrick Valera (flute) there is a far greater depth and diversity to

the sound than previously apparent.

Of course, at the heart of this is still Steven's fluid guitar and deft keyboards, but this time there is more for him to play against and with. He can be belting away with great over the top axework as on "Falling To The Ground", and then Nathan demands to make an entrance and the piece is transformed. There are still heavy Camel influences, particularly with some wonderfully dated keyboard sounds combining with the great guitars. Polished, dynamic, one must wonder what is going to be next for ES. Will the next album continue in the same vein, or will it be back to more of a multi-instrumentalist style? We must wait and see, but until then I will enjoy this polished melodic progressive rock album that is a sheer joy to listen to.
Jan 2017

ELEGANT SIMPLICITY
KICKING THE OLIVE BRANCH
I have known Steven for more than twenty years now, and for most of that time he has basically been a solo artist, adding the odd musician or singer as the need arises. I have always been a fan, so when he said to me he thought it might just be his best work yet. I was intrigued. Certainly, what I didn't expect was the most complete band effort of his career to date. "Timely Reminder" opens the album, with the sax of Nathan Madsen keeping track with Steven's guitar, which immediately made me think of Blodwyn Pig. Then after only a few bars the music was moving and changing, going into new areas, returning to themes and then off again.

The next song contained real flute, care of Noam Goldstein, and by now I realised I was listening to something quite special. Back in the day, Steven would have created all these sounds using keyboards, but here he has brought together a group of skilled musicians that is lifting his music to a whole new level. Although he has used singers in the past, most notably Ken Senior of Evolution, this is an instrumental album and I think Steven is right in what he said, in 2017, after more than twenty full-length releases, he has produced his finest and most complete work to date. I have been playing it a great deal, and the only major fault with this fifty-two-minute-long album is that it is just too short (and hence contains just the one epic, the title cut which breaks the twenty-minute barrier).

Steven has been putting out quality albums for a long time now, but now could not be a better time to discover his music, as this is superb from the very first note to the last.
Jun 2017

ELEPHANT PLAZA
MOMENTUM
This album started life as long ago as 2006, when Espen Mikarlsen (guitars) and Gilbert Marshall (Magic Pie), electric & acoustic guitars, keyboards, lead vocals, started

jamming along to an idea. This led to the song "Naked", and the idea that possibly they ought to make this into a full project. Recording took place when they had the time, and the opportunity to bring other musicians into the project, but neither could devote as much time as they wished due to other responsibilities (including the ongoing success of Magic Pie). But gradually they were getting somewhere, until in 2010 the building where their studio was situated was burned to the ground, and it took until 2012 to get everything sorted and work could commence again.

In 2013 Espen decided that he could no longer contribute to the project, but Gilbert was determined to keep it going to fruition, pulling together a full band that could perform live, and eventually the album was released through Bandcamp in June 2016, as well as being released on CD by Progress Records. I was sent a copy just a few weeks ago, and was somewhat surprised to discover its existence, as I would expect an album of this quality (and especially with the large Magic Pie connections) would have made large ripples within the progverse. But it's here now, and it has been a joy to listen to. Gilbert has been joined in this endeavour by Kim Christiansen (lead electric & acoustic guitars, vocals), John Kamphaug (Magic Pie, bass, vocals), Olav Rygg (Magic Pie Sound Tech, drums, percussion, vocals), John Petter Sæterdal (keyboards, vocals) and Jan-Fredrik Heier (keyboards, vocals) as well as plenty of guests.

As one would expect from an album involving members of Magic Pie, the vocals are wonderful, with great harmonies, and musically this brings in influences from Pink Floyd and The Moody Blues along with great pop sensibilities. There are even elements with female vocals that sounds as if Lana Lane and Erik Norlander are in the house! This is an incredibly well-polished and accessible progressive rock album, and it never comes across either as a project or something that was so fraught, taking ten years to finally be released. It is an album any proghead who hearkens back to music that easy to listen to, but never easy listening, played by masters who never see the need to show off, but who can all take the lead when the time is right, will surely get a great deal from. This is a stunning debut, and let's only hope that the now they are a functioning outfit and have it out the way that they get on with recording and releasing another! Superb.
May 2017

KEV ELLIS
SPACE CADET
Look, anyone with such a great first name, and come to think of it a strong surname as well (my grandmother's maiden name, believe it or not), and I knew I was going to enjoy this. Some of you may be aware of Kev from his time with Dr. Brown (where a certain Mr Huw Lloyd-Langton also played from time to time), Bubbledubble, Sonic Arcana and Spirits Burning as well as working with Judge Trev as the Trev & Kev duo. Apart from some guitar on opening track "Guiding Light" by Grunty

McNaughton this is very much a solo effort this time around. While space rock has had a huge impact on this album, this is more of a homage in places as opposed to an out and out space album with some wonderful pop numbers that owe more to The Ramones than they do to Hawkwind. Just listen to "Super Cosmic Space Age Baby" to see what I mean!

This feels very much like an album from the underground scene of the Seventies, with production and performances that have a naïve charm and attitude. There is something about this that just grabs the listener and brings them in – it sounds as if it should have been released at the end of the Seventies on some dodgy underground label, but instead it is 2014 and has been made available for free on Bandcamp. If you want music that feels as if it has been squeezed out of the underground and isn't sure what it is doing in the harsh light of the internet, then this is for you. Grubby fuzzed guitars, space rock keyboards, harmonica and loads of distortion, I love it!
Jun 2014

EPICA
RETROSPECT
As may be surmised from the name of this album, here we have a collection looking back over a period of time. In this case it was to celebrate the tenth anniversary of the band, and they put on a very special concert to make it a memorable night indeed for their fans. Recorded last March in front of thousands of ecstatic fans at Klokgebouw (Bell Building) in Eindhoven, the Netherlands, the three-hour concert (which included accompaniment from the seventy piece Extended Reményi Ede Chamber Orchestra and The Miskolc National Theatre Choir) was a very special night indeed. As well as using a full orchestra and choir to enhance their own brand of symphonic metal they had Floor Jansen (Nightwish, Revamp) join them for two powerful duets, while they also performed a special performance of their breakthrough single, "Quietus", with founding members Jeroen Simons, Ad Sluijter, and Yves Huts. Released in November as either a double DVD or double Blu-Ray set: what I have here is the triple CD version, which is some three hours long!

Simone Simons has an incredible voice and obviously relishes the opportunity to show just what an incredible performer she is. The arrangements are incredible, with songs such as "Monopoly On Truth" bringing together the power of an orchestra at speed with a rock band, as well as the choir providing support to everything that is going on. Any review of Epica is going to bring forth a comparison with Nightwish, and I found myself doing exactly the same thing throughout. In some ways this album reminds me of Nightwish's superb 'End of an Era', but while both of these are incredible performances by soprano fronted symphonic metal bands, the Nightwish album wins as in my opinion they just have better songs. But, there is no dispute that this is quite an achievement, showing that metal and orchestras can fit well together, and in this case it sounds as if they have always been that way. I can't comment on the visual aspects, but on the sound this has to be a 4* release at least, even though I prefer Nightwish.
Jan 2014

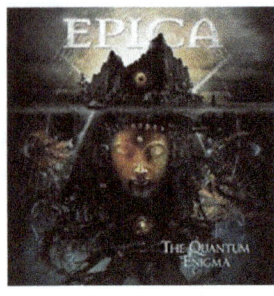

EPICA
THE QUANTUM ENIGMA
There is one word to describe this 2014 album that rises clearly above all others, "Intensity". The production on this album seems to have brought everything together at the highest volume possible, so much so that the listener is quite drained by all of it. Singer Simone Simons has a stunning voice, but to be honest she is sometimes drowned out by the choir and also by the rest of the band so she actually loses some of the impact. This is a real shame, as the album as a whole is an incredible piece of work, much more metallic than the band to which they are most often compared, Nightwish, with the twin guitars locked in and riffing hard. They are also more downtuned and there is the feeling that this a guitar based-band first and foremost, as opposed to keyboard-based. Of course, Epica have a second singer in Mark Jansen who favours death growls as opposed to the 'proper' singing of Marco Hietala, so there is a very different feel between the two acts.

In many ways I actually prefer Epica, as the intensity is palpable: here is a band that are all firing on all cylinders, rushing to the end, taking no prisoners. Sure, I would have preferred to have Simone's vocals higher in the mix, but perhaps I'm being just a little picky? This is a symphonic metal band who concentrate on the latter more than the former, and that's just fine with me. Yes, they slow it down here and there, but it is when they are at full gallop with the band playing hard and the choir singing their hearts out, and Simone striving to rise above it all, that they are at their very best.
Mar 2017

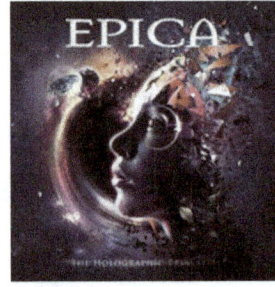

EPICA
THE HOLOGRAPHIC PRINCIPLE
I can't put my finger on it, but there is definitely something that lifts this 2016 album to a higher plane than the one that came out just two years earlier. The intensity is still at the very high level, but Simone seems to be more in control on this one, as opposed to sometimes being swept away. It is bombastic, it is massively over the top, and the guitars have reined in just ever so slightly, although at times they still race off like bolting horses that have been given their heads. It is an overpowering aural assault on the senses, and I love it. The closest way I can think of describing it is like being at a version of Handel's "Messiah" with full choir and orchestra, but with Slipknot involved! I was playing these two albums back to back the other day, and even without looking I knew when this one had started as there is a definite lift, a step up in just about everything. Symphonic over the top progressive metal just doesn't get any better than this. This is not something that can be played as background music, but rather demands full attention of the listener at all times, as this is all-consuming, and not for the fainthearted. I really do hope the guys decide to come down to this part of the world for a show one day, as they must be incredible in concert. This is essential, nothing more, nothing less.
Mar 2017

EPICA
THE SOLACE SYSTEM
2016's 'The Holographic Principle' has been the most successful release to date from symphonic metal outfit Epica, reaching Top 10 chart position entries in the German, Dutch and Swiss album charts. During the recording process the band wrote more songs than were needed, as they wanted to ensure the album was no longer than 76 minutes, but at the same time felt the additional material was too strong to just be used as bonus pieces, so have instead released a six-track thirty-minute-long EP, using songs that were developed during the creative phase of 'The Holographic Principle'. Epica are definitely one of the best, arguably the best, symphonic metal band around. No moves into folk for these guys, this is all about putting metal and classical forms in a way that makes sense. If you enjoyed the last album then this is essential, nothing more and nothing less.
Oct 2017

ESP
INVISIBLE DIN
On the cover the album is credited to Tony Lowe and Mark Brzezicki (Big Country, Procol Harum) and special guests, and on closer inspection, it can be seen that these guests comprise David Cross (King Crimson), David Jackson (Van der Graaf Generator), Phil Spalding (Steve Hackett, Mike Oldfield), Steve Gee (Landmarq), John Young (Lifesigns), Pat Orchard, Alison Fleming (Tony Lowe), John Beagley and electric harp from Yumi Hara (Daevid Allen, Hugh Hopper). So, quite special indeed. David Cross only adds his violin to a couple of songs, but David Jackson is there with a sax and flute for five, but while the guests do add to the overall album, this is very much the work of Tony (guitar, keyboards, vocals) and Mark (drums, vocals).

The best way to describe this album is to think of the more laid-back prog of the Seventies, as many of those bands had an impact here. Imagine if you will 'Octoberon' era Barclay James Harvest combined with Alan Parsons Project, Steve Hackett, and possibly just a touch of Pink Floyd. It is a delicious delight, perfect for late nights, and for drifting away on. There are layers upon layers, and it is all about the arrangements: it is exactly the type of music that punk was supposed to get rid of and failed. Symphonic prog, which has managed to stay on just the right side of being produced to death, so that each instrument can be clearly discerned, and the complexity of the music can be appreciated, yet always it seems almost simple in its beauty and approach. Highly accessible, this is a wonderful progressive rock album that will delight many fans of the genre.
Jul 2017

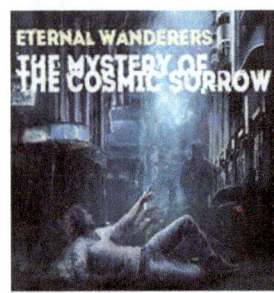

ETERNAL WANDERERS
THE MYSTERY OF THE COSMIC SORROW
This album is my first introduction to the music of Eternal Wanderers, the Russian band led by sisters Elena (lead vocals, keyboards) and Tatyana Kanevskaya (guitars, backing vocals). I wandered over to their site and discovered that earlier this year they played a gig with another of my favourite Russian groups, Lost World Band, and I bet that would have been quite interesting as in many ways they are similar yet also very different indeed. What we have here is a double CD that has very much a science fiction feel to it, so much so that it reminded me less of Tangerine Dream (who have obviously been a major influence), than of Hibernal who in some ways is following a similar musical path. Apparently, the double CD set comes with a fully illustrated booklet (I only have a digital copy), and there is lots of information on the website (which thankfully can be turned to English by clicking on the Union flag) about each song, and what they are about: given that many are instrumental that is certainly a useful facet.

Given that two songs and more than twelve minutes have elapsed before Elena starts singing, it came something of a surprise to hear what a strong singer she is, more alto than soprano, and with plenty of power and emotion. For some strange reason these guys are listed on ProgArchives as neo prog, but they would much better fit within the Crossover genre, although I am sure that Eclectic would love to lay claim to them if they could. What I like so much about this album is that it is just so enjoyable from start to end, and the ninety minutes just flies by: it really is music to get lost inside. The keyboard sounds are all over the place, bringing in quite a few that would normally be at home more in electronic, while the guitars can be there just to provide some counter harmonies or leads, or to crunch out riffs in quite a metallic manner.

There are some amazing bands coming out of Russia at present, and Eternal Wanderers is one every proghead should be looking out for.
Jul 2017

ETERNAL WANDERERS
THE DOOR TO A PARALLEL WORLD
I was having an email conversation with Andy Didorenko (Lost World Band) one day and told him that I had recently heard 'The Mystery of the Cosmic Sorrow' by Eternal Wanderers, and how impressed I had been with it. Shortly afterwards I opened my inbox to find an email from singer and keyboard player Elena Kanevskaya as he had kindly passed on my details to her. We had some conversations, and not long afterwards she sent me their first albums to see what I thought. This their debut was released in 2008, with Elena joined by her sister Tatyana, her husband Dmitry Shtatnov (bass, also in Quorum) and Sergey Nikonrov on drums (with Sergey Alyamkin providing drums on one song). I have been fortunate enough to hear quite a lot of Russian

progressive rock music this year, many of which bring in influences from their homeland, but that is not the case with these guys as they are looking far more to the West, although I am not surprised to find the mighty Polish band Collage mentioned in some reviews.

Much is often made of the fact that the although the rhythm section is male, both the keyboard player/singer and guitarist are female, and they are sisters. But it never matters the gender/race/sexual orientation/age of anyone in a band, it should always be about the music, and right from the beginning one can only be impressed by this. Sergey provides complex drums patterns, while Dmitry uses many different styles to produce not only the notes but also different inflections. Tatyana sometimes riffs in a good old-fashioned neo prog style, although there are others where she provides a melodic lead, while Elena sometimes uses modern sounds and at others looks back to The Nice and Keith Emerson. She has a wonderful voice, but the band are also comfortable as an instrumental unit which sometimes means long passages with no vocals.

The use of a recorder and Jew's harp at the beginning of "Too Close To Heavens" is another example of how they can mix and match styles, as this leads into some delicate bass while Elena has some reverb placed on her voice and is very much to the fore. This ballad is quite reminiscent of Camel and shows understanding of the power of restraint and the requirement for space within music to allow the layers to flow and breathe. This is quite a superb album, and one I have enjoyed immensely.
Oct 2017

ETERNAL WANDERERS
SO FAR AND SO NEAR
2011 saw the second album from Eternal Wanderers, and by now they had increased to a quintet with the addition of Dmitry Drogunov on flute, plus some guest musicians. To my ears this album is more complex than the debut, with Tatyana providing some wonderful guitar runs which show just how important rock can be to the progressive scene. Yes, she knows how to provide widdly widdly with the best of them and can also provide basic backing when it is time for Elena to move to the front, but she has a mastery of many styles outside those normally used within the progressive scene and the album is all the better for it. Having an additional melodic instrument in a flute has also allowed the band to spread their wings musically, while Elena also seems to be far more comfortable providing string keyboard solos when the need is there. If anyone wants an example of just how powerful these guys are then just listen to track two, which not only is the title cut but a ten-minute long instrumental. Using a variety of keyboard sounds (some of which are very Eighties), and complex interplay between the two sisters, it is surprising in some respects at just how well Dmitry and Sergey manage to keep the music grounded, while also playing multi-faceted combinations of their own. They can go from blistering complex symphonic prog with neo elements to Camel at the drop of a hat, then revert into an arrangement that contains multiple layers but is never over-crowded or muddy.

Elena tells me they hope to have the fourth album out inside the next few years, and I really hope that is the case as they are one of the strongest bands I have heard out of Russia, and all their albums are well worth investigating.
Oct 2017

EXCELLION
UNSEAN
No, that isn't a typo in the title, this EP from Mexican-based Excellion really is spelled that way. As singer and guitarist Frozen Chava explains: "There seems to be a lot of people that believe it's a typo and well, it's definitely not, but we expected that too when we decided to name our new work like that. It's a word play where we used "Unseen" and at the same time "Sea" because that's exactly the concept behind this new music. We humans know more about the space than the sea, it's shocking that we only know about five percent of this vast amount of water on the Earth's surface and that's something to reflect about. There is a lot of mystery and things to discover down there, so yeah, that's what UnSEAn is really about."

Musically this is all over the place, with prog shaking hands with djent, mathcore, metalcore, and other sub genres along the way. The guys can really play, of that there is no doubt at all, but I found that there were times when they were just getting too clever and getting in danger of disappearing in a plume of their own ego. The cleverness and styles end up getting in the way of the melody and the music becomes too much of a festival of "look at me, aren't I brilliant?" as opposed to being about any form of musical integrity. It is very clever indeed, but that doesn't mean I want to listen to it.
Jan 2018

EXISTENCE
ORIGINS
I have just taken from my shelves the second Existence album, 'Small People, Short Story, True Crime', which was released in 1999. The CD had made a huge impact on me at the time, as not only had I enjoyed playing it, but it came with a 56-page booklet/magazine! That was a hugely ambitious undertaking for anyone, let alone a band that wasn't known to many within the prog scene, nor a wider music buying audience (and it tickles me that they advertise Mystery within it, they are both Canadian after all). So, a short eighteen years later, and the guys are back with the third album. But, in a very many ways this is full circle, as what is represented here are the roots of the band, hence the album title. When Existence emerged in 1992, their gigs comprised a rock opera, broken into two acts. The first act was recorded and released as their debut album, 'Fragile Whisperings of Innocence' in 1994, but the second act was never recorded as the band moved on. By the time Alan Charles decided to record the second act it was 2010,

and when comparing the recordings, he realised that the right thing to do was to rearrange and re-record everything to make it a consistent whole. Alan provides piano, keyboards, guitar, and bass and returning from the last album is Gérard Lévèque (drums), François Beaugard (violin) and Gaston Gagnon (guitars) and they are joined by Valery Kim Gosselin (vocals) and Richard Ranger (bass).

The booklet may not be nearly as large as the last one, but it has been put together with care and contains all the lyrics with suitable photographs: the focus here is on the music contained on the two CDs. Unlike many progressive bands, the music here is led by the piano. Although turned into a full electric band performance, the piano is always at the heart and soul of Existence, with the lead instrument often being the poignant violin. The hidden instrument in this band is emotion, as the music is dripping with it, from the cracking of the vocals through the arrangements. This makes them very different from other bands within the prog scene, as the approach is towards feelings that are being conveyed, instead of just an aural assault. Complex and complicated, it must have been a compelling experience when the band were performing it live some 25 years ago.

With their two earlier albums released before the advent of the internet and prog sites and forums, back in the day when fanzines like Feedback were the only way to get the news out there as mainstream media ignored or denigrated prog, it is of little surprise that very few people are aware of the existence of Existence. Hopefully the release of this album will gain them many new fans, and we won't have to wait so long for the next one. Well worth investigation.
Dec 2017

EYESBERG
BLUE
It must be said that Eyesberg are a band with something of a back story. They came together in Frankfurt around 1980, with a line-up of Georg Alfter, Michael Buchner, Norbert Podien, Thomas Klarmann, and Malcolm Shuttleworth. Although they wrote several songs, they never released an album, and they all went on to other things. Thomas later enjoyed success as a member of Argos and Superdrama, and this spurred some of the others to revisit the old Eyesberg songs and see what they could do with them now. Malcolm Shuttleworth (vocals), Norbert Podien (keyboards, drum programming, backing vocals) and Georg Alfter (guitar, bass), were joined by Klarmann's Argos bandmate Ulf Jacobs on drums, but neither Thomas nor other original member Michael Buchner were involved this time around.

Given these songs were written more than thirty-five years ago, as opposed to 2014 when they were released, it isn't surprising at all that they have far less in common with modern prog, and the album has a retro feel. This is enhanced by the quite large use of flute sounds from the keyboards, and it certainly makes me think of the type of music Steve Hackett was producing at the time, as well as late Seventies Genesis. It is an incredibly enjoyable piece of work throughout, and the very English vocals of Malcolm

come across as a mix of Gabriel and Roger Chapman, with hints of Peter Nicholls. Overall, this is a very enjoyable album, and I was keen to see if they would stick around to release another.
Feb 2017

EYESBERG
MASQUERADE
Towards the end of 2016 Eyesberg returned with their second album, this time comprising all new songs. There was no use of a drum machine this time, as they managed to secure the talents of Spock's Beard drummer Jimmy Keegan, and this has had a major impact on the music. No longer are the drums just there to keep the beat and provide backbone, this time they have become very much an essential part of the overall sound as Jimmy drives the guys along – he never has been one to be content with just playing the beat, he knows when not to play, and when to force proceedings. No longer are the band performing as if they were around more than thirty-five years ago (although they were), now it is more of that time being an influence on what they are doing, which is far harder and heavier than last time around.

The debut would be best described as retro prog, but this one is much further into neo prog territory, with a more abrasive edge; they have lost the innocence of the debut and are far angrier. The two albums are quite different in some respects, and very similar in others, with Malcolm's vocals playing a key part in bringing them together, along with Hackett Genesis influences still obvious in this one, although more diluted than in the debut. Of the two I prefer the debut, just, but they are both worthy of discovery.
Feb 2017

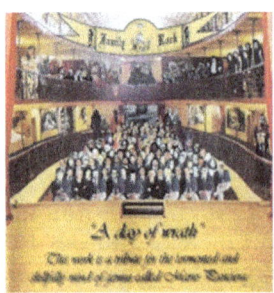

FAMILY FREE ROCK
A DAY OF WRATH
Family Free Rock was a Brazilian band from São Paulo, and this 37-minute-long single-track album was originally released as a very limited CD-R in 2008, Progshine then releasing it digitally in 2015. Interestingly, it is inspired by the works of the band Devil Doll, so much so that FFR state that this includes excerpts from 'Sacrilegium', 'The Girl Who Was... Death' and 'Eliogabalus'. Now, my musical education is sadly lacking as I haven't previously come across Devil Doll but having heard this, I am obviously going to have to rectify that. This was quite some effort from FFR: there can't be many who have released a debut quite like this, it is certainly ambitious. That they sometimes fail can be overlooked as when they get it right this is an incredibly interesting piece of music.

If I was to try and classify the music, then probably Heavy Prog would be the area I would put this into, although there are sections when it is just Doctor Zamboni on vocals,

and Gui on piano, which are quite different, and the additional use of cello as a main instrument also gives the music a quite different edge. While not indispensable, I enjoyed playing this, so why not give a try?
Oct 2017

FAUNCH
DIVE
The story of this 1999 album goes back more than twenty years, to when guitarist Michael McClure left USCD to study theatre in the UK. He wanted to be near Stratford, so attended Warwick University where he met Andy Faunch in late 1978. Along with drummer Dave Blackburn they formed a band, called Tiny Lites (after the Zappa song "City of Tiny Lites") and after Michael returned to the States, he convinced the others to move to California in 1980 "to get the band back together". They had various musical adventures, including working as And And And in the Eighties, but 'Dive' is credited to faunch (all lower case), and all three are heavily involved. Dave provides drums, percussion, djembe, Michael electric guitar, backing vocals, keyboards, and programming while Andy is on vocals, bass, acoustic and electric guitars and programming.

To my ears this is a wonderfully strange yet compelling bringing together of two iconic bands, fittingly one from each side of the Atlantic, as XTC vie with Talking Heads for dominance. It is poppy, it is rocky, it is bright and cheerful, and has plenty of dynamics. It was self-produced (and then mixed and mastered by Dave), yet everything is crystal clear, and it certainly doesn't seem like a low budget production. There is a great deal going on, yet it is always infectious, and there are some wonderful bass lines which show how important that attack can be, as well as the actual playing of the notes. Is there some Hall & Oates type funk in there? Possibly, but there are also some elements of Robyn Hitchcock, and even some vocal tinges of Roy Harper.

It is somehow electronic, poppy, rocky and emotive all at the same time. It was probably dated when it was released, but now it feels timeless, and is a joy from start to finish. It isn't the type of music I normally listen to, but I have thoroughly enjoyed this.
Jul 2017

FAUNCH
VENICE & BEETHOVEN
Just a short sixteen years later, and faunch followed 'Dive' with 'Venice & Beethoven'. By now it was just Michael on electric & acoustic guitars, and Andy on everything else (although Dave did mix a couple of the tunes). This album is even more varied than the last, and we even get the ska/2-tone of "Western Sky" to go with the rock out cover (more of that later). When Michael was asked to describe the album, he came up with "What would

happen if you took all the colours in XTC, 10CC, Kevin Gilbert, Human League, Prince, Richard Thompson, Devin Townsend Project, Porcupine Tree, Robert Palmer, King's X, Peter Gabriel and The Sensational Alex Harvey Band (!), and mixed them all together? Would it inevitably become a steaming pile of funky fudge, or an inventive and curious kaleidoscope of contrasting musical hues?"

As with 'Dive', this just doesn't sound like the work of a few independent musicians, but comes across as people at the top of their field who are working in a studio with a world-class producer to make music that will be loved and known by millions. Instead, what we have are guys doing this in their spare time outside their day jobs but creating music that has a wonderfully rich palette. This is incredibly infectious, and music that makes the listener smile from start to end, and isn't that what music is about? Shouldn't it create an emotional reaction?

All the music has a high pop element, apart from the one cover version, a song I have some relationship with. I was at one of the very first Credo gigs with Mike Varty on keyboards, up in Mansfield, when the guys suggested playing this song in the set to which Mike surprised everyone by saying that he didn't know it! It was a song I discussed with Fish, asking him if he was ever going to get around to recording his own version only for him to burst out laughing and tell me that he had just done exactly that. But the one version that everyone must stand up against is the original, when a Scotsman stood onstage in his white and black hooped shirt and told everyone that he was "The Faith Healer". Given that much of the music until then has had a high electronic or funk element it was somewhat surprising for me when the well-known guitar chords started coming out the speakers. Andy starts with his voice behind the guitar, but then a second guitar comes in and dominance starts to be heard. They haven't tried to copy it fully, but instead have put their own twist on it, yet they keep the keyboard soaring and powerful, just how they should be. So, two very interesting albums from a band new to me. Let's hope that we don't have to wait quite so long for the next one…
Jul 2017

FEN
WINTER
Formed in early 2006 with the goal of producing Atmospheric Black Metal that incorporates elements of post-rock, Fen has, since then, found themselves at the vanguard of a resurgent UK Black Metal scene. With an EP, four full length albums, several splits, and compilations to their name so far, this their latest full-length album (released March 2017) is their most ambitious to date, as they have combined Black metal with many other styles to create something that is very special indeed. Conceptually, they have returned to the roots of their ideology, seeking to embrace and distil all that inspired them when they first set out on this path over a decade ago – that is, to invoke the ambience of bleak reflection and ancient sorrow that permeates the mysterious landscapes of the fens of Eastern England.

According to singer/guitarist The Watcher this album "describes a journey towards sanctity and redemption across a landscape steeped in mystery, hints of forgotten darkness and sorrows long since drowned in the distant past." There are six songs, but the only real way to play this album is to put it on at the beginning and be prepared for seventy-five minutes of music that will take you well away from the comfortable world you reside in, to a place that is far more barren and bleaker, filled with foggy atmosphere and danger. How just three guys (The Watcher is joined by Havenless on drums and Grungyn on bass and vocals) can produce something as majestic and over the top of as this is beyond me. It shows that although the Scandinavian countries had a stranglehold on this type of music for a long time, that is no longer the case. Fen have been going for ten years, and they are maturing and getting even better with age. The record label describes this as "atmospheric Black Metal and delicate, spacious cleans, married with aspects of 70's progressive rock, shoegaze and doom metal". I can make it much simpler than that. This is genius, nothing less.
Feb 2017

THE FIERCE AND THE DEAD
SPOOKY ACTION
There are times when a reviewer's life is not an easy one, and this is one of those. Here I have the second album from an instrumental quartet (who use a couple of guests sparingly – including some great brass from Terry Edwards on two numbers), and I'm not sure how to describe it. Saying it is an incredible piece of work which grows on the listener each and every time they play it probably doesn't give enough information. Saying that they have large math rock influences, obviously have spent a lot of time listening to Robert Fripp and are an incredibly tight outfit also doesn't really state what these guys are about. In Stuart Marshall they have a drummer who can keep it simple or can turn into a demented Keith Moon when the need arises before getting back to business and providing something like a simple drum roll, bassist Kevin Feazey often employs one of the filthiest bass sounds I have heard in a while (think of a distorted Chris Squire), yet he can also tone it down both in sound and attack and knows when not to play at all and provide space for the twin guitars of Matt Stevens and Steve Cleaton. Having a rhythm section that can play such a huge melodic counterpoint gives a great foundation for these guys to go off and have a real blast.

Complex, intricate, all over the place yet always making sense as they go from one motif and style into another, these guys use discord and disharmony as close friends to really stress what they are doing. In some ways this is quite a close relation to free jazz as they bound along and keep throwing musical ideas out here and there and seeing where they will be led. To discover this was recorded in just four days is incredible, but probably explains the life and vitality that is prevalent throughout. If you like your music to be cutting edge, yet melodic, hard rock/metal yet progressive and full of jazz influences, or if you just want to discover yet another amazing band then you need to check these guys out.
Jan 2014

THE FIERCE AND THE DEAD
FIELD RECORDINGS
This may be only just a tad over twenty-eight minutes long but is a blast and a delight from start to finish. The band have certainly grown a lot since I first came across them, and to perform instrumental complex music to a group of people who haven't come across them before takes balls. Taken from the band's incendiary set at last year's Ramblin' Man Festival, 'Field Recordings' captures the band in their element – performing live on stage in front of a crowd who very quickly warm to them. The album features two previously unreleased songs which may (or may not!) feature on The Fierce And The Dead's third album, currently in production. Sometimes the bands are cranking it hard, almost out of tune, and others it is incredible dual harmony guitars with Matt Stevens and Steve Cleaton knowing exactly where the other is going to be.

Add to that the dynamite rhythm section of Ken Feazey (who has one of the dirtiest bass sounds you're ever likely to hear) and Stuart Marshall (who knows his way around all aspects of his kit), and here we have a band that are revelling in the experience. They close with "666…6", and the intricate, almost delicate, introduction provides no hint of the change in style that is to come as firstly the guitars blast, before the bass takes the lead and brings the band back into the melody. There is a back-and-forth style through this, but it is the guitar distortion that really makes it special, turning it into an epic monster, which really lifts the crowd as they segue into "Brainstorm" in honour of Hawkwind who are headlining the festival.

My only complaint is that this is just too short! But it has certainly whetted my appetite for the next full release, and if you have never come across these guys before then here is a great place to start.
Apr 2017

FLAMES OF GENESIS
INTERSTELLAR TRANSMIGRATION PART I
The full title of this album is 'Interstellar Transmigration Part I: A Bridge To Further Realms', and is the debut album by Flames of Genesis, where all instrumentation is provided by The Voyager. According to the website, "The experiences are translated through ethereal cinematic dark ambient soundscapes - each piece telling a part of the story, conveying the experiences of the journeys across vast distances, crossing the border between what is known and unknown, embracing the mysteries and the wonders, transcending all limits and boundaries both within and without." As The Voyager so eloquently puts it, what we have here is a dark ambient album, one that for me works on a great many levels.

Dark ambient is a style of ambient music that features foreboding, ominous, or discordant overtones, and in the case of this album also brings in the feeling of coldness which comes about from being cast adrift in deep dark space. The original Alien film had the

tagline 'In Space No-One Can Hear You Scream', but this music works to provide the feeling far better than the words ever did. To me this is all about being alone in a spaceship, with the engines cut, drifting on the solar currents just knowing that however bad it feels now, it is only going to get worse. Strangely disturbing, yet also compelling, this is a collection of music that will only appeal to a select few, but those few will undoubtedly find it as attractive and essential as I did.
Jan 2018

FLAMING ROW
MIRAGE – A PORTRAYAL OF FIGURE
So, what we have here is the second album from German quartet Flaming Row, but is it? While Martin Schnella (guitars, keyboards, vocals) provided all the music, based on a story written by Kiri Geile (vocals) and then arranged by Martin with Niklas Kahl (drums) and Marek Arnold (keyboards, saxophone), this is way more than 'just' a band album. To be able to do justice to the story of the Third World War they have brought in a couple of guest musicians and the odd singer. Okay, to possibly put that more into perspective, the total singer and musician count on here is more than 30, and with the likes of Dave Meros, Kristoffer Gildenlöw, Jimmy Keegan and Arjen Anthony Lucassen helping out on the music, and the likes of Ted Leonard, Magali Luyten, Simon Moskon and many others on the vocals, perhaps it isn't surprising that this is something a little special.

This is an over the top, multi-layered incredibly strongly produced album which sometimes stays in control as although each musician adds his piece it still somehow manages to remain a bombastic masterpiece instead of disappearing up an ego of its' own making. I challenge any lover of prog metal not to fall in love with this at the very first hearing, and just sit with the booklet and listen to the narration and singers telling the story while marvelling at the melodic complexity that is displayed in front of your very ears. Although sounding nothing like Spock's Beard, it is almost as if they have captured the sheer brilliance of albums such as 'Snow', have then brought in some American melodic metal, combined it with the symphonic power of Nightwish while also ensuring that fans of the dexterity (both musically and lyrically) of Clive Nolan are well catered for.

Simply put, this is one of the most exciting and interesting albums that I have heard so far this year. I fell in love with it just a few bars into the first song and I kept hoping that I wouldn't be disappointed with the rest of the album while I just found more to savour. Each time I played this, new depths have come to light, and this has become for me one of those albums that prevents me writing about anything else as I just want to play it so much! It may be over the top, yet somehow there is enough restraint to ensure that it never really falls totally out of control, but rather shows that sometimes music needs to be more than just a couple of guys in a studio, and by adding so many others with their own techniques and styles it has allowed Flaming Row to create something very special indeed. The only question in my mind, is how on earth do they follow this? I note that in

the booklet they state this is to be continued, so that is something to look forward to indeed.
Jun 2014

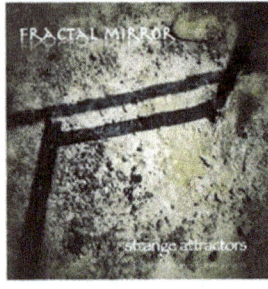

FRACTAL MIRROR
STRANGE ATTRACTORS

The debut album from Dutch band Fractal Mirror has been gaining quite a lot of kudos in various quarters, with its combination of laid-back synth laden prog and alternative pop. Some of the keyboard sounds are very dated, and there is so much space in the music that one could drive a truck through it, and it moves from being incredibly complex to sheer simplicity, so it sounds like just the sort of thing that would have me raving about it to the highest heavens. Well, one might think so. Instead, I find this a very cold album with a simplicity that seems contrived as opposed to naïve, with vocals that I find poor as opposed to emotional. Yes, there are elements of Psychedelic Furs, New Order and Eels in the vocal approach, but with all of the faults and none of the benefits. But, even putting that to one side there isn't enough happening musically for me to find this consistently interesting and enjoyable. Getting to the end of the album the first time was a trial for me, as opposed to an event that I enjoyed, and playing it again was something I had to do to so that I could see if the album grew on me as opposed to just reviewing it out of the box.

But no matter how many times I play this, I keep coming back to the fact that I don't think that it is a very good album, no matter what anyone else says. Plenty of other people are saying this is wonderful, so maybe it is just me (and that won't be the first or last time when I am at odds with everyone else), but I can't see myself ever playing this again.
Apr 2014

FROZEN OCEAN
TRANSCIENCE

Following on from the release of the 'The Prowess Of Dormition' EP, Vaarwel, the person behind the name Frozen Ocean, has produced a guide to what he sees as his kingdom, described as "a traveller's almanac that reveals the breathtaking order within the daunting chaos". 'Transience' is a compilation of fifteen remastered tracks, three previously unavailable, and when downloaded comes with cover art, created by Vaarwel himself, a selection of Frozen Ocean flyers, an original poem that explores the thoughts behind Transience and a set of wallpapers for the 'A Perfect Solitude' album. Vaarwel's musical world is comprised of three kingdoms, the Aether, the Tether and the Nether, with each being formed from a different musical style.

Those three strands are recognisable as Blackened Metal, Dark Ambient and Post-Rock, and musically this is a strong combination of all three. Mostly electronic in its making, this album manages somehow to be mostly laid back and almost soothing, while also containing an edge of menace and darkness that allows the listener to understand that the world may not be all it is supposed to be. Just listening to this makes me feel cold to the bone, even though it is bright sunshine outside and a balmy 25 degrees. When the guitars kick in, as on "Tredje Vind: Håndflate Av Stormen", we are transported from the wastelands to a musical world where evil rules, and there is plotting going on in the subterranean caves. It is in stark contrast to what has gone before yet is also related and forms part of the musical whole.

Frozen Ocean have a wide and diverse discography, and Vaarwel has released this album as a way of providing a way into his project and understanding it (personally I had the same issue with Zappa, never really knew where to start, so in the end just dove in and am now a real fan). As Vaarwel says himself, "Projects with an enormous and varied discography are very difficult to perceive, even at a subliminal level. I could imagine that from the listener's point of view, thus I prepared this for all of you who would like to attune with Frozen Ocean but didn't know where to start. 'Transience' itself is an inherent part of the Frozen Ocean artistic method, so it is completely representative within the choice of songs, including the previously unpublished ones. 'Transience' is a piece of different, good music combined into one block, but moreover it is a safe and convenient passage through Frozen Ocean's meandering discography. Welcome, and follow me..."

Vaarwel is offering this beautiful, expansive guide to the world of Frozen Ocean as a gift to those with the desire to discover, so is available free of charge, and is his way of opening the gates to all who would explore the ice shrouded sounds of his imagination.
Oct 2017

GALAHAD
SEIZE THE DAY
It's been a while since Galahad last released an EP, in fact it has been 20 years since the 'Voiceprint Radio Sessions' came out. I remember listening to it in the car with Stu before a gig at King Arthur's Court, makes me feel very old indeed! So, what we have here are three songs with two versions of each. First up is an edited version of "Seize The Day", taken from 'Battle Scars', and I can see why this was chosen as at just over four minutes long this half-size version really works. It certainly doesn't feel as if it has been edited, and if someone was coming across this as an introduction to the band then they would be surprised to hear that it is normally double the length. There are some wonderful bass lines here which feature almost as a solo, and each time I hear them I see Neil in my mind's eye. The band really come together on this song, with stellar performances from everyone with Spencer and Roy doing their best not to be overshadowed by Dean and Stu, and sometimes they achieve it.

Next up is the full-length version of the same song, which to my ears is definitely the best way to hear it, but the edited version does enough to more than stand up in its own right.

Then there is a 'new' song, "21st Century Painted Lady". In fact, the original version is one of Galahad's oldest songs, but the first time it featured on a recording was on the cassette 'Other Crimes and Misdemeanours', with another version appearing on the second of that series and yet another on the reissue of 'In A Moment of Madness'. Here we have a very different side of the band, acoustic and without the trans-style keyboards of "Seize The Day". The musical accompaniment works so well that the next song is the instrumental version of the same song, and it is interesting to hear yet another styling with Dean really making his presence felt and the whole song feeling quite different. Interestingly Karl Groom also adds some guitars to this track, although not quite in the bombastic Threshold manner one often associates with him.

Then it is time to close with "Bug Eye". It is strange to think that 'Following Ghosts' is some fifteen years old now, and this features the same line-up of the band that originally recorded this back then. It has been updated, with the guitar and keyboards being clearer and more dynamic, and at nine minutes long is the second longest song on the EP. The honour of the longest goes to the live version of the song, which closes the EP, and at more than twelve minutes long they all have the chance to shine. Stu has always been a great live performer and there is an additional edge to his vocals that provide a great contrast to some of the softer moments. Galahad have always been a rock band first and foremost, and this shows that even with different keyboard stylings the Dorset boys are always ready to pound it when the need arises. This is the first in a series of EPs planned for this year. I can't wait for the next one, especially when one considers it is more than 40 minutes long! Not bad for an EP.
May 2014

GALAHAD
30 EP
Majestic. Grandiose. Class. Those are the very first words that came to me as I was listening to this four track EP, which Galahad have released as part of their thirtieth anniversary year. They have taken four of their older numbers, and have re-recorded them in a manner that is both a nod to the past yet very much showing the current and future direction of the band. Three of those involved, Stu Nicholson (vocals), Roy Keyworth (guitars) and Spencer Luckman (drums) were of course involved when the songs were recorded the first time around, Tim Ashton (bass) played on some before taking his rather extended break from the band (22 years!) while "new boy" Dean Baker may not have played on these originally, but he has been around since 'Following Ghosts' (can it really be sixteen years since that came out?).

First up is "The Chase", a song I first heard when Stu and I were sat in my car outside King Arthur's Court before a gig, listening to a pre-release of 'Voiceprint Radio Sessions' (which to my horror I realise was more than 20 years ago now as it was their 8th Anniversary show, with The Morrigan in support, who they had also played with at Whitchurch). This time around I was struck by the space contained within the song, and the way the use of acoustic guitar transforms it. Stu is still singing as well as ever, hitting the higher notes with ease, while the music shifts and moves. Providing bass is Daryl Watts, son of the band's original bassist Paul, and he locks in with Spencer to provide the groove while Roy is playing with more confidence than ever, relishing the opportunity to move the song into a more metallic direction with riffs that are both laid back and strident, while Dean definitely takes the opportunity to shine. Even when he isn't providing the primary melody, there is a great deal going on in the background, so the song has way more depth and power than the original ever did. Something else I noticed on this song, and throughout the EP, is that the production has allowed us to really hear just how important Spencer is to the overall sound. I have played all their songs many, many times, but I have never heard the drums quite so to the fore and hadn't realised just how much of a powerhouse he is.

And so, onto "Chamber of Horrors". I must confess that I was rather worried about this, as this was one of two songs from 'Nothing Is Written'. Not only was it their first ever full length release, but it is also an album that I have saved on my iPhone and still play frequently. For much of the time the band play this "straight", staying fairly close in many ways to the original (although Stu sounds more relaxed and going with the flow than first time around), but when Dean comes in with the keyboard lead with a sound straight from the Eighties all bets are off, with Tim providing some great driving bass in the background. The short break leads into the restrained guitar lead, some lounge keyboards and superb rhythm section, and then we are off and running towards the end.

"Dreaming From The Inside" was the A-side of the band's debut single, and was later re-recorded as part of the Galahad Acoustic Quintet project, but here the use of classical guitar (by producer Karl Groom) and piano (by ex-keyboard player Mark Andrews) combined with great vocals lifts it far higher than it had ever been imagined before. A great deal of thought has gone into this arrangement, and it is the restraint and use of space that makes it now one of the finest songs they have ever recorded. This is quality, sheer quality, of the very highest order with Tim and Spencer having an incredible impact by not appearing until nearly four and a half minutes through. Roy switches to electric, while Dean provides some keyboards on top of the piano, as they rock through to the end. Part of me is torn, as I can't make up my mind if it would have been better to stay with the trio all the way through, but I love it as it is.

"Room 801" is an intriguing choice to end the EP with, as although it has always been one of my favourite songs, this was one that I have always associated with Neil on bass due to the way he attacked this in concert, even though Tim played on the original recording. Here it starts with sound effects for the first minute or so, gradually coming in with a nod to "Close Encounters". One small thing that made me smile, is that on the original there is a distinct percussive sound that strikes out a rhythm, while here the exact same sound is used rather more sparingly. This has been done just for the true Galafan, as those hearing this for the first time won't know the difference, but anyone who has played the original will smile with the recognition. Almost Marillion-esque in its approach, there are multiple layers, and a classiness throughout the eleven minutes, with some great filmatic clips. I hate to think how much Dean had to work on this, as there are multiple keyboard tracks combining to provide a sound that is almost Tangerine Dream or Jean Michel Jarre at times, evoking the feel of "space". He and Stu combine magically, with the rest leaving them to it at times, coming back in to provide a restrained oomph. The guitar lick at eight minutes starts with Roy mimicking what he did all those years ago, before moving away and back again, keeping to the original but also making it very much a new piece with harmonies and layers of his own. Galahad probably first came to prominence to many when they won the Radio One Rock Show Rock Challenge back in 1991. Somehow it seems fitting that the EP ends with the mighty Tommy Vance introducing the band (love the Stephen Hawkings amendment of Mark to Dean) and saying that "Room 801" is an epic song. And do you know what? He's right.

So four songs, just tasters of what will be released later this year, and I can't wait.
July 2015

GALAHAD
EMPIRES NEVER LAST
It is indeed strange to realise that the album I am currently playing is now some 10 years old. I reviewed it back then, but what I am currently listening to is the 2015 remastered reissued version. Instead of a standard CD case, this was released as a digipak, containing two additional songs, while the booklet that appeared in the initial version had also been retained. Although in terms of membership there had only been one change between this album and the previous, 'Year Zero', there had been a gap of five years and the band had been through a great deal in the intervening period. Much of this was reflected in the music, which saw the band move into a far heavier approach than previously. Gone was the naivety of the band of the Nineties, and instead it has been replaced by a maturity and strength that showed the band in a brand new light.

I do have a history with these guys, so it probably isn't surprising that I am going to be raving over this, as I think I have done so with every one of their releases ever since I first came across them some twenty-five years ago, but this is a very different band indeed to the one that won the Radio 1 Rock Show Rock Wars all those years ago, who first came to the notice of many progheads at the same time with their debut CD 'Nothing is Written'. True, in Stu, Roy and Spencer they have the same singer, guitarist and drummer and keyboard player Dean Baker had been there for a while by then now (line-up completed with new bassist Lee Abraham) but it is the depth and presence of the band that is such a surprise.

Galahad are one of those bands who have truly progressed with each album, and have toyed with acoustic and dance among other things, but at their core they have always been a progressive rock band, and here they pushed the rock more than ever before. This is an intense ride, and there is no doubt that having Karl Groom at the controls made a huge difference to the overall sound. 'Year Zero' suffered from a long gestation period, being recorded in multiple places and then being produced by the band themselves, whereas this was mostly recorded at Thin Ice.

With each release showing another side of the band, but here it all comes together in a major tour de force. It may open gently enough with "De-Fi-Ance", and some guest vocals, but this really is just an introduction for the band to kick off blazing into "Termination". Second song in and already Galahad have the listener by the ears and the balls. From here it is a rollercoaster ride of power and emotion, the band kicking together and showing that prog can be a really strong and dynamic force in the hands of guys who really know what they are doing and what they want to achieve. This was awarded 'Album of the Year' in many quarters, and rightly so, as here is a band at the very top of the game with over the top bombastic progressive rock

To be honest it had been a while since I had played this, but given that I now have three copies in my collection (tour edition, 'normal' issue and now the deluxe edition) I really don't have any excuse for not returning to it more frequently. If you want to hear progressive rock at it's finest, then just go to "I Could Be God" and play it loud. Very loud.
Mar 2017

GALAHAD
GUARDIAN ANGEL
During 2014, the guys were busy working towards their thirtieth anniversary the following year, and so made the decision to release three EPs to bridge the gap from their last albums in 2012, of which this is the second. Released in the summer of that year this contains four versions of the song which appeared on 'Euphoria' plus a piano version of "Beyond The Barbed Wire" (from 'Battle Scars'). Galahad have never been afraid to experiment with their own music, and it is interesting to compare the third song on this EP, the ten-minute plus album version, against the opener which has just Dean on piano and Stu on vocals. Of course, stripping a song back to its essentials is nothing new, and something that Martin Orford has been a party to both with IQ and Jadis numbers, but these are so very different that in many ways they come across as totally different songs. Between the two on the EP there is a hybrid version which as it sounds, contains elements of both the piano and the full-on prog version. It's hard to say which I prefer, as they are both damn fine, and it is interesting to see the band experimenting like this.

The same is true of the last number, as with just some reverb on his vocals this is Stu stripped right back with just the Dean's piano to pitch against. There is no hiding place when music is performed in this manner, both must be perfect as any mistakes can so easily be heard. This is still available from the band as both a download and a physical CD and is well worth investigating if you are a fan.
Mar 2017

GALAHAD
MEIN HERZ BRENNT

This was the last of the three EPs from 2014 and was a surprise in a few different ways. Firstly, Stu is singing in German (well, it is a German song after all), it's a cover, and it's a cover of a song by Rammstein, not a band usually referenced by prog bands. There will be a version on 'Quiet Storms', which will be out later this year, but whether it is one of these we will just have to wait and see. The first of the four is a delicate piano and violin version, which really captures a beauty that I think Rammstein threaten at in their own version, but miss with the bombastic attack for which they are so well-known.

The "fully loaded" version is the one that is closest to the original, as the delicate pianos give way to crunching guitars, although there is also a lot of depth here with quite a bit going on musically within the verse, so there is a stronger structure. Of course, Stu's vocals will never quite have the edge of the original as he is a very different singer, but he has always been able to provide menace when he needs to and does it here with aplomb. The other two versions are an English language take on the piano/vocal, and the other is a piano instrumental. This last has a real beauty to it and is something I have really enjoyed playing. In many ways it is simplistic, but simple music can be incredibly hard to play, and Dean produces a wonderful interpretation. If you are interested in Galahad, or Rammstein, then this is well worth getting.
Mar 2017

GALAHAD
SLEEPERS

So, an envelope arrived one day from the UK, and my wife asked me who it was from. When I replied that it was from Stu Nicholson, she asked me what he had sent me, so I showed her the CDs it contained, and she immediately said "Oh, isn't that the dead lady?". Of all the thousands of CDs I've been sent over the years, this is the one where the cover made an impact on her, from twenty years previously. True, the story about the cover did make quite a fuss, and this was in the days before internet or Prog Magazine, but for me the story was always that of the album itself and how it was recorded. After the success of 'Nothing Is Written', winning the Radio 1 Rock Wars, appearing on the Friday Night Rock Show it appeared as if the stage was set for Galahad to burst through into the mainstream in a big way. All they needed now was the follow-up album. 'NIW' was self-financed and had come out in 1991, but the band were starting to make a real name for themselves, and new keyboard player Karl Groom had settled in. They started experimenting with new songs, showing a move into a slightly rockier area, and although the loss of bassist Tim Ashton was a blow, it allowed them to bring in Neil Pepper, who was a force to be reckoned with.

I still remember Stu ringing me in a state of real excitement, as they had managed to secure the services of Tony Arnold to engineer and produce the album: he couldn't believe that a producer of such history and renown would be interested in a small prog band from Dorset. It is fair to say the experience on all sides was not perfect, and the album took far longer to come to fruition than was expected. The band were playing the songs live, and I can remember Stu needing the lyrics to the title cut at one gig as it was the first time they had played it! Some of the guys even went out and recorded an album as the Galahad Acoustic Quintet just to be able to work on something. But the album finally was released in 1995, and even then, I found it strange to review it given I knew all the material so very well indeed. So, what would I think of it now?

The 2015 reissue has been remastered by guitarmeister Karl Groom, has two additional songs not on the original, and has been released as a digipak by Polish label Oskar. What I noticed immediately from the sound is that this is contains far greater balance than the original, and the drums have been given a much greater focus. Karl is known for creating great sound both in a studio and in the live environment, and even though he is a guitarist he has always been adept in getting the best out of a drumkit, and as with the '30' EP he has brought to life all the work that Spencer carries out at the rear of the band.

As for songs, well, we're spoilt for choice as we go from the dramatic and sublime to, frankly, the ridiculous. "Dentist Song" really is a song about a trip to the dentist, and although this seems like a strange subject choice for any lyricist, let alone a proghead, I have always enjoyed this, as the layers of keyboards tie in so well with the guitar on this poppy little number that I have always found it to be a load of fun, although I am fully aware that most proggers don't share my point of view. "Julie Anne" is still one of the finest ballads they ever produced, and with its appearance on a 'Frontiers' CD it also gained them a lot of interest from outside the prog scene. Stu has always been a great singer, and with the right production and minimal backing he has always been able to deliver the goods and is a format the band still use today.

I could go through every song in turn, explaining why I feel that this album is still essential after all these years, but instead I'll focus on a song that is still possibly the best they ever recorded. I first saw them perform "Exorcising Demons" at The Astoria, when Tim was still in the band, and even then, I could hear the band was moving into a more mature style of music. At nine plus minutes long, it is the fourth longest on the album, but it is both timeless and way too short! With keyboards and percussion setting the scene, it always makes me imagine Stu alone in a cavernous warehouse, switching his singing between gentle and menacing. After more than three minutes the bass comes in playing a riff that is picked up by the guitar, and gradually the band starts to pick up speed and the vocals contain more venom, until everything stops so that Stu can sing out "Exorcising Demons" unaccompanied. This is a song that really does build, with lots of layers and complexity, and although it is more keyboard-driven than the live version it is still a powering number.

I have no idea how often I have played this album over the years, but "lots" seems like a good number, and back in the day Stu and I had discussions at gigs when I discovered that they had dropped "Exorcising Demons" for one reason or another. Looking back this is a bridging album in some ways, from the naivety of "Nothing Is Written' to the more

powerful works they were to bring later. It took too long to be released, of that there is no doubt, and the band lost some of the momentum they had been building just a few years earlier. But they got through it, and all these years on is still an album I enjoy playing, and isn't that what listening to music is all about? If you have only come to Galahad through 'Battle Scars' or 'Euphoria' then you will find this quite different, but for someone who first heard them when I played the 'Madness' cassette (which I still have!), then this is something that I dearly love, and would take with me if I was ever stranded on that desert island.
Mar 2017

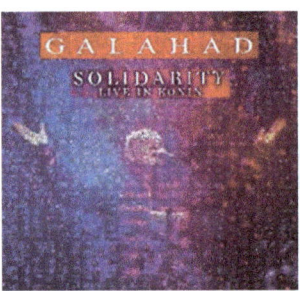

GALAHAD
SOLIDARITY: LIVE IN KONIN
On September 2nd, 2011, bassist Neil Pepper finally succumbed to cancer, and this had a major impact both on the band and all those who had the privilege to meet him. What were the guys going to do after this? They had recorded two albums with Neil, both of which were released in 2012, but how would they perform them live? Actually, they didn't have to look too far, as keyboard player Dean Baker and guitarist Roy Keyworth had been helping out in Twelfth Night, which also featured multi-instrumentalist Mark Spencer. It was soon agreed that he would join them for gigs, and then in 2014 Tim Ashton returned to the fold, so this album captures quite a short-lived line-up. Recorded in Konin, Poland, on 26th October 2013, this double CD and single DVD set finds a band who in many ways are very different indeed to the band I saw so many times in the Nineties. Yes, singer Stu Nicholson, guitarist Roy Keyworth and drummer Spencer Luckman are still very much involved as they were back in the day, but this is an outfit that has progressed in many ways indeed.

At one time, they were very much part of the neo-prog scene, being heavily influenced by the likes of Marillion and IQ, but they have changed quite dramatically over the years, and how have a much heavier and denser sound. Dean has a wonderful approach on keyboards, knowing when to be quiet, reflective, and "progressive" in approach but he also knows what it takes to move into a far more metallic area. Spencer has grown in confidence over the years and has become much more of a rock or even metallic drummer, really pounding the kit, while Roy has turned it all up and provides a much more powerful platform. With all this mayhem going on it probably isn't surprising that Stu's vocals have also gained a depth and breadth they didn't have previously – he still hits all the notes, but now they are quite a different proposition than before.

I am sure a lot of this is down to the person who mixed and edited this album, Karl Groom, who has been working with the band now for some years. There are only a few of the older numbers included in this set, and one of these should be called out for special mention. After everything having been turned up to the max, and the audience blasted into submission, they come back for the encore. Or more truthfully, Stu returns on his own to sing "Painted Lady" totally a capella. It takes a brave singer to do that at any time, let alone after already performing for ninety minutes, and he nails it. Totally. This album

is a great introduction to the Galahad of today, and one that makes me regret now living so very far away, as I am unlikely ever to catch them in the flesh again, and these guys are still proving they are one of the best prog acts around.
Apr 2017

GALAHAD
WHEN WORLDS COLLIDE
Back in 1985 a small group of progheads formed a band, and even though the musical furrow they were ploughing has never been the most popular, somehow, they have persevered and in 2015 they marked their thirtieth anniversary. Through some twists and turns, the line-up in 2015 was 80% the same as the one that recorded their first CD, 'Nothing Is Written', with just 'new boy' keyboard player Dean Baker the only one not there all those years ago. But, seeing as how he joined the group in 1997, possibly the new boy tag is just a little unfair...The concept behind this double CD was quite simple, re-record songs from throughout the band's career, but perform them as if they had just been written. Also involved were previous members of the band (and in one case, the son of a previous member), and co-producer Karl Groom also assisted with acoustic guitar on one song. As for the booklet, they approached various people who had been involved with the band at some point in their career and asked for some memories to be included, so I do have to confess and admit some involvement at this point, so my review is obviously going to be biased...

To my ears this is an amazing album in that they stayed true to the originals in many ways yet have given them a new lease of life. As an example, take the extended version of "Room 801" which in its original form was seven minutes long, but is now nearly eleven. There is a much longer introduction, Dean has provided quite a different keyboard sound in many places, yet stays close in others, while Tim's bass is much warmer, and both Spencer and Roy are kicking it far more than in the original. Of course, back in 1990 Stu didn't have the confidence that only comes from fronting a band for many years, and back then they weren't working with a producer like Karl. A nice addition to this song is the original comments from Tommy Vance that he gave after the song was played on the Radio 1 Rock Show, and he states who plays on the song, with a machine providing the name of Dean as he was the only one not involved at the time.

"Richelieu's Prayer" is another triumph, featuring quite a different piano introduction to the original, but performed by Mark Andrews who was of course the keyboard player on the debut CD. This has always been a personal favourite of mine, and it builds to a climax with the piano being a focal point throughout. It is the confidence of all those involved that makes this album such a triumph. It would be churlish of me to complete the review, though, without mentioning the reworking of "Exorcising Demons". This has been one of my favourite songs since I first heard it performed at The Astoria a million years ago, and Stu and I had discussion a few times back in the Nineties when I realised that it wasn't going to be performed. Stu even made a point of telling me that it was going to be included on this album! It has been deconstructed in some ways, and the fresh arrangement has made it something that wouldn't sound out of place on a new album. Here Tim is putting his own take on what was originally Neil's bassline, instead of the other way around, which was the normal state of affairs.

It's not possible to have a "Greatest Hits" album without at least one true "hit", so what we have here instead is an album of classic numbers that have been reworked and re-recorded to make them more relevant and important to today. If you have never come across Galahad before this, then this is the place to start.
Apr 2017

GALAHAD
QUIET STORMS
Over the years, Galahad have always dared to be different, and deliver music very much on their own terms. This has seen them produce an acoustic offshoot, a dance offshoot, as well as mixing and melding the styles that sees them always moving forward, always progressing. When I first came across them, they had won the Radio 1 Rock Wars, and released their first CD: it seems like a very long time ago, but that's okay because it was. They were the first band I wrote to in the progressive underground (yes, it was snail mail, no other type had been invented yet), the first band I wrote a complete piece on, and the first band I felt really close to. Through Stu I was introduced to others in the scene, and he told some mates of his to contact me which is how I came across the demo of some lads who were calling themselves Big Big Train, but that's another story altogether.

What's different about this album? Well, for starters it contains some already released songs, although they are here in different versions – therefore the booklet contains lyrics only to some numbers, as they are the new ones. But the largest difference outside the style of music (more of that in a minute), is that here Galahad are performing as a trio with guests. A trio? Well, yes, and often they are a duo. This album is based around Stu's vocals and Dean's delicate touch on piano and keyboards, with just occasional percussion from Spencer. There is no room for bass, so "new boy" Tim Ashton, who returned in 2014 after 22 years off for good behaviour has taken a break on this one. But where's Roy? Roy Keyworth was the founder of the band more than thirty years ago, but in March the band announced the sad news that Roy had decided to retire from music. He makes an appearance on the very final song of the album, "Guardian Angel (Hybrid)", which originally appeared on the "Guardian Angel" EP, but that is his swansong. Guitar features on just one other song on the album, and producer Karl Groom provides acoustic on that, somewhat different to his normal crunching day job with Threshold. Sarah Bolter is back as a guest again, providing woodwind and backing vocals, reprising her role on "Iceberg", which appeared on 1994's Galahad Acoustic Quintet album.

Yes, if you hadn't already worked it out, this is a far more pastoral album, one that relies on tone and technique as opposed to force and power. I honestly believe that Stu is one of the most under-rated singers around, and he has lost none of his pitch, breath control and range, while in Dean Baker he has found the perfect accompanist. Their relationship makes me think very much of Martin Orford and Gary Chandler, in that they complement each other so perfectly, and make incredible music without anybody else being involved. Christina Booth from Magenta duets with Stu on "Termination", old boy Mark Andrews appears on "Don't Lose Control", which he originally played on back on that debut CD, while Louise Curtis provides violin on their take on Rammstein's "Mein Herz Brennt" (I much prefer this version to the original).

This isn't a prog album in its truest sense, but instead shows a band that are always confident in their ability and move around in different styles yet deliver the goods time and time again. I think it was more than twenty years ago I confessed that I was losing all ability to write rationally about any release by Galahad, as I love their music so much. The reason I love it so, is because they are always refusing to conform to anyone's expectations, and keep producing works of outstanding brilliance and quality, like this one.

The band still don't know who their new guitarist is going to be, but Karl Groom has kindly agreed to play on 'Seas Of Change', which is going to be released later this year as well. That is going to show a very different side to the band, I'm sure. But for now, play this to your friends and astound them with wonderful music from deepest Dorset.
Jun 2017

GALAHAD
TWO CLASSIC ROCK LIVES
When I was staying at Stu Nicholson's house recently, I was told to go into the studio and have a good luck at the CDs and merchandise and see if there was anything that I didn't already have. I was somewhat surprised to come across this double CD release from 2008, as it was the first time I had seen it! Back in 1996 Galahad released a single CD live set called 'Classic Rock Live' on their own label, and at the time I had quite a moan at Stu as they hadn't included "Exorcising Demons" in the set, to which I was told they could only afford to release a single CD and they couldn't fit everything in they wanted. It has appeared on a couple of live albums since then, but this was their live album released on CD and I did always feel that it was an opportunity missed.

But that has now been rectified by this double CD digipak from Poland's Oskar, as the first CD contains a set from Mister Smith's on 28th October 1994 and the second is the original album, recorded at Rotherham CRS on 22nd April 1995. Given the recordings were only six months apart, there is no surprise there are similarities between the sets, but the earlier set contains ten songs instead of eight, and there are some beauties to be heard here as there is not only 'Exorcising Demons" but also "Parade" and "Lady Messiah" and the wonderful tongue-in-cheek (literally) "The Dentist Song". The last was a number I always felt was much better live than the studio version, as the humour came over much better.

I wasn't at either of these gigs, but this was a time when I was seeing the band regularly and is the line-up I have seen most in concert. By now Neil was making "Room 801" his very own, while the rest of the band had the confidence of having been together a few years and were riding the crest of the neo prog wave (if there ever was such a thing). Listening to these recordings in 2017 there is a sense of naivety and innocence that has long gone from the scene, and the Galahad of 1994/1995 couldn't have thought they would still be recording and gigging more than twenty years later (although only Stu and Spencer are still there). There are times when the sound at Mister Smiths is a little muddy, especially during the bombastic sections of "Exorcising Demons", but this all seemed so very familiar to me, taking me back to venues like The Railway, The Standard, Whitchurch and so many more.

Fans who have come to the band since Dean has been involved may be surprised at how very different they used to sound, and how far they have moved on from their roots and may find this not to their taste. But for those of us who were involved in the scene in the early Nineties in the UK will listen to this with a massive smile on our faces.
Sep 2017

BRAD GARTON & DAVE SOLDIER
THE BRAINWAVE MUSIC PROJECT
Imagine if thoughts could be turned into music without having to physically play an instrument? For the last ten years musician/ neuroscientist Dave Soldier and composer/computer- musician Brad Garton have been experimenting in using EEG machines to do just that. An EEG measures the electrical activity in the brain, and they have developed some software tools that can generate music using this brainwave data. In shows Dave gives a lecture on the brain's cortical activity, Brad explains how this is turned into music, and then they use their own brainwaves or those of guest musicians to "compose" in real time.

This album features four different soloists, who all played on 3 or 4 songs, and they are credited on each as playing their own instrument (flute, Hardanger fiddle, mandolin, or drums) plus EEG. Perhaps unsurprisingly the result is incredibly avant garde, and quite unlike anything I have come across before this. There is no musical rhythm or repetition, yet although it is often chaotic, somehow it does all seem to make sense, which must be right as the soloist is accompanying his/herself, although not consciously. It is strange, at times unsettling, sometimes oriental, and always strangely compelling. This will only be of interest who enjoy their music to come out of left field, as it doesn't get much further from the mainstream than this.
Jan 2018

The Progressive Underground Vol 5

GAZPACHO
TICK TOCK
On 30th December 1935, after 19 hours and 44 minutes in the air, Antoine de Saint-Exupéry and his mechanic-navigator André Prévot, crashed in the Sahara Desert whilst attempting to break the speed record in a Paris-to-Saigon air race. They both survived the crash, but with only rudimentary maps and very little supplies they were in serious trouble. Luckily, after four days they were discovered by a Bedouin, who saved their lives. This near brush with death features prominently in Saint-Exupéry's 1939 memoir 'Wind, Sand and Stars', and in turn forms the basis of this the sixth album from Norwegian act Gazpacho. Released in 2009 this album seems to have fairly polarized opinions with many strong and positive reviews, but also plenty from those who can't understand what all the fuss is about. They are obviously influenced by Hogarth-era Marillion and Radiohead, along with Muse and Porcupine Tree but by the far the most interesting style included here are the short Arabian-style passages. For the most part this album is just too one-dimensional to maintain interest and each time I played it I have found myself looking at the screen to see just how much longer there is left as I want to get onto something more interesting. The musicianship and vocals are very good, and it is well recorded and produced, but for me it is just too flat and ultimately is plain boring. I found the story it is based on, and the short biographies I read of Antoine de Saint-Exupéry far more interesting than the musical result.
Apr 2014

GENTLE KNIFE
CLOCK UNWOUND
This is the second album from Norwegian act Gentle Knife, but the first I have come across, and to try and give some idea of what it sounds like let's look at the line-up. They have no guests, as with this many people they really don't need any more! It must be one of the largest line-ups of a progressive rock band I have ever come across, but each has their place. Astraea Antal (flutes, woodwinds and visuals), Pål Bjørseth (keyboards, vocals, trumpet), Odd Grønvold (bass), Thomas Hylland Eriksen (sax and woodwinds), Veronika Hørven Jensen (vocals), Håkon Kavli (vocals, guitars), Eivind Lorentzen (guitars and synths), Charlotte Valstad Nielsen (sax), Ove Christian Owe (guitars), Ole Martin Svendsen (drums, percussion) and Brian M. Talgo (samples, words, vocals) have put together one of the most interesting albums of the year.

That it is progressive is beyond doubt, but as to what sub-genre it belongs to is more of a discussion. The band have been claimed by Crossover, but they could easily have gone into eclectic if it wasn't for the majestic beauty of some of the passages that transcend all thoughts of prog into stunning classic rock pop. The production has a large part to play on this album, and in many ways, can almost be thought of as yet an additional instrument, as it is the clarity and separateness of all those involved that prevent this from turning into a muddy mess. There is an emotional use of bass saxophone on the fifteen-minute-long title cut where the notes resonate against the gently picked electric guitar with quite devastating effect and impact. They aren't afraid to use volume, driving riffs and screaming guitars when the need is right, or to move from melody into atonal noise where everything crashes together, before moving into yet another space and time.

This is music that is exciting, vibrant and with a controlled chaos that is rarely heard in today's scene. The arrangements are complex and perfectly executed, and in many ways this album is reminiscent of the most rich and fragrant paella one could come across: take a bite, give it a stir, and the next bite could be totally different as firstly one tastes mussels, and the next chorizos, yet at all times the rice is providing a balance and continuity. I think this is the first time I have ever compared an album to food, and I have written many thousands, but this is comfortable, intriguing, welcoming and inviting, just like a good meal. Needless to say, a good drop of South Otago Pinot Noir goes with it very nicely indeed, thank you very much. In some ways very Seventies, and in others very up to date, this wonderful album should be heard by all progheads. It is simply stunning.
Jul 2017

GENTLE KNIFE
GENTLE KNIFE
After I reviewed their most recent album, 'Clock Unwound' the band kindly sent me a copy of their self-titled debut, which was released in 2015. They were only a ten-piece at the time, comprising Astraea Antal (flute, winds and visuals), Pål Bjørseth (keyboards, vocals, trumpet), Odd Grønvold (basses), Thomas Hylland Eriksen (sax and woodwinds), Håkon Kavli (vocals, acoustic guitar), Eivind Lorentzen (guitars and synths), Melina Oz (vocals), Ove Christian Owe (guitars), Ole Martin Svendsen (drums, percussion) and Brian M. Talgo (samples, words and visions. I said "only", as for the next release they had gone to 11 (cue Spinal Tap jokes).

As with their most recent album, I am amazed at how intricate this music is, and how they bring everyone together in a way that makes complete sense without the senses being overwhelmed by the amount of instrumentation involved. Of course, electric guitars and sax should combine repeating the same melody, it provides more force and presence, and allows the keyboards to get on with the job of playing over the top. The arrangements are superb, and somewhat surprisingly, given the number of people in the band, there is a strong sense of space and the use of dynamics. They can be peaceful and laid back, with just rippling keyboards and gentle flute, or they can be doing their level best to blow the woofer out of the speakers. They mix full-blown progressive rock in its truest traditional sense with some psychedelic tendencies to create an album that is immediate, impressive, over the top and that delivers even more each time it is played.
Oct 2017

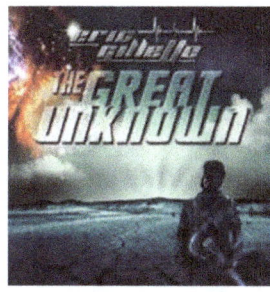

ERIC GILLETTE
THE GREAT UNKNOWN

Apparently, this album came out last year, but it has only just come to my attention. Eric has of course been lead guitarist with the Neal Morse Band for some time, and here he is back with his second solo album. Those expecting prog in the same vein as his "day job" will find a few similarities here and there, but mostly this is melodic prog metal with influences taken from throughout that scene. I convinced myself that the drummer just had to be his NMB compadré Mike Portnoy due to what is going on behind the kit, but further investigation revealed that it was none other than Thomas Lang (John Wetton, Robert Fripp, Glenn Hughes, Robbie Williams, Kelly Clarkson, and many others). Also involved are Haken members Diego Tejeida (keyboards) and Conner Green (bass), so overall this is quite some musical powerhouse.

Those who have seen NMB will know already that Eric is a strong singer in his own right, and this is very much an album of songs as opposed to mass instrumental workouts. Of course, there are times when the note density is incredible, and he does his best John Petrucci impression, but there is way more on here than just Dream Theater complexity and long songs. Of course, he is used to the odd epic here and there when working with Neal, and it would have been surprising for there not to be one included, and the eighteen-minute-long "Escape" is stunning in the way it moves and folds. This is an album that will certainly appeal to those who enjoy prog metal, but it is way more than "just" that, with elements from Haken, DT and the softer sides of Neal Morse all being blended in a way that is both immediate and makes for compulsive listening. This is superb from start to end.
Apr 2017

GLORIOUS WOLF
AQUARIUS

Glorious Wolf is a project by Ruud Dielen, who provides all the instrumentation on the album. Ruud is a guitarist who has been working in various covers bands, and since 2007 has also been part of Perpetual Béta, an improvisational band who were influenced particularly by Weather Report and Frank Zappa. That he comes from a diverse background is reflected in this debut album, as although the roots are often in progressive music, he is moving through many different styles, so much so that it is hard to really categorise. There are times when we have fusion-led guitar solos with minimal backing, others when it is much more Floydian in approach, while we also get slowed-down doom which is almost sludge.

But, at the heart of everything, are pure clean guitar lines, no matter what is going on in the background. Ruud is a fine guitarist, and has an innate understanding of melody, although the songs themselves are just vehicles for him to provide lengthy solos. I would like to see this project morph into a full band, or at least with real drums as opposed to

programmed, but even as it is this is an album that is accessible and enjoyable on first hearing. I sincerely hope that this leads to more music from Glorious Wolf.
Oct 2017

GOBLIN
FOUR OF A KIND

There is no doubt in my mind, and nor in many others I would imagine, that Goblin are the finest progressive rock bands ever to come out of Italy. Their 1977 soundtrack to the cult horror 'Suspiria' is an amazing album, and I was lucky enough to see a version of the band play live in front of a showing of the film in Auckland a few years ago. But there's the issue, their history has been a little problematic, and in 2015 there were two different versions of the band doing the rounds. I am a little unsure if this is a Goblin album, or a 4Goblin album, as it doesn't appear on the discography of their official website, and a "4" appears inside the capital 'G' on all places, and not long before this album came out in 2015 there was a band called New Goblin. In addition, Claudio Simonetti also has a version of Goblin, but he is the only member of the 'Suspiria' quartet missing from this line-up, his place taken by Maurizio Guarini who joined the band in 2003.

Originally released by Backtothefudda in 2015, Black Widow have pulled out the stops with this release as there is a booklet, slip sleeve, and even four playing card aces featuring cartoons of the musicians. But it is easy to see why, as here is a band that may have left the scene for quite a few years, but they are back with an absolute vengeance. The production is spot on, which allows each of the musicians to really shine on this instrumental album. It shouts class from the first note to the very last, and it is incredible to realise that this band was formed more than forty years ago yet is still producing music which is important and relevant today. Massimo Morante has the same delicate touch on guitar as always, and this brings the music together in a fashion which allows the others to create space and depth throughout. This is yet another Goblin classic to add to their canon, and I hope I manage to catch these guys in concert again. Superb.
Jun 2017

SIMON GODFREY
BLACK BAG ARCHIVE VOLUME 1

Released in 2015, this seven-track thirty-one-minute-long album is presumably a collection of material that had been kicking around in the collection of Simon Godfrey (Tinyfish, Shineback), awaiting a suitable vehicle. Due to its very nature, this is quite a fractured set, in that there isn't a cohesive theme throughout, but what it does show is just how Simon's mind works in many different areas. There are songs that are complex, others that are far simpler, some which rely on gentle guitar chord structures, and others that almost drop into the realm of electronic. This isn't

something I would recommend to anyone as a starting point, but if you are already aware of his music then this may well be of interest. All the material is played by Simon, with no additional musicians.
May 2017

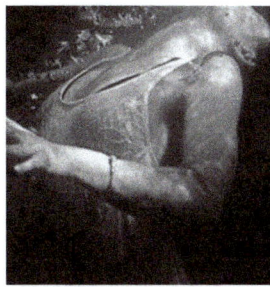

SIMON GODFREY
BLACK BAG ARCHIVE VOLUME 2

Towards the end of 2016 Simon released another collection of material, some of which stretched back as far as 1991, while opener "Teahead" was written for this album as he didn't feel any of the others worked as an opening cut. As with his other compilation, Simon played all the material, but this one feels far more complete, as if the songs were more fully realised than demos. I am quite a fan of "Teahead", and it certainly doesn't sound as if there was a lot of improvisation and stream of consciousness lyrics. I've never been a fan of electronic percussion and would be interested to hear what this would sound like with a full band, as the crunching guitars of the verse and contrast of the chorus are wonderful. Compare that to "Blood In The Milk" from 2001, which has a delicacy and fragility in both the music and vocals that is enthralling. We also have a one-man epic in "The Year", which is more than fourteen minutes long and contains some music originally written for Tinyfish. Thoughtful and dramatic, this works incredibly well.

Although I wouldn't recommend the first archive collection to those who haven't come across Simon, this works well.
May 2017

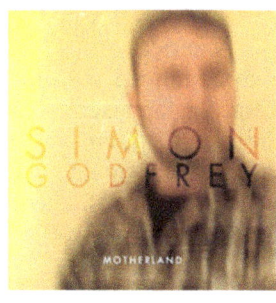

SIMON GODFREY
MOTHERLAND

'Motherland' was released in 2014, and contains eight previously unreleased original songs, as well as three acoustic re-workings of tracks from Tinyfish and Shineback. Spanning twenty years of song writing and featuring some extremely personal lyrics, the album also saw Simon being reunited with long-time writing partner Rob Ramsay (who co-wrote three of the songs and provided some spoken word and harmonica). This was the first album released by Simon under his own name, and as well as having no band name to hide behind he has also stripped back the instrumentation so that often it is just acoustic guitar and his voice. Mind you, I think he would have done even better if he had also left out the drum machine that annoyingly appears here and there.

There is a mixture of self-reflection emotion and numbers that contain more poppy and melodic elements, and the result is an album that is reminiscent of the Seventies while also being right up to date. It isn't all picking and gentleness, there are chords strummed and voices raised, and the result is something I really enjoyed. His vocals are more

delicate than, say, Ian Anderson, and he probably has more in common with Rog Patterson and Nigel Mazlyn Jones, and it is the bringing together of many different styles in a fully open style that makes this so endearing. This is an album that does appreciate being played quite loudly so that nothing from the real world can break into it. Of the three albums of his I have listened to recently; this is the favourite.
May 2017

JEFF GREEN PROJECT
ELDER CREEK
Five years on from his debut solo album, 'Jessica', American guitarist Jeff Green has returned with his second, which this time is credited as a project. When one sees who has been involved this time, it is probably a fairer way of crediting it. While Jeff provides most of the guitars, mandolin, guitar synth and much of the vocals, he is also joined by Pete Riley on drums (Guthrie Govan, Wetton & Downes Icon, Keith Emerson), Mike Stobbie on keys (Pallas and a renowned prog producer), Sean Filkins (Big Big Train, Lorien) provides lead vocals on the title number, Alan Reed provides lead vocals on "A Long Time From Now" (Pallas, various Clive Nolan projects, solo), Garreth Hicklin provides lead and backing vocals (Illegal Eagles), Phil Hilborne guitar (Nicko McBrain's touring Clinic, has played with Brian May, Glenn Hughes, Keith Emerson, Steve Vai), with Andy Staples (bass) and Imogen Hendricks (backing vocals) completing the line-up. Out of all of these, the one name that may seem unusual to progheads is that of Garreth, until one realizes that Jeff is also a member of Illegal Eagles.

'Elder Creek' explores the concept of memory, its loss and the part it plays in our lives, the lives of loved ones and society in general. Using both anecdotal and mythological subject matter, the album raises the question; if memories define who we are, then who indeed are we without them. Many lyrics were based on poems written by Jeff's father. Jeff may have lived in Ireland for more than a dozen years, but it his American roots that come through, especially when he is playing acoustic guitar, as that combined with the harmonies leads the project more into the area of Crosby Stills and Nash as opposed to IQ or Pallas. But the prog influences are also there throughout, and the result is a crossover album that is beautiful, with soaring vocals and great keyboards that accentuate the guitars. This is all about songcraft as opposed to showing just how clever all those involved are when it comes to playing their instruments. They have nothing at all to prove, and this feels incredibly relaxed as it draws the listener in to its heart and soul.

There is a depth and real presence with this album, with some wonderful arrangements and the clever use of repeating melodies on different instruments to provide additional dynamics while staying within the same theme. Immediate, impressive, one can only hope that it doesn't take five years for the next one, as anyone who enjoys great songs with great singers, especially if they enjoy their classic Americana, will find a great deal here to enjoy.
Jun 2014

The Progressive Underground Vol 5

GRIDFAILURE
SCATHED
This is music that breaks the very boundaries of the definition, as what we have here is experimental noise. Since its' early 2016 conception, Gridfailure has released three albums, a collaborative album with Megalophobe, a split with Never Presence Forever, an EP, a compilation track, and other singles. The plans for the rest of the year and early next are more albums and to hit the road in the summer. This is hostile, with off-kilter percussion, unhinged keyboard and synth attacks, carcinogenic bass/guitar tones, white noise, treated and indecipherable vocals, and apparently also Theremin, didgeridoo, xylophone, harmonica, as well as some field recordings. This isn't meant to be comfortable listening, and it isn't, but it is also quite compelling. David Brenner has created a monster with this album, and I don't think it's very friendly. It can be downloaded free from their Bandcamp site, from where it is also possible to purchase it as a CD. Not for those of a weak disposition.
June 2017

GRIDFAILURE
I SHALL NOT SURVIVE ANOTHER WINTER
When I reviewed David Brenner's last release under the name Gridfailure, 'Scathed', I said it wasn't for those with a weak disposition. Now back with a new eight-track EP (more than forty-six minutes in length), where each song is longer than the last that statement is truer than ever. Somehow, he takes elements of jazz, world music, hardcore, industrial and dark ambient music to create something that is important, captivating, and incredibly disconcerting. David provides effects-soaked instrumentation and vocals, guitars, bass, keyboards, analogue synth, harmonica, Theremin, field recordings, acoustic and electronic drums and percussion, among others. He has also used drums and guitar from Richard Muller (Vise Massacre, The Third Kind, Future Hunter), drums from BJ Allen (Full Scale Riot), accordion from Benjamin Levitt (Megalophobe), guitar and synth by Robert Levitt, piano from Christian Molenaar (Those Darn Gnomes), vocals from Mark Steuer (Those Darn Gnomes). The beginning of "It's Too Late For Me It's Too Late For You" incorporates the famous guitar from "Shine On You Crazy Diamond", but it soon turns into something quite different and more sinister.

If you thought the last release was disconcerting, you haven't heard anything yet! Definitely worth investigating.
Oct 2017

HALF PAST FOUR
LAND OF THE BLIND
This 2016 mini album is my first experience of Canadian progressive band Half Past Four, and the only question I have is "where have you been?". My initial reaction to this

was if ever a band was channelling the spirit of classic Zappa with Seventies Rundgren and then throwing in some King Crimson, Cardiacs, Poisoned Electrick Head and others then this must be it! Also, if there are any Max Webster fans out there, then you need to head straight to their cover of "Toronto Tontos" which is more strident, with wider extremes, than the original which featured on the debut album. It even includes squeaky toys!!

The band is comprised of Kyree Vibrant (lead vocals), Dmitry Lesov (bass guitar, chapman stick, vocals), Igor Kurtzman (keyboards, vocals), Constantin Necrasov (guitars, vocals) and Marcello Ciurleo (drums). I had a look at their website, and I loved this statement "Like the best of progressive rock music, the listener cannot predict where the band will take them next. It is this shifting flow of sound and feeling that distinguishes Half Past Four. They are an aural tapestry, weaving 50+ years of musical influences into mellifluous melodies and rhythmic resonances that take their listeners on a journey to states that are both fresh and familiar." This is music that is truly progressive, refusing to sit within one particular style or another, moving and changing so that Kyree can be singing sweetly one minute or virtually shouting the next with a totally different timbre, while the band all of a sudden is based around the piano, whereas at others it is definitely the guitar, or is it the bass, but there again the drum patterns are all over the place.

This is one of the most exciting and vibrant progressive bands I have come across in recent years, producing music that is complex, refusing to conform to what anyone feels should be produced, and is definitely progressing as opposed to regressing. This five-track mini-album is only 26 minutes long, and I can only hope that we will soon hear a full-length release. As for me, I'm going to have to go back and discover their first two albums, as music as good as this screams out to be heard.
Jan 2018

HELIOPOLIS
EPIC AT THE MAJESTIC
I first heard from Kerry Chicoine (bass) after I reviewed the live album of his former band, Mars Hollow, and now here I am reviewing the live album of the band formed by him and fellow Mars Hollow alumni drummer Jerry Beller, along with keyboardist Matt Brown, guitarist Michael Matier, and vocalist Scott Jones. Musically Heliopolis have taken the influences of classic Yes, and then moved into the modern era without losing the progginess. Kerry has a dominant bass sound but tends to play lower on the scale than Chris Squire, so while he is influenced, he is not a copyist. Matt uses a lot of different sounds with his playing, with plenty of Mellotrons, but his style is quite different to that of many, not staying within one style but moving quickly from symphonic into more aggressive, working hard with Michael to provide the melodic counterpunch. Michael himself approached his prog from a more melodic Starcastle style,

with many hard rock elements, which provides a different flavour. Then on top of that we have the vocals of Scott Jones, who seems to be an amalgam of Jon Anderson, Geddy Lee and Steve Perry. He has a strong clear voice, cutting through the layers of sound that are happening around him, and together these five combine to bring to life something very special indeed.

This music just flows, taking the listener and the audience along with it: there is little in the way of tension, as the guys blend and shift what they are doing, interweaving the melodies, almost as if it is coming out of their pores. This isn't musicians playing notes, it is all about bringing to life something that is already there in the air, providing a form to something that is incredibly natural. I have still to hear their debut album, something I will rectify, and have only just come across this, which was released last year, but hopefully there will soon be more music coming from Heliopolis. I have been fortunate enough to hear some incredible albums this year, and this is another of them. If you enjoy progressive rock that is regressive yet also forward looking, easy to listen to yet complex and layered, then this is for you.
Apr 2017

MATTE HENDERSON
THE VENEER OF LOGIC
This is guitarist Matte Henderson's first album and is a collaborative effort with drummer Marco Minnemann. Bad Brains co-founder/guitarist Doctor Know calls the album the world's first "muttcore" release, meaning it explores the universes of post-rock, industrial, metal, and ambient in equal measure – for some reason he didn't include jazz in that list, which is strange as this includes some elements from that genre. Although this is primarily an instrumental album there are vocals, but these have been almost entirely derived from voicemails, surreptitiously recorded conversations, and prison parole hearings. Obviously Matte thought that this was a great idea that would add to the experimental nature of the album and make it seem even more Zappa-esque, but to be honest I found them at best an irrelevance and often an annoyance, as the music is so complex and well played and structured that it really doesn't need it.

"Several tracks are homages to my favourite guitarists," says Henderson. "'Myers Lane' is my bow to Exposure-era Fripp. 'Whirled' and 'ppgf' are nods to Bad Brains, which saved me from a life of jazz-fusion treacle. 'Single Cell Shark' reflects my fascination with David Torn's boundary-breaking work. 'My Whirled' was written for the late Mick Karn, who was scheduled to work on it before his health crisis. As a tribute to him, I went with a Dali's Car vibe for that tune." There is no doubt this is a really good album, but the vocals do detract from the overall for me and I would much rather have heard it without as the guitarwork, and drumming are outstanding, and they just don't need it. Definitely to be heard before purchase, it contains a lot that Zappa would have been proud of.
Jan 2014

HIBERNAL
THE MACHINE
It takes quite a bit to make me stop and play close attention, but I found myself doing just that when I allowed myself to fall headlong into the world of Mark Healy's creation. I'm not quite sure how to describe this, as it is way more than a concept album, and in many ways, is almost a play with the music being an integral part, another actor. This is an album based on an original short story and is all about what happens to someone as they quite literally climb the corporate ladder and the sacrifices they must make to achieve success, although that success is much more in their own eyes as opposed to those of their loved ones. The first time I played this was in the car and I found myself somehow at home, having driven on autopilot for much of it, but before the album had ended. The next morning, I put it on again, but started once again at the beginning so that I could get the full benefit of listening to it all the way through (and making sure that I paid more attention to the road this time).

It is a science fiction story, set at some point soon, with a first-person narration for the most part, along with some additional key characters. Mark has provided all the music, as well as the artwork, but brought in others to play the roles and Rowan Michaels in the lead has done an outstanding job. At times, quite Floydian, and others more Gong or Porcupine Tree, this is something that in many ways in quite a different art form in that it is neither a story or music but is far more compelling and intriguing than both. Sometimes simplistic, at others quite complex, this is the perfect marriage between spoken words and music, so much so that each time I play it I find myself having to almost shake myself when it finishes, as I have been taken so much into Mark's world.
Feb 2017

HIBERNAL
REPLACEMENTS
When Mark Healy contacted me last year about his project Hibernal, and the first album 'The Machine' I did as I always do with 'new' bands, put the album to one side and wait until I can listen to it with an open mind. 'Replacements' wasn't accorded the same luxury, because as soon as I had it, I just had to play it to see if Mark had dared to stay with the same construct as before, and this he has done, except now there is even more depth and presence. There have been many acts who have released concept albums, but there are very few indeed who have provided a story where the actors speak their lines, and the music is there for support. This is cinema for the ears, and science fiction to boot. But what makes this work so very well is that each element is there for the other, each providing the drama and passion that the other requires.

Rowan Salt provides the bass, with Mark all other music, while there are four actors, with Scott Gentle taking the main lead of Artimus. His voice and presence remind me of Humphrey Bogart, with a grittiness and realism that shines through. It is hard to talk about the story without giving too much away, so let's just say it is set in the future and the replacements in the title are human-looking androids who now undertake the mundane tasks that humans don't want to do. But there are a large number of twists within what must be a very short number of words, and Mark has left so much hanging that I don't feel this has yet come to a full conclusion. Whereas in 'The Machine' it would have needed a new story to follow on from the last, this feels much more like a new chapter of the same. When I first played it, I was rather surprised when it finished as I felt the story was only half-told, and I found myself thinking about it even when the album wasn't playing, such is the power of a few carefully chosen words. I concluded that although I can see why the story ends where it does, I would rather have some more explanation of what had previously occurred to Artimus, and how he got to where he was. There are suggestions, but no more than that, what it has done is made me go back to the album time and again.

But hang on, isn't this supposed to be a music review? Well, it is, but on this album, it is about the music supporting the lead players, the actors. Mark riffs when he wants to, or provides gentle Pink Floyd type noodlings, but importantly the music very much stands up in its' own right as well. Mark has so much confidence in this that he has also released the album as an instrumental, so it is possible to hear the music without the words. This is not an album that can be picked at, but rather must be played through to completion each time, and also it needs to be in the foreground as opposed to the background as it is only by properly listening to it that one gets the full benefit. It is possible to order this as a download through Bandcamp, and there is also a CD available with a full colour booklet containing more artwork. I love it.
Jun 2014

HIBERNAL
REPLACEMENTS (INSTRUMENTAL)
Having played the 'full' version of this album so much I wasn't quite sure how to go about reviewing this as obviously I already know the music quite well, but I was actually pleasantly surprised at just how well this stands up on its own. It is also easier to hear just how many different styles are being used throughout, and while I'm not a fan of some of the electronica style keyboards that are used in one section, there is still plenty of Floydian and rock influences going on that makes this a genuine delight in its' own right. What is interesting to me is that this isn't nearly as dark as it appears to be when listened to with the words, which just goes to show how much presence is put into it by the performance of Scott Gentle. But the presence is still there, and the result is an album that I thoroughly enjoyed playing, as it has much more going on than many instrumental projects I come across. It's not whizz bang in terms of notes density but is all about feel and a strange future worldly emotion. Somehow the science fiction feel comes through on this, even there are no verbal clues. So, a solid piece of work, but to get the full picture then one must get 'Replacements'. Of course, if you already have that album then you should get this one as well.
Jun 2014

HIBERNAL
AFTER THE WINTER

The synopsis of this album is "A man who transfers his thoughts and memories to a synthetic body in order to survive an apocalypse seeks to return to his human form". Yes, yet again we are in the world of Mark Healy, which is bleak and post-nuclear war, sometime in the future. Rowan Salt has again joined Mark by providing bass, and it is interesting to note that Faleena Hopkins, who portrayed Sabel in 'Replacements' is back again, this time as Arsha – the first time that one of the actors has returned. There are only two characters in this story, down from four last time and three in the debut, but in many ways, this is possibly the most compelling to date.

When listening to Mark's cinematic visions I have sometimes wondered which author he most reminds me of, but there was no debate on this one, as to me this is Stephen King and the wastelands encountered on the journey to The Tower. But, as always with Mark, there is quite a twist. If we consider this to be the third in a loosely connected trilogy taken from the same world view, albeit at different times, this is the one furthest in the future, and the one that seems to have the most music within it. There are few words in the script outside of the conversations that take place between the Arsha and the lead character, Brant, and his post rock Pink Floyd inspired soundscapes perfectly capture the mood.

This is the perfect combination of two quite different art forms, that of music and of a script spoken by professional actors, so that one enhances the other to make something so compelling that once it has started, nothing else exists. At the end of this album I felt it was more complete than 'Replacements', one where this particular chapter had come to a logical conclusion. There were questions I wanted answered, and I did want to know what happened in the future, but I also felt that the story was concise and ended in a better fashion than the last one. Compelling, enthralling, imaginative and exciting, Hibernal.
Feb 2017

HIBERNAL
THE DARK OF THE CITY

Mark and Rowan are back, and again the story revolves around just two characters, both played by actors who have previously been involved with Hibernal. Scott Gentle took the lead in 'Replacements', while Faleena Hopkins took a minor role in both 'Replacements' and 'After The Winter', but here things have been changed as Faleena is very much the lead. This changes the dynamic, as the script is always in the first person, so the switch to female was surprising and caught me off guard. As with the previous album there appears to be more music, which is many places is quite dramatic, and whereas I normally "see" Mark's stories in full colour, this feels far more black and white, as if it is a classic Hitchcock. Or at least if Hitchcock was directing films that would normally be called science fiction. In terms of timelines of the Hibernal world, this has more in common with 'Replacements', but more of a parallel universe to that one as opposed to the same vision. There is an almost hypnotic state to the music, as it takes control of the senses and drags the listener into a new world, one where Moreeno the cop is undertaking a relentless search for the creature that killed her partner. By chance she comes across her new partner during the evening, and together they finish what had started a few weeks before. I still find it incredible that in so few words Mark can create a picture of Carson City – I feel I understand both it and its underbelly and can envisage what the characters are seeing when the final act is played out.

The post rock riffing combines with Pink Floyd stylings to create a musical soundscape that is at times at the forefront of what is happening, creating the dramatic when there are no words, and at others falling into the background so that the actors are centre stage. This isn't a concept album, nor it is a spoken book, but something that is different from both and instead is a musical radio play for the ears. This is Mark's fourth full album (the previous three are also available in music only forms), and the fourth to which I feel I need to recommend at the very highest level. Go to his page on Bandcamp, pick any of these at random, then sit back and enjoy the experience. I can promise you won't be disappointed.
Feb 2017

HIDDEN LANDS
HALCYON
Back in 2003 a band called Violent Silence released their debut album through Musea, and I promptly decided that I wasn't a fan and said as much at the time. Of course, that didn't stop them, and they have since released a couple more albums, while Hidden Lands came into being in 2012 and this is the third album since then. What is the connection? Well, Bruno Edling (vocals), Hannes Ljunghall (keyboards and guitars) and Philipp Bastin (bass) all appear here and were also all involved with the Violent Silence debut all those years ago. It's only drummer Gustav Nyberg who is the odd one out. I hadn't realised the history of the band until I sat down to write the review, as I always listen to music without any preconceived ideas, and often only read the press release or research the band after I have played it through a few times.

I'm really glad I did that this time, so that my previous dislike for Violent Silence didn't taint my feelings for Hidden Lands: I don't like this one either. I wasn't a fan of the vocals when I first came across them all those years ago, and the same is true in 2017. Also, there seems to be a distinct lack of musical ideas, so the listener often seems to be treading water. Having long songs and being able to play your instruments well doesn't necessarily make your music appealing, and that is what I found here. The guitars aren't to the fore enough, and everything seems to have been suppressed and taken back as opposed to being brought forward and being dynamic. I have seen some rave reviews , but I am used to being in the minority and just can't get on with this at all.
June 2017

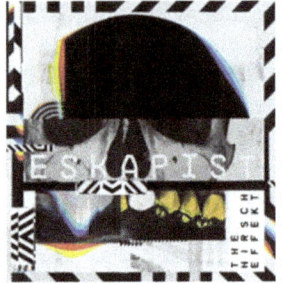

THE HIRSCH EFFEKT
ESKAPIST

Socially critical, caustically political, and musically overwhelming, the fourth album from the Hanoverian band is truly a lesson in progressive metal, prog and core. The one thing that strikes the listener from the first note to the very last is the sheer intensity of this album, it sounds like the trio were wringing wet by the end of each take, putting their very beings on the line as they wreaked havoc on their instruments. All three band members – drummer Moritz Schmidt, guitarist and singer Nils Wittrock and bassist and singer Ilja John Lappin – had an equal share in the writing of the record. The 12 complex compositions, interfused with prog, tech, and sludge metal, continually shift between the different styles and were recorded with Tim Tautorat (who has previously worked with AnnenMayKantereit, Turbostaat, In Flames), Max Trieder and various guest musicians in Hanover, Leipzig and Berlin.

Several songs revolve around social oddities. "Aldebaran" deals with the phenomenon of present-day citizens of the Reich, "Berceuse" highlights the globally growing right-wing populism, as does the haunting "Xenophotopia". In addition to the theoretical, genuine refugees are also discussed in "Natans" on the album. In turn, the 14-minute-long monster "Lysios" deals with the fall of an alcoholic and is probably the bleakest observation that Wittrock, Schmidt and Lappin have ever captured in their music. Escapism, in its many different forms, is the link between the different pieces and what holds the album together.

It is bleak and nihilistic, music that is never a comfort blanket, but instead is all about broken glass and the sound of fingernails on a blackboard. Somehow, among all this it is also melodic, with reason among the madness. Impressive.
Sep 2017

JOANNE HOGG & FRANK VAN ESSEN
RAPHAEL'S JOURNEY

As a founder member of Iona, Joanne needs no introduction as over the years her voice has been at the forefront of everything they have achieved. But back in 2006 she was a new mother and concluded (from personal experience) that adults were more in need of gentle music to go to sleep with than children ever were! So, she started working with producer and musician Frank Van Essen on a project to create and record music that would convey a sense of peace, beauty and comfort and enable listeners to rest, relax and wind down, and then drift away into a contented sleep. This was initially released as download only, with a different cover, and was credited solely to Joanne. However, in 2010 it was finally released as a physical product, at which time new artwork was provided and the crediting was changed to reflect the importance of Frank's contribution.

Joanne's bandmates weren't going to let her do this on her own and they all take part, as does Clannad vocalist Moya Brenna. The result is an album that is beautiful from start to finish. Deliberately designed to be played in the evening, this is something that suits the dark, with the vocals and instruments combining in an ethereal manner that for some reason makes me think of the mists around the Western Isles. It is not unusual for Iona and Joanne to be compared to Enya, but this is stripped down in comparison to that heavily structured style, and it isn't unusual for Joanne to be singing with just delicate piano for accompaniment along with some wonderful string arrangements.

This is a wonderful album, and really does deserve to be heard by a much wider audience. Everyone involved also decided this should be a charity record, and profits from this recording are donated to several organisations that seek to alleviate the suffering of children in extreme poverty.
Apr 2014

HOUSE OF RABBITS
SONGS OF CHARIVARI
House of Rabbits is a self-proclaimed "vaudcore" (hardcore-vaudeville) art-rock band from Los Angeles. The music of House of Rabbits blends dark, theatrical, narrative song writing and lyrics with a variety of musical styles ranging from raucous operatic circus punk to hushed atmospheric bossa nova cabaret. Preferring abrupt tonal changes to a catchy, contrived chorus hook, the members of HoR focus on creating challenging, interesting and impossible to categorize music that constantly defies genre while remaining accessible with their infectiously dance-worthy rhythms. In 2014, after the avant-art-metal project, FEASTofFETUS, went through a major line-up change, the remaining three members (Jess Gabriell Cron - vocals, Mike Caffell - drums, Ian Malcolm - keyboards) found themselves collaborating with guitarist Andy Kovari and bassist Eloy Palacios on material which began to take an entirely new direction. They began experimenting with a different kind of heavy sound, trading the distorted metal guitar chugging for a signature sound more akin to a piano falling downstairs. Thus, HoR was formed.

I was fortunate to come across these guys when they were recommended to the Crossover team on PA, and as soon as I heard the album, I fell in love with they are doing. That the guys are all obviously insane is not even worth debating, that they love Zappa and are taking him to extremes is also true, but after that it all gets a little complicated. The music has a highly visual element to it I am sure, and many of these songs formed part of their sold-out fringe shows, which garnished much critical praise from LA Weekly and won several nominations and awards (The Encore Producer's Award, theTVolution.com Platinum Medal/Best of Fringe). This really is something that must be heard to be understood, as while it is highly melodic, it is incredibly hard to define. The guys all know what they are doing, and interweave musical spells, but is this more a studio recording of a stage show than a pure studio album and that therefore there are bits missing that would add value to the listener? I'm just not sure, but I am sure that I find this an incredibly interesting and enjoyable piece of work which is both pushing many boundaries and somehow hitting into mainstream like Mumford & Sons at the same time.

This is something out of left field that is well worth investigating further.
Mar 2017

STEVE HOWE
THE RELATIVITY YEARS

It must be said that apart from Rick Wakeman, the solo careers of Yes members outside of the band has been a little hit and miss. Steve Howe of course found major success with Asia, and with GTR (although criminally not to the same extent), but his solo albums haven't always been the outstanding success that one might imagine. Here, Gonzo have brought two of his best albums together in a single package which is an inviting proposition to anyone who doesn't already own them. 'Turbulence' was released in 1991, and features Steve playing not only everything with strings, but also some keyboards and anything else he feels benefits the overall sound. His core band is based around Bill Bruford and Billy Currie (ex-Ultravox), although Nigel Glockner provides drums on three songs and Andrew Lucas organ on one. This is an instrumental album, but one that feels far more a band effort as opposed to as solo, one that makes musical sense as it goes through the ten different songs, with a style that is instantly recognisable to anyone who has followed Steve's career. It is bright, it is exciting and invigorating with plenty of energy, and to my ears is the finest "solo" album of his career to date. There are details as what inspired each song, who played what instrument on each one, as well as further details of the actual guitars used by Steve.

Two years on from 'Turbulence' and Steve released 'The Grand Scheme of Things'. Here he put together a band including two of his sons, plus the mighty Nick Beggs plus others. But I only know this as I researched it as there is no information for this album in the booklet apart from a song listing, a photo of Steve and a thanks list. I presume this is because the original contained very little information, but surely some minor research could have been done and that added to the booklet? Unlike the previous album, which was instrumental, half of these songs contain vocals from Steve himself, and while he hasn't an unpleasant voice, I have always felt that it far better when he is using it to provide harmonies as opposed to taking the lead role himself. What saves this album is the sheer diversity of styles being displayed, so while he does at times return to what made him and his bands so famous, he shows that he is comfortable playing in multiple different genres, although always bending them so that they manage to fall within the prog field. Using Nick to provide Chapman Stick on some of the songs was also inspired, as the different sound and textures that provides enabled Steve to compose some interesting counter melodies and balances. Overall, this is definitely a release that any fan of Steve, or any band he has been involved with, should grab with both hands.
Oct 2017

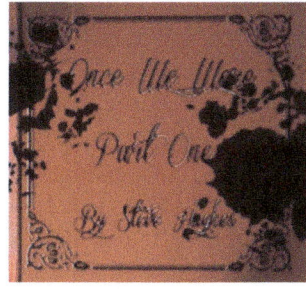

STEVE HUGHES
ONCE WE WERE – PART ONE
Towards the end of 1991 I received a demo tape from a young Dorset prog band who wanted to know what I thought of their music. That band was Big Big Train, the tape was 'From The River To The Sea', and their drummer was Steve Hughes. In the very dim and distant past, I saw Steve perform with both Big Big Train and The Enid, and consequently always thought of him as a drummer. So, when this album arrived my initial reaction was "surely it can't be that Steve Hughes", but indeed it was. This is the first of two albums, if you hadn't worked it out from the title, and this was released in May 2016, with part two following in December the same year.

I fully expected that Steve only provided drums and vocals, so I was somewhat surprised to see that he also provided bass, keyboards, and guitars. He did of course also utilise some guests, and some names immediately stood out for me such as Dec Burke (Frost*), Keith Winter (Shakatak) and Alex Tsentides (The Enid), and the overall feeling is very much of a band, not a project. With a few guest guitarists, it isn't possible to say just how much of the guitar on this album was provided by Steve himself, but I do know he is the only keyboard player, and is no mean slouch in that area at all.

Amazingly, the album starts with a song that is more than half an hour long! What is immediately apparent right from the off is that here is a musician who not only knows exactly what he wants to achieve but can make that happen and ensures the listener is taken along for the ride. This is progressive music touching on many bases, from eclectic through crossover and fusion into a rhythmic drum-driven style that I have only previously come across in the music of Bill Bruford. Drummers think of music in a quite different way to other musicians, and there are passages that could only be written by someone who has that as a first instrument with a rhythmic attack where the other instruments must keep up. There are elements of Camel at time, but really this is quite unlike anything else around and is one hell of a long way from when I first heard him. Superb.
Apr 2017

STEVE HUGHES
ONCE WE WERE – PART TWO
In December 2016, Steve followed up May's 'Part One' with 'Part Two', and one can see why, as musically it follows a very similar style to the first one. The line-up is pretty much the same as well, although we are down to just two additional guitarists this time around (Dec and Keith), and Steve provides all the bass himself as Alex Tsentides didn't return. Nine songs at more than fifty minutes in total length, but no massive epic this time, and only one song breaking the ten-minute mark. This is an even more accessible album than 'Part One', and again there are some incredible passages (such as on "Life's A Glitch") where the syncopated rhythmic attack really lifts this

album to quite a different level.

ProgArchives classify Steve as neo-prog, and I totally understand why that decision has been made, but if it was sent to me to evaluate for Crossover then it would be a strong yes from me as it has such superb melodies within it. This is totally accessible and enjoyable prog music that just makes me smile every time I play it. There are hints of Jadis, hints of Camel, hints of Bruford, and even hints of fusion at times, but overall, this is just an incredibly solid, incredibly enjoyable prog album. I haven't heard Steve's debut album, but on the basis of these two I am going to have to go back and discover that, as both the 'Once We Were' albums are wonderful from beginning to end.
Apr 2017

HUIS
DESPITE GUARDIAN ANGELS
When I came across the debut album from this Canadian band, I was immediately extremely interested to see that the guitarist is none other than Michel St-Père from Mystery. I have been racking my brains but can't think of another band he has played with, and he is here as a full member, not a guest, so it shows just how invested he is in this. Huis ("home doors" in French, and "house" in Dutch) was formed by Pascal Lapierre and Michel Joncas in 2009, after a trip to Holland. They soon found other musicians to make this band a reality, and as well as Michel it features William Regnier and Sylvain Descôteaux. Musically here we have an album that is straddling the worlds of neo-prog and melodic rock, which undoubtedly will upset a lot of purists, but when it comes to listening to music for sheer pleasure then this ticks the boxes for me.

William and Michel J keep the bottom end good and tight, while Pascal is a strong keyboard player who keeps to the role mostly of providing strong rhythmic accompaniment with the occasional flourish, but the standouts here are singer Sylvain, who has a wonderful melodic voice and Michel S. His guitarwork is the strand that pulls this album together, always fluid and emotional, and these elements combined with great songs means that this is an album that non-progheads will enjoy as much as those who think that 7/8 is much more than just a mathematical fraction. This is a very strong debut indeed, and I look forward to the next one with great interest.
May 2014

IAMTHEMORNING
~
Somehow, I totally managed to miss the debut album by this Russian duo, and I first saw the name when reading a post by Second Life Syndrome on ProgArchives. A short while later he asked if I would mind reviewing their material, so I wandered over to Bandcamp and picked up "~", (I know the symbol is called a "tilde", so don't know if that is the name of the album or if they just prefer the symbol). Anyway, this is a Russian duo of Gleb Kolyadin (piano, keyboards) and Marjana Semkina (vocals, backing vocals) along

with some additional musicians, and after releasing this in April 2012, they revisited it and remastered it and then reissued it at the end of that year, and it is available both on CD and through Bandcamp.

There is seriously just one word that fits this album, and that is "beautiful". Marjana has a fragile delicate voice that at times reminds me of Kate Bush, while Gleb has a wonderful touch on piano, and often these two are the main source of all the music. They do use other guests effectively, particularly with strings, and although there are also electric guitars and percussion these are used very sparingly indeed. Apparently, they describe themselves as "a neo-classical vocal indie band... that ...combine non-typical but easily perceived vocal parts of progressive rock with a distinctly classical musical approach", but I prefer just to think of it as majestic and powerful, yet fragile and delicate at the same time. It is possible that this is one of the finest albums by a band you have never heard of, although if you ever check out the top 100 lists by year on ProgArchives then you may have come across these already, as they are currently sat at #2 for 2012. That puts them ahead of most of the Top 10, so they are above Motorpsycho, Big Big Train, Echolyn, The Tea Club, The Flower Kings, Magma, Silhouette and 3RDegree! This is an incredibly impressive debut, full of grace, full of beauty, and is absolutely essential.
Jun 2014

IAMTHEMORNING
MISCELLANY
Gleb and Marjana are currently working on the second album, but to prevent fans from having to wait too long they released this EP at the beginning of 2014 that contains some new songs, along with reworked versions of songs on the first album. Yet again I am struck by the quality of their performances, and it is also worth commenting on the arrangements as they seem to intuitively know what they need on each song to maximize the potential, So there may be a few drums here, or additional keyboards, or strings, but always at the very heart of this is delicate piano and fragile vocals that draw the listener in to a wonderful world. Kate Bush mixed with Enya, with control and passion and never ever falling into New Age.

It is incredible to think these guys are virtually unknown outside of a small circle, as in many ways they are one of prog's best kept secrets which is just criminal as music as controlled and beautiful as this really does deserve to be heard by a much wider audience. I found myself enthralled with this EP, the production is superb, and I was drawn into a world of their making each time I listened to it. These guys are one of the best bands I have come across this year, with consistent high quality and a majestic presence that really belies what they are doing with the fragile and delicate music. Surely it can only be a matter of time before they get picked up by a major as this is a rare beauty indeed.
Jun 2014

ICHTHYANDER DAD'S ONLY DOLPHIN
AT ONE MUSIC FEST 2014

One of the joys of having been involved in the scene for such a long time is that every so often I get approached by a band I haven't come across before, asking if I would like to review an album of theirs. This is exactly what happened here, as guitarist Dmitry Dorosh contacted me, and I'm sure I wouldn't have come across this otherwise. The name of the band, wait for it, is Ichthyander Dad's Only Dolphin, which has to be one of the most interesting names I've come across. Unfortunately it reminds me of Ken Dodd's Dad's Dog's Dead, who I never did manage to see in London in the Eighties, but often saw them listed as "coming soon". According to the bible that is ProgArchives, the band were originally formed in Ukraine in 1994, but broke up before the turn of the milennium having released just a demo. Fast forward to 2014 and original members Dmitry, Oleg Vorona (bass), and Viktor Sirotin (drums), put together a new version of the band with violinist Olena Yeremenko and keyboard player Sergei Kadenko.

They performed a reunion concert in their home town of Kirovograd, and they have now made a recording of this available through Bandcamp. The more perceptive would have noticed there isn't a singer listed, which is because this is an instrumental band, and to be honest there just wouldn't be any room for vocals. To say every person is a master of their instrument is something of an understatement, and this strange, eclectic music is completely enthralling. They are often likened to Frank Zappa combined with classic King Crimson (the only cover is a version of "Starless"), but there are also sections that could be classic Beatles, while Ozone Quartet also springs to mind. There are times when the music is in standard 4/4 time and restrained, while others it is mixing and melding at great speed and intricacy, taking melodic leaps that one thinks will never make sense but somehow always does. Sometimes classical, sometimes eclectic art rock, sometimes compelling, but never boring, I look forward with interest to hear what these guys can do in a studio.
Mar 2017

IF
MORPHO NESTIRO

Even before making it onto the player this 2008 album makes quite a statement as the artwork is both stunning and enticing. The band is still in existence in 2014, but with a different line-up and name, as they changed from If to Ifsounds in 2009. But listening to this album does make me wonder what I have been missing out on all these years. Formed as long ago as 1993, this Italian act started out as a covers group and they broke up for four years before reforming to record their debut in 2004, and this is their fourth. By the time that this was released they had already won accolades for classical, easy listening and progressive rock so it is safe to say that here is a band that isn't content to easily sit firmly within one genre. They may have tried a bit too hard to be Floydian by using recordings of people talking between the songs, but that aside here is an extremely polished and enjoyable album.

There are times when they almost move into AOR/melodic rock, especially on the bouncy "Poison" where one can imagine guitarist Dario Lastella recording the piece with a huge smile on his face as he is allowed to whack out some distorted rock riffs, but there are plenty of others where the music is far more peaceful and reflective with some beautiful piano and keyboards. It really is a huge melting pot of music, never in the face of the listener, but somehow it is compelling and brings the listener in closer. Mind you, listen to "Naked" and you will think that you are playing a long lost song from 'The Wall', but mostly they follow their own path and a mighty interesting trip that is. If the rest of their output is as good as this, then here is a band really worth discovering.
Jan 2014

ILUZJON
SILENT ANDROMEDA
This 2009 release was the third from Polish band Iluzjon and saw them with a four-man line-up for the first time. Grzegorz Nowak (drums) and Michal Dziadosz (keyboards/vocals) had been joined for the second album by guitarist Slawomir Jaros after the departure of bassist/guitarist Paul Sierakowski, by now they had brought on board Marcin Drumew (bass/stick). The addition of Marcin enabled the band to move more fully into the King Crimson style of prog that they were experimenting with on the debut, as his presence certainly adds some fluidity and presence to the overall sound. The vocals are clear, and there is plenty of space within the music for everyone to play their part, so even though Michal can be singing sweetly against his gentle held-down chords, the other three can be playing all around and over the theme. That they are all good musicians is never in doubt, but the songs themselves aren't always as powerful and intense as they could be, although they do have their moments. The result is an album that is both enjoyable and disposable at the same time. I just wish that they had allowed themselves to push the music to the edge, as there are too many times when it is just too pleasant, too restrained. It is interesting music to play in the background, but for me that it is all that it will ever be.
Dec 2016

THE INTERSPHERE
INTERSPHERES<>ATMOSPHERES
Formed in 2006 in Germany, this four-piece have found themselves being marketed into different musical areas over the years, and this 2010 release was no different as here they were being portrayed as a progressive act. I do have some sympathy with that viewpoint, as the band they have most in common with is probably Muse, although with far less dynamics and passion, mixed with some of the softer elements of U2 and Incubus. There is a huge amount of alternative within their overall sound, and my 20-year-old daughter summed it up by

saying that this was music designed to appeal to teenage girls who wanted to rebel against their parents and thought that this was a way of doing it! She also told me that in some ways they reminded her of a boy band, but even I thought that was a step too far.

Even though they are trying to come over as powerful, with plenty of The Edge style riffing guitars, for some reason this just feels lightweight and plastic – they know what they want to do but aren't quite getting there. Apparently their more recent albums have been well received (I haven't heard them), so possibly this was just growing pains, but it isn't one to which I will be readily returning.
Dec 2016

INVESTINMOLDEN
INVESTINMOLDEN
Hearing this self-released EP takes me back in time to the early Nineties, when I seemed to be sent quite a lot of this type of material. Of course we were in the heady throes of neo-prog at that time (although the mass music press of course refused to say that prog existed in any form whatsoever), and there were plenty of new bands coming out showing what they could do. Acts such as IQ and Pendragon had already been around for more than ten years, and the new guard were trying to break through, and anywhere you looked there was another band with a tape they were using to self-promote so that they could get gigs and more fans. Of course, some of those bands are still here today (Big Big Train are virtually unrecognizable from that first tape) and now we have a new 'new guard'.

Investinmolden are a Polish band who although formed in May 2009 didn't play their first gig until some four years later, also releasing this demo in the same year. The name was taken from a sketch by Monty Python's Flying Circus, which includes the phrase "invest in Malden", but a simple typo when registering the name has given them a slightly different version and a story that the Pythons would surely enjoy. At the time of recording the demo they didn't have a drummer, so all drums are programmed, but now they now have a settled line-up of Michał Ambrożkiewicz (bass), Krzysztof Deskur (guitars), Mateusz Pawlukiewicz (drums) and Kacper Wojaczek (vocals, keyboards).

This is all about a band at the very start of their progressive journey, and while the vocals may not always be as clean and as in key as they might be, and there are some clunky moves between the keyboards and guitars, overall this shows great promise and certainly stands up extremely well with the demos I have heard in the past. I encourage you to give these guys a chance as while they are at the very beginning of their journey, I can see them doing some interesting things in the future.
Mar 2014

INVISIGOTH
NARCOTICA

Following on from 2007's 'Alcoholocaust', it is hard to believe that this 2009 release is the work of just two guys, with Cage providing all the music and Viggo Domino all the vocals. When I first started listening to the album, I thought I had it pegged as Steely Dan style Seventies rock, but it didn't take long for those thoughts to be blown away. Musically this is all over the place, from Gabriel and Porcupine Tree through Styx and Floyd, Flower Kings, It Bites and many others. It is strange, yet easy to listen to: it is complex and chaotic, a ramshackle mess of music that somehow works incredibly well. The very first time I played this I fell in love with it, as there are so many changes of styles that it just shouldn't work, shouldn't gel, but somehow it does, and I have no idea how that can happen.

Just sit back, turn it on, and enjoy the ride, just don't have any preconceived ideas before you do so, they even bring in middle eastern elements when they feel the time is right! In some ways, it feels more like a project than a band, but it certainly never sounds like the work of just two people. There is light, there is passion, and they are pushing the boundaries and refusing to accept they must stay inside the lines, and all power to them for doing that. An incredibly solid album, and one I enjoyed immensely.
Dec 2016

IQ
THE ROAD OF BONES

When this album arrived, I didn't put it on the player straight away, but instead looked at the artwork and booklet, and kept thinking about Schrödinger's cat. I so very much wanted this to be a great album, and until I put it on the player (and I still haven't read single review about this album as I needed to ensure that I wasn't being swayed one way or another) this was both a great album, and a poor one, both at the same time. I first saw IQ in concert sometime in the Eighties when they supported Magnum at the Hammersmith Odeon and have seen them quite a few times since, the last being on the 'Dark Matter' tour. During that time I built up a strong relationship with Martin Orford and saw him play solo a few times as well as with Gary Chandler and of course with Jadis as well, but after I moved to NZ, he told me he had left the band of which he was a co-founder. That shook me, and by the time IQ released 'Frequency' some five years after 'DM', Paul Cook had gone as well. I wasn't a fan of that album (and I totally understand that this could be due to emotions as opposed to quality of music), so what about this one? Great or poor?

Five years on from 'Frequency' and yet again there have been changes in line-up. Paul Cook has returned, but perhaps the biggest surprise is that JJ is no longer on bass, but instead has been replaced by the man he himself replaced in the first place! Tim Esau is back, with his first album with IQ since 1989's 'Are You Sitting Comfortably?' I have always been a real fan of his playing and methods of attack, as he can easily move from fretless bass to many different styles: just check out "Screaming" from 'Nomzamo' to see what I mean. Then on keyboards we have none other than Neil Durant. Neil may well be an unknown to many of you, but we have been friends for well over twenty years as he sent me the very first Sphere demo back in 1992 (and Neil knows I still have it, potential blackmail is a wonderful thing). A second demo followed in 1994, and they belatedly followed it up with a CD release on Cyclops in 2002, and it always amazed me that Sphere didn't become far more well-known as they were/are all great musicians. I even managed to see them gig once in the Nineties, but here at long last Neil is able to put his talents to use on a larger stage.

So, of the five members, four of them played on the first two totally classic IQ albums, so what would the band sound like in 2014, with one brand new member and two who had left (for very different timeframes) only to return? Absolutely brilliant is the way I would describe it.

When opener "From The Outside In" really gets going it reminded me of the very first time I heard 'Ever', when the band was again returning after a period of unrest: that time with a returning singer and a new bassist, four years after their previous release. Neil has always been a very fine keyboard player indeed, and here he has tempered the jazz influences he normally displays to fit in and has also incorporated a lot of keyboard sounds that fans of the band will recognise from days gone past. He isn't Widge, and doesn't want to be, but he has made the seat his own by bringing in enough of the old to combine with the new that it doesn't alienate the fans of the original band yet starts to move in a slightly different direction. This is a dark album in many ways, and this comes through in the artwork as well as the album itself. In many ways this feels like a logical follow-on from 'Dark Matter' or 'Subterranea' as opposed to 'Frequency', and that has to be a good thing in my book.

This is an album I have fallen in love with as everything is right from the musicianship to the songs, from the production to the artwork. This is solid IQ, with everyone firmly gelling and producing more of the incredible music we have learned to expect from them, from rockers through to ballads, simplicity and complexity combining in a way that many have attempted to copy, but few have ever managed to achieve the heights. I have the double disc set, 11 songs at just over 100 minutes long, and it absolutely flies by as one classic leads into another. It would be wonderful to be able to see these guys play live, but I guess that isn't going to happen for me as I live so far away, so I'll just have to keep playing this. Again. And Again.

And as for that cat I mentioned at the beginning. He is purring and stretching, ready to jump out of the box and take on the world. IQ are back where they belong, at the very top.
May 2014

ISPROJECT
THE ARCHINAUTS
This is the debut album by Italian duo Ivan Santovito (vocals, keyboards) and Ilenia Salvemini (vocals), who have been joined by Giovanni Pastorino (keyboards, programming), Simone Amodeo (guitars), Andrea Bottaro (bass guitar) and Paolo Tixi (drums), along with special guest Martin Grice (flutes, saxophones) (all of whom, apart from Andrea, are in Z-band). I am a little surprised to see these guys listed on ProgArchives as being RPI in nature, as apart from being Italian and Progressive I personally think that description is tenuous at best. Firstly, all the lyrics are in English (which is often an automatic disqualification), and much of the music is much cleaner, simpler, and less layered. But there are times when they do bring in that style and approach, but for me this isn't the pervasive sub-genre. Just goes to show that although we all attempt to categorise music, sometimes the best we can do is to say whether it is good or bad, which is always a subjective opinion even though every effort is made to be as objective as possible.

Putting all that to one side, this album is a delight from start to end. The vocals are fresh and not forced, and the arrangements are quite superb. There are times when they are symphonic in nature, and others where the piano is the most important instrument. There is a strong use of space, leaving plenty of room for the atmospheric nature of the music to come through. For the most part this is a very modern sounding album, rarely looking back to the Seventies, and the duo have obviously followed their own course as they bring in elements of electronic and pop, so much so that at times I was reminded as much of Savage Garden as I was of IQ. The use of different keyboard sounds and textures is important, while Simone's guitar is sometimes non-existent and at others providing an incredibly dynamic solo, again adding to the textures. This is a modern progressive album that has been released on CD by AMS but is also available through Bandcamp and is one of the best new projects I have heard from Italy in quite a while.
Feb 2018

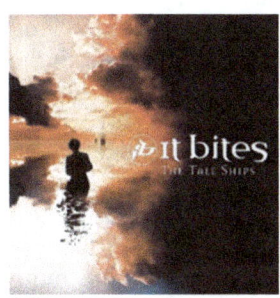

IT BITES
THE TALL SHIPS
When it was first announced there was going to be a new It Bites album in 2008, but that the band wasn't going to involve Francis Dunnery, there was more than one person wondering what on earth was going to happen. True, keyboard player John Beck and drummer Bob Dalton were still going to be there, but who was going to be the new frontman? Step up John Mitchell, who is probably best-known for his incredibly long-running stint in Arena (in the early days the standing joke was that if you wanted to stay in the band then you shouldn't be at one side of the official press photo, as there was a rather fluid line-up back then). Now, John has a wide and varied repertoire and can put his hand to anything (I once saw him, Paul Cook and JJ act as the backing band for a Canadian singer-songwriter), but It Bites? Here is a band that is probably more loved now

than in their heyday, so what was going to happen?

The three of them were going to produce an almighty success, that's what. I saw the original line-up support Marillion on the Misplaced Childhood tour sometimes a million years ago, and I remember being distinctly unimpressed (although in fairness, all I knew of theirs at the time was "Calling All The Heroes"), but here I was grabbed right from the off and stayed with it all the way through to the end. This reminds me so much of the days in the early Nineties when I seemed to be in a permanent state of wonderment about how many great bands there were in the scene, and how many stunning albums there were to listen to. This has been a constant returnee to my player since it was released in 2008, and I have only just realised that I never wrote anything about it at the time!! This has everything anyone could want from It Bites, with poptastic melodies and harmonies and the synthed layers of the opening "Oh My God" dares the listener to turn it off – impossible.

John's singing fits the music perfectly, and in many ways, it really does sound as if It Bites have never been away. So many styles, so many flavours to savour, and there is even a thirteen-minute epic to close with. If somehow this album has passed you by, then you should seek it out immediately.
Dec 2016

ITS.TRUE.MENTALITY
INSOMNIA
This 2008 album was the debut by Polish prog metal outfit Its.True.Mentality. It's not just the punctuation in the name that is unusual, as while prog metal bands aren't exactly uncommon, it is certainly strange to come across one that is totally instrumental, and happy to move as far away from riffs as these do at times. The line-up of Andrzej Lebek (guitar), Grzegorz Haasa (drums), Anna Weyna (keyboards) and Arkadiusz Doroszuk (bass) can certainly crunch the riffs when they need to, but there is a great deal of light within the album as well. The use of older keyboard sounds also provides warmth, and the result is a five-track twenty-nine-minute-long album that just makes me want to keep coming back for more. Bass and drums sit in the background quite a bit but aren't afraid to be forward and demanding when the time is right, but for a lot of the time it is Anna and Andrzej who rightly take centre stage. They have a strong solid understanding of each other, so they can duet and provide strong interlinked runs, or they are also content to let each other take the lead.

This is music that is incredibly solid, as one would expect from the genre, but there is also a great deal of light and space which then allows for contrast against the more metallic elements when they make their presence felt. The solos aren't pure solos in the traditional sense, but more that they are taking the musical lead at that point. It is more reflective than many in the scene and has been influenced as much by melodic guitarists such as John McLaughlin as much as they have by Karl Groom. Highlight is the final song, "Mistificated Paranoia" which has a wonderful warm introduction with some beautiful fretless bass notes that gradually just builds into a swirling epic.

I feel there are times when they lack the musical depth and power that they need, and some of the compositions are a little weak in places, as if this were a work in progress as opposed to the finished article. But this was a self-released demo, so possibly they were looking for some recognition and record company support. Sadly, I believe this was their only release, their sites are no longer active, and their Facebook page hasn't been updated since 2009. That's a real shame as this showed promise and is worth picking up if you come across it.
Jan 2017

IZZ
THE DARKENED ROOM

Izz was formed in the Nineties, and even though this album is from 2009, those Nineties influences are plain to hear. This is symphonic progressive rock from a band at the very top of their game and given that since this album they have recruited former Gentle Giant and current 3 Friends guitarist, Gary Green, into the line-up, I am incredibly intrigued to hear what they are doing now. Harmony vocals? Yup. Plenty of intricately woven melodies? Check. Music that makes the listener stay through to the end and then hit repeat? Double check. This is one of the most exciting albums I have heard from the States since I first came across Spock's Beard, Glass Hammer, Discipline, Timothy Pure and Iluvatar back in the day. It has that sort of impact, and whatever passage I am listening to, of whatever song, is the best bit. There is some beautiful bass on this album, and while they rarely come across as anyone else, there are times when it sounds as if Chris Squire has his hand on the frets.

They're not afraid to slow it down and bring in just gentle piano and vocals (and a triangle – when was the last time you heard one of those on a prog album?). "Can't feel The Earth (Pt.1)" is incredible from start to end, with as much owed to modern classical music as it does to traditional progressive rock (although there are a few Gentle Giant tendencies it must be said). The more I played this the more I kept telling myself that these guys are still active, and released four studio albums before this one and three afterwards (as well as a live album and a DVD) so what are the others like? I feel I have been missing out, yet at the same time am excited that there is so much more great music to discover by these guys. They released their debut album some eighteen years ago and are still going strong, which is quite some achievement.

Quite simply, if you enjoy progressive rock, then this is an album that you just must get, and once you have fallen in love with this as I have, then there is plenty more out there to discover.
Jan 2017

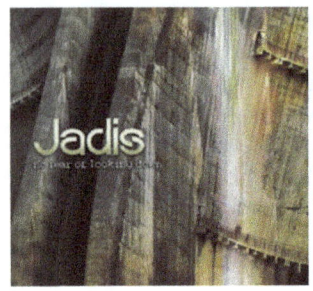

JADIS
NO FEAR OF LOOKING DOWN

The last release before this one, 2012's 'See Right Through You', was seen as one of Jadis's best albums, and rightly so. But, for me there was a key element missing and at least for this album, he's back. Jadis has had some great musicians play with them over the years, but it has always been built around the voice, guitar, and songs of Gary Chandler, and he has been aided and abetted for more than quarter of a century by Stephen Christey on drums. These two were joined by Andy Marlow (bass) and Arman Vardanyan (keyboards) for the last album after the departures of the IQ boys, but although Andy is still there, Arman has left to be replaced by the incomparable Martin Orford. This is Martin's third stint with Jadis, and it is wonderful to see him back again, as I know from conversations with him some years ago that he had felt the need to leave the scene and was planning never to return. But, one thing led to another, and here he is again, rekindling a relationship with Gary that is very special indeed. I was lucky enough to see Jadis play live quite a few times, both with and without Martin, and also caught some of Martin and Gary's duet gigs, which were always incredible.

Although this album was released towards the end of 2016, I have only just got my copy, and to say that it is something I have been eagerly awaiting is something of an understatement. But would it live up to expectations? Of course it would. From the first note to the last, this is solid, classic Jadis. They are a band that sound like no other and have kept true to their roots for many years, with everything built around the vocals and guitar and then layered and built from there. The drums have a rawer sound than normal, while Andy's bass is quite a long way back in the mix, but with Gary and Martin harmonising vocally, and providing the backdrop for each other musically, this could only ever be Jadis. I only have a few criticisms, namely the album is only forty-five minutes long, we had to wait four years for it, and they're never likely play New Zealand, so the chances are I'll never catch up with them in concert again! While this is playing, I am transported to another world, and I am just so pleased to have yet another Jadis album that I can return to time and again. Let's hope we don't have to wait quite so long for the next one, yet again this is quite superb.
Mar 2017

JAM IT!
FOLLOWING THE UNKNOWN

I feel incredibly fortunate at present, as I am being introduced to many Russian progressive rock bands, and here is yet another that has passed me by in the past that I am grateful to hear now. Formed in St. Petersburg in 2006, they have been operating as an instrumental outfit since 2010 and this 2015 release was their third (and latest) album. The quartet of Alexey Vostrikov (drums), Dmitry Medvinsky (bass), Konstantin Ilin (guitar) and Roman Savelyev (keyboards) are obviously influenced by the jazz rock fusion boom of the Seventies, but here it is firmly within the realm of progressive rock, and there are also some metallic influences which bring it right up to date. There should also be a special mention here of the treatment of the drums within production, as it often feels that instead of four instruments being blended together, that it is three plus one. The drums and cymbals are vibrant, bright and direct and given the versatility and musicianship being displayed by Alexey there is a major impact on the overall feel of the album.

Normally one would expect the rhythm section to be more controlled in this style of line-up, but here just Dmitry has that role, with Alexey doing his thing, and then Konstantin and Roman both taking it in turns to provide melody and lead lines. It certainly never feels like a self-released album, as it is vibrant and fresh, never too self-indulgent but twisting and changing in a manner that is always interesting and fascinating. The metallic approach that is brought to bear at times is never too over the top or intrusive but has a part to play in creating dynamics and emotion. Overall, this is an enjoyable album which is well worth discovering.
Jul 2017

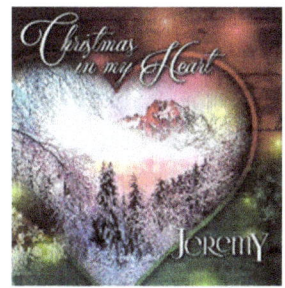

JEREMY
CHRISTMAS IN MY HEART
In many ways it is somewhat surprising that it took until 2015 for Jeremy to release a Christmas album, as at my last check he has released more than fifty albums in one musical form or another, and given that he is also a church minister it does make a sense to bring the two things together. Anyway, here it is, and regarding musical stylings this finds Jeremy very much in the area of power pop as opposed to his progtastic releases. I found one review that likened his influences to The Beatles, The Byrds, Big Star, Pink Floyd, The Hollies, The Kinks, Teenage Fanclub and another that pointed to the Undertones and Phil Seymour, but while bits of all these bands do make sense, there is no single band that can be heard to be prevalent above the others.

This is psychedelic power pop that is taking everything that came out from 1967 – 1970 and melding it together in a fashion that is both enjoyable and fun, and makes for instantly accessible music. Some of the songs are more evangelical than others, but the one thing they have in common is that they don't really sound like any other Christmas song you've come across before. My favourite, though, has to be "Here Comes Christmas" which use the Batman theme to great effect, and must be heard to be believed. Overall, yet another fine release from Jeremy Morris.
Mar 2017

JEREMY
NOT OF THIS WORLD
Before I started writing the review I thought I'd get the CD down from the shelf, so started looking through my collection of Jeremy CD's and it took a while to find it. A

short count later and I realised that I have thirty of his albums on CD, plus another four from the days when he was releasing albums on cassette, and I don't actually have everything he's done by a long way! The album starts as if it is one of his power pop albums, with a more evangelical nature, but the lengthy "Clouds Are Lifting" soon turns into something quite different, as mandolins are riffed and dramatically change the feel of the whole piece and then we are into delicate piano and the realisation that this is an album that is looking back to his classic 'Pilgrim's Journey' in many ways, as it is refusing to conform into any particular style. There are a few guest musicians helping out here and there, but for the most part this is Jeremy doing everything himself. The rhythm section of Dave Dietrich and Todd Borsch may only be involved on a couple of numbers, but they have dramatic input into "I Am The Eye" which is driving rock number, again with many influences and stylistic switches and changes. There are strong hints of The Beatles in particular, moved and pulled in many different directions and styles.

There is a refusal to conform, so the listener never really know what to expect or what is coming next, although this is never harsh or grating. The jangly Byrds-style guitar at the beginning of the title song leads into a pop melody that in turn is twisted into something that could have come out of Sgt. Pepper. Jeremy has really pushed himself with this album, and it feels his most complete work for some time. This will appeal to those who enjoy both his progressive rock and power pop works as here it stretches both and delivers them in a manner that is always enjoyable and entertaining. This is a refreshing and uplifting album which is well worth hearing.
Mar 2017

DUŠAN JEVTOVIĆ
AM I WALKING WRONG?
Originally from Serbia, Dušan has established himself as an accomplished, articulate guitarist in Barcelona, Spain. This album was recorded mostly live with just bassist Bernat Hernández and drummer Marko Djordjević, and there is no doubt that all three are consummate musicians, but to be honest I don't really 'get' most of this album. They are being experimental and trying to extend the boundaries of jazz and prog but for the most part I felt that it often sounded as if they didn't know where they were going. That in itself isn't generally an issue in improvisational music as long as they find their path in the end, but for most of the time that just isn't the case here. It is a wonderfully presented album with a fold-out digipak and interesting notes but for the first nine songs this became an abrasive hard-edged album I was listening to because I had to, not because I wanted to.

So, the last song on the album "If You See Me Again" was a complete shock to me as it is totally different, in every aspect, to what had gone before. Here was something that was constructed around an acoustic guitar with beautiful fretless bass that just took me in

and held me close. If the whole album had featured material like this then I know I would be raving about it, but as it is then it isn't one to which I will often be returning.
Jan 2014

DUŠAN JEVTOVIĆ
NO ANSWER

It must be said that I wasn't the world's biggest fan of Dušan's last release, 2013's 'Am I Walking Wrong', and I think it was probably the first time I had ever given a Moonjune album a poor review, but I just didn't get it. So, when this arrived in the post one day, I wasn't immediately over-enamoured, but I opened the digipak and realised the drummer was none other than Asaf Sirkis, someone whose work I highly admire. The line-up was completed by Vasil Hadzimanov on acoustic piano, Fender Rhodes electric piano and Mini Moog bass, and I was immediately intrigued. Further investigation led to the discovery that the album was recorded in just two days last February and knowing they had toured together in different incarnations, as opposed to being put together for a studio project, made me think that this could be quite a special album indeed.

I put aside any preconceived ideas, and as soon as the first notes came out of the speakers I was transfixed. Here were wonderful guitar lines, perfectly accompanied by different keyboards with both lightness and strong bottom end, and then there was Asaf who was acting as if he was the lead player in the band. There are many times during this album where Vasil is valiantly managing to keep it all together, as both Dušan and Asaf attempt to be the man in charge. This is simply a wonderful album, full not only of wonderful melodies but great interplay between all those involved. Ideas bounce between the trio, and there are so many things on here to enjoy, from brightness and sparks to reflective and delicate, such as on the emotional "Yo Sin Mi". Dušan's guitarwork is exemplary throughout, as he switches styles and tones, yet there is always clarity and finesse. This is not a guitarist who feels the need to prove his skills by playing five thousand notes to the bar, but instead shows it every time he uses sustain. This is one of the most interesting and enjoyable instrumental albums I've come across in 2017.
Jul 2017

JOLLY
46:12 OF MUSIC

Bear with me a second. Here is an American band that want us to be happy, and consequently, within this album they have embedded various forms of brain wave stimulation known as Binaural Tones. These tones are scientifically proven to enrich feelings of relaxation, focus, creativity, and happiness through inaudible changes in audio frequencies. Apparently. I don't know about feeling happy while playing this, but I found it to be quite a choppy mixed-up album that is somewhat confusing to listen to.

They can go from Meshuggah style polymetric passages into Muse soundscapes without warning and the result is I came away thinking that they were very clever at what they are doing, and they are good musicians. Didn't like it a lot though...

For me this is too all over the place, and that there is no real rationale behind it. Now, I can listen to "unusual" music more than most, and in many ways, this is mainstream, but I found myself getting frustrated and unsettled as opposed to being put into some sort of artificial nirvana. Some of the tricks such as the sound of a needle on vinyl at the beginning of "Peril" I found annoying, and as for the sounds at the end of "Inside The Womb" they just went on for way too long. I listened right to the very end just in case something interesting happened, but it didn't. I am sure that there are many out there who will hail this as a masterpiece, and I have seen a few reviews comparing them to Riverside, but while there are some musical similarities at times, the Polish band is so far removed in terms of material to be on another planet. Not one to which I can see myself returning.
Jan 2017

NIGEL MAZLYN JONES
RAFT
This has been way too long coming, in fact this is the first acoustic based album from Nigel Mazlyn Jones in thirteen years, I just hope that we don't have to wait so long for the next one! This contains his trademark use of 12 -string guitars and Glissando bowed techniques, and he has here been joined by some guests including Guy Evans (who has worked with NMJ for more than 30 years now) of Van Der Graaf Generator on drums and percussion, Rog Patterson on Chapman Stick, fretless bass and acoustic (and it's about time he released some new solo material as well!), Jo Lucy on violin, Oscar Morse on sax, Jim Nield on electric guitar, Rob Phillips on fretless bass, Margaret MJ on piano and Dave Reeves on harmonicas.

The only word to describe this album is "beautiful", as the listener is entranced by the sounds coming out of the speakers. There are long instrumental passages where one is taken to a new world by Nigel's deft 12-string technique, and others where they are more songs-based and the guests come in and out of the music as they play their part and then leave again. Only a few of the songs have four people involved, while three are just Nigel. For those who have never come across NMJ before, his style is a cross of Anthony Phillips and Roy Harper, with just a touch of Gong and Steve Hillage here and there. The result is a world of incredibly well-arranged music where space is a permanent fixture, and one is allowed to breathe in the notes and live in NMJ's world. Inspired as ever by his love of the Cornish coast, this album is essential for anyone who enjoys great music. The last words belong to Nigel, "We sail the tiny raft of our lives, and this small planet Earth is the raft that carries us all. Rafts are fragile, not permanent, and held together with hopes and dreams. So, I set my sails well . . . What say you my friend, let's strike out for the ocean?" Released as a digi pak with an insert, this is truly essential.
Apr 2014

The Progressive Underground Vol 5

JPL
MMXIV

So, no prizes for guessing when Jean Pierre Louveton, aka JPL, released this album. He of course made his name with Nemo, surely one of the very finest progressive bands to come out of France, where he provided guitars and vocals, while here he is pretty much on his own, with just a few friends helping here and there. As would be expected, this is a complex album, with many layers, and with most of the vocals in French I found myself treating these as another instrument. This is progressive rock music that is based around complex and often quite heavy guitar, and that works just fine for me.

JPL can slow it down, such as on the introduction to "L'un Contre L'autre", where he allows the guitar to sing and shine with vibrancy, or he can turn it up and provide a much heavier style of music, with multi-tracked guitars, and while it never quite moves into prog metal territory there is plenty of bite and attack. It is this contrast that makes this album such a delight to listen to. True, his vocals are emotional and fraught, and provides a fragility and humanity that work well with the more complex and structured music. There is a feeling that he is on the edge, and it is the music that keeps pulling him back from the abyss, from the darkness, although he does allow just some of it to feed into the album. He has a wonderful guitar sound, rich and warm with plenty of depth, no shallow or single attack for him, this is all about structuring complex music so that it is warm and all-encompassing. This is a superb album, that needs to be investigated by all those into good music.
Apr 2017

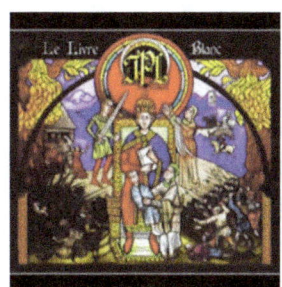

JPL
LE LIVRE BLANC

And so, onto the brand-new release from JPL. In between this and the last one there has been a Nemo album, and another solo work, and this time he is back with additional musicians (including two of his Nemo bandmates in Guillaume Fontaine and Jean Baptiste Itier). Mind you, that is no excuse for Jean Pierre to sit back and relax, as he still provides all guitars as well as bass, vocals, keyboards, programming, and percussion. There is a strength in this album, nearly a harshness, as the vocals are full of passion. Combining this with the multi-layered and incredibly well constructed and arranged music creates an atmosphere where the listener is soon inside a world very much of JPL's making. There is some wonderfully fluid and complex piano underlying some of these songs, and this provides a solid basis for JPL to multi-track guitars so that he then has somewhere to lay some inspirational solos against. "L'ermite" is a case in point, where music goes from layered and bombastic to simple and almost acoustic, before coming back with a real bang.

I feel at home inside the album, able to curl up and let the warmth, power and passion

wrap itself around me, as if the rest of the world no longer exists. I keep coming back to it and finding more to enjoy each time, as if I am slowly unwrapping the layers. There is a groove at times, and at others it is more thoughtful, demanding you to pay attention. Complex but never over the top, this is always accessible and completely enjoyable. Yet another great work from Jean Pierre Louveton.
Apr 2017

JPL
RESTROSPECTIONS VOL II
As with the first album in this series, this album is based on unpublished music written by Jean Pierre Louveton between 1992 and 2005, although this does also include songs from his first three albums which have been rearranged and re-recorded by the musicians playing live with him, as these would form part of the set list. Released in 2016, this doesn't feel like a put-together compilation, but rather that this was an album which was conceived as an entity in its own right. Some of the songs feature just JPL, whereas others are by a full band, and we move from hard rock through progressive to areas that are more acoustic, but always with passion and forethought.

The drummer on the album is Ludovic Moro, who of course played with JPL in Wolfspring, while Nemo's keyboard player Guillaume Fontaine is also very much in evidence, both musicians who have played with JPL for a large number of years, and this comes through very much in the music. It would be possible for this release to be seen as a "stop gap" between 'MMXIV' and 'Le Livre Blanc', as it follows on from the 2008 album, but that would be incredibly unfair as this is a dynamic and enjoyable album in its own right, and flows and rocks, and in no way sounds like a collection of material from times past.

I have always enjoyed JPL, both solo and with his various bands, and this is yet another incredibly strong addition to his canon.
Apr 2017

JUMP
THE BEACHCOMBER
One of the very few downsides of living on the other side of the world is that I am unable to see Jump in concert. Easily one of the hardest working bands around, they must have played thousands of gigs by now and always used to be prolific in their releases. However, it took five years from the release of 'Faithful Faithless' in 2005 for them to return with this at the beginning of 2010. The core line-up is basically the same, with the one and only John Dexter Jones on vocals, Steve 'Ronnie Rundle' on guitars/vocals, Steve Hayes guitars/vocals, Andy Barker drums and Mo on keyboards. But bassist Andy Faulkner has been replaced by Phil Mayhew, plus a few guests.

Jump have always had a very hard sound to define, progressive but not really, neo but not really, crossover but not really. In fact, the only way to think of them in my mind is as a band that plays English rock (a statement guaranteed to upset the very passionate Welshman who is the frontman). They really are one of the undiscovered joys of British music, a band that always put their all into their gigs and who consistently produce wonderful albums. I have been lucky enough to hear all of these, and to my ears they generally deserve at least a 4* rating, and with this their eleventh studio album in nineteen years they have yet again delivered the goods. "On Bended Knee" is a wonderful song, and is a fine example of the album, with guitars restrained yet full, with everyone working hard to ensure that the vocals are accompanied perfectly, complex yet with simplicity. Jump concentrate on producing well-crafted songs, small stories with the perfect backing, and here are another 11 that are going to gain them new fans and please the old.
Apr 2014

JUMP
THE BLACK PILGRIM
July 2013 saw the 12th studio album from Jump, one in many ways that they have been working towards throughout their career. Steve 'Ronnie' Rundle has taken on the bass role in addition to his normal duties, and the only guest this time is Alice Atkinson with violin on a couple of the songs (she also played on the last album). But this time Mo is also contributing accordion as well as keyboards and the two Steves have gone acoustic while Andy isn't as prominent as is usual. Yes, Jump have moved far more into the realms of acoustic folk, although to be honest the overall sound isn't as far removed from their normal sound as one might expect. As I have said before, I have always viewed Jump as an 'English' band as opposed to progressive, and with this album they have shown that they have much in common with the mighty Show of Hands, another band who have always stuck to their own agenda, playing hundreds of gigs and producing one wonderful album after another.

There is purity to this album that is hard to define, with one great song after another, full of emotion and wonderful music, while JDJ shows yet again why he is so highly regarded as a singer. Whatever song I am playing is my favourite, and I have found myself returning to this album time and again as it is such a delight from the start to the very end. Beautiful songs, extremely well-constructed with great arrangements, careful thought being given to the amount of space required between the instruments and between the notes, with room for John to add to the magic. Back in 1991 Jump released their wonderful debut, 'The Winds of Change', and some 22 years later and countless gigs four of the six people who performed on that album are still there. Over the years their music has changed, and they have changed with it, but unlike many they have continued to grow and with this, in many ways their simplest and most roots-based album, they have created the finest of their career. Indispensable.
Apr 2014

JUPITER SOCIETY
TERRAFORM
'Terraform' was the second album from the project led by keyboard player Carl Westholm (Carptree, Krux, Candlemass) who brought together friends and colleagues from his other bands plus some others to follow on from where the debut left off (given that 'First Contact/Last Warning' only came out the year before perhaps that isn't too much of a surprise). Musically here is someone who has been heavily influenced by Devin Townshend, but then brought in some Ayreon to produce something that is full of balls and wall to wall guitars but also with a real progressive sensibility. It is intense, extremely well produced, and the singers manage to just about stay in front of the music as everyone here is determined to make themselves heard.

Given that both Carl and singer Mats Levén (also Therion, Malmsteen, Krux etc) are in Candlemass it is probably no surprise at all that these guys really know when and how to really belt it out. But, as well as the monstrous riffs (with superb bass and drums in support) from both guitars and keyboards, there is also room for more quiet and gentler interludes that emphasise the heaviness that is going on. This is prog metal that is slightly more metallic than it is progressive, but with plenty of both to make this of interest to anyone who wants their progressive rock to be anything but introspective and restrained.
Jan 2014

KARDA ESTRA
FUTURE SOUNDS
This was the second EP released by Richard Wileman in 2015, following on from 'The Sea and the Stars'. Ileesha features with her wonderful haunting vocals on one number, clarinettist Amy Fry appears on two and drummer Paul Sears on another, but for the most part this six song album is just Richard and whatever instrument he believes is right for the moment. I have long said that Richard is one of our greatest modern classical composers, with more than a hint of film music about what he does, and this is even more cinematic than normal. There is an incredible amount of space within the music, and a haunting ethereal edge that reminds me a lot of some of Roger Eno's work. It is deeply compelling, and is a world where the dominant instrument is a slightly phased poignant electric guitar that is both beautiful and disturbing at the same time. As always with Karda Estra, this is music that really does benefit from being played on headphones: it is important to pay full attention to what is being played, as only then will the listener fully understand the complex yet simplistic world.

I can imagine being lost in space, wondering at the majesty of the stars, with this being played as the backdrop, Cinematic, enthralling, beguiling, beautiful Karda Estra.
Jan 2017

KARDA ESTRA
THE SEAS AND THE STARS
This 2015 EP apparently "chronicles the collision between the Andromeda galaxy and our own Milky Way, the eventual end of everything, a celestial intervention and a return to where everything began - viewed from an impossible, empty shoreline." I couldn't have put it better myself. On this release, Richard provides acoustic, electric, classical, prepared and bass guitars, keyboards, melodica, accordion, kalimba, Appalachian dulcimer, rastrophone, bouzouki, glockenspiel, percussion, while Ileesha gives us some of her stunning vocals, and Amy Fry assists with clarinet, alto saxophone and flute. I have found this one of Richard's more difficult releases to review, as each time I try to write about it I find myself spending way too much time listening to it and not enough time capturing any words!

Having the words above saying what this EP is about is a great help, as on this release, as with much of KE's output, this is incredibly visual, and I find myself playing a film in my head while listening to this. One unusual aspect is that Ileesha sings some words, whereas normally her vocals are wordless and eerie, but they definitely fit with the very science fiction feel of the whole piece. This may only be some twenty minutes long, but within the layers and depths the majesty and hypnotic style takes the listener to a far different place. Yet another essential release from Richard.
Mar 2017

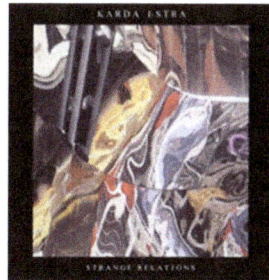

KARDA ESTRA
STRANGE RELATIONS
2015's 'Strange Relations' was the eleventh album to be released by Richard under the Karda Estra banner, and although it is still recognisable as such, there is a much larger jazz element contained than normal. This is because the first six (of eight) tracks were a partnership between Richard and drummer Paul Sears (The Muffins). Given that it's not unusual for drums to hardly feature at all in Richard's work, having a jazz drummer involved is bound to give a very different feel to proceedings. This time around Richard uses electric, acoustic, classical and bass guitars, keyboards, samples, percussion, zither and rastrophone while Caron de Burgh provides oboe on three songs and cor anglais on two, Amy Fry clarinet on three and sax on three, Mike Ostime trumpet on one, Kavus Torabi (Knifeworld) electric guitar on a song while of course Ileesha Wileman provides her delicate wordless vocals on a couple as well.

There are times when the drums do really add something to the overall sound, there are others where I felt that they were too intrusive, and the music would have benefited from less of them. The structure of Richard's music is often classical in approach, and this style doesn't always marry well with a drummer, and that is sometimes the case here. But there are times, such as on "Strange Relations 6", where they come together in a manner that is perfect and the differing styles blend and create something very special indeed.

Although I would hesitate to recommend this as a starting point for Karda Estra, it is still a very fine release indeed and an interesting addition to his canon.
Mar 2017

KARDA ESTRA
INFERNAL SPHERES

Richard is back with his fourteenth album, and I made the mistake of playing this in the car the very first time I listened to it, and only realised afterwards that I had driven more than sixty kilometres with no real recollection of having done so! When Richard is in his comfort zone of mixing and melding classical musical soundscapes with progressive overtones, then there really is no-one else who can match him. I defy anyone to listen to "Obelisk of Cruithine" and not been drawn into a labyrinthine world of melodies, dissonance, simplicity and complexity that defies description, yet makes complete musical sense always. How Richard manages to understand exactly what notes he needs where, and which instruments are to be used to play them, is just beyond me. Apart from Helen Dearnley providing violin, this song, amazingly, is one where he provides virtually all the instruments himself (he lists himself as providing acoustic, classical, electric, bass and prepared guitars, keyboards, samples, percussion, rastrophone, bouzouki, Appalachian dulcimer and zither on this album).

Yet he brings in guests on bass clarinet, oboe, cor anglais, violin, clarinet, tenor sax, bass trombone, tenor trombone and trumpet where he feels the need. There are also drums, but only on two songs, while Ileesha provides her amazing wordless vocals to just three numbers this time. I have known Richard for more than twenty years now, and I have yet to hear anyone else achieve what he manages with Karda Estra. He still surprises me in so many ways, as he moves so many different styles, yet all with a common theme of being visual: I always "See" his music as well as hearing it. It may be his fourteenth album, but he shows no signs at all, of slowing down, and this is his finest yet.
Mar 2017

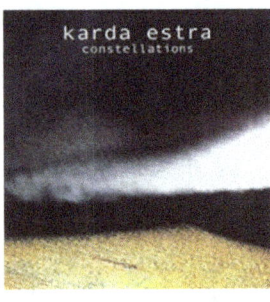

KARDA ESTRA
CONSTELLATIONS

This review is part of my attempt to catch up with some of Richard's albums I missed the first time around for one reason or another, and here we are back in 2003. Within his musical chronology this was the follow-up to his collaboration with Artemiy Artemiev, 'Equilibrium', which is my least favourite of his albums, but really this should be viewed as the follow-up to 2001's 'Eve'. Between the two albums there has been just one change in line-up, with the addition of Sarah Higgins on cello, to add to the violin and viola of Helen Dearnley and Rachel Larkins respectively, and the line-up completed by Caron Hansford (oboe, cor anglais), Zoe King (flute, alto & soprano saxophones), Ileesha Bailey (wordless vocals) and Richard of course providing everything else (classic & electric guitars, bass, keyboards, percussion).

This album epitomises to me just what Karda Estra are all about, providing thought provoking modern classical music that is enthralling, beautiful, poignant and dramatic. Richard is rarely the lead musician, allowing others the opportunity to shine, with the woodwind often taking the melody line. This is an album to fall deep inside of, and then to be carried out along drifting on the currents of melody without any understanding of time or thought. It is simple, with loads of space and plenty of contrast, yet is also complex, with incredibly strong arrangements. One unusual aspect of this album is that there is also a cover here of Steve Hackett's "Twice Around The Sun" where Richard has allowed himself to Karda Estra-ise a song so that it is both true to the original and to his own style. 14 years on I have finally heard another true gem from Richard Wileman.
Apr 2017

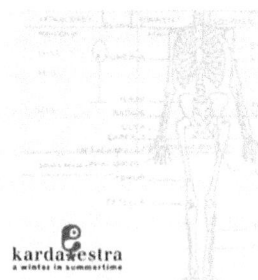

KARDA ESTRA
A WINTER IN SUMMERTIME

In 1997 Lives & Times released their final album, 'Hoarse', on their own No Image label: at the time they were a duo, comprising Richard Wileman (all instrumentation) and Ileesha Bailey (vocals). A year later they were back in a new incarnation, Karda Estra, being joined now by Zoe King (flute, clarinet) and Rachel Larkins (viola). 'A Winter In Summertime' was their first mini album, with seven instrumental tracks and just over twenty-seven minutes long. For some strange reason, I never heard this when it was released, so some nineteen years on I'm coming across it for the very first time.

Right from the off this is classic Karda Estra, as Richard combines all the instrumentation plus Ileesha's wordless vocals into something quite magical and special. This is a soundscape, a musical feast for the ears. Richard, to my mind, is one of the most important composers of modern classical cinematic music, creating images and drama with wonderfully layered arrangements and perfect juxtaposition of different instruments and sounds. Using Ileesha as another instrument adds to the other worldliness of the album, and combining this with gently picked classical guitar and a lighter curtain of sounds is simply wonderful. There is so much depth within this album, it just draws in the listener so that nothing else exists except the new world of Karda Estra. It goes from lulling to something more frantic, and the switch between the end of "The Excavation Site" and the introduction to "Transference" is quite mean, as I found myself quite rudely awakened from a dreamlike state. I may be nearly twenty years late to the party, but I am so very glad that I finally got there.
May 2017

KARDA ESTRA
YONDO

'Yondo' is one of those rare things, namely a digital single, and it's also free! Taken from the 'Time & Stars' album, Richard released it as a freebie Halloween special back in 2015 and never took it down so it's still available on Bandcamp for the bargain price of zero, nada, zip! Inspired by the weird story 'The Abominations Of Yondo' by Clark Ashton Smith', it features Richard Wileman (guitars, bass, keyboards, samples, percussion, effects) and Amy Fry (clarinet), and is a perfect example of why I love his music so much. It is deep, it is dramatic, cinematic, modern, dramatic and thought-provoking. If for some strange reason, you don't already own any Karda Estra albums then grab this five-minute-long piece of musical oddity and mastery. It's free!
May 2017

KARNATAKA
THE GATHERING LIGHT

In the dim and distant past I travelled to a Sleeping Giant gig, intrigued to see what the ex-So & So's were doing, and aware that Steve Rothery would also be appearing. But they weren't the headline, that honour belonging to Karnataka. To be honest, I wasn't exactly impressed with what they were doing, and spent more of their set outside chatting with Dave Foster and wasn't overly surprised when I heard they had broken up a while later. But bassist Ian Jones kept hold of the name while others departed to The Reasoning and Panic Room, and eventually put together a brand-new band using the same name as before. The first time I heard this 2010 album I was amazed, as here was real power and depth, a vibrancy and passion that immediately made an impact. Lisa Fury has a great voice, while the rest of the guys (Ian Harris (drums), Gonzalo Carrera (keyboards, piano) and Enrico Pinna (guitars)) are wonderful musicians.

There are obvious similarities to bands such as Mostly Autumn, and when listening to their use of uilleann pipes, I had a little smile to myself and thought "There's Troy Donockley", and yes it was. They also use a "real" string section as opposed to synthesised, and I note that one of these is Hugh McDowell who I first saw on TV playing with Wizzard more than forty years ago but is probably best remembered for his years with ELO.

The album starts with an emotional, atmospheric prelude, where held-down keyboard chords provide the backdrop for Troy to place his magic. "State Of Grace" commences with some beautifully clear guitar lines, and then the band start to build and really project. This album is a delight from the start to end with elements of folk combining with symphonic progressive rock to create something that is quite special indeed. The band seem to be just at home playing light and gentle or over the top bombast, and it is this contrast that highlights the different aspects of their music. The opening prelude, "The Calling…" is an instrumental, as is "State Of Grace", which is nine minutes long, and it is only a minute into "Your World" that Lisa finally makes an entrance, as the band move into a more syncopated style. Up to then the listener thinks there can be no room at all for a singer as the music is so complex, and after that one asks why were they not using her previously?

I may not have been a fan of Karnataka in their previous incarnation, but I like these guys, a lot.
Jan 2017

KARIBOW
FROM HERE TO IMPOSSIBLE
I don't often receive CDs these days, a combination of many labels now using digital downloads for promotional purposes and living at the bottom of the world. So, I was pleased to firstly see a padded envelope, and even more pleased when I saw what was inside, it as this is a beautifully put together release. A digipak, with great artwork, there is also a twelve-page booklet with all the lyrics, even more art, and details of who played on what song. This time Karibow have brought in some guests, but to all intents and purposes this isn't a band release but a project being run by Oliver Rüsing, who on some numbers provides virtually all the instrumentation as well as the vocals. Most of the songs feature Oliver and just one or two others, but as he is involved to such a high degree it does mean that there is continuity and a band feel.

The seventy-two-minute-long concept album is a neo-progressive masterpiece with great songs, wonderful vocals, and lots of different styles being displayed, with influences from IQ and U2 through Porcupine Tree and Steve Hackett. From the beginning to the end there is a feeling of direction and depth, with different effects being provided to provide emphasis. This could be the delicate use of saxophone, or wonderful duets between Oliver and Monique Van Der Kolk (Harvest). The result is a well-produced modern progressive rock album that will appeal to all fans of the genre.
Jul 2017

KONCHORDAT
ENGLISH GHOSTS
Konchordat were formed in 2009 by Steve Cork (bass, piano, keyboards, acoustic guitar) and Lee Harding (vocals, piano, keyboards, acoustic guitar, drums, programming) and with some guest guitarists set about recording 'English Ghosts'. But, when listening back they realised the quality was so poor that it was pretty much unusable, so Steve asked one of those guitarists, Stuart Martin, if there was anything he could do to salvage it. Eventually they realised that a remix wasn't going to achieve anything so Stuart and Steve set about re-recording most the album again, apart from some of the keyboard parts, and this is the result. In some ways, it is quite surprising to

realise that this release is as late as it is, as in many ways this feels that this is from the early Nineties. It is good solid neo prog, with some lengthy numbers (the title cut is nearly twenty minutes long).

What lets this down though, are the vocals. They just aren't strong enough, and the impression is that this would be a much better band altogether if they had a real singer, and it is of little surprise to me that Lee hasn't been involved in the band since this. Musically they have been paying close attention to bands from the early Nineties, and while Citizen Cain are one of the bands that are obvious, as are IQ, the biggest influence is Galahad. There are signs of real promise within the music, but there is always the feeling that this isn't the full article and there are things which could have been done to make it better but given the issues they had suffered during the recording it is amazing they got it out at all.

Solid, with some good points here and there, but not essential.
Jan 2017

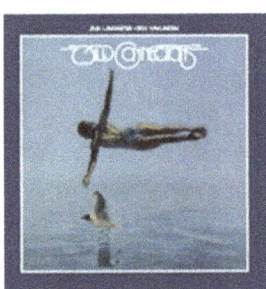

JACK LANCASTER & RICK VAN DER LINDEN
WILD CONNECTIONS
When I saw this listed in Gonzo as a new release last year I was immediately intrigued as I remember Jack from Blodwyn Pig, while I knew that Rick van der Linden was a Dutch keyboard player. When I discovered the album was originally released in 1979, and apart from drums (Barry Morgan from Blue Mink) and a choir, everything was played either on a Yamaha GX11S or a lyricon (electronic wind instrument that triggers patches), then I knew I had to hear it. Just how far out and experimental would this be? In fact, the answer to that is not very, as although this was all cutting edge at the time, that is 35 years in the past. But, instead of something that is now breaking the boundaries of music what we have here is an excellent synth album that doesn't really show its age at all.

This album is a sheer delight from start to end, with Rick and Jack in such harmony that often it isn't possible to tell which one is playing where. It is multi-layered and multi-faceted, and in many ways reminds me of some of Rick Wakeman's lighter albums (lighter as opposed to his New Age works which are quite different again). It may only be 36 minutes long but is of such quality that I am extremely surprised they didn't record any others together. Rick of course has had a long solo career, as well as being with the group Ekseption since the late Sixties, but this album is just so good I really wish that they had undertaken more together. As it is, all praise to Gonzo for making this available again as this certainly passed me by when it was released, and it deserves far more than that.
Mar 2014

LISA LARUE PROJECT 2K9
WORLD CLASS
Lisa is a keyboard player who has been influenced by progressive rock since a young age, and this was her fourth album, released in 2009, although she did call it a project which then led to the forming of her band Project 2KX. When I noticed that John Payne (Asia) was one of those involved I became very interested indeed, but the more I played it, the more disillusioned I became. There is a real lack of focus over the course of the album which leads to it seeming very disjointed indeed, and actually quite hard to follow. There are some really good progressive instrumental numbers where Lisa often finds herself in the supporting role to the very fine guitarwork of Steve Adams, but then these are broken up with some AOR songs and the result is the sum of the parts is very much less than it should be. If Lisa had concentrated on just an AOR album, or just an instrumental progressive rock album, then I am sure that either would have been more preferable than the end result. Well produced with some fine songs and performances, it isn't something to which I will often be returning.
May 2014

LAVA ENGINE
LAVA ENGINE
Originally formed in 2006, this Swedish progressive band had already been through a few different line-ups by the time they self-released this their debut EP in 2008. At this time, they were Magnus Florin (vocals & guitars), Ronnie Jaldemark (guitars & vocals), Christian Karlsson (drums) and Ian Varjanne (bass). Yep, although they originally had keyboards, this had changed by the time they came to record, although their progressive approach hadn't: I think the lack of keyboards is probably why they have been tagged 'prog metal', but I believe that 'neo' is much closer to the mark. They have obviously been influenced by Porcupine Tree as well, and the quality of the four songs on offer (especially "Blood", which is more than ten minutes long), would have had me believe that a lengthy career was on offer. However, it appears that another EP a few years after this one was all that would appear from these guys, and the website certainly hasn't been updated in a while. A real shame, as this EP shows promise, and I would very much have liked to have heard a full album. They deserved more than just leaving behind two EP's.
May 2014

THE LAZARUS TRIO
OPEN LETTERS
Back in 1998 I received a package from Malcolm Parker at Cyclops: that wasn't unusual as this was in the days before digital downloads, and I used to get packages nearly every day from record labels and bands, and Malcolm used to send me everything he released. Nothing prepared me for what I would hear when Cyclops CYCL 075 made its way onto

The Progressive Underground Vol 5

my CD player. The album was 'The Robbery of Murder', the band was Salem Hill, and I was entranced. Here was a concept album with a twist, a different way of looking at a car accident and the impact on the child, and music that was dynamic and powerful. The album made such an impact on me that it is still on my iPhone some 19 years after I first heard it and is one that I return to time and again. But what has that to do with The Lazarus Trio? I have kept an eye (and ear) on what Carl Groves, singer/songwriter/instrumentalist has been doing since those days and was delighted when he became lead singer of Glass Hammer for a while, as well as still working with Salem Hill. Then when I discovered he was involved with a new project, I had to hear it, and here we are, with The Lazarus Trio.

Just to clear a few things up though, firstly this isn't a trio, but a duo comprised of Michael Koeniger (vocals) and Carl (vocals and everything else). Michael is a composer and struggling musician who has never recorded professionally until now, a schoolteacher and military veteran who writes music in his spare time. Mike and Carl have been friends for decades and started working on this project during a joint family vacation. They have multiple musical influences; both share a fondness for progressive artists from Kansas to Haken as well as being fans of Kevin Gilbert.

This is a musical odyssey that started in the mind of a 17-year-old hitchhiking home on a rainy evening, and when the concept was presented to Carl Groves, the music started to solidify into the work presented on the final CD. Carl patiently worked with the "former 17-year-old" to get the musical ideas out of his head and into a listenable form. He also contributed many of his own musical ideas improving on the originals, and adding new compositions. These are the musical musings of two men who see the world through the lenses of family, fatherhood, philosophy, theology, partnership, military service, and mortality.

Given that all the music is played by Carl, it perhaps isn't surprising that in many ways this feels like a new Salem Hill album, yet there are enough points of difference that one can easily hear this is a quite different band. There are many harmony vocals, and this dual approach works well when they are both singing, or when it is just one as it creates dynamics and impact. Musically this covers many bases from Crossover progressive rock through some progressive metal, neo and symphonic. There are times when Carl really crunches the riffs and there is a very heavy bottom end, while at others he provides gentle accompaniment on acoustic guitar and piano.

I do find it hard to fathom that Michael hasn't recorded prior to this, as he has a wonderful voice, and his long-term friendship with Carl has also had a great impact as this feels like a complete album. There are no signs that this is a project, and that there is only one instrumentalist involved, as this feels like a full band, so all credit to Carl for the amount of time he must have put in on this multi-tracking all the different instruments.

Back in 1998 I heard an album that had a major impact on me, and only time will tell if in twenty years I am still playing this one, but do you know what? I think I might be, as I

love it, from the first note to the very last, and the more I play it the more I get out of it. Let's hope that it doesn't take thirty-five years for the duo to record another album together, but that they get their act together much quicker than that! Highly recommended.
Jun 2017

LEGO LEPRICONS
JUDITH, CALL SECURITY
One of the joys of having been writing about music for so long is that I often hear from bands asking if I would mind listening to their music, so I get to hear a lot of material that otherwise would have passed me by, and Lego Lepricons are a case in point. I haven't heard much progressive music from Israel (although I have some), and while this EP was released in 2012 it only came to my attention when the band contacted me towards the end of last year. So, I downloaded it and put it into my review list, and a few months later finally got around to listening to it. To say I was blown away was something of an understatement, so I did some more digging to discover where on earth this band had come from.

They describe themselves as post rock/space rock (they are much more the former and progressive than space) and were formed in 2011 by singer and musician Yair Ziv, keyboard player Shlomi Maya with their manager Leo Yaish. Shlomi Maya has played with many of the most influential Israeli musicians and singers (Hemi Rudner, Yirmi Kaplan, Shiri Maimon and many more), and is currently working with Haim Zinovich who produced and composed music to many well-known TV series such as 'The Sopranos', 'Sex and The City', 'ER' etc. Yair Ziv's career was formally launched in 2004 with the release of the single "Boee (come to me)" which went on to become one of the most popular songs in Israeli music history. So, both these guys have a real pedigree within their own country but have now turned their attention to creating something a bit different, with all lyrics in English, that owes a great deal to Radiohead, Muse and Elbow.

This is dynamic sweeping music, with a singer who knows he is good, really good. This means that there is a confidence throughout everything that they are doing and the reason this sounds like a seasoned band as opposed to a debut is that all those involved have been around for so long. The line-up for this EP was Yair Ziv (vocals, guitars), Roy Messiah (drums), Nitzan Berger (guitar and percussion), Shlomi Maya (piano, keyboards, and programming) while they brought in guest Yonatan Levital to provide the bass.

My only hope is that given it is so long since they released this EP they will soon have a full album to share with us! Powerful, dreamy, full of space and great emotion, this is a wonderful collection of songs that needs to be listened to by a far wider audience.
Apr 2014

LION SHEPHERD
HEAT

One day I was talking to my good friend and fellow writer Olav Bjørnsen in Norway, and he told me he had a duplicate of the new album by Lion Shepherd, and would I be interested in hearing it. A while later it turned up in the post, and I was impressed even before hearing it as here was a fold out digipak that opened out, so it formed a cross, with plenty of information on all sides, the booklet pasted into the top section, and the CD in the middle. A lot of effort and money had gone into this, and it is rare for a band to have that much spent on them unless they are quite special.

I undertook some research and was somewhat surprised to discover that the guys were Polish, based around singer Kamil Haidar and Mateusz Owczarek (electric guitars, acoustic guitars, Irish bouzouki). They were joined on the album by Łukasz Adamczyk (bass), Sławek Berny (drums, percussion), Kasia Rościńska (backing vocals) and Wojtek Olszak (keyboards). The reason I was surprised was that musically this certainly sounds as if its roots are in the UK and the US as well as the Middle East, and I firmly expected the band to come from one of those two countries.

They themselves describe their music as a "mix of world music, trance, progressive rock, blues, and Middle Eastern motifs. In addition to traditional European instruments, there is the Syrian oud lute, the Persian santur, and various Indian and Arabic percussion instruments." It is like nothing else I have ever heard from Poland, mixing and melding styles from many musical forms into something that is layered, polished, melodic and almost poppy on the first hearing, but with percussion and underlying musical motifs that transcend any particular genre or culture.

That this album is a masterpiece is never in doubt, that it is firmly one of my albums of the year is also something which isn't even up for debate. Each song brings a new delight, a new style, a new passion, and is one of those where the class and power shines through from the beginning to the very end. I knew it was special when I saw the packaging, I just didn't know how very special it was. This is essential.
Nov 2017

LIQUID SHADOW
SPECTRUM

Liquid Shadow were formed in 2000, but after four years decided to call it a day. Guitarist Przemek Drużkowski became part of well-known Polish act Millenium for their 2004 album 'Déjà Vu', while singer Sabina Godula provided backing vocals on the following year's 'Interdead' and later became lead singer with Loonypark, with whom she has now recorded four albums. Originally released in 2004, and then remastered in 2008, this is a collection of recordings made by the band between 2001 and 2003. Given that for the most part the music is either progressive rock or prog metal, there is a surprisingly large number of songs, fifteen for 67 minutes running time. Just a couple of these are sung in English, with the rest in Polish, and it isn't surprising to discover this is a collection of songs as opposed to a "proper" album, as there isn't a real flow throughout.

But, while the band may have said that they were influenced by Dream Theater, for the most part this is a much more commercial affair, and is an album that can be enjoyed on the first hearing. There may not be incredible depth to it, but there is certainly enough to be gained from playing it repeatedly. It is well-produced, the songs are quite catchy (even those sung in Polish), Sabina has a great voice and there is good interplay between guitarists Przemek and Jacek Bardo and keyboard player Krzysiek Lepiarczyk. I keep thinking that "Barok" is going to burst into a straight-out polka, as the music shines – this couldn't be from anywhere else than Poland. This probably wasn't easy to get hold of in 2008, and even less so now, but it is well worth hearing if you ever come across it.
Jan 2017

LITTLE TRAGEDIES
THE CROSS
I have heard a couple of other albums by Little Tragedies, but it is safe to say they didn't impress me nearly as much as this one did. Inspired heavily by the Seventies, and by ELP, this has a complexity and togetherness that is rarely displayed by other prog bands. It is full of dynamics, with gentle guitar and synthesised flute combining with fretless bass and rim shots to create a certain mood, yet at the next they can all be off and flying with every musician pursuing note density and complexity while always making perfect musical sense. It is more Western than Eastern, with just the vocals (performed by Gennady in a spoken style, in his native Russian) creating something that is obviously different. In some ways, it is the vocals that spoil this for me, as there is so much going on that they could easily have made this a fully instrumental album, and not bothered with the vocals at all. There are large sections where the band allow themselves to fully push themselves, with no words to heard, and it is here when they fully come alive.

The longest track, "The God Abandoned", is nearly twenty minutes in length, and vocals are there only for a small part of it, yet the song just flies by as the listener is taken deep into an incredible world of soaring keyboards and guitars, with majestic interplay between all those involved. Their site is available in English, and I urge every proghead to discover the joys of Little Tragedies.
Jan 2017

LIVES & TIMES
RATTLEBONES
Lives & Times were formed in 1988 by Richard Wileman (guitars, keys, percussion) and Lorna Cumberland (vocals). For the next three years they recorded demos, wrote songs, and played gigs with various line-ups but never succeeded in getting a record deal. In January 1991 they split through frustration and later that year Richard formed the No Image label with musician friend Nick Weaver. The first release was a compilation of material by Nick and Richard and Richard then contacted Lorna and they recorded four old Lives & Times songs. As it went so well Nick decided to start a new project, Eternal Energy, and Richard and Lorna resurrected Lives & Times.

'Rattlebones' was released in 1992, with Teresa Griffin joining on bass while Richard provides the rest of the instrumentation. Lorna's voice is clear and pure, immediately bringing forward thoughts of Kate Bush and Maryen Cairns. The music itself moves between straight pop, classical and even New Age, truly a Crossover band if ever there was one. The vocals and music combine well together, but it is the voice to which the listener is really drawn. All the songs here are good, but nothing really stands out, and while enjoyable is probably the weakest album they released. But given the scarcity of all their material if you see it, then grab it!
Jan 2014

LIVES & TIMES
THE PULL OF A TIDE
'The Pull of a Tide' came out in 1993, with Chris Brown now the resident bassist (although Teresa Griffin did play on a few tracks). The song writing had improved and broadened into new directions. "Who Do YOU Live For" starts with classical guitar but then turns very nearly into a rock song. Strong guitarwork and harmony vocals work well to create a standout track. "Kicking Against Nothing" is another example of the harder edge of L&T with a strong riff and chorus. That being said, this album is just as experimental as the first but songs such as these serve to really emphasis the point. Yet again there are some songs here that point to Richard's later (and current) work with Karda Estra, with "Evolution" being a fine example of his more classical style, albeit with synths and piano. Lorna's angelic vocals and Richard's fine accompaniment making this a real joy. If you enjoy good singing and don't want crashing guitars or complicated prog, then L&T provided well-structured songs that showed Lorna's voice off to best effect.
Jan 2014

LIVES & TIMES
WAITING FOR THE PARADE

'Waiting For The Parade' was the third album from L&T, and saw them sign with the Dutch label SI Music, who at the time was certainly one of the most important progressive labels in Europe. Phil Legende (of Lorien) is the only external musician, providing acoustic percussion on five of the nine tracks, while bass is provided this time by Richard himself. Right from the off the hallmarks of the earlier L&T albums are there, but for some reason they appear more accessible. The 'live' drumming definitely helps as well as it adds something to the songs. However, the most beautiful song on the album is "Deadline" where Richard on classical acoustic guitar provides the perfect backdrop for Lorna's haunting voice. Mind you, "Divide" comes a very close second as it gradually builds and builds while "Corners" again hints at the future, while also bringing in loads of influences from Steve Hackett and IQ.
Jan 2014

LIVES & TIMES
THE GREAT SAD HAPPY ENDING

This was the fourth album under the L&T banner, with multi-instrumentalist Richard Wileman again joined by singer Lorna Cumberland, with Andy Kittral providing bass. Lorna's vocals are reminiscent of Kate Bush and Maryen Cairns, and the music is the perfect foil as moods and atmosphere are created with seeming ease. It is this atmospheric interpretation that is the basis of their music: no room here for crashing guitars or pounding drums, but rather well thought out material of extremely high quality. Listening again to this album after so many years one thing I find interesting is there are some non-vocal numbers and passages that show that Richard was already starting to musically spread his wings, which of course would eventually lead to the demise of this band and the commencement of Karda Estra. In fact, "Wired to the Moon" could indeed be a KE number as opposed to L&T with its long orchestral filmscape feel.

Much of the album is devoted to providing superb accompaniment to Lorna's vocals, often with as little intervention and intrusion as possible, letting her really shine. It is an album full of space, depth and complexity, with the guitars often sounding quite frenetic but as they are kept low in the mix they don't take over. There are definite Hackett-ish qualities to much of this, and the result is an album that I have fallen in love with all over again, the best part of twenty years since I first heard it.
Jan 2014

LIVES & TIMES
THERE AND BACK AGAIN LANE
This was L&T's fifth album, and at the time I said I felt it was their most complete work to date, and I see no reason at all to change that opinion now. As with the previous album Andy Skittrall provides bass, Lorna Cumberland vocals and Richard Wileman everything else. Released in 1995 this was very different indeed to the rest of the British underground prog scene at the time (and yes, it was very much underground with only fanzines daring to write about prog at all, totally different to today), but they never felt they needed to follow anyone else and indeed travelled their own path. The album opens with an air of menace on "Why Do I Watch?" which leads into a characteristically atmospheric number. The tempo is increased along with the volume and menace, but Lorna's voice still rises like a soaring angel above it all. Classical guitar plays an important part in this song, adding little touches here and there which manage to emphasise the electric riffing guitar. The music is often complex but never wanders into realms of self-indulgence.

"Darker" shows a totally different side to their music, with overlaid vocals and a musical background that switches themes and style, yet with the melody underpinning it all. Again, this is a portent of things to come with Karda Estra, combining loads of different musical elements with vocals being just part of that. Hackett is again a main influence, and overall, this is a superb piece of work.
Jan 2014

LIVES & TIMES
HOARSE
After two CDs on their own No Image label, two more on SI and another on Cyclops, L&T released their sixth (and final) album back on their own label. Richard Wileman is still there of course, along with Andy Skittrall on bass (his third album for the band) and Phil Legende who guested on drums on their third album 'Waiting For The Parade', but the most important aspect to note is that vocalist Lorna Cumberland was no longer with the band! Her place was taken by Ileesha Bailey, who heralded a slight musical shift. This is now a more forthright songs-based outfit producing songs that wouldn't sound out of place either in the charts or on any singer-songwriter connoisseur's playlist. There is far more emphasis on guitars and much less on keyboards. Some of the songs such as "Let The Clouds All Melt Away" are commercial with only a few (such as "Landmarks") sounding rocky and more challenging.

The result is the most immediate album to date from the Swindon swingers and it is one that will appeal not only to diehard fans but also to many others who like female vocals and, most importantly, good songs. Of course, what no-one realized at this point was that this was going to be the final album from Lives and Times as Richard decided to follow a different musical direction and formed a new project, Karda Estra. Richard and Ileesha

still work together, but her voice is used in a very different way indeed, and I'm sure I'm not the only one who looks back at these albums and wonders why they were never well-known, as it was certainly deserved.
Jan 2014

LOONYPARK
EGOIST

Polish band Loonypark was formed in 2007 by Krzysztof Lepiarczyk (keyboards) and Jakub Grzesło (drums). They soon found the right singer in Sabina Godula-Zając (who had previously been in Liquid Shadow with Krzysztof and had sung with Millenium), and Krzysztof then looked to another of his previous bands, Meteopata, for guitarist Piotr Grodecki and bassist Piotr Lipka. For a debut album, this is a polished affair, but given the guys had all been around the scene for a while that probably isn't too surprising. Unlike Liquid Shadow, here all the vocals are in English, which immediately makes it more accessible for those who don't understand Polish, and the music is also quite different in that here it is far more reflective, and not nearly so in your face.

It contains elements of symphonic prog, mixed with good strong melodies and sensibilities while also using some wonderful Camel or Jadis-style guitar lines. There is a real warmth to the keyboards, and Sabina has beautiful control and timbre that gives the music a depth and quality sadly missing from many bands. It certainly doesn't come across as a debut, there is far more power and passion, but all restrained and dealt with in the right manner. Guitarist Maciek Tomczyk, who later turned up in the Polish avant-garde metal band Luc Occulta, is a guest on this album for some of the songs, and it is hard to imagine that he later became more abrasive as here his guitar sings gently and sweetly, combining with some wonderfully dated keyboard sounds to create something quite special. Poland has long been a haven for some amazing progressive bands, and Loonypark are yet another strong act.
Jan 2017

LOONYPARK
UNBROKEN SPIRIT LIVES IN US

This was the third album from Polish act Loonypark, and in the intervening years there was just the one line-up change with drummer Jakub Grzesło departing prior to their 2011 release, 'Straw Andy', being replaced by Grzegorz Fieber. In many ways, this is quite a different album to the debut, which perhaps isn't surprising given there were seven years between the two, as the band were by now confident in what they were doing, and it is this confidence that shines through in everything they touch. It is more symphonic than before, and whereas the power was somewhat restrained in the past, here it is allowed more freedom. Sabina hits the notes she wants to, and maintains them without a quiver, standing proud to the world, showing she knows she has the voice, and is going to use it.

The delicate guitar lines that were the trademark sound of the debut are still here, but not as frequent as they once were. The band have shifted so that Krzysztof's keyboards are even more important than they were previously: they are much more integral to the overall being that is Loonypark. He isn't afraid to play delicate piano if that is what is needed, or use the sounds of a harpsichord, while Piotr Lipka brings in a fretless bass to give that extra warmth, or they can easily move into all-out bombastic over the top symphonic prog. There is a real sense of space within the music, so the listener can move between the interweaving strands and concentrate on whatever seems to be the most important. "Treasure" is a real highlight, with so much delicacy at the beginning that it feels as if a gossamer thread is being woven, before being blasted away just in time for them to start the process all over again. I became a fan of Loonypark when I first heard their debut all those years ago, but this album is just so much more than I could ever have imagined they would become. Awesome.
Jan 2017

LORIAN
VIRGINAL MIND

Recorded in 1994, this is the only album from German band Lorian, who appeared to make it through that decade before vanishing without trace. This isn't a newly reissued lost masterpiece but was sent to me to see if I would consider them for the Crossover sub-genre of ProgArchives. The answer to that was "no", as this is a melodic rock/neo-prog album, very much of its time, but not one that would fit within the sub-genre I'm involved with. Given what Lorian were competing against back in the day, they certainly stand up against the bands that were also starting to become active at that time, and the recording and release quality is good even by today's standards.

But, while they were a class above many who were also attempting to break through, they are still a very long way from bands such as Galahad, IQ, Pendragon, Pallas, and the like. The songs are frequently passive and miss out on the energy that is needed to drive this style of music forward. Of the previous four, it is probably with Pallas they are most similar, and it is possible that their music would have progressed onwards if they had managed to stay together, but we will never know.
Sep 2017

LOS RANDOM
PIDANOMA

According to their website, Los Random are an experimental trio from Tucumán, Argentina, who mix distant sounds from all quarters and kinds, creating their unique, eclectic, and unpredictable music, which they define as "Incorrect". Starting in 2009, they

have to date released one other full-length release and an EP, all with the same line-up of Pablo Lamela (bass), Raúl García Posse (guitar, vocals) and Marcos Crosa (drums). Musically this is all over the place, blending free jazz with Faith No More, Tool with Meshuggah, Art Zoyd and Hawkwind, and the result is a chaotic musical maelstrom where there are no rules, and all that matters is the music and following the path even though there appears to be no rational reason for doing so. In many ways it reminds me of the first time I listened to Axis of Perdition, as although I knew I was part of only a small group of people who would really appreciate it, I also knew I had to keep listening as I was almost mesmerized by what was going on.

The use of sax on "Me Chango" is inspired, giving the music a very different feel, and it would have been interesting to hear more of that, possibly on a fully instrumental album, to allow their space rock feel to really come through. This is progressive in its' truest sense, as it attempts to break through what many people would even believe what is music at all, let alone the subgenres and pigeonholes. Play this to most people and they won't see it through the first song, it is only a few of us that can get inside these guys minds and understand that what they are bringing to the scene is something new and incredibly exciting. Miss this at your peril, but you may not like it very much.
May 2014

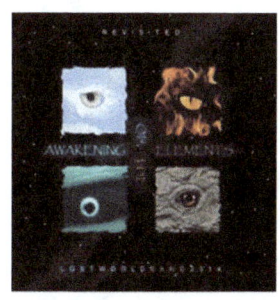
LOST WORLD BAND
AWAKENING OF THE ELEMENTS – REVISITED
Back in 1990, three friends at music college formed a band, calling themselves Lost World. It took until 2003 for the debut album to be released, 'Trajectories', and after 'Awakening of the Elements' in 2006 the guys made a slight change to the name and added 'Band'. Although there had been some line-up changes over the years, the original three, Vassili Soloviev (flute), Andy Didorenko (acoustic and electric guitars, bass, acoustic and electric violins) and Alexander Akimov (keyboards, percussion, programming, sound design) are still there (and indeed all played on the most recent album, 2016's 'Of Things and Beings'). But 2011 saw the guys working with a new drummer, Konstantin Shtirlitz, and Andy's thoughts started to turn back to their second album, and wondered what it would sound like if they re-recorded the drums, added violins and then remixed it.

Well, it came out so well they released it. I don't think I ever heard the original Musea CD, but I am so glad that Andy thought that I might like to hear this version! Russia has produced some amazing progressive rock outfits, and Lost World Band have been a strong favourite of mine since I was sent the debut all those years ago (and looking among my racks I see I still have it). Influenced by the likes of King Crimson and UK, they can easily switch lead instruments from electric guitar to violin or flute and given they met at music college it is of course no surprise at all that they are all masters of their instruments. But it is the arrangements and interplay that makes this album such a delight to listen to. There is a confidence and maturity that is pervasive, and Konstantin knows exactly what to add to provide emphasis and contrast to the melody. It can't have been an easy task taking on the role he was asked, but the result is something that is complete, fresh, and totally enjoyable from beginning to end.

They can be bright and energetic, or laid back and thoughtful, while the opening title cut comes across as a mix of Kansas and Jethro Tull, with some more rocky guitar and a delightful Seventies feel as well as leads from both flute and violin. This is a great album, that flows and moves, so much so that the listener is never really sure where they are going to end up, but it doesn't matter as the journey is always so interesting. If you've never investigated Russian progressive rock then you should, and Lost World Band and this album are a great place to start.
Jul 2017

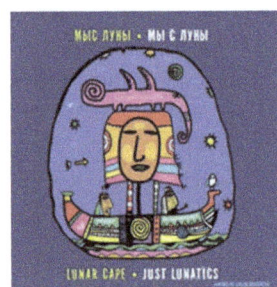

LUNAR CAPE
JUST LUNATICS
Formed in Moscow in 2011, this is the debut (and so far, only) album from progressive rock/jazz fusion instrumental outfit Lunar Cape. The line-up is Petrovsky Nikolay (Electro-Nick) on guitar, harmonica, alto recorder, Olga Scotland on flute, mandolin, alto recorder, sopranino recorder, Paul Bulak (SadFat) keyboards, guitar, sound effects, Andrey Shashkov – bass guitar, basso recorder, Mikhail Zolotarev, drums, and Ilya Myasin – soprano recorder. Yes, there is a lot of woodwinds on here, most unlike many other bands around. Although there are times when they do come across as similar to Jethro Tull, due to the way the lead flute is being played more than anything else, they have also been clearly influenced by Gentle Giant in particular, and western Seventies prog in general. For some reason, I also kept thinking of Camel, just because of the way they approach the music, but they sound nothing like them at all.

From the first time I put this on I found I had a smile on my face, as this album truly is a delight from beginning to end. I find it hard to believe they have yet to be picked up by a label that can do them justice, as this is timeless music that certainly deserves to be heard by a far wider audience. It can be in your face, or reflective and gentle, and although it may never turn into rapids, this is a babbling stream of musical water that has a great deal to offer. The song "Motorbike" commences with influences from South America, before gradually turning into something both more Cuban and Celtic, as if Clannad or Enya have been on holiday to warmer climes. The more I play this the more I like it and have discovered that this is music that really does benefit both from headphones and having the eyes closed, so it can be fully concentrated on with no distractions whatsoever. A beautiful album, I can only hope that there is enough support for another one soon.
Nov 2017

MACHINE MASS feat. DAVE LIEBMAN
INTI
There has been a change to both the band name and line-up since Machine Mass Trio's debut in 2011, as although Michel Delville is still here on guitars and electronics, and fellow douBt colleague Tony Bianco is still providing the drums, they have a new saxophonist/flautist in the shape of legendary Dave Liebman. Known as one of the hardest working saxophonists in jazz, he has released more than a hundred albums as either band leader or co-leader, and has guested on many hundreds more, with credentials that are second to none. Note, there are only three musicians, and this album was recorded in a single afternoon, with first takes used for the most part. Both Michel and Tony trigger loops and sounds while they are playing, using computers to assist with the load, and some of the loops are themselves more than 100 bars long. It certainly never seems that there are only three musicians involved, and certainly not that the whole thing was recorded without any overdubs.

That they are all consummate musicians is never in doubt, and the way they support each other within the framework of a song is quite astounding. The drumming on "In a Silent Way" really takes the song to a totally different level, with Michel and Dave playing quite gently and in a very controlled manner, which is the total opposite of what Tony is delivering from behind the kit. It is this dichotomy of sound, the use of structures and arrangements that should never really fit together that makes this album work as well as it does. This is a fresh landscape, new, exciting and vibrant. There are vocals on just the one song, "The Secret Place", which are provided by Saba Tewelde, and while it is interesting, I did find this is something of a distraction to the rest of the album as there isn't the same feeling of adventure and vitality. But that is just a minor niggle, as overall this is an album that fans of modern jazz really ought to be seeking out.
Jun 2014

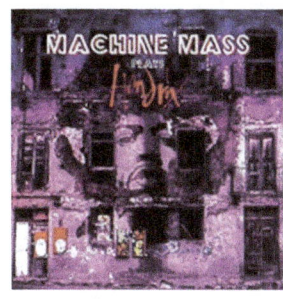

MACHINE MASS
PLAYS HENDRIX
Yet again there have been some changes in the Machine Mass camp, and here founder members, guitarist Michel Delville (The Wrong Object; douBt; Alex Maguire Sextet) and drummer Anthony Bianco (douBt; Elton Dean; Dave Liebman) have brought in keyboard player Antoine Guenet (The Wrong Object; Sh.TG.N; Univers Zero), to assist them in their adventures. As a starting point the album is quite simple in its intent, namely that in one day last March the trio recorded some Hendrix songs live in the studio to celebrate the 50th anniversary of 'Are You Experienced?'. It's just from there that it gets more complex.

Everyone has their favourite Hendrix songs, and probably also their favourite Hendrix covers. For me there has always been something whimsical and emotive about 'The Wind Cries Mary", while I still believe that The Hamsters monumental album from 1990,

'Electric Hamsterland', takes some beating. But what we have here is something that Hendrix himself would have probably appreciated, namely three top musicians taking his songs as a starting point and then improvising, twisting and melding them into something that is barely recognisable yet paying true homage to the craftsman who created them initially. Whenever a guitarist dares to cover a song created by a master they are putting themselves up to fail, but what Michel has done here brilliantly is not only show that he too is a genius with his instrument but has filled the interpretations full of jazz intensity and experimentalism, to create something that cannot be directly compared as it is just so very different indeed. While fans of Jimi will enjoy hearing what Machine Mass have managed to do with classic Hendrix songs, this album is also very much for those who may not be close to the originals. Antoine uses some wonderful Hammond sounds as Anthony tries to keep everything under control while Michel sounds like he is deconstructing his guitar while somehow keeping sounds emanating from it. This album is incredibly impressive on every level, from the musicianship and arrangements through to the way they have ripped this material to pieces and then put it back, lovingly and with honour, into a brand-new format. And that they finish with "The Wind Cries Mary" is the icing on the cake. Superb.
Jul 2017

MAGENTA
THE TWENTY SEVEN CLUB
Yet again Magenta are working as a core trio, with Christina Booth (vocals), Chris Fry (guitars) and Rob Reed (everything else) plus a guest drummer in Andy Edwards. Now, I have known Rob for many years and even put Cyan on the cover of Feedback in another lifetime and have followed his musical adventures with interest. But it has been with Magenta he has made his name within the neo-prog scene, and this album will only do more to enhance that reputation. This is a concept album in the sense that each of the songs is about a different musician who passed away when they were 27, so for example we start with "The Lizard King" and end with "The Devil At The Crossroads", and throughout we are treated to some wonderful soaring progressive rock, and while Rob is at the heart of what is happening musically it is Christina who will always be the star of the show.

She has a wonderful voice, with great range, control, and emotion, with a timbre not unlike Steve Nicks in her prime, yet with more soul and passion. Rob knows how to write material that is going to highlight this, and together they have combined to produce another album that is sheer class from start to finish. Chris's guitar provides the cut through that provides the additional edge that is needed, the harsher solo that takes away any thoughts of saccharine, the rock riffs that provide the depth. Andy Edwards proves yet again why he is such a sought-after drummer with a powerful performance, while Rob is everywhere, providing fills and solos in whatever instrument he is using.

This is a band with a large sound, and in Christina they have one of the finest singers around, combined with music that is always searching for a way forward. Some may

condemn this as just another neo-prog album, as for some reason that is a sub-genre which purists often look down upon, but I and many others really enjoy this as a musical form, and there are as few as adept at it as Magenta. It may not be in quite the same league as 'Seven' but is a fine album all the same and one I enjoyed immensely.
May 2014

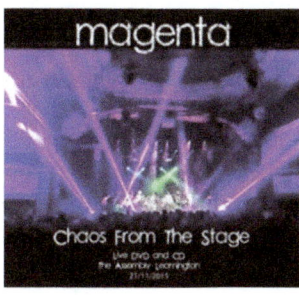

MAGENTA
CHAOS FROM THE STAGE
Recorded live at The Assembly, Leamington Spa on 21st November 2015, this DVD + CD set takes its title from the final song on the set, "The Lizard King". I don't have the DVD but have heard that the picture and camera quality is excellent and given how good the sound is on this recording I wouldn't have expected anything less. Since they first started working together in 2001, singer Christina Booth and multi-instrumentalist Robert Reed have continually produced excellent albums, and it is a particular regret of mine that I never managed to catch them in concert, especially now I have heard this. Joining them in the band is Chris Fry (guitars), Dan Nelson (bass) and Andy Edwards (drums) and the over-arching feeling that one gets from playing this is that here is a band in total control at all times.

They all understand their roles, when to hang back and let someone else take the spotlight, so there is always a feeling of space. The harmonies and some of the arrangements could have come from Floyd, other sections could have come from Yes, but in reality, it is solid Magenta, showing there is still plenty of life in Seventies-style progressive rock. "Lust", taken from the mighty 'Seven' (can't believe that album came out 14 years ago) moves all over the place, with the bass taking the song into new places, hoping the drums will manage to keep up while Rob and Chris have a delicate battle. Then there is Christina, a singer who never fails to deliver, both in emotion and pitch, always in control. She lets the boys have their fun, but then comes in with poise and grace, taking the song to another level. There is no doubt that Magenta are still one of the very top prog acts in the UK, and if you have somehow missed them then is the place to start.
Jan 2018

NICK MAGNUS
CHILDREN OF ANOTHER GOD
Nick first started his musical career with The Enid, but it will be with Steve Hackett with whom he will always be most associated with. He toured as part of his band, and of course provided keyboards on albums such as 'Spectral Mornings', 'Highly Strung' and 'Defector'. In many ways, the opening title cut could have come from the last of these, and given that Nick of course is on keyboards, with John Hackett (flute) and Steve Hackett (guitar) very much in evidence perhaps that isn't

too surprising. This isn't a Steve Hackett solo album, but it can be heard from just this one song how important Nick's contributions were to those seminal works, with very similar keyboard sounds being utilised to what we all know so very well. Vocals on that number is by Tony Patterson (probably best known for his time with ReGenesis), but another ex-'Defector' luminary takes that role on "Doctor Prometheus", which to my ears is much more of an Alan Parsons Project romp and is great fun with a bouncy singalong style.

It is an incredibly diverse album, with one of the highlights being "The Others", which is far more orchestral in feel, with some delicate acoustic guitar and wonderful vocals from Linda John-Pierre. Quite simply, this is a beautiful song that sounds as if it has been taken from a stage musical, where it is the closing finale of the first act. Restrained passion and power never sounded quite so good. Nick provides vocals himself on "Identity Theft", and while this is in many ways the weakest song on the album his voice is pleasant, and I am sure he could have undertaken more of this role if he had wished to. This is an album that is solid but not brilliant but does contain some glorious moments. Well worth hearing if you get the opportunity.
Jan 2017

MAJESTIC
ARRIVAL
In 2004, multi-instrumentalist Jeff Hamel (from prog-metallers Osmium) started working as Majestic, working mostly on his own with just the occasional guest singer. After releasing a couple of albums, he joined forces with vocalist and lyricist Jessica Rasche, and together they worked on 'Arrival', which was released in 2009. There are only four songs, but with an album length of over 77 minutes you can work out for yourself that they are a little long. In fact, there are only two real epics, with the two in the middle being 'just' nine minutes each. At no point this this seem like a project, as there is a real band feel to the proceedings and there is also a great deal of restraint so that all the music makes sense as opposed to self-indulgency, which can creep in on some projects. Another thing that really hits home is the lack of fat within the songs. The first time I played this I was astounded when I realized that "Grey" has been playing for more than twenty minutes as I had the impression that it had only been on the player for a very short period of time.

Symphonic, yet with plenty of prog metal overtones, elements of Floyd mixed with some of Dream Theater, this is a heck of an album. If you go to the website and sign up to the newsletter you can download some albums free of charge, so why not give it a try?
May 2014

MAYAN
ANTAGONISE
There are times that when a band is described as being part of a sub-genre that in itself is part of another sub-genre that one just wants to not bother listening to the album, as how

on earth can that be right? Well, back with their second album Mayan prove again just how wrong that idea can be, as what we have here is a Symphonic Death Metal band who are exactly that. Originally this started as a project conceived by Mark Jansen (Epica) and his old friend, Jack Driessen (ex-After Forever), and they put together a band with some guest singers (including current Nightwish vocalist Floor Jansen). Well, Floor is back again for this album, but there has been a firming of the ranks and there are now seven full-time members, three of whom are singers. Songs such as "Insano" allow soprano Laura Macri to show her paces, but for the most part her role is to provide support to the main leads of Mark Jansen (grunts and screams) and Henning Basse. Musically there is a great deal going on, and the guys aren't afraid to bring out the acoustic when the time is right, but for the most part this is brutal metal with keyboards being orchestrated to bring an over-the-top appeal to the material. It is polished, and extremely complex, but there are times such as with "Human Sacrifice" where the symphonic passages are used to highlight just how heavy and strong these guys can be when they want to.

There have been a few albums in this style recently, and when bands get it right, I am stunned at just how bombastic and intense this can be. To say that Mayan have it right is something of an understatement as this is everything one could wish for with an album, with great songs, wonderful musical performances and vocals, while the production is also top rate. This is definitely worth discovering.
Jun 2014

MICE ON STILTS
AN OCEAN HELD ME
When I was first asked to join the Crossover team on ProgArchives I was intrigued enough to say "yes", the result of which has been that I now spend way too much time listening to bands and working on the site as opposed to just writing reviews. But the huge positive is that I get to hear bands that otherwise would pass me by, and MOS is a case in point. They were recommended to us to see if we felt that they would be a worthy addition, so I added them to the list and jumped over to their Bandcamp site to play the album. 34 minutes later I was in quite a state, as I had just played a debut EP that honestly is quite different to most of the music I am sent to listen to. Then the realization slowly came that these guys were Kiwi, current, and playing in and around Auckland! Now, to be fair to the local music scene I don't get out much, as I live in the middle of nowhere some 70 kms north of Auckland (although I pay rates to Auckland Council even though I'm not on the mains water or sewage system and have a gravel road and no streetlights or public transport – of course I'm an Aucklander!! Yeah, right). But I had never come across this band at all, and that was a loss to me, and if I wasn't finding out about them when I live in a small country, who on earth would have heard this name outside NZ?

I'm getting ahead of myself. Locally recorded and produced, this was released on the local Triple A Records (Allgood Absolute Alternative) as a digipak, with a booklet and is a great presentation, which makes it worthwhile getting this instead of just the download. The band was put together by Ben Morley (guitar, vocals) and contains a large and interesting musical line-up, with the rest of the band comprising Sam Hennessy (viola), Aaron Longville (saxophone/trumpet), Rob Sander (drums), Sam Nash (bass), Nick Wright (piano/Rhodes/vocals) and Joseph Jujnovich (vocal effects). Yes, you did read that correctly, here is a seven-piece band trying to make a name for themselves in small venues. Also, did you note that it contains both brass and strings? Lastly, what about having someone who provides vocal effects and what exactly does it all mean?

Only five songs, but they create a world where nothing else exists apart from the music and vocals. I have been trying to think who they remind me of, and in some ways, it is early Pink Floyd, Muse, Radiohead, VDGG, Peter Hammill, Roy Harper and others, but mostly it is Mice On Stilts. Here we have a band that are a stated seven-piece but in fact are an eight-piece with that incredibly important musician, Space, used effectively and throughout. Just because there are many musicians doesn't mean they are all necessarily playing at the same time (although they can and do), and it is this use of silence as an important musical layer that assists in the dramatic shifts that can take place. "Vulnerable Vader" goes from sublime to chaotic and both styles are affected by the presence of the other. Joseph is also playing an integral part, as his use of effects often brings together different styles or provides that over the top element that is just what the song needs. The longest song is the closer, "Tuatara Lawn" at 12:36 (for those who haven't come across that word before, and to be honest I hadn't before coming here, tuatara are reptiles endemic to this country and which, although resembling most lizards, are part of a distinct lineage), and the only issue I have with the song is that it is actually way too short! The only thing that keeps my sanity is putting the whole album on repeat and playing it time and again.

Of course, once I had discovered them, I had to go and see them live so last month I managed to catch up with them at a local venue, and I and 50 other brave souls saw an incredible performance with the guys hardly having any room to move on stage yet somehow managed to reproduce music that is incredibly deep, moving and emotional. The only thing that let the evening down, was when I was approached by someone who thought that the only reason someone of my age would be attending would be because my son was in the band!! That night I did learn that these guys are actually even more powerful in concert than on record: they did remind me of a young Pink Floyd building and working at their craft, and if they had suddenly dropped "Interstellar Overdrive" into their set I wouldn't have been surprised (they didn't). I am going to see them again in a couple of days at a rather larger festival, and I can't wait to see them in a bigger setting as if they can do that when they have to stay rooted to the spot what are they going to do when they have some freedom?

Too often these days music can be shallow and one-dimensional, but this is multi-faceted and contains a maturity that should not be overlooked.
Mar 2014

MILLENIUM
VOCANDA 2013 LIVE IN STUDIO
2013 saw the fifteenth anniversary of Lynx Music, quite an achievement for a label that concentrates on progressive rock. To mark the event, Ryszard Kramarski decided that his band Millenium should undertake a special performance of 'Vocanda', which they released in 2000. Obviously, they needed to rehearse for such an event, and a month before the gig they congregated at the studio and recorded the rehearsal so they could play it back and check if anything needed amending. The concert was well received, but wasn't professionally recorded, so Ryszard thought that it would be a nice idea to make this available for fans, in a strictly limited numbered edition. It isn't a studio album, nor is it a live album as there is no audience but has the band playing the new arrangements with no overdubs, so in many ways it is a combination of both.

Having played this quite a lot, I feel I am very fortunate to have been introduced to this band all those years ago as I have many of their albums in my collection and each and every single one is a joy. There are many neo influences in what they do, especially IQ and Pendragon, and Ryszard understands the need for rock guitar as part of this so doesn't hog the limelight but ensures that Piotr Płonka has plenty of time centre stage. Singer Łukasz Gall's voice is as powerful and strident as it was when he first sang this all those years ago, but guest Karolina Leszko also has a major part to play, and she provides lush harmonies or the occasional lead when the music is right.

Poland has had some great progressive bands over the years, with Collage and SBB being of particular note, but Millenium more than stand up with them, and this is yet another wonderful album from the guys, even more impressive is that it is live in the studio. Highly recommended.
May 2014

RICK MILLER
HEART OF DARKNESS
Less than a year after I reviewed 'Immortal Remains', here I am writing about Rick's 2014 release 'Heart of Darkness'. This is his fourth in four years, and his ninth since 2003, but there is no sign at all of him having an issue with quality control, as this one is better than his last! This is an incredibly emotive album, extremely deep and full of passion, even when there are just a few instruments being used, as it is the arrangements that really make such a difference. Guitars can be duetting with the wonderful flute of Sarah Young (whose contribution to this album cannot be overstated), or there can be just gentle drums and keyboards, all I know is I find myself drawn into the world that he is creating time and again. Some may say there are elements reminiscent of classic Floyd or Camel, but I also found large elements of John 'Rabbit' Bundrick, especially his 'Moccasin Warrior' albums as the flute is often used more as a native

instrument than as if it were being wielded by a bug-eyed one-legged madman.

My 17-year-old got into the car the other day when this was playing, and her normal reaction is to grab the iPod and choose something that she wants instead (normally Bowling For Soup), but after a few minutes she actually turned up the volume and said, "you know what, this isn't bad". High praise indeed from this teenager (even though her first ever gig, at the age of 9, was The Flower Kings where she sat on the corner of the stage). "Castle Walls" is simply a beautiful song, with wonderful, orchestrated arrangement and acoustic guitar that allows Rick to sing his heart out. I keep being reminded of some of the classic Sixties pop numbers and could imagine The Small Faces or Cat Stevens having a go at this.

There is no doubt that this is a great album, a real breakthrough in so many ways, and now all that is needed is for others to try it out for themselves.
Jun 2014

MINDFIELDS
ONE
Mindfields were a Polish five-piece who recorded just the one album back in 2007, and then no more. Well, that's not exactly true as drummer Tomasz Paśko (who also provided the lyrics, which are all in English) has a day job in the wonderful Millennium, while guitarist Marcin Kruczek has appeared in Moonrise, and he and keyboard player Rafał "Karmel" Muszyński provided the music. The line-up is completed by bassist Wojtek Famielec (later in Redemptor and Disperse) and singer Rafał Gołąbowski. So, was this ever meant to be more than a one-album project? Hard to tell this far down the track, but what they have left behind is an album that is certainly worth searching out for those who enjoy great songs, heavily influenced by the likes of Camel and Alan Parsons Project.

Like those bands, this album contains music that has plenty of space within it, and a lightness that combines with melodic, almost pop, sensibilities. Although the rhythm section has an important part to play, the ear is drawn mostly to the deftness of touch displayed by Marcin. This guy can play, really play, but this is far more than just shredding, it is all about playing exactly the right notes in the right style to create the impact. Rafał also has a wonderful touch, and this is clear when he is playing piano as opposed to keyboards. This is a multi-layered sound, music that is both timeless and ageless, and although the vocals have their part to play, and are sung in a delicate manner, I found myself happier when listening to the lengthy instrumental passages. Ideas are bounced between the two main protagonists, and when the time is right the guitar crunches hard, but that is just to provide the counterpoint to the next delicate passage. Five proper songs, with three vignettes (one of which, "Sunrise", is a beautiful demonstration of what is so good about acoustic classic guitars), there is a great deal of depth, a wonderful world to be discovered.

This is a beautiful album in just so many ways, and now that ten years has gone past, possibly the time is right to do another? Please?
Jan 2017

MIND PORTAL
½: THOUGHT AND MATTER

There aren't many instrumental quartets playing prog metal, yet here we have a Russian band back with their second album doing just that. I've been able to find out very little about them, and that is a real shame, as when music is as good as this then there is a requirement for people to know about it! Hailing from Voronezh they liken themselves to acts such as Liquid Tension Experiment and Joe Satriani, and I for one can also hear plenty of Steve Vai in some of the shredding and arrangements. Guitarist Grigory Kuronov also provides all the music, although it is then arranged by the band, but this isn't as much a guitar fest as one might imagine from that as he ensures that Vyacheslav Bessonov (keys) also has the opportunity to shine and they often duet, or one gives major support to the other. The rhythm section of Vitaly Zotov (bass) and Roman Gorodnyansky (drums) is extremely tight, and this allows the other two to crank it up and have some fun.

Although they are wonderfully melodic (with more than a touch of the Seventies AOR scene at times), this is first and foremost a band that is happily more into metal than rock. They run through the crunching guitars, with loads of complexity when it is the right time, but they don't ram their musical virtuosity into the throats and ears of their listeners. Vyacheslav has more than a hint of Don Airey about what he does, providing the musical finesse and cream that allows Grigory to really crunch the riffs when he wants to, or shred like a demon at others. This is a real gem of an album, one that is accessible the first time it is played and just keeps getting better.
Jun 2014

MIRIODOR
COBRA FAKIR

Miriodor formed in 1980 in Québec City and have been through some different band formats since then but are currently a trio comprising founding musicians Pascal Globensky (keyboards, synths, piano) and Rémi Leclerc (drums, percussion, keyboards, turntable) along with long-time member Bernard Falaise (guitars, bass, keyboards, banjo, turntable). Miriodor have long been members of the international RIO movement, but what I find amazing is just how immediate this music is, although it is complex in the extreme and some would find it incredibly challenging. To my ears it is a staccato world where not only am I welcome, but it is somewhere I want to stay as long as I can.

They have given this album the right title, as a cobra fakir is a snake charmer, who uses carefully concocted melodies to put the mighty reptile into a trance from which there is no escape. That is the same here, as once this hits the player nothing else exists. Imagine Gentle Giant and King Crimson combined at their most eclectic and not allowed out of the studio until they have come up with something that is breathtakingly brilliant, and you may be close to what this is all about. There is no doubt in my ears that this is one of the most important albums ever to come from the wonderful Cuneiform stable and here is something for everyone into RIO, prog, avant music, jazz and/or they have an open mind as to where music can take them. In many ways hard to describe, and certainly hard to ignore, this is a compelling piece of work.
Jan 2014

MIRIODOR
SIGNAL 9
So, the Canadians are back with their ninth studio album, and a slight change in line-up as they move back to a quartet, but as all the guys play multiple instruments anyway there isn't a noticeable difference in that area. As with the excellent 'Cobra Fakir', the first word that springs to mind is "staccato", as this is music that is rapidly moving around and for the most part doesn't have time for long held-down chords but just wants to get on with it. Coming from a RIO/Avant background, they have been listening to some of the early Canterbury bands as well as to King Crimson and Art Zoyd to create something that is always interesting and complex, and just a little different to much that is available within the prog scene, let alone mainstream.

It is the type of album that will polarise opinions, as those who like it will enjoy it a great deal, while others will fall into the "what on earth are you listening to" camp and won't give this album the time it both needs and deserves to get the most out of it. This is complex, with lots of melodies and countermelodies, with Bernard Falaise often crunching the guitar against myriad keyboard sounds, but that can all change in an instant. It is music that does demand respect and attention, and those prepared to do just that will get a great deal out of this, as it is incredibly rewarding.
May 2017

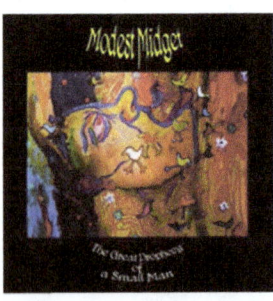

MODEST MIDGET
THE GREAT PROPHECY OF A SMALL MAN
Modest Midget was a project put together by Lionel Ziblat, a classically trained composer, multi-instrumentalist, and singer. This the debut album was released in 2010, with Lionel playing most of the music himself, along with a few guest musicians (most of whom aren't named or recognised, so it isn't possible to even say how many people were involved). This really is one of those albums that is a reviewer's nightmare as not only are the songs quite different to each other, but there is such a fractured

mix of styles going on that it is hard to pin down what is happening, apart from knowing it is excellent (and then being frustrated at not having the words to hand to describe it). The one band these guys do get compared to more than any other is Gentle Giant, but of course they sound nothing like them, although I can understand where some people may say that given some of the arrangements. It is spiky energetic music that at times brings in Zappa and Cardiacs, as well as plenty of British pop. I can imagine The Kinks having fun with this, but really have no idea why, nor why Traffic should also be included. But I swear that if you hear this then it will all make sense, maybe.

It is progressive, but in its truest sense, and mixed with so many Sixties pop sensibilities that one can almost see the Carnaby Street suits and swagger. It certainly sounds like an album that has come out of London, with some American influences, and not from an Argentinian who lived in Israel before settling in Holland. Confused? You should be, but all you need to know is that this is awesome.
May 2017

MODEST MIDGET
CRYSIS
Although some EPs were released in the time following their 2010 debut album, it took until 2014 for the second album to be made available on Lionel Ziblat's own label. This new album illustrates life, portrayed as a cycle consisting of several inner cycles, and each time a cycle ends, another one starts, and these movements are often frightening, painful and traumatic, but they also offer a chance for change and for growth. The named musicians joining Lionel in this were Tristan Hupe (keyboards), Maarten Bakker (bass guitar/keyboards) and Willem Smid (drums) with yet more guests who are un-named. I love this quote from the band, which probably does a better job of summing up this album that I can, "It might seem impossible at first to have a grip on the band's musical style. How would one go about trying to explain an inconceivable mixture of Rock, Soul, Baroque, Ska, Jazz, Punk, Symphonic Rock, Sicilian Tarantella & Romanian Gypsy music? Still, it is the great pride of the band having chosen not to succumb to any particular existing category and to simply embrace music in all its glory."

As one can easily see from the list above, this is music which is defying all attempts to categorise it, apart from throwing it into crossover progressive rock as that is really the only place that fits with their refusal to accept any musical boundary and then bringing in melodic pop as well! This is vibrant, exciting, and their quirky ska-style take on "(Oh) Pretty Woman" must be heard to be believed. It's awesome. Towards the end of 2015 Lionel issued the following statement, "In case you were wondering about the band these days, I personally took some time off to work on several different projects, composing and arranging music for different ensembles and other productions. But I'm also contemplating recording a couple of new albums. When the time comes, you will know." I only hope that we do see him back with more material at some point as Modest Midget are a quirky, nonsensical great band.
May 2017

MOGADOR
CHAPTERSEND

When I first started playing the fourth album from Italian band Mogador, I was struck by just how similar they were to Kansas, but it is possible that I was influenced by guest Ida Di Vita who provides violin on that song, but sadly not on any of the others. But, although there is a strong use of Hammond organ on this album, it is more influenced by British and American bands than it has by many of the prog acts from Italy. I have seen some criticisms of Marco Terzaghi's vocals, but those reviewers must have been listening to a different album from me as he is in fine voice, more of a classic Wetton or Lake style singer than those who want to hit the high notes. For that they have brought in Jon Davidson (Yes, Glass Hammer) who guests on "Josephine's Regrets" which is one of the highlights of the album. Here we have controlled picked acoustic guitar combining with delicate piano, but I did wonder if the use of Jon was just to get more people to write about the album as he is singing in a lower register than many would expect from him, and I am sure that Mogador could have done it quite well without him.

The more recognisable influences on Mogador are bands such as Gentle Giant, the aforementioned Kansas (even without a violin) and John Wetton and manages to keep on the more progressive side of melodic rock so much so that it is wonderfully enjoyable the first time, and that feeling doesn't diminish with repeated plays. There isn't much information on either the band or label sites, but at least it tells you how to buy it!
Oct 2017

MOLOKEN
ALL IS LEFT TO SEE

Formed in Umeå, Sweden, in 2007, Moloken want to create progressive experimental music that has a basis in metal, particularly the black metal scene. I was a massive fan of Rakoth when I first heard them many years ago, and both bands have a similar approach to their music. Here though, we have quite a short album, which was their first release in four years when it came out in 2015. Comprised of eight songs with a total length of less than half an hour, three of these are themselves shorter than 90 seconds, with one of these less than a minute. What is amazing then, is the amount of emotion they manage to cram into everything they do. The vocals are raw, and kept surprisingly low in the mix, so that the twin guitars of Kristoffer Bäckström and Patrik Ylmefors are at the front, with the rhythm section of Jakob Burstedt and Nicklas Bäckström right there in your face. It is raw yet polished, basic but intelligent, and is always hammering into the brain with a feeling of ice and power. Just playing this album makes me feel cold, although as I write this, I am in the middle of a Southern Hemisphere summer. I look out at the evening bright sunshine yet am chilled to the bone.

This is powerful stuff, and it is only by playing close attention that the listener gets the

most out of it. In some ways, it would be incredibly easy to dismiss this as "just" another black metal album with ideas above its' station. But listen to the complexity of the arrangements, especially to the drummer's polyrhythms and shuffles, and one realises that this is quite a special piece of work. But are we going to have to wait four years until the next one? I hope not.
Jan 2017

MOONRISE
THE LIGHTS OF A DISTANT BAY
It never ceases to amaze me at just how much great music continues to come out of Poland. This is the debut album from Moonrise, who have put out two more since this was released in 2008, yet there is just one constant, namely Kamil Konieczniak. That's because this is a one-man band, with Kamil providing all the music with Millennium singer Lukasz Gall brought in to provide lyrics and vocals. Perhaps it isn't surprising that much of this album is instrumental, what is surprising though is that this never comes across as project as it really does feel like a band. He is no mean guitarist, but it is the keyboards where he shines, with some beautiful touches, especially on piano. This is fine neo-prog, with influences from Hogarth era Marillion, IQ and Pendragon vying with the likes of Jadis and Camel to be heard.

Although for the most part the guitar sound is quite different, it is with Jadis that he has the most similarities; but that is far more to do with the arrangements and approach than the domination of any single instrument. Lukasz is renowned for having a great clear voice, and here he shows off his best Paul Menel/Gary Chandler/John Wetton stylings, providing an additional level of class to an album that is already rich with it. This is something the listener can drift into and get a great deal from, whether it is the wonderful arrangements, the melodies, or the clarity of thinking. Poland as a country is an incredible melting pot for great music, especially for prog, and there seems to be no end of bands that need to be discovered and heard by a much greater audience. Time to add Moonrise to that ever-growing list.
Jan 2017

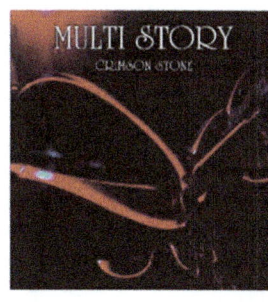

MULTI STORY
CRIMSON STONE
Back in the Nineties I was running Feedback fanzine in the UK and was fortunate enough to be in contact with the wonderful Larry Kolota who ran Kinesis, a record label who released both modern progressive rock (I was always very fond of Iluvatar) and reissues. One of the albums he sent me was 'East West', the debut by a UK act Multi Story, which was originally released in 1985. It gained a lot of attention at the time, and the band even toured as support to Magnum on the 'Storyteller's Night Tour'. But, by the time they went back into the studio to record the follow-up singer Paul Ford

had left, replaced by Grantley Nicholas, later of Feeder. 'Through Your Eyes' didn't build on the success of the debut, and soon the band was no more.

So, when I saw they had a new album out it is safe to say that I was somewhat surprised! I still have the debut on my shelves and recognised the name straight away. Original singer Paul Ford and keyboard player Rob Wilsher had been writing material together, and it was decided to turn the project into a band and resurrect a name that had disappeared a mere 29 years earlier. It perhaps isn't surprising that the material they have produced here sounds like a cross between neo-prog and Eighties prog, as that is the era they are from. They had the same influences as the likes of IQ, Pallas and Marillion, but whereas those bands have all moved on since then, Multi Story have stepped back in time, just with modern recording techniques. The result is an album that although not ground-breaking, is still a lot of fun and enjoyable for those who miss the "old" days. For me it is strangely familiar, yet new at the same time, and while never essential is still an album that is well worth investigating.
Jan 2018

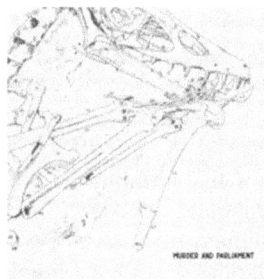

MURDER AND PARLIAMENT
MURDER AND PARLIAMENT
This may be a new band name to some, even if the concept isn't, but this is a project from none other than the quirky steampunk himself, Tom Slatter. He has been joined on this jolly jape by jazz bassist Alun Vaughan and Chrissie Caulfield on violin, and together they have conspired and perspired to bring us an incredibly varied instrumental album. For me it is full of Tom's sense of humour, even although there are no words to convey them, as he weaves melodies and counter melodies which evoke feelings of Poisoned Electrick Head and The Cardiacs while never sounding like either. We sometimes have delicate melodies, while at others it is all about intertwined electric guitars that somehow manage to make sense, even if some of the lines are distorted. They slow it down, they speed it up, and then decide to do it all over again! I don't know why I am writing the review in this style, but it just seems right. I can imagine Matt Deacon from The Bob Lazar Project just itching to get involved with his labelmate, as they do sometimes follow similar musical paths, complex and sometimes avant garde, and always with passion and integrity. There are times when it is heads down and riff to the end, with guitar melody over the top, and Alun is adept at either providing a rock-solid grounding or a counter melody all his own, while the keyboard sounds often sound as if they belong to the Eighties as opposed to the current day. The first time I played this I managed to fall asleep and only awoke after it had finished (it was stupid o'clock in the morning and I was on a plane on the way to Australia), which seemed such a waste, especially when I started playing it again when I was slightly less comatose and realized just how much fun this is. At times straight rock, others almost RIO, others straightforward prog, there is so much going on in this album that there just isn't room for vocals. For this and other releases from that really nice man with a beard, visit his website.
Jan 2018

MY ETERNEL
PURSUIT OF A HIGHER THRONE
According to the label, VoA Voxyd (piano/keys) (Ad Inferna) and Melissa Ferlaak (vocals) (Plague Of Stars, ex-Aesma Daeva, ex-Visions Of Atlantis) "have united to create music to transcend to another place and time where true home exists in the hearts of those on their personal journey towards an eternal existence" and they categorise this album as falling into classical romance, ambient and atmospheric while their backgrounds are gothic, metal, dark electronic and symphonic metal. So, there you have it. What we have here is a delicate album, where a trained soprano sings over the top of music that is often just piano, sometimes combined with some overlaying synths to give it a more orchestral feel.

While there are some New Age stylings to this, the album does a very good job of creating a wonderfully peaceful and tranquil world. It is not one to be played in the car, but rather music that needs to be played when the listener has the time and inclination to gently drift away. There is a small dark undercurrent that provides an edge and some Gothic overtones, but it is the delicacy and space used within the notes that makes this such a great piece of work. Indeed, when the piano is pushed more to the background and the drum machine comes in with more synths, there is a feeling that this is an unwanted intrusion and I found myself looking again for the purity of the piano. This is an album that I have really enjoyed playing, and one for those who don't always want the music directly in their face and ears. And yes, I have spelled the name correctly (Americans...).
Jan 2014

MYSTERY
SECOND HOME
Some 19 years ago I had my first ever email conversation with someone outside the company I was working for, and that someone was Michel St-Père, guitarist and leader of Canadian band Mystery and the label Unicorn Digital. They have had some interesting times since then, including engaging and then losing Benoît David (with Mystery from 1999 to 2013, as well as being in some band called Yes from 2008 to 2012). The person undertaking that role now is Jean Pageau, and if he has any nerves of following in those shoes, then he certainly isn't showing it on this live album, which was recorded at Progdreams V Festival, Zoetermeer, Netherlands, April 3rd, 2016.

Mystery released this album in August, and they did release their other live album 'Tales From The Netherlands' only three years ago, but that was with Benoît, and in between they released the mighty 'Delusion Rain'. Five of the songs are featured on the audio version of 'Second Home' (it is also available on Blu-ray/DVD), and he shows that he has just as much power in concert as he does in the studio. But what makes this band so very special indeed is that they really are an incredibly strong group of musicians who function together as a very powerful unit. Michel is a great guitarist, and he is often at the forefront of the arrangements, while in Sylvain Moineau he has a sparring partner who can provide power chords or additional widdly as the need requires. In Benoît Dupuis they have a keyboard player who instinctively knows not only what style but what sounds he needs to be using, while in bassist François Fournier they have someone who wants to follow the melody either directly or as a counterpoint: he certainly doesn't want to just provide foundation but add to the symphonic sound. Then, to top it all, at the back there is Jean-Sébastien Goyette who obviously doesn't know he is in a progressive band, or at the very least thinks he is in a prog metal outfit. He is a driving force of nature, hitting the skins as if they have offended him, and ensuring that the complete kit is getting the workout it deserves.

This is a monstrous live album, one that all progheads should have in their collection. It is a great introduction to the band if you've never come across them before, and while many of us were sad to see Benoît David leave, the future for Mystery looks very bright indeed.
Oct 2017

NAXAL PROTOCOL
THE GUILTY GET WHAT THEY DESERVE
When I am confronted with something that is out of the ordinary, I start from the position that the fault for not understanding the music lies with me, and that I need to persevere and in time I will come to understand. This has stood me well with artists such as Art Zoyd and musical styles such as free jazz. But to be honest, I don't get this at all. Formed out of Cazzodio, they are back with an album that even the label describes as "a crushing & unrelenting neural assault that will be remembered for ages to come". Note that they say nothing about music. This is noise, nothing more or less, and in the end, I stopped playing it as I was starting to fear for my hearing and the small elements of ambient majesty certainly do nothing to abate the assault that has nothing to do with musical form, and everything to do with chaos.
Mar 2014

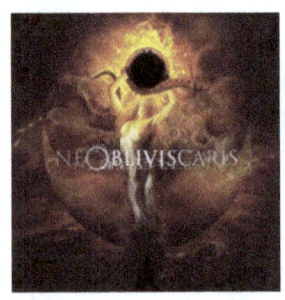

NE OBLIVISCARIS
URN
Founded in the Australian coastal city of Melbourne in the year 2003, Ne Obliviscaris took the inspiration for their name from the proud motto of Argyll, Scotland's Clan Campbell which means "forget not". From the start, this collective made it clear that they did not intend to follow any trends or walk on well-trodden paths. This is their third album, and again shows their refusal to fit into any pigeonhole, but instead is out to prove that music (at least in its truest form) is indeed a living beast but isn't something that will conform to anything in particular. Listen to certain sections of songs and one will be convinced that this is an out and out death metal act but listen to others and it is obvious to anyone that they are acoustic folk, but to be honest Ne Obliviscaris are one of those incredibly rare things, a progressive band operating out of Australia.

For my sins, I have to go to Melbourne about once a month, and I see I need to keep an eye on their website and tie one of these trips in to catch these guys in concert, because if this album is anything to go by, they are a force to be reckoned with. Each of the musicians is at the top of his game and seems able to cope with any and all musical forms. Daniel Presland is a dab hand at powering the band from the back and is in full control of the double bass drum pedals, while guest bassist Robin Zielhorst has an incredibly warm and pronounced style (his impact is so strong that I do find it hard to understand why he isn't a full member of the band). Matt Klavins and Benjamin Baret provide the twin guitar attack, riffing or shredding as the needs prevails, although they can also go acoustic. This then leads the twin frontmen of Tim Charles and Xenoyr. The latter is in charge of the crushed larynx approach while Tim is a clean singer, who also adds violin, but often in a full out frontal attack with the guitars as opposed to something gentler and more melodic, although he can do that as well when required.

This is a consummate act, and one that has produced an incredibly complex album which proves (if it was required) that those who enjoy playing music loud enough to burst ear drums often also have a great deal of musical talent and make their own rules. This isn't gently straddling the lines between quite diverse genres but is stamping all over them and proving that music is whatever the purveyor wishes it to be. There will be some who say that this is too progressive for their extreme metal tastes, while others will say that the guitars are too much, and the drum attack is upsetting them. Me, I think it is bloody excellent and look forward to hearing a great deal more from them.
Dec 2017

NEMEZIS
NEMEZIS
Nemezis came together in 1996, and although they did have some local success, they never completed their debut album and broke up. After recording an album with Mindfields, guitarist Marcin Kruczek felt it was time that the songs written by Nemezis finally saw the light of day, so he put together a brand-new band to do just that, none of whom had played in the original line-up. Krzysztof Lepiarczyk (Loonypark) provided keyboards, and the music is credited to him, Marcin and original bassist Grzegorz Wojtasiński, who wasn't involved this time around. The line-up was completed with Karolina Strużycka (vocals, who also provided all the English lyrics), Piotr Lipka (bass), Waldek Kowalski (drums, percussion) while Metus provided guest male vocals on one song.

This certainly doesn't sound like a project, but rather a well-rounded band who have been playing together for years. Karolina is a beautiful singer, with just a faint hint of accent that provides an edge to her voice, enhancing and not detracting. However, in many ways this is a vehicle for Marcin more than anybody else, with everyone else playing a backing role. On some songs, he does provide chords, but for the most part he is providing some plaintive soloing that is either the main focal point of the passage, or as a direct counterpoint to the vocals. Krzysztof is well-known as a keyboard player, yet here his role is to provide a melodic backdrop for Marcin to play against. The result is a neo-prog album that may have hints of Camel, Jadis and Pendragon among others, but is quite different to most of what was in the scene.

This 2008 album was sadly the only release from Nemezis, although Marcin and Krzysztof did play together on the solo album by Millennium singer Lukasz Gall. Produced by Millennium keyboard player Ryszard Kramarski, Nemezis released an album that is a highly regarded part of Poland's impressive progressive rock scene.
Jan 2017

NIGHTWISH
SHOWTIME, STORY TIME
Back in 2012 I heard that Nightwish were going to be coming to New Zealand, and me and one of my daughters knew we just had to be there. I had loved 'Imaginaerum' and felt the band had come a long way since they replaced singer Tarja Turunen. Her final performance was captured as 'End of An Era' and is something that I had played time and again but felt that Anette Olzon was a better fit with the way that the band had changed into something that was more bombastic and metallic. But I was surprised to hear that after just two albums Anette was no longer in the band, and that she had in turn been replaced by Floor Jansen from After Forever. But, although she had performed well in the studio, the live performances I had seen seemed to show someone who possibly wasn't fully in tune with the band and what they were trying to achieve. So, what would the concert be like with Floor?

Simply put, it was brilliant. Floor has the controlled soprano that is required to perform the classic Nightwish numbers but is also very much a rock performer and knows there are times when an edge and roughness are required to provide the emphasis. The other surprise that night was the appearance of veteran Troy Donockley, who is now a full band member. I first came across Troy when he was a member of Iona for their classic 'Book of Kells' and have heard some of his solo work as well as other band performances, and he certainly provides the group with additional styles with his pipes, flutes and whistles.

But why am I talking about a concert and not reviewing the album I have before me? Well, that is because this is a recording of their appearance at Wacken later the same year. By now Floor had really settled in (bear in mind that Anette's final performance was September 29th, 2012, and Floor joined the band for their performance on October 1st, having learned and rehearsed the vocal parts on the flight from Holland to Seattle!!), and the whole band seems comfortable and relaxed. It will always be Tuomas Holopainen's group, he writes the material and provides all the symphonics with his keyboards, but for me the most important person is bassist/vocalist Marco Hietala who provides the brutality and depth in his powerful singing as a total contrast to Floor. My one gripe about the gig is they didn't perform "Bye, Bye, Beautiful", which is easily the most played song on my phone as I have both the studio video and a live performance loaded and I play both multiple times each week. But given that it was about Tarja, possibly they didn't feel that performing it after Anette had left would be the right thing to do.

But if you enjoy symphonic metal then it really doesn't get much better than this. It is quite a contrast to 'End of An Era', and this is very much the one that I prefer.
Mar 2014

CLIVE NOLAN
KING'S RANSOM
Clive and I started talking to each other at the time of the first Shadowland album, and I have been fortunate to review most of his recordings since then, through multiple bands and projects. I missed the musical 'She' (one of the problems caused by moving to the other side of the world), which was released under the name 'Caamora', but did come across 'Alchemy' which used many of the Caamora Theatre Company but was released under his own name. Here he introduced us to the world of Professor Samuel King, and his battle with Lord Henry Jagman to solve the mysteries of Anzeray. I, like many others, log everything I play on the LastFM website, and according to their records I have played this album more than any other since I started logging my plays at the beginning of 2007 (the next two are 'The Snow Goose' and 'Snow' as you didn't ask). One of my daughters loves this almost as much as me, and it is often chosen to be played in the car, with "The Unwelcome Guest" being especially favoured (and consequently the most played song according to the same site).

So, when I heard that Clive was releasing another album in the same series I was intrigued. It just so happened that I was back in the UK in August for the first time in more than five years, and somehow the planets aligned for myself and Clive to meet for the first time in aeons. Sat in his music room, talk soon turned to the new album, so he passed me his bound copy of the lyrics and he then started to play highlights to me, explaining the story and thinking behind it. The events in this musical follow on from 'Alchemy', albeit a few years later, and does include some of the same characters. Interestingly, although many of the musicians have played on both, very few of the same singers are involved again. Also, although there are a couple of small mentions of things that happened on 'Alchemy', there is no need to have heard that release as this stands up in its own right. But, if one has heard the first one then there are both lyrical and musical repetitions designed to make the listener smile, as if they have been let into a secret.

One criticism I have heard of 'Alchemy', which had also reached Clive's ears, is that in many ways it is too dark, with too much death. Consequently, this album has been made deliberately lighter, with some quite comedic numbers. My favourite character is Captain Fergus Maunder, and it is obvious that Alan Reed (Anel Ganz, Pallas) had an absolute blast playing the role. For anyone who knows him, his Scots accent isn't nearly as strong as he lays it on here. There are too many musical highlights to mention, but "Haunted" always makes me smile, while "Nostalgia" reminds me of "Half Of Sixpence". Yes, in many circles Clive will always be known for progressive rock, and as I write this, he has just returned from playing with Pendragon in Japan, but with his theatre productions he looks far away from the prog field and looks instead to classic British musicals of the past.

Clive has stated that he feels that this is the first steampunk musical and has released three short videos to provide just a taste of the show. At the beginning of September some lucky souls could see a performance of 'Alchemy' one night, and then 'King's Ransom' the next. Of course, I was back in NZ by then!! Yet again he has created a masterpiece, and only time will tell if this one gets played as much as the last. Also, he has left the door wide open for a third, and I hope there is enough interest in these for that one also to be written and performed. This is for anyone who enjoys musical theatre, particularly British, or just wants to hear some great songs well performed. This is a masterpiece.
Oct 2017

THE NONEXISTENT
SPACE ROC
The Nonexistent were formed following on from a discussion between Chris Gill (Band of Rain) and Steve Palmer (Mooch, Blue Lily Commission). They had been working together on some of Steve's band projects and thought that it might be an interesting concept to record a session where they performed improvised space rock and see what came out of it. With Chris on guitars and Steve on bass, plus drummer Andy Hole, the first session went so well they recorded another two. From these they broke the sessions down into separate tracks and Steve added synth to the first two sessions while Chris did the same for the third. They then divided the album into two, with one disc featuring the rockier numbers (called 'Roc') and the other the more spacey elements ('Space), with Chris then adding two more numbers to 'Roc' and Steve two more on 'Space'.

The live sessions were sent straight to a digital recorder, and there is something about improvised music being captured that shows just how good/bad the musicians really are. There must be a connection between the guys for this to work at all, as otherwise it just becomes meaningless noise, and it shows they have all been working with each other over the years as they understand what they are doing and where the music is leading them. Recorded in a local village hall the guys were all able to see each other and bounce ideas, while also having that live ambience that is so important. One wonders how the drum sound was captured without too much bleed over, given that both Chris and Steve were playing through amps, and no-one was using headphones, but the sound mix is surprisingly good.

Released in DVD-style box as opposed to a jewel case, with a printed insert containing details of the sessions and some photos, this is worth hearing if you enjoy space rock.
Apr 2014

NOSDRAMA
ÄES

This 2010 album was the third full-length release from Finnish rock band Nosdrama, who describe their music as "melancholic progressive metal", and I totally understand where they are coming from. But, I do think the word they are missing in there is "melodic", as while this is dark and sometimes quite Gothic in overtones, there is also a real sense of melody that makes this album attractive the very first time it is played. There is a real intensity, but it never overpowers, so the listener feels more drawn into the unusual yet somehow familiar material. Apparently this is a concept album, based on the Cudgel War, which was a 1596/97 peasant uprising in the kingdom of Sweden (in the part that is now Finland). which was suppressed brutally and bloodily. The lyrics are in English, but I didn't concentrate on them too much, but instead let the music just wash over me in a wave. Imagine Type O Negative crossed with Muse and Threshold, then it might just give you an idea of what this sounds like. Others have also likened them to Opeth, Anathema and Katatonia, and they certainly share the darkness and bleakness that the last of these permeates.

The four-piece of Janne Haka-Risku (keyboards), Ari Niemi (guitar, vocals), Mika Hiironniemi (drums) and Janne Haapala (bass) have managed to create an album that is over the top, bombastic, and intense yet incredibly easy to listen to, all at the same time which is no mean feat. This album is dark and light, moody and fun, and I really enjoyed it.
Jan 2017

NOVELISTS
NOIR

Novelists are a progressive metal band from Paris who were formed in 2013, when Florestan and Amael Durand met former A Call To Sincerity members Matteo Gelsomino, Nicolas Delestrade and Charles-Henri Teule. After a series of singles, they released their debut album in 2015, and following on from touring Europe with the likes of For Today, Breakdown Of Sanity, Dream On Dreamer and Silent Planet they are now back with their second. Keyboards and sax play an important part on some of the numbers, such as the atmospheric "Monochrome", but sadly the press release doesn't say who else was involved, which is somewhat strange.

What is also unusual is that unlike many bands in the genre, they are coming at it from the view of Meshuggah and throw in elements of hardcore and death as well as the more usual progressive stylings. But, instead of sounding like a mish-mass, musically this always seems to make sense. Although French they sing in English, and this does make the album easy to approach from a lyrical point of view, and Matteo has a melodic voice that certainly fits in with what is going on with the rest of the band. This feels fresh and exciting, and with the support of Arising Empire behind them it will be interesting to see

what happens with these guys over the next few years.
Nov 2017

NY IN 64
THE GENTLE INDIFFERENCE OF THE NIGHT
Justin Hock (guitars) and Thomas Schlatter (bass) were both originally in 90's screamo band, You And I. After a rather lengthy break from writing music together they again started collaborating and brought in Chris Alfano (drums) and Seth Rheam (guitars) (both from progressive act East of the Wall) to create a new instrumental band, NY in 64. This is their second album, (six songs, a fraction under thirty-three minutes in length), and with two pairs of musicians from quite different musical backgrounds it is probably not surprising that in some ways this comes across as a rather strange combination of hardcore and progressive metal. The former is the most prevalent, but what makes this so interesting is that just when the listener feels that the energy and raw aggression is about to be taken to a whole new level, they can suddenly change tack and become something far more akin to shoegaze! At times, they all combine to provide slabs of sound that wouldn't sound out of place from Kyuss yet can still channel Life of Agony when the time is right. This won't be for everyone, but is interesting, and as well as being released on vinyl can also be streamed so why not give them a listen?
June 2017

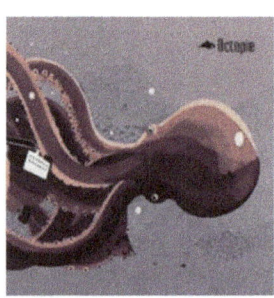

OCTOPIE
OCTOPIE
This is yet another band I came across when I was asked to evaluate them for ProgArchives, and I was quite blown away by this four-track EP. Hailing from Finland, this is their second toe in the water of releasing material, and I can only hope that they will soon be picked up by a label and given the time and resources to record a full-length album as these guys have real promise. They have definitely been listening to 'War Child' era Jethro Tull (and that can never be a bad thing in my book), and although their use of flute is much more clear than the breathy tone often deployed by Mr Anderson, that is not the only thing that reminds me of that period of time with chunky keyboards (including mellotron of course, and Hammond) and a singer in Tom Tamlander who was obviously born in the wrong decade. Here is not a singer who is going to sit quietly in the background, but instead not only sings but really lives what he is doing, putting loads of emotion into everything. Consequently, the band have to be on top form to be able to stay the course and they are definitely up for the task.

The music is quite laid-back at times and has been recorded in a way so that every instrument has plenty of space and the ability to shine but not so distant from each other so that they also can blend and complement what each is playing. There are long

instrumental passages where they all have the chance to take the lead role and show that many other classic prog bands have also had an impact on their sound (early Genesis, Gentle Giant, Yes, to name a few). Definitely one to keep an eye on, this EP can be streamed from Bandcamp, so it is possible to try before you purchase.
Apr 2014

OPENSPACE
OPENSPACE
Openspace came together in Poland towards the end of 2003 with the core of Rafał Szulkowski (drums), Marcin Zahn (guitars) and Robert Zahn (bass). Over the next few years some other musicians came and went, then in February 2006 Marcin Korzeniewski joined on keyboards and vocals. After positive reviews for their demo recordings, they signed to Lynx Music who released this their debut in 2008. Although this contains the high level of melody one has come to expect from Polish progressive bands, these are very much more into the prog metal end of the spectrum, but they don't crunch like Threshold or have the delicacy and intricacy of Dream Theater: this is much more like a heavier version of Enchant. There are hooks aplenty, and although they come together like a well lubricated rock behemoth at times, there is also plenty of space within the music for emotion and vitality to shine through. They're also not afraid to mix up the keyboard sounds, so it can go from Hammond and Mellotron styles through to something far more modern while the guitars can be gently picked, riffed, or take the lead with some soaring Gary Chandler style lines. They use piano, when necessary, plus fretless bass, as well as moving through musical styles, and it is this diversity of approach combined with some great melodies that makes this such an interesting and compelling piece of work.

They did release a follow-up album a few years later, but both Marcin and his brother Robert Zahn have left the band, so I'm not sure of their current status, which is a shame as this album showed some real promise.
Jan 2017

OPETH
SORCERESS
I still remember the impact 'Ghost Reveries' had on me when I first heard it back in 2005. It was Opeth's eighth album, but the first I had come across, and it totally blew me away. I then sought out the earlier albums and was intrigued to see how much they had changed over the years: what would that mean for the future I thought? This is their fourth album since then, and features the same line-up as 2014's, 'Pale Communion', namely Mikael Åkerfeldt (guitars, vocals), Martín Méndez (bass), Martin Axenrot (drums), Fredrik Åkesson (guitars), and Joakim Svalberg (keyboards). But, of that line-up only Mikael was a full member on 'Reveries' (Martin played on just one

song), so in many ways this isn't the same band, so perhaps it isn't surprising that the band have moved in such dramatic fashion from their death metal days. But what does that mean for the fans who followed them?

I found I kept thinking of classic Uriah Heep, but on steroids, as the guitar is that much sharper and the solos more powerful, but the way the organ keeps thing moving and repeating motifs is very much of that style. When I told someone, I was finally getting around to listening to this album, which came out in September last year, he said he would be very interested in hearing what I thought of it. In the end, I told him that in many ways I think this is a good album, but it's not Opeth. And there's the rub, looking at the cover art does one really notice that the peacock is displaying his tail feathers on a mound of skulls? The skulls may be where they have come from, but are they now a bird with an annoying cry? Do they look good, but there is little substance and no taste?

Musically this is all over the place, but early Seventies is where it is most at home, and songs such as the acoustic "Will O The Wisp" would be more at home on a classic Jethro Tull album than Opeth. But, and it's a big but, take the word "Opeth" off the album cover then I and probably all other reviewers would be looking at this in a different light. What will fans be wanting when the band play live? Will it be the older material or this? I know what I think. This should probably have been released as a solo album by Mikael, as there is too much risk of disengaging fans who have been with the band for years. The question is, how many of them will turn up for gigs, and how many will buy the next album? I enjoyed this on a pure musical level, but it isn't what I expected at all.
Jul 2017

ORANGE CLOCKS
TOPE'S SPHERE 2
I'm not quite sure who to blame for this, but I'm going to start with David Elliott from BEM, moving on to the band themselves if I can't find the evidence needed. From start to end this is a brilliant pisstake of an album, and I love it. It is combining HHGTTG with Gong, throwing in some bits of Hawkwind and a feeling of the Clangers with the Bonzo Dog Doo Dah Band and there we have it. This is a comedy album, which really is funny, as well as some excellent songs and performances. The wonderful thing for me is that a back story has been provided so this all makes sense, and I have seen reviewer after reviewer falling for it: I can just imagine the band and label sitting there reading some of the comments and killing themselves with laughter, when a quick search for some of the names would provide realisation that they only appear about these guys. This is what the band have said about themselves and the album.

"Orange Clocks hail from a shed in the depths of East Northamptonshire and specialize in music of no fixed genre; improvising and jamming for long periods, pausing only to consume lots of tea and biscuits. They have been in their current incarnation for a little over two years, although the seven band members have played together in different musical incarnations for many hazy years, united by a love of psychedelic and hypnotic music (amongst other things).

Originally devised in 1973 by eccentric producer Tomska R Huntley and destined for German TV, Tope's Sphere was set to be a ground-breaking animation featuring a live soundtrack by 1970's UK/Germany supergroup, Klementine Uhren. The series followed Tope, the knitted monkey protagonist, with his sidekick Chode on their outer-space adventures accompanied by lush layers of psychedelic music. Unfortunately for Tomska, Klementine Uhren was unhappy with the final mixes. They promptly disappeared with all the tapes for an 'extended session', never to be seen again. Tomska was bankrupted and his dreams shattered; he dumped what was left from Tope's Sphere into a skip and vanished into the depths of the Himalayan mountains. After the discovery of the fragments of video tape, stage props and art from Tope's Sphere, Russ Russell (Producer Extraordinaire of Parlour Studios) recruited Orange Clocks to re-imagine the soundtrack, taking what details they could find from the scraps of script rescued from the skip to bring the unique comic-book adventure back to life."

Even I can work out that the supposed supergroup name translates closely to "Orange Clocks". I love this album, as it is packed full of early Seventies humour and fun, yet is also a bloody good album, and one I have really enjoyed playing. I love it when a band don't take themselves too seriously, but I truly hope they don't end up being tagged with a "novelty" label as they deserve much more than that. I'm not sure how the humour will translate outside of the UK, but if anyone loves psychedelia and space rock mixed with prog and loads of laughs, then this is brilliant.
May 2017

OSTA LOVE
GOOD MORNING DYSTOPIA
Osta Love are a studio project that has been put together by childhood friends Leon Ackermann (drums) and Tobias Geberth (guitar, vocals, keys and bass). They started Osta Love in 2010, and this is their debut album, showing they have been heavily influenced by Porcupine Tree, Muse, Pink Floyd and other more emotional and dreamy bands. There may not be too much in terms of rock within this prog rock album, but there is enough so that it doesn't become a blancmange of sound. There is just enough diversity and contrast to keep the listener involved and become emotionally invested in what is going on. Lyrically the album is dealing with urban life, surveillance and escapism, and the image on the front cover is incredibly striking. Why are they covered in red? Who is she/he? What is their purpose? This doesn't feel like a project, but very much as a band album, and it will be interesting to see how they develop as if they are going to take this onto the live circuit then of course they will need more musicians, but will that change the sound? At present this is brooding, compelling and interesting stuff.
May 2014

OVRFWRD
BEYOND THE VISIBLE LIGHT
I was recently contacted by keyboard player Chris Malmgren, who wanted to know if I would be interested in hearing the instrumental progressive rock band he was part of, which is how I came across Ovrfwrd. Formed in 2012, as well as Chris the band is comprised of drummer Rikki Davenport, guitarist Mark Ilaug and bassist Kyle Lund. Five songs, with a total length of forty-eight minutes, this is a light-hearted and interesting debut. When a band is fully instrumental then of course there is no room to hide behind a singer, and what impresses me about this 2014 release is the sheer variety of styles and sounds they are bringing to bear. They aren't a fusion act, but there are some elements of jazz here and there, and although the guitar can be gently picked, there are also times when the only thing to do is to shred. When this is undertaken on "Stones of Temperance" I found it interesting that drummer Rikki is the only one keeping up with Mark, blasting around the kit, while Kyle kept everything grounded and Chris was playing piano.

They interweave melodies so there is always balance, and even when the music is delicate and almost fragile, there is a strength that holds it all together. They know when the time is right to rock it out, or bring it all back in, when they need to use piano or keyboards, when to riff or gently play leads. The result is an album that is immensely listenable to, and enjoyable on the very first playing.
Apr 2017

OVRFWRD
FANTASY ABSENT REASON
There aren't many bands who go out on a limb and finance a vinyl release of their second album, so all power to Ovrfwrd for making this available either digitally or as a real honest to goodness record. The album kicks off with the sixteen-minute-long title cut, which allows the band to show all the tricks they have available. They are very much their own band, but some of their most important influences are on display on this song, with Discipline and King Crimson well to the fore. They move from bombastic and discordant to gentle and reflective without a pause for breath, from prog metal to piano-led gentleness, going wherever they feel the music is taking them. Rikki concentrates on cymbals when the time is right, hardly touching the rest of the kit, while swirling keyboards can provide accompaniment to the melody leads of electric guitar and piano.

That this is the highlight of the album is never in doubt, but the rest of the songs also stand well up to muster, with "Brother Jack McDuff" having a late-Sixties feel with plenty of Hammond organ sounds on clear display. The joy of both these albums is that the guys clearly know what they want to achieve and have a diverse approach to getting

there. I know they are currently working on their third album, which I am eagerly awaiting, as both of their albums to date are well worth investigating and I know that the next one will surely build on what they have been doing to date.
Apr 2017

PANDORA SNAIL
LIVE AT BABOONIUMFEST
No prizes for working out that this is a live album, which was recorded at a festival in St. Petersburg on 6th November 2016. This was my first introduction to this eclectic progressive band, although they released a studio album in 2015, which I haven't heard. There are some interesting bands coming out of Russia at present, bringing together multiple different styles, and these guys are yet another that is totally out of left field and producing something that is a million miles away from the mainstream, yet is also accessible (at least to me) and enjoyable the very first time I played it. What we have here are five people who are all incredible musicians and have the jazz confidence in their bandmates that comes from many hours of playing together, are combining that with modern classical influences and then bringing in elements of RIO and the more complex areas of progressive rock music to create something that is refreshing and new. No Genesis clones here!

In terms of instruments, we have keyboards (which is often piano), bass, drums, electric guitar and violin (plus a guest trumpeter on two songs) with no vocals. If there are boundaries in music, then these guys aren't just stretching them but are trampling them underfoot as if they don't exist. If I was to liken to them to another band then possibly After Crying, but I can also see Frank Zappa getting a real kick out of what they are doing, and would it be too much to bring Art Zoyd into the equation? It doesn't sound as if they were playing in front of a mass crowd, but those who were there were certainly provided with a musical treat. I look forward with great interest to hearing more from Pandora Snail.
Mar 2017

PANDORA SNAIL
WAR AND PEACE
Having really enjoyed the Russian band's live album from last year, I have now finally come across their debut studio album from 2015. Yet again I am amazed at the quality of the music and just how enjoyable this is the very first time I played it, growing to love it even more with each repeated play. Virtually instrumental, the band that one immediately starts to compare them with is Kansas due to the way that the violin is often taking the lead role, but they are influenced by way more than just one band and acts as diverse as King Crimson, Art Zoyd and Frank Zappa have all had their part to play with this album. It is complex and highly structured, with melodies and

counter melodies repeated on different instruments (always nice to hear pure piano take a lead role), yet there is a vitality and breath of life through the whole piece. It is music that in some ways does take a lot of listening to, to gain the most benefit, yet at the same time is also immediate and transparent.

This album certainly never comes across as a debut, and I have heard that it took five years from the recording for it to see the light of day, and if that is the case then that is nothing short of travesty and tragedy as this is a superb piece of work. There are a great many bands coming out of Russia at present, and Pandora Snail should be viewed as being at the vanguard of the progressive rock movement as this is wonderful on just so many levels. I can only hope that given the reviews I have seen of both this and the live album they soon follow up with another visit to the studio.
Sep 2017

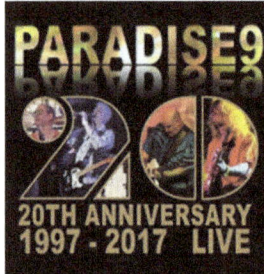

PARADISE 9
20TH ANNIVERSARY 1997 – 2017 LIVE
Here we have an album that pretty much does exactly what the title suggests, namely that it is an album comprised of live recordings taken from the band's 20-year career to date. The first CD is subtitled 'These Days' and includes tracks recorded in 2016 at the Blind Cat and Kozfest Festivals with the current line-up of Gregg McKella (vocals, guitar and synth FX), Tyrone Thomas (lead guitar, backing vocals), Neil Matthars (bass) and Wayne Collyer (drums). The second disc is "Those Days" and includes ex-members Andy McDonald, Steve Teers Mufa, Carl Sampson, Jonas Golland, and Jaki Windmill plus special guests the legendary Nik 'ThunderRider' Turner, Jeanette Murphy, Tracey Morais, Mike Mishra and Kev Ellis. The CD also comes with a tour poster and family tree, to help make sense of the comings and goings. But at the heart of this band is Gregg McKella, who has been the driving force from the very beginning when he formed Paradise 9 in 1997 at the Acoustic Revolution songwriter's nights with bassist Andy Macdonald.

Although we don't have any recordings from the very first year, we do have one from 1998, which shows that Paradise 9 have been following the same path of psychedelic space punk rock for a long time now. That they have been influenced by Hawkwind is never in doubt, but it is a more punk-influenced 'Wind than the standard space rock copyists. They have worked with Judge Trev and Nik Turner alike and have a great deal of punk and edginess in their music, almost as if they were coming to it twenty years earlier than when they did. This is independent underground music that will never hit the charts, but the refusal to conform is one of its strengths. I first saw Neil play bass with the Casuals some twenty-five years ago, and I did smile when I realised that not only was Carl Sampson on the album, but that Mike Mishra also guests on one song from the Nineties.

Paradise 9 are now a staple on the underground and festival circuit, and one of the delights of this collection is the diversity of the songs on show, as well as the way they

were arranged with the different line-ups and guests. This is undoubtedly the best way to discover one of the hidden gems of the British music scene.
Nov 2017

MATTHEW PARMENTER
ALL OUR YESTERDAYS

This 2016 album was a long time coming, as Matthew's last solo album "Horror Express' came out in 2008, but good things come to those who wait. This is the first of the three to feature Matthew on the cover and he is shown with the make-up he normally wears with Discipline. This isn't the only Discipline reference, as he is joined on this album by bandmate Paul Dzendel who provides drums on four of the songs, while Matthew provides everything else. If there is just one word that captures this album, it must be "maturity", as here is an artist comfortable in his craft who is just going to let the music speak for itself. His vocals are reminiscent of Peter Hammill combined with Geoff Mann and Robert Wyatt, and musically this feels quite tied to the early Seventies with Wyatt, VDGG, Procol Harum and the Canterbury scene obviously having a major impact.

This is mostly based around piano and vocals, with additional instruments used as necessary, and a special mention must be made of the overall sound and production, as it captures the power and dramatic passion effortlessly. I firmly believe that Discipline are one of the most important bands to come out of the American prog scene, and that they have never really been afforded the acclaim they deserve, and the same is very true of their leader as while there are a select few who know of his brilliance, it should be far more widely recognised.

Some albums leave one feeling that there is something missing, something that could and should have been added, like having a Chinese meal and then wanting a burger a short while later. That is not the case here, as this album is so full of musical sustenance that when it ends the listener needs a break, a space before going back to investigate further. It is a feast, a banquet for the musical soul, with passion and emotion contained in a few notes and chords, and vocals that are breaking. Now he has signed with the British label Bad Elephant I trust that they will ensure that this album gets the publicity it deserves, as this is quite some achievement. Let's hope we don't have to wait quite so long for the next one.
Mar 2017

ROG PATTERSON
FLIGHTLESS
Back in the early Eighties Rog Patterson went to Nottingham University to study Philosophy, and as luck would have it, he soon made the acquaintance of a large hairy person by the name of Greg Smith, a fellow twelve-string player and Ant Phillips fan. They were finally convinced to leave the halls of residency and play some proper gigs

and made their live debut in a church hall in Billericay, as Twice Bitten. The ensuing sequence of lucky breaks saw them playing their fourth gig in front of a thousand people, supporting Roy Harper: and their fifth, seventh and eighth at the Marquee in London. Although they were playing acoustic twelve strings with nary a keyboard between them, they were soon accepted into the then-thriving progressive rock scene, supporting Twelfth Night, Solstice, Pendragon and others. They released some cassettes, played numerous gigs with Haze, but by 1986 enough was enough.

Rog decided to keep performing as a solo artist, touring, and playing in other bands as well, and even released some material. Of course, by being on tour so much it made sense that he became involved in the other side of proceedings, so in 1988 was asked to join Pendragon's crew, as a favour, for one gig: he soon became tour manager and sound engineer, as he didn't have enough to do. He released this album in 1989, and was soon on the road again, in Britain, Holland, France and Germany supporting Pendragon. I first met Rog in 1994, as somehow, he had got himself involved with Mark Colton and his new band Credo. By this time, he had almost given up on ever recording another solo album, as now he had a strong reputation as sound engineer and tour manager for bands such as Murder Inc., L7, Lawnmower Deth, Mordred, and Rage Against The Machine. But he was still incredibly pleased and proud of his album and gave me a copy, which I still have, to this day. So, some twenty-eight years after it was released, and some twenty-three years since I first heard it, yet again I am reviewing the album, which has just been reissued by Bad Elephant on CD.

The album features just Rog on mostly acoustic guitar, and conjures up thoughts of Ian Anderson, Roy Harper and Jay Turner. Some people think that an acoustic guitar means no power or vitality, but they ought to listen to Rog belt his way through "Ergo Sum". A twelve-string guitar has never suffered so much punishment. He is an outstanding guitarist and can play in many styles, so "Ergo Sum" manages to convey many passions and emotions, just with different styles of playing. Double tracking enables him to harmonise vocals with himself on "Party Piece" to good effect, and this is an incredibly impressive piece, although part of the music was "borrowed" from Jethro Tull's "Up To Me". I bumped into Rog at a gig not long after I had written the original review and sent it to him, and I was more than a little nervous about what he would say regarding that comment. But he told me that I had it bang to rights as he had been playing Tull while searching for inspiration one night and it just happened! What was originally the second side of the album featured just two songs, "Conclusion" and the title cut. The latter is more than twelve minutes long, and is lyrically the strongest, as Rog opens himself up for examination.

But wait, there's more! To quote Rog himself: "In a last-ditch attempt to avoid recording my 'new' solo album, I have somehow persuaded those fine but rather silly folk at Bad Elephant Music to release the old one again, including demo versions of three tracks which would have been on the next album had I ever got around to recording it. That's still imminent, though as '30 years late' is intrinsically funnier than '28 years late', I wouldn't hold your breath." So, we have three additional numbers, "Alien", "Couldn't Happen Here" and "The Name of the Rose", which feel both slightly drier and more polished than the rest of the album. But they fit in well with the overall feel, and it will be interesting to hear what they sound like if they appear on the new one!

Although Rog and I haven't met up for probably fifteen years or so, we have been in email contact quite a bit recently, and he tells me that it is possible that we could be having a pint together in NZ next year talking about the new CD. I do hope that is the case as a) it will be great to meet up with him again after all this time and b) it has been far too long since he last released any music, let alone a solo album. If he does release a second, then it will have taken even more time than it did Credo, and that's saying something. I love this album, have done so for many years, and I urge all fans of Anthony Phillips and Roy Harper to seek this out at once, if not sooner.
May 2017

PARZIVAL'S EYE
FRAGMENTS
Parzival's Eye is the name that Chris Postl from RPWL (vocals, bass, guitars, keyboards) gave to his solo project when he released this album in 2009. He was joined by singers Christina Booth (Magenta), Alan Reed (Pallas), as well as guitarist Ian Bairnson from Alan Parsons Project, fellow RPWL'er Yogi Lang on keyboards, drummer Hannes Weigend and more guitars from Ossi Schaller. The result is an incredibly polished album that contains the fluidity and grace one would expect from RPWL, along with some wonderful guitar passages and solos that definitely are more into the neo-prog and Steve Hackett arena, but really for me this is all about the quality of the songs and the guys singing them.

I have been a fan of Alan since his days with Abel Ganz and have followed him through Pallas and many projects through the years. He has a wonderfully clear voice, able to hit seemingly any note with ease then provides as additional warmth to the tone. On this album he has a female compatriot who is able to match him and harmonise when the need arises or take on the lead as she has on so many incredible albums. Chris has managed to bring together a group of players that bring his songs to life, provides them with a vibrancy and passion, and the result is a neo-prog album that is immediate and enjoyable, and just gets better the more I play it. There are times when it crosses into melodic rock, but that isn't a bad thing when an album is as classy as this, and it just goes to show that 4/4 can be used as a valid time signature in prog!
May 2014

HENNING PAULY
BABYSTEPS
Henning has long been a favourite musician and composer of mine, and he has released some wonderful albums under his own name, plus various bands/projects such as

Frameshift, Chain, Shadow's Mignon and Roswell Six. But, for some reason I had never listened to his 2006 "opera" until now. For this album Henning provided all the music himself, apart from piano by Marcus Gemeinder on three songs, plus a guitar solo by Ian Crichton (Saga) on one and a piano and keyboard solo by Jim Gilmour (Saga) on another. He used four different singers this time, Jody Ashworth (Trans-Siberian Orchestra), James LaBrie (Dream Theater), Michael Sadler (Saga) and Matt Cash (Chain). He has previously worked extensively with James, Michael and Matt in various bands, but I believe this is the first time he has worked with Jody, who plays the lead role.

Henning has always referred to this as an opera, and that is probably a good way of looking at it, as this is a story of four characters. Based in a rehabilitation centre, it tells of Nick (Jody), a professional athlete, who is withdrawn and has lost faith in life and people in general. Another patient, Matt (Matt), tries to befriend Nick get him to change his outlook, but to no avail. Nick was having issues with his doctor (James), and meetings weren't going well, but he kept going back to the café and talking with Matt, who introduces him to his own doctor (Michael). After this, things go well between Nick and his own doctor, and he and Matt celebrate with a cup of coffee. Musically this has elements in common with TSO and Savatage, yet that is sometimes cut through with the incredible guitar attack that Henning is known for, and at others with a simplistic piano and bass.

This was the seventh album in three years for Henning, and he was providing all the instrumentation himself, and I wonder if this was just a step too far. The album was based on a true story, and is obviously incredibly personal for Henning, and I am sure that is the reason it doesn't gel as well as it should. There are sections, such as the guitar solo on "A Place In Time", where everything comes together and is sheer brilliance, but there are plenty of others where the words and music don't quite fit as they should. Metallic, progressive, over the top: it is all these things, but I can't help feeling that if Clive Nolan had been brought in to advise then it would have been a different beast altogether, and much the better for it. I may be wrong, but I don't think that Henning has released a solo album since this one and hasn't released many albums at all in any form and is now concentrating on running a studio, which given his work rate prior to this album is quite something.

I still love Henning's work, but for all the great moments and performances on this album, it is the one to which I will be returning least out of all his canon.
Dec 2016

PBII
PLASTIC SOUP
Michel van Wassem (keyboards, vocals), Ronald Brautigam (guitars) and Tom van der Meulen (drums) are all well-known within the progressive scene for being founder members of the mighty Plackband, a highly regarded Dutch group who sadly never

The Progressive Underground Vol 5

reached their full potential. Here they are back together (hence the band name), and they have been joined by Harry den Hartog on bass. It is strange to think that the core of this band started playing together in the Seventies, as this has much more in common with the neo prog scene of the early Nineties, than what was around twenty years earlier. Musically this is an incredibly powerful piece of work, with great performances from all four. Ronald's guitar style is incredibly reminiscent of Alan Morse, and "In The Arms Of A Gemini", in particular, contains some Spock's Beard moments, but there are also strong elements of Galahad and Pendragon as well as more American melodic stylings. This is strong stuff, with some crunching guitars, great over the top keyboards, and a dynamic rhythm section. Harry sometimes provides gentle fretless bass as a counterpoint, while at others it is a fretted plectrum-led attack that gives the music a totally different feel.

The vocals for the most part have a slightly harsher edge, they haven't been smoothed out too much, and that is totally in feeling with this concept album, as this is a call to arms about the state of our environment, and what we are doing to our seas. The term "plastic soup" refers to the way carrier bags react when they are in the sea. Dutch minister Jacqueline Cramer said "I think it's great PBII chose plastic soup as a topic on their new album! The more people know about it, the better!". The longest song, at nearly thirteen minutes, is the title cut and contains the thought-provoking lyrics "It's plastic soup, it chokes the oceans, while all of mankind fails, will we ever hear again, the singing of the whales."

Musically and lyrically, this is a wonderful piece of work that anyone into melodic or neo prog will get a great deal from. Well worth investigating.
Jan 2017

PERFECT BEINGS
PERFECT_BEINGS
When Johannes Lulley (Moth Vellum) told me he was working on a new project I was instantly intrigued, as not only did I enjoy the music he had undertaken with his previous outfit, but I was also a fan of his excellent solo album. When the recording was completed, he sent me a digital copy and asked me what I thought, and to be honest I wasn't quite sure what to say. From the very beginning it is obvious that here is an album which is daring to be different in so many ways, and yet is also familiar and reassuring. I have seen elements of this release likened to XTC, The Beatles, Genesis and Pink Floyd and I would agree with all of these, but somehow that misses what this album is about for me.

To my ears the guys have decided that they are going to perform in a pop/prog format, which at times is much more the former than the latter, yet never loses the complexity within all the apparent simplicity. Musically there is a great deal going on, with some significant performances from everyone involved, yet at times they come across almost as if they were Coldplay, or The Byrds, or a band founded in the psychedelic era. The music is timeless, and the production is quite superb, allowing the listener to fall into the sonic landscape they have created knowing full well that the multi-layered notes will catch them and transport them away. There is a small drum fill during "Walkabout" which only lasts a few seconds, yet the way it has been treated in the mix really allows it to shine through and create a very different feel.

The harmonies are superb, the hooks constant, yet there are sections where they allow themselves to remember they are a prog band at heart and throw in different styles and complex musical motifs. One could argue this is a prog album for those who would never say that they were progheads, as there is plenty on here that could well get radio play, but they do forget themselves a few times and allow themselves to have a stretch out to more than eight minutes on a couple of numbers, But, there are also some which are under three, including opener "Canyon Hill" which is pure English classic pop. More than happy to change time signatures during songs if the mood takes them, let no-one con you by saying that this is a pop album with prog pretensions, but rather is something that is carefully crafted and has feet firmly in both camps and the result is something that will be enjoyed by many.
Apr 2014

PERSONA GRATA
REACHING PLACES HIGH ABOVE
Persona Grata are from Bratislava, Slovakia, not an area really known as a hotbed of progressive rock bands, but perhaps it is all about quality as opposed to quantity, because take it from me this is a debut album which is just going to blow you away. Back in 1999 keyboardist Adam Kuruc and lead guitarist Martin Huba started working together, and in time this band came together, heavily influenced by Yes, Dream Theater, Muse, and others. This is complex prog metal with a focus on melody and allowing all the musicians plenty of room to shine and be heard. The full line-up is Martin Stavrovský (vocals, guitar), Jana Vargová (flute, vocals), Martin Huba (lead guitar), Adam Kuruc (keyboards), Timo Strieš (bass) and Ján Šteňo (drums – who says he is personally heavily influenced by Mike Portnoy, and it shows).

What makes this band so interesting is the way they move and thrust in so many different musical directions and time signatures, and whatever they are doing makes complete musical sense as does the transition from one section to another which often is quite diverse from what has been going on before. In many ways this is quite a tiring album to play, as it is amazingly intense and demands a lot from the listener just because it has to be listened to, as it downright refuses to be accepted as background music. Here is a band that are going to hammer it into your ears and face until you accept that they are the masters and that you will listen all the way through to the end.

For me the over-riding questions have to be such as "why aren't these guys signed to a

The Progressive Underground Vol 5

major label?" or "I wonder if they will ever come to NZ for a gig?". While the latter is unlikely in the extreme, I am convinced the former must be close at hand. These guys reached out to reviewers and asked if we wanted to hear the album, have provided press kits and have a professional website yet are doing this all on their own. It certainly isn't what one expects from a band with a self-released debut.

Powerful, intense, compelling, complex, brash and full of confidence, this is a band to be reckoned with. One wonders how they are going to follow this up, especially as both Adam and Martin have left the band since the album was recorded, but replacements are already on board and the guys are convinced that they are ready to take it to the next level. Based on this, I believe them.
Jan 2014

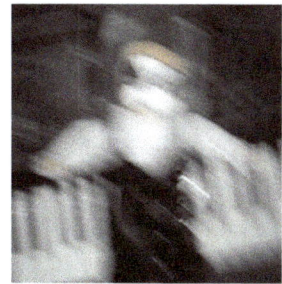

PERSPIRE
EXIT PLANET LUST: EMBRACE/CRUSH/DREAM/DESTROY

This twenty-six-minute-long EP features six instrumental pieces of work that I have found quite fascinating in their simplicity and emotion. Perspire is a composer, producer, conceptual artist and guitar shredder for hire residing in Brooklyn New York, and his work has appeared in XLR8R, The Wire and more. According to his biography, on this work he draws influences from Derek Riggs, Can, Geoff Barrow, Brad Fiedel and Tangerine Dream. To be honest, I don't know all of those listed, but I certainly see the influences of Can and Tan Dream on this. I wasn't surprised to see he is a conceptual artist as well as a musician, as in many ways this seems to have more in common with the former than the latter – as if it is conceptual art for the ears. The cover artwork is deliberately blurred, and there are few details to be found about Perspire on the web, which ties in with the label not even having a website (Eternally InDEADed is an art and record label created by ArKane in late 2015, based in Greenpoint, Brooklyn. The label specializes in short run vinyl, cassettes, zines, objects of beauty, and ephemeral happenings. Artists include Dead Ryan, Giorgio Moroser, Unwashed, Halford Witchcock, and Perspire.).

I honestly think the best way to appreciate this is by sitting in a room where the walls, ceiling and floor are painted brilliant white, and there is harsh lighting. In the middle of the room is a painted wooden chair, and the music is directed to that point, to the listener. I can't explain why I feel that way, but know it makes sense to me. This is an interesting and intriguing piece of art.
May 2017

THE PILGRIM
THE SOLAR PILGRIM

I am always trying to discover new bands, so when a collaborator on ProgArchives dropped me a note one day asking if I had heard of Auckland band The Pilgrim, I knew I had to investigate further. He had kindly provided me with a link to their Bandcamp page,

and I could see they had released this album in 2016 and another earlier this year. So, I grabbed both and then attempted to contact the band, failing miserably. I searched for information on them online, but to no avail, and eventually decided the bible of Aotearoa music, www.muzic.net.nz, would be bound to have a listing for them, but again I was wrong. All I know for certain is they are based in Auckland but can't be sure if it is a solo project or full band (I suspect the latter), have no idea how many people are involved. If they play gigs then I have been unable to find any record of it, haven't been able to discover any reviews, and a search of Facebook proved fruitless.

All I can say with confidence is that this is an instrumental album, with song titles going from "Sun" all the way out to "Pluto". They play a type of metal that is heavily influenced by mathcore, but there are also some progressive elements within it as well. That Meshuggah have had an influence is not in doubt, but they seem to be more like a melodic Protest The Hero in many ways. They do repeat riffs and melodies at time, and this provides a naïve innocence to what is happening. The bass sometimes takes the lead, with a strong use of plectrum that gives a hard edge to proceedings, while the guitars are often at the forefront. I found that I really enjoyed this and find myself incredibly frustrated not to know any more about a local band. Well worth investigating,
Sep 2017

THE PILGRIM
STAR CYCLES
Obviously keen to stay with the same theme, the album released last month has songs that identify with either spaceships or stars. There is a little more information this time, in that they tag their music as being hard rock, heavy metal, metal, metalcore, progressive and rock, but apart from that there is no indication about who is involved, while they do state that they are from Auckland (New Zealand's largest city and main hub for transportation. Located in the North Island, it is also the most populous urban area in the country with a population estimated at 1.415 million in 2016. The 2016 population of 1,415,550 in Auckland accounts for 33.4% of the country's population. I may not be able to tell you anything about the band, but I can copy off the internet like a good 'un).

Yet again this is an instrumental album of high-quality progressive rock and metal blended with a healthy dose of mathcore. The songs between the two albums are interchangeable, and don't show much distinct difference between them, but given they were released only eight months apart that isn't surprising, and it is obvious they are viewed as a pair by the band, given both the album and song titles. I haven't given up hope of contacting them as this is a band/project with real potential, and I do look forward to hearing more releases by these guys.
Sep 2017

The Progressive Underground Vol 5

POCKET SIZE
VEMOOD: CLEANING THE MIRROR VOLUME 1
Towards the end of 2016 I was contacted by guitarist Peter Pedersen, who asked if I would be interested in hearing the latest album from his band, who combine psychedelia with progressive rock. Well, it sounded interesting, so of course I said yes. What I didn't expect was a live album that it many ways sounds as if it has far more in common with the 1967-1970 period than anything that was being played and produced nearly fifty years later.
'Vemood: Cleaning The Mirror Volume 1' has at its heart rough and raw rich sounds that are so broad that I felt the notes coming out of the speaker are almost visible and that by just grabbing one I would be lifted up to the ceiling, such is their weight.

In many ways, the bands I kept thinking of were Cream and especially Blodwyn Pig, but more in approach as opposed to musical style, which owes far more to the likes of Jefferson Airplane. There is a Hammond B3 at the very heart of the band, and then three guitarists, a rhythm section and a saxophonist/flautist combining to make musical sense of what is going on. There are times when it feels a little basic, but it is played with such heart and soul that the listener just gets caught up in the passion and feeling of the whole thing. There is room for everyone to take their own solos, and the others happily take a back seat and provide the perfect accompaniment, so that in some ways it is quite jazzlike in its nature. Not as overtly heavy as one might expect from different guitarists being involved, and notes are often picked as opposed to heavyweight chords, but there is such a density and intensity to the work that it just doesn't need it. Overall, this is a superb work.
Dec 2017

PRAVDA
THE CLARITY OF CHAOS
This is my first experience of Pravda, although this is their fourth full-length album and was released in 2012. At the time they were just a trio, and all three of them supply vocals with harmonies being an important part of their style. In fact, there are times when they remind me of Gentle Giant, although the music itself is not nearly as complex as that of the classic Seventies act.
The more I worked my way through the album I felt they have possibly been inspired more by Spock's Beard, who of course were inspired by GG, as there is quite a lot within their music that could sit within the more melodic, and less overtly progressive, of that band's music. As I started listening to this, I was trying to decide in my mind of that was a five-star album or a four star, so I was somewhat surprised to discover that the more I played it the less I actually liked it. There are loads of great sections on this album, and the vocals are really good, while musically they are all on the top of their game, but there is something about this that just really doesn't do it for me and for the life of me I can't work out why. Each time I play it I find myself doubting my own views as I really enjoy it but the more I get through. the more I feel that

I really want to be playing something else. That's just not the normal reaction for me on any album.

Melodic, symphonic, very American but with some British influences, this is a prog band that sometimes veers into the prog metal territory without fully being a prog metal act. They have some wonderful songs, some great vocals, but to my ears they might have been better off using an external producer as some songs such as "Second Hand" could have done with some judicious editing. They are worth hearing, but this album just doesn't really do it for me, although I feel it should.
Jun 2014

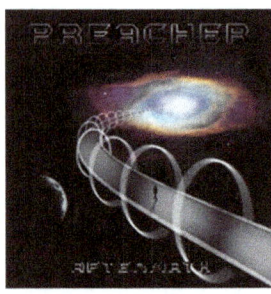

PREACHER
AFTERMATH
Preacher is a band new to me, but apparently, they have been around since 2007, and this 2016 release was their second album, following on from 2014's 'Signals', which I have yet to hear. Hailing from Scotland, the line-up is rather unusual in that they are an octet, with two backing singers very much included as part of the band. Martin Murphy's voice is one of the highlights for me, as while he is closer to Roger Chapman and/or David Bowie than David Gilmore, his vocals blend the three together in a way that provides real character to the songs. As to the music itself, it would be very easy to say that these guys have been influenced by 'Dark Side Of The Moon' and leave it at that, but to be fair to them they don't always come across as Floyd, but instead have taken a host of different Seventies influences to create a very special classic Seventies rock sound.

These are far more than mere copyists, and any band that writes a song dedicated to one particular recorded medium, "Vinyl", is always going to find favour among people such as myself. They say they are influenced by Purple, Floyd, Yes and Led Zeppelin, and that may well be the case in their ears, but we all know it is Floyd that is closest to their heart. But and it is a big but indeed, they have taken it as a starting point and moved with it so fans are getting brand new music for their money, as opposed to just copying what happened all those years before. Highly recommended.
Jan 2018

PRESTO BALLET
THE LOST ART OF TIME TRAVEL
This band was put together by Kurt Vanderhoof (Metal Church) with the intention of bringing back the glory days of progressive rock. They state, "Presto Ballet combines the melodic and harmonic old school aspects with the neo progressive rock sound of today," and that "they are bringing back the classical influence in rock and the sense of composition that was so very popular in the early 70's". Presto Ballet is Neo Classic Progressive Rock."

So, that's their views, and mostly they manage to hit those points well. That they have been heavily influenced by the likes of Kansas, Deep Purple and Uriah Heep is never in doubt, although the guitars are much heavier and modern sounding. But the one element that did surprise me is the amount of Styx influences one can hear, both in the vocal melodies and the music itself, although this is far heavier than anything they ever attempted.

The album is packed full of melodic hooks, and although there are a couple of lengthy numbers (including one at fourteen minutes), there is always plenty going on and one is wondering what turn the race is next going to take. The music is often played at pace, yet never provides the bite that one would expect from the involvement of an old-school thrasher like Kurt. Overall, this is a polished and refined album, but it could have done with just a bit more roughness and rawness to make it shine.
Jan 2017

QUANTUM FANTAY
TERRAGAIA
By the time I came across this Belgian band they had already released four studio and two live albums prior to 'Terragaia', which came out in 2014. I was a little surprised that they managed to escape my attention for so long as these guys have been heavily influenced by one genre in particular, and one band especially, the mighty Ozric Tentacles. Given just how long the Ozrics have been around, perhaps it is surprising that there aren't more bands that have decided to create their own version of a sound which is instantly recognisable. They aren't mere copyists though, and have brought in some more ethnic and folk elements, particularly on songs such as "Azu Kénè Dékè Lepé" which contains some wonderful tribal drumming combining with clear guitar lines.

There is an energy and passion contained within the music, and the listener is soon transported into a magical world where woodwind, keyboards, guitars and drums combine to create something that is very special indeed.
Oct 2017

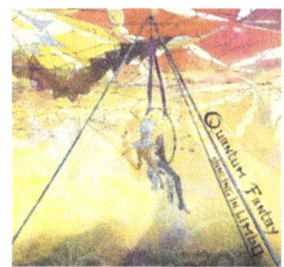

QUANTUM FANTAY
DANCING IN LIMBO
Quantum Fantay's 2015 album was interesting in quite a few respects. Firstly, they had a new guitarist in Tom Tas, and secondly, they had used more guest musicians than previously, one of whom was Ed Wynne! Given that these guys have been more than a little influenced by the mighty Ozrics that is a huge compliment to what they are doing. Lastly, instead of a series of songs of different lengths we are this time treated to four songs that are all basically 11:15 long. I hate to think just how many albums I have listened to over the years, but I am sure that is a first for me, as bands tend to have the songs as long

as they need to be as opposed to attempting to keep them to a particular length (apart from the old days when they had to be three minutes or less to be played on the radio).

This album takes a more direct approach than the previous one, with a more rock approach and less folk, but still with plenty of swirling keyboards and space rock stylings. Its straightforward approach means that this is instantly appealing, and there is less thinking to do with this music, just let your ears open up and then drown in the sensations. Yet again this is indispensable for anyone into space rock in general and Ozrics in particular.
Oct 2017

QUANTUM FANTAY
TESSELLATION OF EUCLIDEAN SPACE
This really is a band that wants to both stay true to its roots and progress at the same time, so for 2017 the band has expanded from a four-piece with guests to a six-piece working on their own. No more using a guest flautist, as Jorinde has joined as a full member, as has Nette Willox who brings in saxophone and vocals. Don't worry, they haven't suddenly turned into a band with a lead singer, the vocals are just another effect they use when the time is right as opposed to now being a band providing backing music. They are still very influenced by Ozrics, but they have started to expand away from the core sound, especially with the use of the saxophone. In many ways, they have turned up the complexity with a great deal of layering within the sounds and have also gone back to a more normal format of song writing as opposed to the experimentation that existed on the previous album.

Although each of the three albums are quite similar in many ways, they know what people expect from them and are going to continue to keep delivering it, they also know they need to move on to succeed and thrive and that is very much the case with this one. It is the strongest album of theirs that I have heard to date, and I am starting to realise I need to go back in time and listen to their very first ones, as so far everything I have heard from the Belgians has impressed me immensely.
Oct 2017

RC2
FUTURE AWAITS
RC2 was formed in Caracas, Venezuela, during 1999 following the break-up of Radio Clip, a popular act that released four albums in Venezuela between 1988 and 1994, selling thousands of albums, having number 1 singles and Gold records on the Venezuelan charts. Radio Clip started off as quite a pop-oriented outfit, but became much heavier throughout their career. After three of the members left, Arturo Torres (bass) and Félix Duque (lead vocals) decided that they wanted to keep working together,

and brought in some more musicians and the group moved more into a progressive rock direction, and they changed the name. It was again put on hold when Arturo moved to the States, but the rest of the guys decided to continue, and the line-up stabilised with Félix, Eduardo Benatar (drums), Demian Mejicano (guitar), Rafael Paz (keyboards) and Pedro Misle (bass). Their history is rather unusual and complex, has involved such minor things such as people moving to Spain, playing their first concert only after they had been together for four years, then later landing the opening slot for Dream Theater in Venezuela only for their current guitarist to be unavailable, so their previous guitarist (who hadn't played with them for five years) rehearsed with them for three days to get the job done!

'Future Awaits' was their second album, and the first to be performed in English. Apparently the debut, which was released some five years prior to this one, was very much in the prog metal camp, but this is much more symphonic in nature. Mauricio Barroeta had replaced Demian, but the rest of the line-up remained the same. I wasn't sure what to expect from a Venezuelan progressive rock act, but it certainly wasn't a delicate and symphonic album with as much strength and depth as this one. The drums and bass are much higher in the mix, and Eduardo in particular has produced an incredibly dominant performance – he understands the impact he has, so there are complete sections where he doesn't play at all, and others where he is providing much more of a polyrhythmic performance than one would normally expect from this style of music.

All the songs are infectious, compelling, and totally enjoyable on first hearing. It is hard to imagine that apparently the music was written and recorded with none of the lyrics or even the melody lines worked out beforehand. The instrumental "El Diablo Suelte" is a load of fun, and is easily the most South American thing out there, with some wonderful picked guitar lines, and is that a ukelele I hear? There is a lot here to enjoy, and fans of bands such as Genesis, Kansas and Styx and even The Flower Kings will get a lot out of this.
Jan 2017

RED BAZAR
TALES FROM THE BOOKCASE
Red Bazar formed in 2007 with Andy Wilson on guitar, Paul Comerie on drums and Mick Wilson on bass and keyboards. The trio released their debut instrumental album 'Connections', in 2008, and followed it up with 'Differential Being' in 2010. After they released the three track EP 'After The Ice Storm' in 2013 they realized the increasing use of keyboards was making it harder for them to play live, so looked for a separate keyboard player, which saw the recruitment of Gary Marsh. With his addition, the band thought that possibly it was the time to try something different, so started a collaboration with singer Peter Jones, (Tiger Moth Tales), and this 2016 album is the result of that.

I haven't heard the earlier albums, so can't comment on what they sound like, but this is solid neo-prog, with a heavy guitarwork, so that at times they do remind me of the original Freewill line-up when they included keyboards. But this is neo-prog as opposed to prog metal, as there are plenty of times when Peter assists them in taking it down a step and to move more into IQ territory, but it's just that when Andy puts the hammer down, he really does! It is a diverse album in many ways, with picked guitar almost as prevalent as riffs, and the production is quite superb, allowing the space between the layers to be felt really cleanly. It does come across as a lost gem from the Nineties as opposed to the present day, but speaking as one who was solidly immersed in that scene at the time, I'm not viewing that as a bad thing at all! This is something that progheads should be seeking out.
Jan 2018

RED JASPER
THE GREAT AND SECRET SHOW

A few years back I was thinking about Red Jasper one evening and decided to google them to see what they were doing. Shortly thereafter I found myself having email conversations with D.C. (David Clifford), and we soon started talking about the potential for reissuing their albums on CD. I suggested he talk to Peter Purnell at Angel Air, and a short while later I found myself writing the booklets, and the conversations turned to potentially a new album? Well, here it is, released at the beginning of 2015. Original frontman Davey Dodds had decided that he no longer wanted to be involved with the music scene, but in drummer D.C. they already had a replacement as by now he had been making a name for himself as a singer with Clive Nolan's Caamora company and had one of the lead male roles on the incredible 'Alchemy'. The rest of the gang were all on board for the journey, but as D.C. felt he was no longer a drummer they brought in Nick Harradence, who was drummer with Shadowland when the two bands toured together some twenty years earlier! It was obvious that Red Jasper were going to sound very different to how they used to, as D.C. is such a different singer, and Davey also used to provide mandolins and whistles, so could they carry it off?

Thankfully the answer to that is a very strong and emphatic "Yes"!! Musically they are a different beast, and have moved more into a neo-prog area, but it still contains the folkier elements for which they were known. The biggest difference, though, is in the approach and style of the vocals. Not only does D.C. sing in a higher register than Davey, but he is also more used to a theatrical style of singing, where there may or may not be good microphones and there is a need to project. As opposed to someone just using their vocal cords with not much effort, here he is putting his all into each song so that each one becomes much more of a performance. Of course, the Jaspers were also always well-known for the power of Robin Harrison's guitars, and he has lost none of the knack of enthralling listeners with either gentle notes or hard-struck power chords. This is particularly true on "The Time Is Right", where the use of a guest sax also adds an additional element. Interestingly, the sax player is none other than Pat D'Arcy who was in an earlier line-up of the band and was with them when they released 'Sting In The

Tale'. DC's daughter Sohelia duets with him on "The Time Is Right", just as she did for the original live performances of 'Alchemy', and their voices work well together.

Jon Thornton (bass) and Lloyd George (keyboards) tie in with Nick and Robin in a manner that belies the truth that this is a band that hasn't performed for eighteen years. I mean, really? Somehow, I never saw them play live back in the Nineties, although Davey and I used to catch up every so often, and now they're back playing, and I live on the wrong side of the world! But this comeback album is an incredible statement, the Jaspers are back and long may this continue.
June 2017

RED JASPER
777
So, after the minor gap of eighteen years between albums, the Jaspers decided to take just a year to come back with the next one. Nick Harradence had only ever joined the band to help on the previous recording, and by now he had been replaced by Florin Werner on the drum seat. Sohelia came back to provide vocals on another song, and although there was no Pat D'Arcy, interestingly there was a guest appearance on guitar from Tony Heath, who just like Pat had been a member of the band for the 'Sting In The Tale' album, so there is a nice synergy and feeling of completeness.

As with the previous album, this is very much the 'new' Red Jasper with a very different musical approach to how they were in the Nineties, more "straight progressive" (if you get what I mean), but still with folky elements. I can't imagine another band performing a song such as "She Waits" as it starts with a very British almost "oom pah pah" feel before becoming a commercial rocker, and switches between the styles throughout. It is commercial, it is packed full of hooks, and such great fun! There are times when they do remind me somewhat of Credo but given my incredibly long affiliation with that band, I can't really say that is a bad thing. This album is a real grower, and Florin and Jon have already built up a strong relationship, with Jon having one of the lightest touches on bass that one will come across, with great effect. This partnership allows both Lloyd and Robin to build and throw melodies, solos, and swathes of sound around: it certainly sounds as if the guys had a blast recording this, while D.C. is still there at the front providing his different theatrical vocal approach.

D.C. has told me to expect yet another album soon as the guys just can't stop writing music together, and with such a long gap in their history it really does seem as if they have never been away.
June 2017

ALAN REED
HONEY ON THE RAZOR'S EDGE

It must be nearly 25 years since I first came across singer Alan Reed, probably with Clive Nolan's project 'Strangers On A Train', although it could have been Abel Ganz. This far along it's difficult to be sure. Alan of course made his name with Pallas, with whom he was frontman for more than 25 years, but he has always kept working with Clive as well, and earlier this year took one of the lead roles on 'King's Ransom'. The album starts with a strong keyboard pattern, and my immediate thought was, "Surely that's not Mike Stobbie?", but yes, it is, and a quick check of the musicians revealed some other very well-known names such as Jeff Green (guitars), Steve Hackett (harmonica), Scott Higham (drums) and a few guest singers such as Christina Booth from Magenta.

There will be many who will be bundling this into the neo prog scene, but its place in that sub-genre is probably more due to history than it is to the reality of what is featured on this album which sits best within crossover, moving between genres but always providing plenty of melody. One of the real joys is that it doesn't seem like a solo album, but like a band effort, with Jeff in particular being given plenty of room to show his style. But it's not all bombast, as Alan has a deft touch on guitar himself, and when the fancy takes him, shows a far more pastoral side. This is an album of great depth and breadth, and at the very heart are the pure clear vocals of Alan, capturing the listener and taking them on a journey. I enjoyed his solo debut, but this follow-up contains far more powerful and strength within it. Superb.
Dec 2017

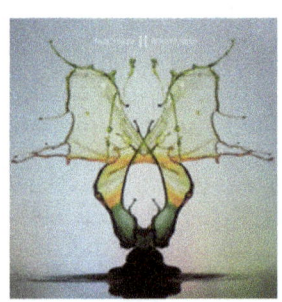

ROBERT REED
SANCTUARY II

Between 1991 and 2006 I was fortunate enough to run Feedback fanzine in the UK, and my constant cry in the early days was "I need artwork!". In 1993 I decided that one way to provide this would be by cutting out (literally) photos of album covers sent to me on press releases and make a collage. One of the albums reviewed in that particular issue, and included on the cover, was Cyan's 'For King And Country'. That 1993 debut release featured a young Robert Reed who provided everything. After a few more Cyan albums, and a dalliance with fellow Welshmen Ezra, he of course made his name with Magenta. But he is still a true multi-instrumentalist, and in 2014 released 'Sanctuary', following it up with the inventively titled 'Sanctuary II' in 2016. The version I have here is the double CD, which features the two songs that make up 'Sanctuary II' on the first, that album remixed by Tom Newman (yes, the Tom Newman who produced 'Tubular Bells') plus some additional songs. There is also a version available with a DVD as well.

Robert doesn't hide his love of Oldfield, especially considering he has Simon Phillips on

drums and Leslie Penning on recorder, both firmly associated with that artist, and he does actually list tubular bells among the instruments he himself provides. But, although this is heavily influenced by Oldfield and his style (especially when he brings in the distorted guitars), this is still Robert producing the music that he wants to, writing the songs and performing them in a certain manner. There are many bands out there who are heavily inspired by Genesis, King Crimson, IQ etc., but there are few who have truly managed to capture the style of Oldfield and turn that into something as dramatic and interesting as Robert has with this album. I just think it's wonderful, and an album I really enjoy playing as it is so vibrant and exciting.
Jan 2018

ROBERT REED
SANCTUARY LIVE
Following on from the success of the two 'Sanctuary' albums, a decision was made to bring a band together to perform both albums in their entirety and to record that for posterity. The event took place on October 8th, 2016, at Peter Gabriel's Real World Studios, and it was then released as a CD/DVD set. There was no way that Rob could provide all the instrumentation, so brought in friends to help, including Chris Fry, Martin Shellard, Dan Nelson, Jiffy Griffiths, Tim Lewis, Nigel Hopkins, Simon Brittlebank, Angharad Brinn, Christina Booth, Fran Murphy, Lorraine King and Ffion Wilkins. Now, this is music to be taken in and enjoyed, so although there is audience noise between the songs, everyone is calm and collected during the performances themselves. That everyone does a great job, nailing all their parts so that it comes across as very close to the original studio versions comes as no surprise, so it only leads to the question "so what was the point?".

But the point of this was showing that music isn't just a studio creation but can be taken out and performed. True, that does mean having quite a few guitarists all playing at the same time at certain points, but I don't really have a problem with it when the music is as solid and strong as it is here. Oldfield also has to surround himself with musicians when he tours just because there are so many layers, and that same is true with Rob Reed. That he isn't spoken about in the same context apart from those in the know is nothing short of sacrilege, as I have enjoyed this and Robert's other albums just as much, if not more, than many of those by Oldfield. Plus any album that has Christina singing on it will always be something to relish. Yet another truly glorious album from the Welshman.
Jan 2018

ROBERT REED
VARIATIONS ON THEMES BY DAVID BEDFORD
This EP sees Rob re-interpret three songs by David Bedford, surely not only one of the most important musicians to come out of the Seventies but also now one of the most forgotten. I only have three of his albums myself, one of which is probably his most well-known, 'Nurses Songs With Elephants', and the title song from that album is one of those

The Progressive Underground Vol 5

that has been re-interpreted by Rob. Terry Oldfield is involved, as is Les Penning and Tom Newman, and the EP contains "Rio Grande", "King Aeolus", "Nurses Songs With Elephants". These songs are then provided again as Newman remixes, and then two of them are repeated as more stripped-down versions.

Rob says, "I have been a huge fan of David's work for many years, which was a massive influence on Mike Oldfield, with whom he worked in the 1970's. I really think without David's influence and encouragement, we would not have Tubular Bells. David was equally at home in the classical and the rock world and had successful careers in both. I really want people to discover his work, which can at times be challenging, but at other times also very melodic. As a composer his maverick approach to music is sadly missed, so I've taken the original arrangements of 3 of his pieces and re interpreted them, using modern recording techniques. My mission was to do justice to his legacy while also trying to amplify their melodic and emotional context." He has certainly achieved that, and the vocals of Angharad Brinn on the second song is quite inspired.

I firmly believe that Rob has achieved everything he wanted to with this EP, making fans aware of the music of David Bedford, re-interpreting the originals, and then providing his own Oldfield-style flair to them all. This is yet another essential purchase for anyone who has ever cast an ear to 'Ommadawn' or 'Tubular Bells'.
Jan 2018

XAVI REIJA
RESOLUTION
Xavi is recognized as being one of Spain's top jazz drummers, and over the last fifteen years has built his reputation by working with artists such Steve Hogarth (Marillion), Gary Willis (Tribal Tech), Monica Green (The Supremes), Caco Senante, O 'Funk'illo and Pep Sala Joaquin Calderon. But he has also been working on his own bands, releasing 'Two Sides' with DX Project, two albums with the Xavi Reija Electric Quintet as well as trimming that down to the Xavi Reija Electric Trio who prior to this had released a DVD. Now he is back, again in a trio environment, with Bernat Hernández on bass, and Dušan Jevtović on guitars. Bernat also played with Dušan on the latter's album 'Am I Walking Wrong' which was released last year.

When I first started listening to jazz as a child, it was bands led by drummers that I became most interested in, and the very first jazz album I ever bought with my own money was by Gene Krupa. There is something about music being geared towards the complexity and freedom that comes from a powerhouse at the back that really lifts the overall, and if you normally listen to metal then you would have to agree that Testament's recent stunning live opus just wouldn't be half as dynamic if Gene Hoglan wasn't behind the kit. Only four of these compositions are group numbers, with the other seven all scored by Xavi, but the common theme throughout is the sheer amount of space these guys have given themselves to work with. That they are all stunning musicians is never in doubt, but they know the importance of simplicity as well as complexity and the right time to deliver what is required, with fuzzed distortion adding to the overall sound.

The three musicians work off each other, and the result is an avant garde album that combines improvisation with funk and melody, distortion and feedback with clean struck notes, polyrhythmic sounds with simple timekeeping, so much so that the listener never really knows what is coming next. A very strong production tops off yet another incredibly powerful release from the Moonjune label.
Jun 2014

RETROSPECTIVE
STOLEN THOUGHTS
This 2008 album was the debut from Polish group Retrospective, and is a concept about the growth of a child into adulthood, and the loss of imagination, innocence and carelessness that comes with it. I was incredibly impressed with the follow-up 'Lost In Perception', which came out in 2012, but it has taken me a while to look backwards, and I am glad I did. Musically they have been heavily inspired by their counterparts Riverside, yet there are also elements of Muse and Porcupine Tree in music that is often dark and mysterious. It is strange to think there are two guitarists at play here, as it is all about bringing the right emotional content to the music as opposed to crunching out the riffs. Łukasz Marszałek on bass is also very much a key player to the band, as he underpins what is going on with wonderful counterpoint, while guitarists Maciej Klimek and Alan Szczepaniak are often matching him. The production on the drums of Robert Kusik is strong and clean, while keyboard player Beata Łagoda uses many different styles, switching to piano when it is the optimum time to do so.

So, the music is both powerful and emotional, and it needs a very special voice indeed to rise over this, and here there is the lustrous rich and edgy baritone of Jakub Roszak. Many singers cut through music like a knife, thin and powerful, reaching heights that many cannot imagine, while here Jakub is a thick carpet – joined to the music beneath him, and with a power and breadth that cannot be contained. Will there ever be an end to the amazing prog bands coming out of Poland? I certainly hope not.
Jan 2017

RETROSPECTIVE
RE:SEARCH
It took four years from the debut for Polish Prog Metal act Retrospective to release their second, and then another five for this their third, so let's hope that they don't keep on this progression as I really don't want to wait for six years until the next one! There is a real mix of melody and metal combined with rock sensibilities and passion that makes this album stand out from many others within the genre. It is just about impossible to make a comparison with other bands, but possibly the closest would be Muse or Porcupine Tree,

but even that's not fair on either band. One of the things that makes this album is the way they have managed to bring so much space into the compositions, so much so that there are times when the instruments seem miles apart, as opposed to all being in the same room. This allows the listener to listen to the music as well as all the minute details of what everyone is doing.

This is real "grown up" progressive music, that has so much to offer anyone who enjoys the genre. Good vocals, with all the lyrics in strong English, this is an album which deserves to be given full attention, as opposed to something being played in the background. I've lost track of the great Polish bands I've heard over the years, and only hope these guys will gain the attention they deserve, as this is a goody.
Mar 2017

MARKUS REUTER
FALLING FOR ASCENSION
Since the late 1990's, Markus Reuter has steadily made a name for himself as a formidable player, a gifted improviser and a composer for both rock and classical music ensembles. As one third of Stick Men, he tours extensively across Europe, Asia, Australia, and in North and South America alongside King Crimson's Tony Levin and Pat Mastelotto. In 2013, his large-scale composition for orchestra, 'Todmorden 513' received its world premiere performed by the Colorado Chamber Orchestra. Here he is working with Switzerland's post-minimal quartet, SONAR and live electronics specialist, Tobias Reber.

Reuter leads this ensemble through a series of compositions that are amongst his earliest, having all been written between 1985 and 1987. "For me the striking thing about this album is that the themes and melodies and rhythms that you're hearing were written when I was 14 years old," explains Reuter. "I had these little motifs set aside for such a long time and I never knew what to do with them." Recorded in just one day under Reuter's direction, the pieces were prepared as modules, most of which contain a 12-tone row and assigned to an individual player. "They had the freedom to decide when to move to the next stage within the module, independent of each other," says Reuter. Within each module, a finite number of choices are available. "The choice is limited to the 'when', not the 'what'. There's a specific thing asked of you, but you can decide when to move to the next element in the series." Personally, I've had real issues with this album, as when I think I'm just about getting to grips with it the feeling goes away and yet again I think it's dire. But I honestly think that is more down to me than it is to the album itself. This is incredibly repetitive, but there are similarities with Can, and for some reason I found myself thinking of Art Zoyd, although they sound nothing alike. This is something that takes perseverance, and at the end of it I'm still not sure if the effort was worth it. This is music that needs to be worked at, and certainly won't be to everyone's tastes.
May 2017

YUVAL RON AND RESIDENTS OF THE FUTURE
RESIDENCE OF THE FUTURE

Although this album was originally released in 2009, it was remastered by Yuval in 2012 and then promoted towards the end of last year. It's quite strange in some respects as this album is now available free of charge from Yuval's website. This is mostly an instrumental album, the music being supplied by Yuval Ron (guitar), Aviram Gottfried (keyboards, laptop), Yaniv Shalev (bass) and Yatziv Caspi (drums) although there are also some female vocals here and there care of Dorin Mandelbaum. They describe their music as a constant emphasis on harmonic richness, rhythmical sophistication, dialogue between the players and an extensive use of synthesizers, laptops, and other electronic instruments. It is certainly a breathtaking mix of styles with fusion very much at the heart of all they do, but while Yuval provides the main melodic lead it is obvious the rest of the guys are all incredible musicians.

The keyboard sounds being deployed often have more in common with electronica than prog, and in many ways, this feels at times as if it has been transported from the Seventies, a lost album if you will. Yuval has an incredibly fluid style and McLaughlin has obviously been a major impact on him, but they are also bringing in elements that are more progressive, and even some that are metallic. The album is a combination of carefully thought-out compositions with improvisations, and I just found myself listening and smiling, gently moving with the beat as I fell under its' spell. Even the drum solo didn't distract me (I normally hate studio drum solos with a passion) as it seemed to be just so in keeping with the rest of what was going on. The simple piano work on "Watching Over Shizutani Kou Bay, Pt 1" is incredibly compelling.

So, there you have it, a fusion album that originally came out a few years ago which is now being made available as a free download if you sign up to Yuval's mailing list. What have you got to lose?
Apr 2014

YUVAL RON & RESIDENTS OF THE FUTURE
FUTURISTIC WORLDS UNDER CONSTRUCTION

This EP was released back in 2004 and was the first music made available by Yuval Ron & Residents of the Future. Given that it was another eight years before the debut album came out, and there has been nothing official since (although the band regularly tours, and has also released videos), they aren't exactly the most prolific act around, but don't let that put you off from discovering their music. This is an instrumental five song EP, clocking in at some thirty-three minutes in length, and somewhat surprisingly for a band led by a guitarist, starts with lots of synths. But, from here on in we have a band that is cooking and are very much a band as opposed to a backing outfit for Yuval, who is indeed one helluva guitarist. The interplays between him and keyboard player Ofir Shwartz are reminiscent of how John McLaughlin and Jan Hammer used to play off each other, with each providing the backdrop for the other to solo against, while Yaniv Shalev (bass) and Yatziv Caspi (drums) are also given plenty of opportunities to show just what they can do.

This is jazz fusion, played by exponents of the art who know what they want to achieve, and can do just that. Moving forward to the current day, and Yatziv is still there with Yuval, although Ofir and Yaniv are not, and they are still very active and touring and playing internationally. This is incredible music, and there are more details on this plus everything else that is going on at his website. This is great music, and if you love electric jazz/fusion/prog then this is simply indispensable.
Apr 2017

THE ROOM
BEYOND THE GATES OF BEDLAM
I was having a conversation with David Elliott from BEM recently, and he asked me if there were any bands in the back catalogue that I would be interested in reviewing, and one of those I requested was The Room. I wasn't sure why but knew I had heard about them from somewhere, but for the life of me couldn't remember why. As soon as I started playing this it all came flooding back, as the man on vocals was Martin Wilson, ex-Grey Lady Down, a band I saw many times back in the Nineties, and whose original demo I still have (blackmail anyone?). The other musician I also knew was Steve Anderson, who was latterly in GLD, but who I know from Sphere, the band he was in with Neil Durant (now in IQ). The line-up for this their second album is completed by Andy Rowe (bass), Steve Checkley (keyboards) and Chris York (drums).

This is music that hearkens back to the Nineties, when everyone involved in the UK progressive rock scene really felt that things were about to explode into the mainstream, as there were so many good bands that could be heard virtually every week in London. GLD, as with many others before them, played at The Marquee (with Jump as support on the night I saw them), yet as with most of the neo prog scene didn't make the leap into the big time. A large part of the album is neo-prog, although there are also strong melodic rock tendencies, and there has been a great deal of thought with the arrangements.

Steve is an interesting keyboard player, one who is prepared to solo when needed, or stay more in the background playing the perfect accompaniment, and that comes through particularly on songs such as "As Crazy As It Seems", which is far more laid back than one might expect from a band like this. There are lots of different influences in what they are doing, and perhaps it isn't surprising that GLD is one of these, but bands as diverse as Credo, Marillion and Magnum all have a part to play as well. Martin's vocals are perfectly suited to this style of music and provide a significant point of difference, with emotion being very important indeed. This is a really solid piece of work, and I look forward to hearing more from The Room.
May 2017

The Progressive Underground Vol 5

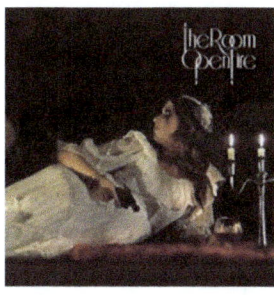

THE ROOM
OPEN FIRE

Having recently reviewed The Room's 2015 album 'Beyond The Gates of Bedlam" I now find myself listening to their 2012 debut, 'Open Fire', which is available through Bandcamp (I believe it was originally released in the States on Melodic Revolution Records). I don't know why it took them three years to follow up on this debut, but it certainly wasn't down to lack of quality or songs as yet again this is another really strong release. Martin Wilson has a memorable voice, and this melodic rock crossover neo progressive rock sound gives him plenty of room to shine. Andy Rowe and Andrew Rae keep the rhythm section nailed down, knowing when and what to play to either provide the others a backbone or dramatic emphasis, while guitarist Steve Anderson and keyboard player Steve Checkley are both adept at providing harmonies or solos as required.

It may have been released in 2012, but the heart of this album belongs twenty years earlier when the progressive scene was insular, robust, and full of vigour. True, it was often the same people attending all the gigs, but back then there were loads of gigs to go to! With no internet, and virtually no press, the only way to get people to hear the music was by getting out there and gigging, and this music is very much at home with what was being released back then. Of course, Martin and Steve Anderson were very active during that period, and with this album it is as if the years in between just never happened. I can "see" The Room out there playing with Grace, Galahad, Landmarq and all the others from back then, and it is wonderful to know that music like this is still being performed and played with such passion today, and that The Room are a gigging outfit getting out there and showing the crowds that progressive rock is as relevant as it ever has been. If you doubt me why not go to their Bandcamp site and listen to this and see if you agree.
May 2017

ROZ VITALIS
OVERCOMING-UP

This release is something of a strange one, as it was recorded and mixed between April 2007 and September 2008 and had been completed long before the 'Revelator' and 'Patience of Hope' albums from 2011 and 2012 respectively yet was only released in 2014. To add to my confusion Ivan Rozmainsky (keyboards, percussion, samples, tenor recorder) sent it to me at the beginning of this year to review, although to be fair he did try to send it to me back in 2014 and I said I was too busy back then. The line-up of this instrumental outfit is completed by Vladimir 'Energoslon' Semenov-Tyan-Shansky (bass), Sydius (aka Igor Pokatilov) (guitar, samples) and Vladislav Korotkikh (flute), Yes, here is a band that has no use for drums.

Listed on PA as RIO/Avant, that is definitely the right sub-genre for them to be included in, yet this music is surprisingly melodic and incredibly easy to follow. It all makes

musical sense, with the different instruments and sounds melding together in a fashion that has far more in common with modern classical, yet with an emptiness and bleakness that is incredibly powerful. Not everyone must be playing at the same time, and there is no need for anyone to show off their skills, this is all about playing the right notes, in the right manner, at the right moment. Ivan has a wonderful touch on piano, and this combined with the flute are the driving forces of the band. They have even the temerity to include a song that is more than twenty minutes long, which works incredibly well. Their music is peaceful and restrained for the most part, but the introduction of "Thorns of Forgiving" could almost be from a different band altogether, as it is strident and more mainstream progressive, and the repeated melody on an organ provides a far warmer feel. I don't know why it took so long to release this, but I'm happy it has finally seen the light of day as it is yet another strong album from these guys.
Mar 2017

ROZ VITALIS
PSALM 6
This is so completely different from 'Overcoming-Up' that one would expect this to be by a totally different line-up, but although there have been some changes Ivan is still very much at the helm on grand Bluthner piano, electric keyboards and metallophone, while Vladislav still provides flute and Vladimir has moved to guitars from bass. They now have a drummer in Philip "Phill" Semenov, a new bassist in Ruslan Kirillov, a second guitarist in Vladimir Efimov with Alexey Gorshkov on trumpets and acoustic guitar, plus some guests providing percussion and bass clarinet. Apparently this thirty-three minutes long EP is about spiritual quest and the emotional upheaval of a human being in a situation of strong stress. Mind you, given that this is totally instrumental as with all their work, it's a little hard to get all that without any lyrics.

I think this is the third or fourth release I've heard from this Russian outfit and is easily the most varied. There are times when I think I'm listening to Mike Oldfield, at others there are hints of early Barclay James Harvest and at others King Crimson. All this from a band that are supposed to be RIO/Avant. Ivan is always at the heart of everything that is going on, as would be expected, but this is very much a band as opposed to a project. His piano doesn't seem to be as far to the fore as in other releases, and certainly the guitarists and trumpets start the album off with such a bang that I wasn't even sure I was playing the right one! With hints of jazz, loads of melody, and a stronger move to the mainstream progressive field than many might expect, this is an album that will certainly intrigue many listeners who may not have wanted to listen to Roz Vitalis in the past. There is still plenty of space and tone within their music, and given that this is on Bandcamp why not wander over and give it a try?
Mar 2017

ROZ VITALIS
AT LAST. LIVE
So, Roz Vitalis are back with another live album, which is taken from two different performances in St. Petersburg in December of 2016. What we are presented with here is the full live line-up of the band, which includes trumpet, flute and low whistle, electric and acoustic guitars, keyboards, bass, and drums. Here is a band where the arrangements are crucial, and some of the instruments are only used sparingly, which mean that from one song to the next the band can be quite different in their sound and approach. But band leader Ivan Rozmainsky knows exactly what is needed for each piece and maintains a continuity throughout. Much of the material being performed has yet to appear on an album, while others are older yet have also never been released in that format.

Musically the band they have most in common with, at least to my ears, is Karda Estra, as they bring together classical music and progressive rock so that a style is created that will appeal to fans of both areas. The largest difference between the two is that Ivan is firstly a pianist, and many of the songs rely on his delicate touch, while another significant difference is the use of trumpet. This is played as if it is being directed by an orchestral conductor as opposed to someone from the jazz scene, and the result is long notes that hit hard and pure, no sliding or strange stylings. Alexey Gorshkov has great breath control, and there is little sense of vibrato or strain, just clear sounds that take the music in a different direction. This brass feel is quite at odds with the flute and low whistle of Vladislav Korotkikh which is much warmer and friendly.

I have long been a fan of this Russian band, and each release cements that even more. I look forward to the next studio album to see what they do with some of the songs included here, and highly recommend this to anyone into the more orchestral style of progressive rock. As this is on Bandcamp, it is also possible to give this a listen before purchase, so why not give them a try?
May 2017

RSC
AKA FLYROCK
RSC made a huge impact when they started in the Polish progressive scene in the easily Eighties, and with the violin being of major importance, they soon became known as the "Polish Kansas". After the debut, there was a gap of ten years before they then released a series of albums, only to disappear from the scene again until 2008, when 'Aka Flyrock' was released. The first thing one notices from looking at the personnel involved is that only singer Zbigniew Działa and keyboard player Wiktor Kucaj are still there from 'Fly Rock', released in 1983, but guitarist Waldemar Rzeszut first made his appearance on 'Czas Wodninka' in 1996, so the only new boy is guitarist Marcin Percel. With no violin, the sound is obviously quite different from what many

will be looking for, but the result is something that is still enjoyable on first hearing.

For a band that has been around for so long, albeit with some large gaps, one might expect there to be a much larger Seventies influence on the music, but the most prevalent decade is that of the Eighties, as they bring the electronic pop sound of bands like Thompson Twins into a more progressive arena, mixed with American style AOR. The result is an album that is surprisingly accessible, even with all the lyrics in Polish. Strongly crossover in outlook, as opposed to the AOR prog style with which they made their name, this is an enjoyable album for those that want their music to be light and fluffy as opposed to dense and complex.
Jan 2017

RUBYCONE
PICTURES FOR SUSCEPTIBLE HOUSEWIVES
A Fifties-style cover and an interesting album title gives nothing away about what one will find when one puts this on the player, and song titles such as "And The Perfect Yellow Walls Will Show You The Magic" doesn't exactly lend themselves to interpretation. But all becomes clear when one finally listens to the music as here we have a band that are refusing to conform in any way whatsoever. The basis of this could probably be best described as instrumental prog metal, but there are huge jazz influences at play as well. They move between electric and acoustic instruments with ease, each having its own place in the collage of music they present, and while they can riff out in true Dream Theater style with plenty of counterpoint and aggression the real joy of this album is never being really sure what it likely to come next.

With 11 songs and only just over 41 minutes long it is a concise piece of work, with the one lengthy number, the closing "When The Rain Is Over I'll Say To You: Hasta La Vista" (with some sound snippets from a certain film) which is eight minutes, but generally they keep their musical journeys short and to the point. Overall, this is quite a debut from this Moldovan quartet, and some five years on from its release I am amazed that there hasn't been a follow-up. I just hope that doesn't mean these guys are no more as this is well worth investigating. The music is so tight there isn't any room for a singer or keyboards, and the rhythm section manage to keep it going so that the two guitarists can interweave the melodies. Superb.
May 2014

SALVA
SIGH OF BOREAS
This 2016 album was the fourth studio release from the Swedish band, who are based around multi-instrumentalist and singer Per Malmberg. It had taken five years since their previous release and is the first time I have come across them even though they released their debut back in 2004. I have seen some reviews where they complain about the vocal style, but I found it quite refreshing and different to the normal gentle style beloved by

many. Musically this is all over the place, from the bombastic and over the top prog metal to folk and everything in between. It doesn't sound as if it is a recent album but is far more reminiscent of the vibrant neo prog scene from the Nineties. They have used IQ as a reference point as much as they have Yes, particularly in the keyboard runs, and I soon found I was smiling while listening to it.

Any band that starts with a fifteen-minute-long song is always going to get my attention, especially if it takes a long time for the vocals to start, and I thoroughly enjoyed the melting pot of styles that is going on here. It really is all over the place, yet somehow always works. For example, the dual picked acoustic guitars combined with over-the-top staccato keyboard chords make total sense in the title song, as it does when it segues from that straight into a more reflective and gentle section. The flute is a wonderfully delicate touch, and I admire the restraint in some of these songs as there is the distinct threat of them turning it up and blasting through, yet they are always in control and when they do strike the riffs it is always in the perfect place. Stefan Gavik is a fine guitarist, and to hear him let rip over the top of delicate piano is quite something. I can see I need to seek out more of their material.
Feb 2018

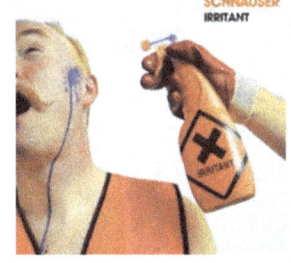

SCHNAUSER
IRRITANT

With a twelve-year history and five full albums to their name, Alan Strawbridge, Duncan Gammon, Holly McIntosh and Jasper Williams are veterans of the music scene, and now they have embarked on the next step of their journey by bringing on board saxophonist Dino Christodoulou and by signing with those nice chaps at BEM. Vocalist and guitarist Alan Strawbridge says: "We're all really looking forward with Bad Elephant; enthusiastic and like-minded chaps with great taste and even better facial hair." This is my first experience of Schnauser, and I am already starting to wonder what the other albums sound like, as this strange hotch-potch of styles is incredibly appealing, even though I'm not sure why.

Trying to describe this is, um, difficult. Okay, so let's get the obvious ones out of the way first – they're heavily influenced by the Canterbury scene, and I am sure the addition of the sax has exacerbated this, but there are heaps of musical references taken from the psychedelic scene of the late Sixties. Add to that a power pop sound that has elements of The Mothers of Invention, as well as the beat scene, and a wicked sense of humour then you may be getting close. I think I deserve a prize for picking up on the single melody line from "Roobarb" which appears on "Re-Mortgaging The Nest of Hairs" (did I mention humour?).

This is a very British album, there is just no way that any other country could bring together a mess of influences like this and make it into something that is quite special.

There is a real "indie" feel to much of this, and there will be plenty of progheads aghast at this being described as progressive, as they sound nothing like Yes or Genesis. No, they don't, they are Schnauser, and they're great.
May 2017

NERISSA SCHWARZ
PLAYGROUNDS LOST
I first came across this album when it was suggested to the Crossover team on ProgArchives that Nerissa would be a worthy inclusion. It didn't take long for us to agree, and she was duly accepted, and I discovered this was an album that stayed with me, one that had so many hidden layers and depths that it required repeated plays to try and understand the music that was contained within. Nerissa first came to attention to many as harpist with the progressive band Frequency Drift, and although she has also worked elsewhere this is her first truly solo album where she provides electric harp and Mellotron in what is a truly atmospheric and reflective melancholic album. There are times when the music is really very dark indeed, and I wouldn't recommend playing this late at night after too many gins, as it might not put you in a mood you would relish. But, playing it late at night with a glass of Man O' War Exiled Pinot Gris is a different matter altogether, and I would recommend that as an interesting exercise. I also found this really is an album that benefits from being played on headphones, as the listener mustn't be distracted by any other sounds, but instead needs to be taken deep into her world. That the cover is a photo of a person in woods is not an accident I'm sure, as for me this album evokes feelings of walking deep in forests allowing my mind to wander (and not too sure if it will ever really come back). Sometimes the dappled light comes though the leaves, providing some relief, while at others it is deep, and the canopy is a ceiling that cuts out the birdsong and contains just that hint of threat. If ever an album repays being paid close attention to, then this is it.
Jan 2018

SEASONS OF TIME
CLOSED DOORS TO OPEN PLAINS
For numerous reasons, most of them concerned with line-up changes, it has taken 17 years for Seasons of Time to return with the follow-up to 'Behind The Mirror'. Dirk Berger (bass, keyboards, vocals) has been there since the beginning, while Malte Twarloh (vocals, guitar, keyboards) also sang on the debut but prior to coming back for this recording left the band in 2006, with the line-up now completed by guitarist Florian Wenzel and drummer Marco Gruhn. Here we have a classic case of an album that could be great, but has failed on a somewhat important hurdle, that of the vocals. While musically this is a tight outfit with a lot going for them, the vocals just don't work for me. I have tried, really tried, and managed to get to the point where they are almost bearable, but they are just nowhere near the standard of the music that is playing

underneath. I haven't heard the debut, so can't state if they are the same there, but when the singer has problems keeping on a note, obvious issues with breath control for sustain, then one must wonder.

It is almost as if there are two sets of recordings here, with a top-notch band recording some great music in a studio, while the vocals have been added from a demo tape. It is incredibly frustrating as if they had turned this into a pure instrumental album then it would have a lot more going for it, with neo-prog moving into a more prog metal territory. It has taken them an age to record their second album, but unless they change their approach, I can't see there being a great deal of demand for a third.
Jun 2014

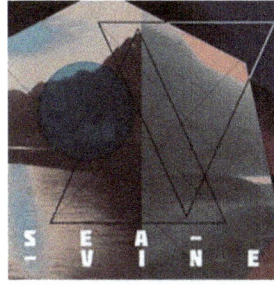

SEA-VINE
SEA-VINE
Although this is being portrayed as a band album, for the most part this is the work of keyboard player Michal Cywinski, who also provides drums (ok, programming) on five of the six songs. With a guest guitarist on one, a drummer on another, and a singer only on a few, one wonders why he hasn't put this out as a straight solo project and why did he get the others involved at all? Michal has a wonderful touch on piano, and the production is quite superb so that one has a great presence of being with him in the room. What I do find strange is that on the solo piano piece, "Going Anywhere", there are a few wrong notes, so I wonder why that has been kept in?

It appears that he is more at home with piano than electronic keyboards, as the sounds being deployed are often very dated, and without the passion and emotion that comes through when he is playing more naturally. There are times when this album does cross into the more Tangerine Dream electronic style, and not always in the best way possible. The major issue I have with this album is with singer Milena Szymanska who for the most part does a fine job with her clear vocals, but there are passages where she is obviously struggling. I could understand that appearing in the final product if this was a live album (with no re-recording, not that anyone ever does that...) but there is no excuse with a studio effort. So although there were parts of the album that were really quite pleasant, it was rarely more than that and at times it was worse, so this isn't something to which I will often be returning.
May 2014

SECTLINEFOR
ANOREXIC INSECT
When I recently started reviewing music again in earnest, I contacted bands and labels to let them know that I was back in the land of the living, and one of these was Piton from Ygodeh. He soon wrote back to me and told me that he had been working on a new project, Sectlinefor, and would I be interested in hearing the debut they had released recently? Like Ygodeh, Sectlinefor is a trio based around bassist Aal and Piton

(everything else), but instead of Serberus, this time we have Jared providing vocals. I can see why it was decided that this was a new band instead of just a new album, as here we have something that is very special indeed, creating a form that I found both incredibly compelling and immediate.

Imagine if you will System For A Down mating with Throbbing Gristle, and bringing to life a bastard offspring that not only contains elements of both bands (and Serj Tankian's orchestral exploits to boot) but also the brutal force of death metal. Sonically this is immense, with Jared singing perfectly in key at some points, and only managing to get his vocals out through gritted teeth at others, struggling to even hit any sort of notes as he fights the restraints of the straitjacket he has been wrapped in. Here we have music that is pushing the boundaries, creating something that is vibrant, brutal, and uncompromising at all levels, and I love it. The more I play this the more I find within it, as the layers open – there is no way that this should make nearly as much sense as it does, but for those who don't want their music to be 4/4 and boring then look no further than this. Available through Bandcamp I urge all those who enjoy music from left field to at least stream this and give them a try. What have you got to lose? And you have plenty to gain. Then if that wasn't enough, I have to give special kudos to the press release, repeated below so that you can enjoy reading it as much I did. Sectlinefor are a band that should be on everyone's radar.

"Trawling through the freezing swamps and slicing his legs open on poisonous shrubbery, Piton realised he was about to die. Hungry parasites were suckling upon his organs and mosquitos the size of his fist were devouring his blood until no quantity of food or water could sustain his survival. For a whole he could no longer remember why he had embarked on this mission in the first place, but as his bones withered into twigs, none of these things mattered anymore. He was so lost and worn that his knees began to betray him, and he fell into the muddy ground, disinterested in the life he once treasured so preciously, ready to surrender his person into death. But what he didn't know, was that he was being watched.

An external force by the name of Hypno-frog had been keeping an eye on Piton for quite some time now, admiring the man's ambition whilst waiting for the perfect moment to introduce himself. That moment came when Piton stumbled a few feet away from a dusty cabin and crawled inside to find warmth and shelter from the elements. There, Hypno-frog revealed himself to Piton, complementing the boy on making it this far and then delivering a proposition. He handed Piton a guitar and requested that the two of them lived together in that very cabin without speaking, giving up their voices to communicate only via the means of music, the epitome of expression. Piton eagerly agreed, happy to abandon the cold in favour of his bloody fingers using strings to represent the soul he had trapped inside for so long. And for a while, life was good again, the translation of spirit into an extrinsic audio force building health to both parties, each finding a mutual love (and hate) in the technical aggression of metal structures and cosmic atmospheres.

However, all things must pass, and eventually Hypno-frog instructed Piton to step back and witness what he had created. For before them was a full-length album, written and arranged, almost fleshy enough to be released beyond the constraints of the cabin. At first, Piton was confused as he did not know how to approach this discharge, but once again it was Hypno-frog who offered a solution. He suggested they should build a small army, one which could help sharpen these sounds into a more direct spike to pierce virgin ears with more precision. Piton not only understood the benefit of such an idea, but also knew exactly the right soldiers to do it. Enter Aal, a beast who explored bass frets like he was reading brail. Piton knew all too well that these passionate creatures were each born with their own unique sets of powerful skills, as together they had fought many wars in the past, formulating a chemistry they had named YGODEH, a separate audio project created from a consistency so potent that any sorcerer would shudder at the smell. They were already a team, and as soon as they assembled, they knew they were almost ready to charge into battle. Except they were missing one crucial piece to complete the message. They needed a voice.

After a tiresome search, they stumbled upon an abandoned child by the name of Jared. Depressed and confused, this boy was known to shout at the heavens in great anger, with no place to focus his elaborate tales of the earthly horrors he had witnessed. Recognising his dire need for adoption, the group presented Jared to Hypno-frog, and received his blessing, just like the scripture had foretold all those centuries ago. And with that, Sectlinefor was conceived like a baby in the womb, ready to be cut out and dismembered, a small piece for every person in the world. Every fairy tale needs a hero, and every fairy tale needs a villain. And at this early hour in our story, not even SECTLINEFOR know which side they are fighting for." 'Nuff said.
May 2017

SECURITY PROJECT
LIVE 1
What we have here is a very special band, comprising members of King Crimson, Shriekback, and Gabriel's original band coming together to bring some of Peter Gabriel's classics into the live arena. Seattleites Trey Gunn and Michael Cozzi join esteemed drummer Jerry Marotta and NY keyboardist David Jameson to harness the core of these songs. Added to the pedigree of these players is the voice of Brian Cummins, whose interpretations add haunting authenticity to the performances. With David also providing the eigenharp (an electronic hybrid instrument akin to a computerized bassoon) and Trey on his 10-string touch guitar, it is hard to even comprehend how just four musicians create the majestic tapestry that is there for Brian to sing against. He may not be exactly like Gabriel, although he isn't too far off, but it is the music being performed that blows the mind.

These aren't always note for note reproductions, as the guys put their own twists on the interpretations but given how many layers were placed on the originals it is incredible that just four people are able to recreate this. Each song on this album truly is a classic, from "Lay Your Hands On Me" to "Biko", and there is even a nod to Genesis. I was

amazed at just how relevant and real they are – vital, alive, with a coming together of world music and progressive rock in an incredible fashion. Some of these songs are forty years old now, but here they have been made fresh by guys who really care about what they are doing. I was blown away when I heard this, and I know that anyone who enjoys Gabriel will feel the same way.
Apr 2017

SECURITY PROJECT
LIVE 2

After such a brilliant album in 'Live 1', the only sensible thing to do was release 'Live 2'! This features the same line-up as the debut, but musically they have spread themselves wider in that we get two songs from 'Lamb' right up to 'OVO', all of them played with the same care and delicacy that made the debut album such a delight. I am generally not a fan of tribute bands, but I can't even think of these guys as such as they are playing the music with such love and vitality that it is all-consuming. Just listen to "Moribund The Burgermeister" to see what I mean as it shifts from delicacy and superb percussion through to a rock number with ease.

I could listen to this album all day, as the songs have real life and passion, and that's what makes them so immediate and essential. One can hear the audience getting restless when they hear the piano introduction to "Lamb", as if they are wondering is this really going to be performed? Then when Jerry hits those cymbals, they know it's a reality, and Brian sneers his way through the song, giving Rael a much greasier edge than he used to have. I've discovered that I can't play this album without smiling all the time, as it is just so much fun with classic songs being given a new lease of life by musicians who are not only masters of everything they touch, but also care about the music very much indeed. I know it is unlikely that these guys will ever play down in my neck of the woods (although Hackett is here later this year, so anything's possible), so until I get to see them live, I'll have to keep playing these two albums and enjoying them immensely.
Apr 2017

SECURITY PROJECT
FIVE

The latest release from Security Project is a five-song sampler that allows listeners to hear new singer Happy Rhodes, which has allowed the band to start stretching their wings away from just Peter Gabriel although that will remain the focus of their attention. Happy is an American singer, songwriter, instrumentalist and electronic musician with a four-octave vocal range. She has produced eleven solo recordings, and Jerry Marotta and Trey Gunn play on a several of them. In fact, her husband percussionist Bob Muller, was a key partner of Trey's in his solo band, and he has known her for quite some time.

The five songs contain four Gabriel classics ("Games Without Frontiers", "No Self Control", "I Have The Touch" and "Rhythm of The Heat") plus "Mother Stands for Comfort" by Kate Bush (originally from 'Hounds Of Love'). Of course, Gabriel and Bush have worked together, so this is an interesting song to include, and it allows Trey to provide some emotive touch guitar behind Happy's breathless vocals. This comes across as a simple, yet highly complex piece, and works incredibly well. Happy can put her vocals to just about anything, moving between styles with ease, which will enable the band to become even more diverse. Given their output in a very short period of time, I am certainly intrigued to see what comes next. I urge anyone who enjoys this style of music to visit their site and investigate further. You won't be disappointed, I assure you.
Apr 2017

SECURITY PROJECT
CONTACT
Security Project has once again reinvented itself, this time with vocalist Happy Rhodes. Together with Jerry Marotta (drummer from Peter Gabriel's first five records), Trey Gunn (King Crimson), Michael Cozzi (Shriekback) and NY keyboardist David Jameson, the group continues reimagining the early work of Peter Gabriel (and on this disc Kate Bush), but with Happy's impressive four-octave vocals adding an entirely new dimension.

To say this is incredible, just doesn't do the word justice. It is hard to imagine Gabriel's music given a more imaginative and careful re-interpretation, with stunning vocals, beautiful harmonies, and great arrangements. No-one knows how to provide the passionate drumming that Gabriel required like Jerry Marotta, while Trey's touch guitar adds a wealth and depth of sounds, and he links in with Michael Cozzi, whose guitarwork is stunning, and then there is David Jameson. There can't be many keyboard players who have a PhD in Computer Science, and who founded a software company to develop audio plug-ins (which he uses on stage to recreate classic synth sounds). Happy has a stunning voice, but it is also the use of others as lead singers that makes this band so special, especially when they interplay as they do on songs such as "Intruder".

Yes, this is a covers band, but they aren't trying to reproduce the music exactly as it was originally played, but instead are showing that the music from nearly forty years ago (I feel very old) is as relevant as it was when Gabriel was driving music through to a new frontier. If you have ever been involved in a discussion as to which of the 'Peter Gabriel' albums are best (I personally tend towards 'Melt', but it's a tough call), then this is the album for you.
Dec 2017

IL SEGNO DEL COMANDO
IL VOLTO VERDE
Well, it has been quite a while since I have had the opportunity to write about Il Segno Di Comando, as their last album was released in 2002 and I reviewed it in August of that

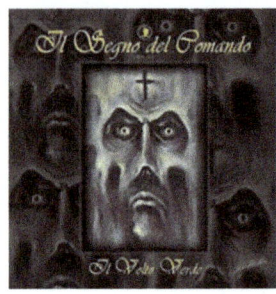
year. There followed a long period of activity until Diego Banchero put together a new line-up in 2010, with just himself remaining. Perhaps the most prominent change from the listener's perspective is that there is now a female singer in Maethelyiah, and with the musical approach also changing somewhat it isn't hard to say that in many ways this is a brand-new band as opposed to the third album. Anyway, putting such matters to one side, what we have here is an album that is looking back to the classic Seventies progressive movement, especially the mighty Goblin, but also bringing in some lighter and symphonic moments that offset the darkness and drama that one might expect.

For the most part Maethelyiah is a revelation, but there are some places, such as when she is providing vocals behind the guitar on "Tremodia delle dolci parole" that it just doesn't work, and she actually detracts from the rest of the band. But when she is at the forefront and is singing the lead then she is full of confidence and the rest of the guys support her admirably. If this was a debut then I would say that it was showing promise, and to be honest that is probably the best way to look at it, but if we see this as a continuation from 'Der Golem' then I have to say that I much prefer the former. There are some really strong passages here and there and some good songs, but overall, it just doesn't contain the same presence and power of their last work.
Jun 2014

7 OCEAN
DIAPAUSE
7 Ocean is a band from the former Soviet republic of Belarus. Forming in 1989, they released four albums before breaking up after the death of one of the founding members in 1994. Some years later they reformed and released the first album with the new line-up in 2008. Since then they have released two more albums on download only and have now returned with their latest 'Diapause', which can be downloaded from their site and has also now been released on physical CD by Mals. All the music and lyrics are provided by Alexander Eletsky (keyboards, vocals), who has been the driving force behind the band since their inception some 25 years ago. All lyrics are in Russian, but that just adds to the very Eastern European feel that this album has.

It is symphonic, but there are some elements and stylings that show where this music has originated from, especially with some of the traditional folk that is obviously a major influence. If someone had asked me to pick a country of origin without knowing, I would have guessed Poland, and as they share a boundary with Belarus, I don't think I could have been accused of being too far away. One quite unusual part of this album is there are a lot of keyboard sounds utilized that I would have associated far more with the Eighties than the present day, and there are times when pop seems to be making its way into the prog. There are many dreamy sections, and the result is something that in many ways is quite atmospheric and pleasant, while also being somewhat dated. Some of these songs

could be used as background music in films, but I don't really view that as a positive in their case.
Jun 2014

SHADOW CIRCUS
WHISPERS AND SCREAMS

One of the things that can put the listener off certain prog bands is that they very much forget the "rock" part of the term "progressive rock". That isn't something that can be laid at the door of Shadow Circus as the combination of frenetic drumming and repeated riffs of the opener "Captain Trips" makes one incredibly aware that here is a symphonic progressive rock band that means business. Serious business. To show just how serious they are, "Captain Trips" is part of a seven-section number called "Project Blue" (inspired by Stephen King's 'The Stand') which has a total length of nearly thirty-four minutes (each section is separately named and split on the album). Strangely enough, although they sound nothing like them whatsoever, the band they most remind me of at times is Gabriel-era Genesis, while at others it is Spock's Beard, or Kansas, and this is one of the joys of this album, in that they don't come across as anyone else at all and are striving to create their own direction.

This 2009 album was the second from the Americans, and they have released just one more since then, as for some reason they have stayed quite low under the radar although it appears that nearly all those who have heard it and have reviewed it have the same opinion about it that I have, namely this is an album and band that have an awful lot going for it. There are times when it is almost straight ahead rock, but it is when they morph into Gentle Giant with complex interplay and strange time signatures that they come into their own. Every time I play this album, I find that I am discovering even more layers, but as I peel this particular onion there are no tears but plenty of smiles. Solid, symphonic, exciting, and a blast throughout.
Jan 2017

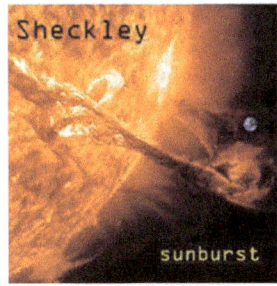

SHECKLEY
SUNBURST

Sheckley are basically a duo, created by Phil Jackson (keyboards, percussion, also in Paradox One) and Richard Gorman (guitar, vocals, percussion), although they are joined by Thierry Sportouche (Silver Hunter) on one song where he provides keyboards and vocals. This is music with a great deal of space within it, and a rawness one rarely finds within progressive rock. At times I am reminded of Gong, at others Robert Wyatt, while Hawkwind have also been an influence. It also has a lot in common with the more ambient workings of Brian Eno, but never falling into the trap of New Age. This isn't always easy music to listen to, with songs such as "Solar Flares" channelling a RIO feel to proceedings with repetitive and contradictory musical themes,

with drums that make an appearance here and there almost as an afterthought, but having an important part to play. By the time I had finished playing it the first time I couldn't actually say that I enjoyed the album, possibly more "endured", but there was something about it that did make me go through it again. It really is quite compelling, even though it is hard to put it into words. With this one it really is a case of listening to it and everyone making their own decision.
May 2017

SHEPHERDS OF CASSINI
SHEPHERDS OF CASSINI
The more I discover about the local NZ music scene, the more impressed I am by the quality and diversity of what is available down here. Shepherds Of Cassini are another case in point. Hailing from Auckland they were formed in 2012 by Omar Al-Hashimi on drums (from Pilgrim's Pyre), Vitesh Bava on bass (from Pilgrim's Pyre), Felix Lun on electric violin (from An Emerald City) and Brendan Zwaan on guitar and vocals (from Flood). Imagine if you will Ozric Tentacles using violin instead of wind and bringing in stoner elements as they experiment with sound, then you may come close. Of course, you need to add to that list the tribal rhythms and especially the Middle Eastern influences and then you may get somewhere close.

The first time I played this not only did I not understand what I was really listening to, I actually didn't like it at all. The songs often were over-long ("Eyelid" is eighteen minutes), I couldn't work out why I was playing it (apart from being asked to) and it just didn't work. But I determined the fault was probably with me as opposed to the music, especially as I kept hearing good things about them in the scene, so I persevered, and it was only on the third time through that it started to make sense. From there on in every play has just cemented my view that this is an incredible piece of work in so many ways. For the most part this is pure instrumental and sounds as if the guys were playing this live in the studio, working with each other and bouncing ideas. Instead of being too long, the songs were now too short, and the simple almost naïve complexity really brought me in. I'm not overly sure of the drums sound, as to my hearing the snare is too high in the mix, but that really is just being picky. This is never going to be an immediate album, but is definitely worth persevering with, and can be streamed from Bandcamp before purchase so if you want to try something that is definitely more than a little different then this may well be for you.
Apr 2014

SHIBALBA
PSYCHOSTASIS – DEATH OF KHAT
Shibalba is Acherontas V.Priest (Acherontas), Karl NE/Nachzehrer (Nåstrond) and Aldra -Al-Melekh. Their music is saturated with the mysticism of the East. It's richly detailed and multidimensional, while layered with chanting and broadly defined elements of traditional ritual and shamanic music. Apart from contemporary synths and guitar drones,

the band makes use of bones and skulls as percussion instruments, Tibetan horns, Tibetan singing bowls, bone and horn trumpets, darbuka's (goblet drums) as well as ceremonial bells and gongs. The band's intention, in their own words, is to "guide the subconscious of the individual to dream beyond the skin of matter & to dream in ecstasy and exult". The album was recorded by the band themselves in Greece and Sweden, and the label itself describes this as meditative dark trance/ambient/shamanic music. I know I haven't heard anything quite like this before. I did find myself being reminded of Negură Bunget in some ways, and Burzum in others, with Gregorian chanting also making an entrance in what is an album where voices are used as another instrument. It is hard to explain the depth of this album – when it is playing it is as if no other plane exists, and that darkness has taken over the world. There is a drone-like feel, and the listener is taken to a place that is alien in nature, a dark monastery in the Himalayas where the monks aren't exactly wanting to bring joy to the world. This is a compelling album, one I really did enjoy, just because it was so different to anything I have ever heard before. It won't be to everyone's liking and is as far removed from the mainstream as anything I have ever heard, but I feel musically enriched by coming across it.
Apr 2017

SIIILK
ENDLESS MYSTERY

There are times when one comes across an album that is perfect in just so many ways that it is hard to quite know what to say about it, or how to describe it to give it justice, and that is what I am faced with right now. Siiilk are back with their second album, following on from the highly rated debut 'Way To Lhasa' and I have no issue at all with saying that this is better. It is a songs-based album, built around the vocals and acoustic guitar of Richard Pick, but what provides the depth is the quality of all the musicians involved and how they all know how to best utilise both space and dynamics.

It is a dreamy, reflective album, bringing together elements of Pink Floyd, Seventies Barclay James Harvest, Camel, Caravan, and so much more. This is music that takes the listener to a place that only exists between the ears, music to get lost in, music to be transported by. There are times when the full band are involved, (and they also bring a couple of guests to add some additional nuances with clarinet and Indian tablas), and it is the arrangements that make all the difference as often there will only be one or two others involved besides Richard, with everyone knowing their place and how their contribution reflects overall. Catherine Pick has a beautiful voice, sometimes taking the lead, but often providing sympathetic backing and the restraint and control demonstrated throughout the album is considerable. This is simply stunning and essential to anyone who enjoys this style of progressive rock.
Sep 2017

SILHOUETTE
THE WORLD IS FLAT AND OTHER ALTERNATIVE FACTS

For me, I will always associate Progress Records with Hansi Cross, who sadly passed away earlier this year. But, although Hansi is no longer with us, the label he left behind continues to release albums of incredible stature and worth. That is definitely the case with Dutch band Silhouette's fifth studio album. 'The World Is Flat and Other Alternative Facts'. Somehow, I missed their last studio album, although I did manage to hear their live album which was released earlier this year. I gave a 4 * review to their third album 'Across The Rubicon' which came out in 2012, and there is no doubt in my mind this is superior.

This has everything I want from a prog album, great melodies, wonderful musicianship, soaring vocals, layered arrangements that can appear almost simple at times, and never forgetting that the music always must come first. They may all have wonderful virtuoso skills, but how does that fit in with what is needed? Brian de Graeve (lead & backing vocals, 12-string guitar), Daniel van der Weijde (electric & acoustic guitars), Erik Laan (keyboards, bass pedals, lead & backing vocals), Jurjen Bergsma (bass, acoustic guitar, backing vocals) and Rob van Nieuwenhuijzen (drums, percussion) have created something that contains elements of Yes and Neal Morse alongside more melodic rock elements, as well as plenty of prog. The vocals are superb, and everything somehow gels together seamlessly. One can't imagine another instrument or note needed anywhere, yet there is nothing superfluous in what they are doing. This is majestic, soaring prog that makes me smile each time I play it. And I have been playing it a great deal indeed. When discerning progheads compile their top albums of the year list soon, there is no doubt that this will be one to reckon with. From acoustic 12-string to heavily layered arrangements to rock guitar, this has it all and so very much more. I love it. This is simply essential to anyone who dares call themselves a progger.
Jan 2017

SILHOUETTE
STAGING THE SEVENTH WAVE

In 2014, Dutch band Silhouette released their fourth studio album, 'Beyond The Seventh Wave'. In 2016, they were filmed and recorded performing the album in its entirety, and this has now been released as a DVD and CD set, along with a few additional songs on the DVD. They wisely had a few guests make appearances, the most important of which is an additional guitarist who was there for the whole set (he did try to stay at the back of the stage and out of the way), who assisted in providing some additional heaviness to proceedings, allowing Daniel van der Weijde to provide some delicate solos on his seven-string guitar.

Although their sound is more in common with bands such as Saga than IQ, I did keep

being reminded of the former in the way they set up the stage, the use of a backdrop film throughout, a keyboard player who also provides superb vocals when needed, and a rhythm section that keep it locked down so the others can take centre stage. Brian de Graeve has a gentle vocal style, never showing any strain, while Erik Laan uses a myriad of keyboards and sings in a similar fashion, so that when they harmonise, they do so with aplomb. This is a powerful album, with lots of drama and dynamic shifts in the music as they tell the story of what happens to the main character (which has been reproduced in the centre of the digipak so that even those who haven't heard the original knows what is happening). Somehow, I have managed to miss all of Silhouette's albums apart from 2012's 'Across The Rubicon', a situation I am going to have to address. The concert footage is well filmed, with multiple cameras and angles, and this is a great introduction to the band.
June 2017

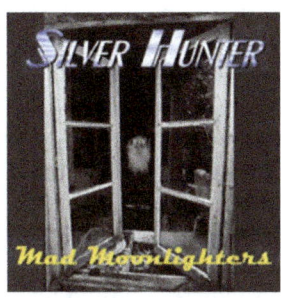

SILVER HUNTER
MAD MOONLIGHTERS
Silver Hunter is a collaboration between Tim Hunter (who has released many albums on his label) and Thierry Sportouche (Silver Lining), so no guessing where the name came from. I have known Thierry for at least twenty years, but not as a musician but instead as the driving force behind Acid Dragon, probably one of the longest running progzines around. Here he provides vocals and keyboards, while Tim provides vocals, guitar, keyboards and drums. They are joined by some other musicians and female backing vocals to give this English/French duo a real band feel.

In some ways, this is quite a strange album, as although it is firmly within the progressive camp, there are so many different influences and styles in play that the album switches all the way through. "The Silver Key" talks about the Silver Hunters, so is the closest they have to a theme song, and feels heavily influenced by Steve Miller, not someone who often features in prog reviews. There are spoken word sections, and I particularly love "Dr. Beyond and the Prisoner of Dreams" which is about the Asylum of Musical Delusion – we all know people and full bands who belong there. The story is spoken against a musical and sound effect backdrop and is quite simple but is stunningly powerful. I also like how in another song Thierry announces he is "High Priest of Prog" – in France that could well be the case. This does feel like an independent release, and there are times when it is quite raw, but it is also strangely compelling. The first time I played it I wasn't too sure but found there were bits and pieces which stuck with me, and the more I persevered the more I found that to be the case and sometimes find myself singing snippets of the songs on here, which isn't something that usually happens. This doesn't appear to have had much in the way of reviews so far, even though it came out last year, and that may well be because it doesn't really fit in with most people's idea of prog and is quite Seventies in approach at times as well, but overall, I found this is an album I really enjoyed. I hope there is enough interest to release another one soon.
May 2017

SILVER HUNTER
CONCRETE HEARTS

This is the latest EP from the Anglo/French partnership of Tim Hunter (guitars, synthesizer, keyboards, sequencing, drums, lead vocals (4)) and Thierry Sportouche (lead vocals (1-3), flute (3)). On this four-track EP they have also been joined by Jasmine Isa Butterworth (backing vocals) and Phil Jackson (keyboards). I am a little confused with this release in a few ways, as it is named after the song that appears third, and the lead off number is a cover of "Avalon". The issue with taking on a song that is as well-known as this, is that it is bound to be compared with the original. Now, I believe Roxy Music released far better material than this during their existence, but this is the song that was played to death on the radio back in the Eighties so I, and many others, are incredibly familiar with it. While musically it isn't a bad take, Thierry's vocals don't work with this. The trace of accent, along with production that is too dry, means that one must wonder why it was undertaken. Ferry's vocals were given a great deal of reverb, and this should have also been the case here.

The second song, "Ode a Emile" also doesn't work as well as it could for some reason, as it jars, but the third song (which is the title track of the EP) is quite the opposite with some strong guitar and delicate flute and the vocals definitely stronger, and a strong melody. "Ys – The Lost City of Brittany" is the longest song of the four, and in some ways, is the most reminiscent of the album, but also isn't as structured and well-arranged as I would expect. While Silver Hunter should be commended for releasing physical product, and none of the songs on this EP are currently available elsewhere, I would have preferred it if they either hadn't covered "Avalon" or had different production, and they should have actually led with the title song as that is the strongest of the four.
Oct 2017

SIMAKDIALOG
TRANCE/MISSION

At the beginning of February, Leonardo Pavkovic of Moonjune released the following statement. "On January 13, 2017, I have lost one of my closest friends, the Indonesian piano and Fender Rhodes maestro, an accomplished composer, arranger and musicologist, the Indonesian music icon - Riza Arshad. Riza was a special friend of mine since 2000, a man of great humanity and immense musical talent. In 2003, on my first of 25+ trips to Indonesia, Riza was the really first person whom I met in the Indonesian capital, and he virtually introduced me to 'everyone' on the Indonesian music scene. 20 releases of Indonesian artists on MoonJune Records wouldn't be possible without Riza's input. I was looking forward to seeing simakDialog at the upcoming JavaJazz Festival the first week of March and discuss with Riza 2017 releases of his band's new studio album, as well the release of his new solo album recorded in Los Angeles in two sessions (in September 2013 and November 2016) with Ernest Tibbs on bass and Chad Wackerman on drums. It's a sad moment for me, but the life goes on and

Riza Arshad's legacy must live forever. There is no better way to celebrate my friend's music than listening to my friend's music, and I invite You all to do the same, to listen to the great music of my dear late friend, and music visionary, Riza Arshad. Rhodes to Paradise. R.I.P. Riza Arshad (November 2, 1963 - January 13, 2017)." To celebrate his music, Leo then made available for free download the four albums simakDialog had released through Moonjune, plus an earlier album originally only released inside Indonesia. I already had the latest album ready for review, but it seemed fitting to visit those I had yet to hear and review them all together. Riza Arshad was a great talent and will be sorely missed by those who have heard his music.

Formed in 1993, simakDialog were an Indonesian fusion band who released their first album as long ago as 1995, with 'Trance/Mission' being their third in 2002. Throughout their career their music centred around the soloing and fluidity of the keyboard player Ravid Arshad and guitarist Tohpati, combined with local Gamelan music to create something that was incredibly accessible to Western ears, yet also stayed very true to their roots. The fluidity and melody of Ravid and Tohpati is incredible, relying far more on intricate runs than the use of chords, with each both being prepared to take the lead, duet with the other, or even take a total break from the music altogether. It isn't unusual to find one of them totally absent for long periods of time, just to give the other more space to move and breathe. Tohpati always makes me think of John McLaughlin, and strangely so does Ravid although he is playing keyboards, which is probably why they work so well together.

Ravid uses an electric organ to great effect on this album, with my favourite number probably "Throwing Words" where Tohpati lets Ravid get on with it, until he comes back with a slightly distorted guitar which is totally at odds with what has been going on before, really shifting the timbre and style of music. Indro Hardjodikoro has a delicate touch on the bass, providing warmth and filling the gaps between the melody makers and the percussion. There are four guys playing a variety of Indonesian instruments that provide an authenticity and realism to the music, a total fusion not just of jazz and rock, but world music and the west.
Mar 2017

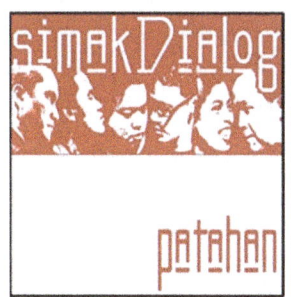

SIMAKDIALOG
PATAHAN
'Patahan' was their first live album, released in 2005, and there had been quite a change in line-up between this and the last studio album, 'Trance/Mission', with just Ravid and Tohpati plus percussionist Endang Ramdan still involved. When one first starts playing this it is hard to realise that this is a "live" album as the audience is so quiet, and there is no introduction or announcement, but straight into "One Has To Be", which is a piano tour-de-force. This is all about Ravid, a maestro in total control of his instrument, with the rest of the guys happy to provide the gentle percussive background which is all that is needed. When Tohpati finally takes centre stage, it is restrained, almost as if he is having to pull the notes up from great depth, showing great

control and sustain, Hackett combining with McLaughlin.

There are just five songs on the album, but with the shortest at eleven and the longest at nearly twenty there is plenty here to enjoy. It isn't always gentle and reflective, and there are times when the band feels far more menacing, such as on "Kemarau", where the riffs give way to repeated piano motifs while the percussionists build the scene ready for Tohpati to take it to another level. We've gone from the delight of bands such as Santana into something that could almost be from 'The Exorcist', albeit with a tribal background. Here is a band made up of consummate musicians, working together to produce something that is very special indeed. Fusion in it its truest sense, this is indispensable.
Mar 2017

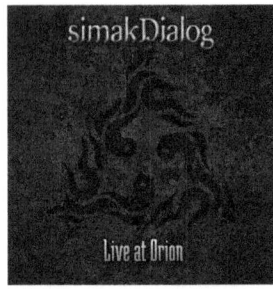

SIMAKDIALOG
LIVE AT ORION
Recorded live on September 7th, 2013, at The Orion, Baltimore, MD, this was to be the final release for simakDialog. Looking back to their previous live album from 2005, Ravid, Tohpati and Endang were still there, with bassist Rudy Zulkarnaen and additional percussionists in Erlan Suwardana and Cucu Kurnia. This release is a double CD, and again none of the songs are less than eleven minutes in length, and the band are determined to stretch their wings. "Throwing Words" is very different in the live environment to when it was released some ten plus years earlier, with Tohpati demanding centre stage and taking firm control. The band had been together for twenty years by this point, and the way that Tohpati and Ravid swap roles and bounce off each other in superb.

Here is a band where everyone is a master of their instrument and knows exactly where each of them needs to be musically, but the coming together of Western and Indonesian styles and sounds allows them to sound both incredibly tight and loose at the same time. Just listen to the combined runs of Tohpati and Ravid at the beginning of "Stepping In" to see what I mean, as while they are hitting each note in perfect unison at great speed, the percussionists are creating a sound storm beneath them. This album is a perfect introduction to a great band, who never really gained the kudos they deserved outside their native country. Discover this, and then go back and listen to their other releases to see why I am such a fan.
Mar 2017

CARSTEN SINDVALD
MOONSCAPE
This 2016 release was a follow-up to Carsten's 2011 solo album 'The King's Chamber'. I first came across Carsten due to his work with Robin Taylor, and he was originally trained as a classical saxophonist at The Royal Danish Academy of Music. In addition, he is organist at the Odense Valgmenighedskirke and second organist at Ansgar's Church in Odense where he performs daily. He is also a freelance musician and composer and is

conductor of the Odense Teaterkor. Perhaps it isn't surprising that on this instrumental album he provides piano, keyboards, soprano saxophone, tenor saxophone and clarinet, but what is surprising is the sheer number of styles he follows across the length of this release, and the number of guests (sixteen) he uses to turn his vision into a reality.

Carsten himself says he incorporates elements from jazz, tango, flamenco, and classical chamber music, but given how these in themselves include so many different styles one can understand just how diverse this album is. I have always thought of Carsten first and foremost as a saxophonist, but what makes this album really work is the delicacy of his touch on piano. With this number of guests, it would be easy to get lost in the maze of myriad styles but the piano cuts through it all, and this is the real driving force. Of course, the sax also is often the main instrument, but it could also be an accordion, or strings. In many ways, it is a very complex and quite heavy album, but it is also incredibly fresh and light. It is a wonderfully bright New Zealand Autumn morning as I write this, and the album is the perfect accompaniment. All I'm missing is a glass of North Canterbury Pinot Gris and I'll rectify that as soon as I put this review to bed. This is another incredibly enjoyable album from Carsten, and I feel enriched from having had the opportunity to listen to it. Let's hope that we don't have to wait another six years until the next one.
Apr 2017

SKY ARCHITECT
A BILLION YEARS OF SOLITUDE
When I first came across this Dutch band and their 2010 debut, I was incredibly impressed, feeling they were taking me back to the days when SI Music was consistently releasing great albums. But now they have stepped it up a notch and are moving quite a way from where they were before. There are still the swathes of keyboards that give a strong Seventies feel as a backdrop to much of what they are doing, but they have obviously been paying attention much more to Dream Theater and have definitely increased the note density. There are times when this is a much more metallic album than they have produced before, but they can just as easily drop into a funk groove or provide us some Riverside or Porcupine Tree touches before going off in yet another direction.

The only term that could ever be used for these guys is "progressive" as they are pushing boundaries in what they are doing, although not exactly King Crimson in approach, there are definitely some similarities with their outlook. And whenever you see a flugelhorn listed in the instruments you can pretty much guarantee you are in for something quite out of the ordinary. When Tom is singing one wonders why they don't use him in that facility much more, then when they are in full blast as instrumentalists one wonders why they bother with vocals at all. They seem able to put their mind and skills to anything they want to do, but also manage to keep it reined in so the music always still makes sense and doesn't go off onto long meaningless tangents as is always the risk.

Somehow, they manage to keep this open and free, not constraining what is going on but letting the music take flight: where some prog bands want to be insular and controlling, these guys act more as conduits and move wherever they are driven. Yet another great release from the flying Dutchmen.
Apr 2014

THE SKYS
JOURNEY THROUGH THE SKIES
This 2015 album was the third studio release from Lithuanian act The Skys. Joining Jonas Čiurlionis (lead vocals, guitar) and the boys on this album are some notable guests including Snowy White (Thin Lizzy, Pink Floyd etc.) and Rob Townsend (Steve Hackett). This is another where the vocals have come in for some criticism which is somewhat unfair to my mind, as I do think they add an additional quality to the music. True, they may be more spoken than sung at times, with an accent, but to me there is pleasure to be gained in that this allows the band to create their own identity and stand more alone. Keyboard player Bozena Buinicka also provides vocals at times, and there are some female leads, but I really enjoy what Jonas is doing here.

Musically they are heavily influenced by Pink Floyd, but from more than one era, so that while one could argue that 'Animals' is the more important album, there are also elements of 'Dark Side' and from the very early days as well. There are times where they bring in sitar, distorted guitars, tablas etc., and this all adds to what is a very interesting album indeed. The Skys, for some reason, have never really gained the recognition they deserve, as this is an album that progheads really ought to seek out.
Feb 2018

TOM SLATTER
THROUGH THESE VEINS EP
If you go to Tom's website, you will be greeted with "Hello! My name is Tom Slatter and I write the sort of music you'd get if Genesis started writing songs with Nick Cave after watching too much Dr. Who." So, there you have it. As if that isn't enough, what about this? "What could be more prog rock than a concept album? 'Two concept EPs and a concept album,' is Tom Slatter's answer. In his continuing effort to jump on the prog rock bandwagon, Tom has made the commercially savvy decision to dedicate the next twelve months to composing and recording two EPs and one album about the same story, including a twenty-minute epic to crown the whole project off sometime in the Autumn. The first step in this cynical, conceptual sell out is 'Through These Veins', an EP that tells the story of a rogue surgeon who starts turning her patients into macabre living sculptures. "My songs are usually driven by narrative, and this is no

exception. I was thinking about albums like 'Outside' by David Bowie, or 'Operation Mindcrime' by Queensrÿche. Plus, I saw all these English prog rock guys coining it in with their long songs and concept albums and I thought – I need a piece of that. Matt Stevens drives a limousine you know. Alan Reed takes a private jet to the studio every single day," said Tom."

Okay, so the last time I looked Alan was working at the BBC, so I think some of the above statements are a little tongue in cheek, but it does give an idea of the sort of thinking that goes on inside the very strange world that is Tom's brain. This music should be very carefully labelled, as take it from me this is not something that will immediately make the listener think it is essential and will more likely elicit the "this is awful, what are you doing playing this?" response. Luckily for me my brain is used to me ignoring my ears and playing music more than once, and the more I played this the more I got inside Tom's twisted, dark, and surreal world. As I kept playing it, the more I realized the great depth there was inside, and apart from the insidious and annoying drum machine I found I was enjoying this a great deal. It is definitely music from left field, and Tom's vocals definitely fit with the overall feel. I realize that all things included, this is a rather lengthy review for a four-track EP that is only eighteen minutes long, but hopefully this will entice you to give this a chance, as music as out there as this deserves to be heard.
May 2014

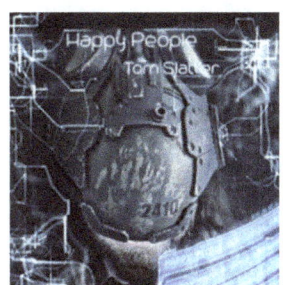

TOM SLATTER
HAPPY PEOPLE
Back in 2014 Tom asked me to review one of his EP's, but until now that was the only music I had heard of his, so when this his fifth full-length studio album arrived, I was looking forward to seeing what else he had been up to. As I was undertaking some research, I managed to come across an old press release of his, where it states "What would it sound like if Nick Cave started writing songs with Genesis after watching too many episodes of Dr Who? How many songs about replacing your body parts with mechanical alternatives is too many? Does the world need a steampunk/sci-fi inspired prog rock act? Tom Slatter set out to answer none of these questions, but accidentally did. Described by the Steampunk Chronicle as, 'an experiment too far', Tom's music sits somewhere between folk singer-songwriter, prog rock and indie rock of the Radiohead and Mansun ilk."

I think the best way to describe Tom's music is as "English", nothing more or less. It is progressive, very much in the crossover vein, but it is hard to imagine this music being delivered by anyone who hadn't grown up in that green and pleasant land. He has an acute observation that is reminiscent of Geoff Mann and John Dexter Jones (note: I am fully aware that JDJ is Welsh and would be traumatized at being called English) and a musical style on this album that is very akin to Jump in their prime. It is quite difficult to do anything else while playing this album (I soon gave up on my book when listening to this the first time), as it drags in the listener, demanding they pay attention. There is the feeling this album has been crafted from finest mahogany by a skilled artisan, as opposed to having plastic poured into a mould by automaton.

It is quite different to most of the prog that is around, and all the better for that. All in all, this is a special album indeed.
May 2017

MICHAEL SØBYGGE
MELODIC MELTDOWN
MICHAEL SØBYGGE
NO WORDS NEEDED
MICHAEL SØBYGGE
DR. JEKYLL & MR. HYDE

'Melodic Meltdown' was Michael's first album, released in 1997. Rather confusingly he later formed a band called Melodic Meltdown, which was more of a traditional hard rock band, but when he first started it was all about him and his guitar. On some of the songs he is joined by Lasse Wintehr Wehner on bass and Joe Clancy on drums, but there are also plenty of times when it is just him and his guitar. What is somewhat surprising when listening to this is the number of different styles at play here. Michael is comfortable playing classical acoustic (indeed, one of the songs is called "Andante Op. 1 No. 1") whereas on others he is full on shred. Listening to this on my iPod I had to do a double take when "Stonehenge" started as it really is full on, and although it does temper back a bit, there is no doubt that here is a guitarist more influenced by Vai than Bach. Although some of the production and arrangements do leave something to be desired, this is a solid album that fans of the guitar would certainly enjoy.

Joe stuck around for the next album the following year, and allowed himself to be much more to the fore while Michael added the role of bass and piano to his repertoire. This starts with a mighty kick to the nether regions as "Awakening" really blasts from the speakers. Production-wise there has been a step change since the debut, and there is never any doubt that this is an album by a guitarist, with all the arrangements designed to have him front and centre. As with the debut, this is much more than just a heavy metal shred fest, and "Spanish Interlude" works incredibly well with a real depth of feeling and emotion through the classical guitar. It is an album that refuses to stay within any single genre or musical form and is the better for that. Although not always as inventive as the debut, this is a more complete piece of work overall.

For his third solo album, released in 2000, Michael changed things around a bit. Martin Bech joined on drums, while Lasse returned on bass and he also brought in a singer for a few songs, Lars Binderup. Of the three albums this is the most frustrating, as it does feel that Michael has decided that he needed a singer to move more into the mainstream and when Lars is singing, he takes more of a back seat, only letting rip when Lars isn't involved. Thankfully that isn't a great deal, as not only does Lars prevent Michael from

playing as he should, but he also isn't a very good singer and has a detrimental impact on the whole album. On the plus side, Michael is playing better than ever and when he lets go, he shows he can shred with the best of them, but obviously he was now looking forward to being part of a band and when 'Second Skin' came out a few years after this it featured Michael, Lars and Martin (and a new bassist) but it had the bandname Melodic Meltdown. All three of these albums have their merits, but I would probably turn to 'No Words Needed' first and then to the debut, before the third. But Michael's shredding on the third is in a different league to that on the first two, so it really depends on what you think of the vocals, but if you ever come across these albums, they are certainly worth hearing.
Jan 2014

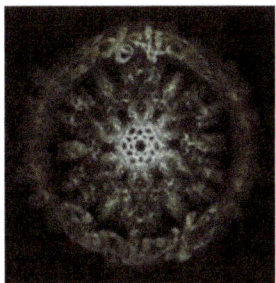

SOLSTICE
SPIRIT

No-one can accuse Solstice of being one of the more prolific progressive rock bands around. Their debut album, 'Silent Dance', was incredibly influential when it was released in 1984, but they didn't release their next two albums until the Nineties, and this 2010 album was only their fourth. Guitarist Andy Glass has been the only constant through their career, but at least singer Emma Brown was still there from 1997's 'Circles'. Apart from these it is a brand-new band, as they are joined by Jenny Newman on violin and viola, Pete Hemsley on drums (I still have to pinch myself that the previous incumbent was Clive Bunker, originally from Jethro Tull), Steve McDaniel on keyboards and Robin Phillips, bass. No matter who the musicians are, this is still polished music, in quite a laid-back style. Solstice are often called 'neo prog', but this album is not nearly as punchy as that style often suggests.

Andy's guitar and Emma's vocals are often to the fore, and out of everything it is the vocals that lets the album down as although they are often excellent there are just a few places where she doesn't sound quite on key, and each time I cringe and wonder why they didn't just re-record those few words. The violin also doesn't get as much of an outing as one would normally expect, and the result is a prog album that in many ways is incredibly well polished, and has a lot going for it, with some strong melodies and interplay, but I do feel this is more of an opportunity missed than one being grabbed with both hands. Their debut is a masterpiece, which I still play to this day, and I doubt they will ever match it. This is superior to their previous outing, but I prefer the 1993 'comeback' 'New Life' to this one as well. Andy is a fine guitarist with a deft touch, and his lead melody lines are what make Solstice who they are, and if you are already a fan, you'll probably enjoy this. If you haven't come across Solstice previously then you're missing a treat, but there are a couple of other albums of their that you should pick up first.
Feb 2017

SONIQ THEATER
HEROES OF THE PAST
Another year, and another Soniq Theater album. It is incredible to think that Alfred manages to keep producing albums at such a rate, as this is his fourteenth in fourteen years, with everything played by the man himself. He has revisited his archives again for this one, and two of the twelve numbers were actually recorded back in 1987. Yet again we can hear Wakeman influences here, combined with Vangelis and Jean-Michel Jarre. There isn't so much Emerson in this album, which generally has a lighter feel, but again it is music that one can get inside quite easily and there is almost some new Age in some of the sounds. It is refreshing, easy to listen to without ever becoming easy listening and it is interesting to hear the difference in the older song "Lemuria" against the rest as it contains a darkness and emotion that is often missing from his more recent works. I have been fortunate enough to hear all of Alfred's works and this is yet another worthy addition to his catalogue...
May 2014

SONIQ THEATER
GUITARISSIMO
As with all of Alfred Mueller's releases this is available as a low budget CD-R, or as a free download through Bandcamp. What isn't normal though, is that this isn't a solo keyboard-based release, but instead is a collaboration between himself and guitarist Stefan Grob. Recorded back in 1990, and only now being made available, this is very different to what I would expect from Alfred, and it suffers for it. There are times when the guitars work well, and others where the keyboards are quite superb (love the Vangelis sweeping stylings on "Beach of a New World" for example), but rarely do they totally gel together, and the result is an album I was quite disappointed in. But Alfred keeps to as high release schedule of an album a year, so given that this came out in 2015 there are more for me to be listening to.
Mar 2017

SONIQ THEATER
GLOBALICED
Alfred's 2016 album is the first since 2012's 'Overnight Sensation' not to feature any old recordings from his time before he worked with Rachel's Birthday, and with no guests involved this time we are down to just Alfred and his trusty keyboards (including of course programmed drums). I have said previously that Alfred's playing reminds me of Rick Wakeman combined with Vangelis and Jean Michel Jarre, and this album is again on very similar lines. There are times when the music is progressive, others when it is more New Age, but never really moves into pure electronic

territory. It would be interesting to hear "Ayers Rock" with a strong proper rhythm section behind it, as I think that additional vitality would make an already interesting song even more so. Working in a band framework with live instruments would make this album even more appealing, if Alfred maintains full control and keeps doing what he is already. Yet another interesting album from Germany's Soniq Theater, and worth investigating from Bandcamp where it is possible to download this free.
Mar 2017

SONIQ THEATER
THE JOURNEY
As surely as day follows night, January 1st brings with it a new Soniq Theater album, and 2017 is no exception, with Alfred's seventeenth release under that name. This one is back to the old traditional style of artwork as well, back when everything was being released on CD-R, but now he uses Bandcamp so in many ways the artwork is even less important. There are a few vocals on here, but for the most part it is Alfred and his keyboards, with a mix of some up-tempo numbers and the more New Age style with which is he is most commonly associated. This is a "classic" Soniq Theater album and is quite safe in that it isn't doing anything dramatically different to what he has done before, but if you enjoy that then you will most definitely be interested in this one as well. One of my few complaints is that I do wish that "Short Trip To Space" could have been extended, as the keyboard sounds being used and the melodic feel of this demands much more than the amount of time it was allocated, and it would be interesting to hear a full album going down that path. As always, it is possible to hear the album in full (and even download them at no cost), so why not give Soniq Theater a try?
Mar 2017

SOUL ENEMA
OF CLANS AND CLONES AND CLOWNS
It is a long time since I last came across Israeli act Soul Enema, who were formed back in 2001, and released their debut 'Thin Ice Crawling' back in 2010 through Mals and Musea. It gained a lot of positive reaction at the time, but for some reason it has taken some seven years for them to release the follow-up. That of course may have to something to do with the fact that only keyboard player Constantin Glantz is still there, so in many ways this is a brand-new band. Singer Noa Gruman is a real find, as she is at home in whatever musical style the band are prepared to throw out, and there are certainly plenty of them. The easiest way to describe these guys are as progressive, but progressive rock in its very truest sense as they bring in elements of melodic rock, metal, ethnic, psychedelic, jazz-fusion, prog, symph-rock elements etc., with a somewhat theatrical approach to the lyrics.

There are times when I find myself thinking of Orphaned Land in the way they approach some of the music, and a closer inspection of the guests shows the appearance of Yossi Sassi (ex-Orphaned Land, Yossi Sassi Band), as well as Arjen Lucassen (Ayreon, Star One). The album was mixed by Jens Bogren (Opeth, Devin Townsend, etc.), so as well as being intriguing in a musical sense, the production allows every instrument and nuance to shine, showing how important each element is to the overall sound. I haven't heard much from the Israeli music scene, and if this is an example of what is being produced out of that country then I really need to hear some more.

This album is intriguing, and musically all over the place, so if the listener doesn't like what is going on just wait a minute as it is going to be changing soon. I love this album, and sincerely hope we're not going to have wait another seven years until we get the next one.
Jun 2017

SOUL SECRET
FLOWING PORTRAITS
This 2008 release was the debut album from the Italian prog metal band, who originally started out playing Dream Theater covers back in 2004. They have certainly come a long way since then, as this is far more commercial and direct than anything to come from the Americans, but still displaying incredible virtuosity. While the harmony voccals may not always be absolutely spot on, the result is something which feels more 'real', and far less contrived. The interplay between guitarist Antonio Vittozzi and keyboard player Luca Di Gennaro is an absolute delight, while bassist Lucio Grilli and drummer Antonio Mocerino lock it all together. What is somewhat surprising is that singer Mark Basile, who is key to the overall sound and success of the album is here only as a session singer (formly with Mind Key, he is now active in DGM) – the band's singer Michele Serpico was unable to record due to ill health, and he was replaced after they had been in the studios so Mark was only brought in for this album.

One of the things that is readily apparent is the quality not only of the songs, the vocals and overall performance, but also that of the production. So, it wasn't much of a surprise to see that although it was originally recorded in Naples, it had then been mastered by none other than Threshold's Karl Groom, and certainly some of the crunching riffs could have been laid down by the Thin Ice guitarmeister himself. It contains plenty of space, and the songs flow and move as if they are a living breathing being, effortlessly going from one melody to another, but always with real feeling of passion and depth.

This is an incredibly powerful album, very nearly flawless, and if one is into prog metal of any type then this should be played immediately, if not sooner.
Feb 2017

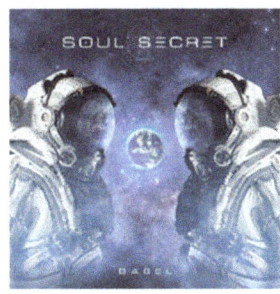

SOUL SECRET
BABEL
Soul Secret are an Italian progressive metal band based in Naples who released their debut album "Flowing Portraits" back in 2008, with Mark Basile (DGM) as guest singer. This is the only album of theirs I had heard prior to this and remember thinking it was an incredibly strong debut. Obviously, I wasn't the only one as it led to them playing with the likes of Pendragon, Vanden Plas and Subsignal. They have been through a few line-up changes since then, and are now back with their fourth album, a concept telling the story of Sam and Adriel who are sent to space to find God, helped by logOS, an on-board computer providing cutting-edge technology to the mission. When they finally find the City Of Gods, they find it empty...

This album is full of strong songs, but I found the concept and spoken links were getting in the way of my enjoyment of the music, and after the first few plays it was getting harder and more difficult to get into the music. That is a real shame, as there are some strong performances on here. The vocals are superb, and there are some djent influences in the music at times, which is certainly a departure from the norm in terms of progressive rock. Possibly it is necessary to see the full release, and I only have a digital download to gauge my opinion on, but for me this just doesn't have the impact and power of the debut, and I expect bands to keep improving, not taking a retrograde step, which is a real shame.

It is light, pleasant, melodic progressive rock with some interesting influences, but not challenging or interesting enough for me to maintain my focus throughout, and the additional elements that have been put in that link that album are superfluous and over the top (although even I must smile when the code word is "Pendragon").
Jul 2017

SOUNDRISE
TIMELAPSE
This Italian band started as a covers group back in 2003, but only guitarist Dario Calandra and singer Walter Bosello are still there from those early days, with the line-up changing a few times over the years. They released their debut (and so far only) album themselves in 2012, and again here is a band that came to my attention when they were suggested to the Crossover team at PA for evaluation. When one looks at their site, and how they promote themselves, it is obvious it is being undertaken at a very professional level so the question remains as to how on earth they can get the publicity that they deserve, as yet again here is a very fine album indeed from a band most people will have never heard of.

This is progressive rock that is also bringing in elements of AOR and melodic rock with neo and other genres, resulting in a crossover which is truly that, with pop tendencies and feelings but also plenty of hard rock and balls. This is one of those bands who haven't forgotten that the second word of the definition 'prog rock' is "Rock"! I enjoyed this immensely from the first note to the last, with great vocals and harmonies and hooks that are so big that one could hang a coat and hat on them and know that they would stay there.

It is a fun album, nothing self-indulgent or navel gazing here. If that is what you are looking for then move along, but if you want progressive rock that makes the listener smile from start to finish then this is it.
Apr 2014

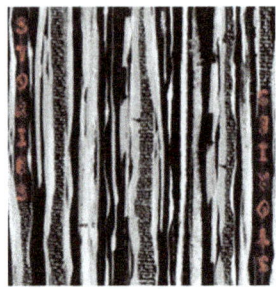

SOUNDS LIKE THE END OF THE WORLD
STORIES
Sounds Like The End Of The World are an instrumental Polish post rock band formed in 2012, and this is their second album, released in March this year. Mind you, their website doesn't contain any updates since 2015 so the album isn't listed there, there are no details on who played on it on the Bandcamp page, and the press release only provides the names and details for four musicians, none of whom play keyboards, but there are obviously keyboards present. According to Bandcamp this was recorded live in the studio, so now you all know everything I do about this.

There is a feeling of togetherness, so I'm not surprised that it was recorded live, as they are all feeding off each other. There is plenty of angst and rawness as they strive on discord and disharmony, but there are also moments where they are more reflective in nature with some definite Pink Floyd elements. The highlight of the album is undoubtedly "Obsession", where guest violinist Jan Gałach can really let rip. This is the only song on which he makes an appearance, and if I had any say in proceedings then I would make him a full-time member of the band as his roughness and stridency takes the music to another level. While not totally essential, this is still an album that is well worth hearing and is interesting. Why not give it a listen.
Apr 2017

SPIRAL KEY
AN ERROR OF JUDGEMENT
It's early in 2018, yet Spiral key have already put a stake in the ground for progressive metal album of the year: it is going to take something quite special to be better than this. Formed in 2012, this is their second release, but their first for Pride & Joy. The band features the distinctive voice and intricate guitarwork of David McCabe and the bass of Ken Wynne (Cut the Wire). After a short hiatus following on from their debut, they brought in drummer Chris Allan (ex-Malefice, now session/independent) and guitarist Dan Carter (Belial) and hit the stage in 2016 supporting several bands across

the spectrum including Kingcrow and Votum. Back in the studio they brought in guests John Mitchell (Frost*, It Bites, Arena) who contributes a guitar solo to the track "Dark Path", vocalist Miguel Espinoza (Persefone) on "Possessive", while Dan Carter displays his inimitable style on the track "Sanctimonious". Interestingly there is no mention of who provides keyboards, which are an important part of the overall sound.

When I first started playing this my immediate thought was Threshold, and each time I played it I came to the same conclusion. But that is more to do with the music and the style being performed, as when it comes to the vocal melodies, they are undoubtedly quite different. But given how long Threshold have been at the peak of the prog metal scene in the UK it isn't surprising that another band from the same country has been influenced by them. The songs are hard, heavy, and always incredibly melodic and I found myself continuously being drawn back to this album. It is interesting to see John Mitchell being involved, as it shows just how much melody that the band are providing as his name isn't one that would normally come to mind when discussing this style of music.

This is something that those into prog metal really need to seek out.
Feb 2018

MARTIN SPRINGETT
THE GARDENING CLUB
Martin Springett is probably best-known as an artist, but over the years he has also released some albums, and this one from 1983 has just been reissued by Gonzo. I had not heard of Martin, and it was only because I had read a review in the mighty Gonzo magazine (what do you mean you don't read it? As Jon says, "It's stylish, it's witty, it's subversive, it's free. It's everything you want from a music magazine). I was intrigued, and knew I had to find out more, so soon had a copy sent to deepest darkest New Zealand. To say I was blown away on hearing it is something of an understatement. That this is a classic isn't even up for debate, the only question in my mind is how on earth has this been missed by progheads? It all must be down to timing, if it had been released ten years earlier then it would have been written about by the mainstream press, but back in the early Eighties it was hard to discover any prog unless you had a frontman called Fish – even Twelfth Night and Pallas suffered, so an ex-pat living in Canada didn't stand a chance.

But, thanks to Gonzo we all now have the opportunity to relish this. Think 'Breathless' era Camel, combining forces with Steve Hackett and Anthony Phillips, and is an album which made me smile from the first song to the very last. I must make mention of Bob Brough, who contributes some very fine soprano sax, and makes instrumentals such as "The Traveller" very much his own. There is a great deal to discover and enjoy on the album, with songs making way for instrumentals, 12-string acoustic guitars to electric, always with a strong sense of melody. It is dreamy, it is reflective, it is pastoral, it is very simply bloody excellent! This is simply one of the finest reissues I have ever come across

in terms of pure musical enjoyment. To find out more about Martin, his art, and his music, then visit his website. All progheads should have this: I personally could play it all day and not get tired of it.
Jan 2018

Note: It was this review which had Martin seek me out, since when we have become firm friends and it is his artwork which adorns the book you hold in your hands.

LYNN STOKES & SOL SURFERS
TERRA NOCTURNE
Although this may sound like a duo, Sol Surfers is actually the name of Lynn Stokes' band, which includes both a saxophonist and a flautist among others. Now that is out of the way, what about the album title? 'Terra Nocturne' can be translated to "nocturnal land", while of course 'nocturnal' translates to "done, active, or occurring at night". So, we have a land at night, hence the picture of the moon on the cover, or is perhaps a bit more than that? Often, bands are influenced by those who have gone before, some more than others, but it is somewhat unusual to come across a band who seem to have been influenced by just one album from that band. Yep, here we have a group who are influenced not just by Pink Floyd, but very much by the classic 'DSOTM'.

Part of me feels this is a sacrilege and that this 2008 album should be taken out and destroyed, however there is a larger part of me who is really enjoying listening to this and that is the side that wins! This album passed me by at the time, and the same must have been true for everyone else as this appears to have been their only release, and their website no longer appears to be active. That is a real shame, as although heavily influenced by Roger et al, this is an original piece of work and in the lack of the masters themselves is something any Floyd fan would enjoy.
May 2014

SUBJECT TO THOUGHTS
THE CULMINATION
Subject to Thoughts is a two-man band from Brownsville, Texas & Weirton, West Virginia. It actually started as a solo project from Mark Mendieta as long ago as 1999, and it was only in 2007 that he was joined by Brandon Strader, who provides lead vocals and guitar solos. There is an almost naïve approach to the sound, as if they have attempted to catch a DIY ethic which is quite different to the norm and makes them stand out from the rest. The first time I played this it put me off and I found I wasn't enjoying it very much, and the same goes for the vocal approach, which is unusual in many ways. But, as Mark says, his aim is to produce thought provoking progressive rock music and I found that this album definitely achieved that as I challenged myself to understand what was happening and to get inside the thinking of Mark and Brandon.

The more I played it, the more I got from it, and their doom/acoustic laid-back progressive/new age/metallic approach definitely works. The DIY feel adds to the overall impression, and the end result is something that in many ways is quite simple but stands up very well indeed against what else is being released in the market and is better than many. Released in 2010, this their fifth album is certainly interesting, and as I write this in 2014, I know the next one will soon be out, and I look forward to that with great interest.
Apr 2014

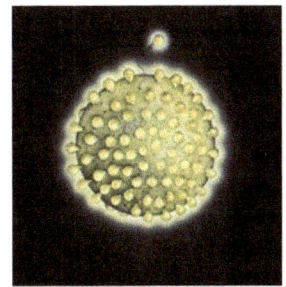

SUNRISE SUNSET PROJECT
SUNRISE SUNSET
According to Facebook, Sunrise Sunset Project is a multi-genre progressive rock band from Saint-Petersburg, Russia, a combination of classical progressive and art rock, electronic music, jazz, trip-hop, ambient, atmospheric rock. The only result to date is this debut album, which was released in 2009. It is instrumental, so there are no lyrics, and instead each page of the booklet contains a painting representing a song. This care and effort in the presentation is carried through into the music as well, which is very Floydian in nature, although there are also some elements of Wakeman. It is dreamy, ethereal, dynamic, beguiling and entrancing all at once. The more one plays this, the more there is to hear, as layer upon layer becomes apparent.

It is a complex and extremely structured album where the guitar is often the instrument that cuts through to provide edge and power, but the arrangements are always sublime, and it takes no effort at all to gain a great deal from listening to this. Unfortunately, their website and Facebook pages don't appear to have been updated for quite some time so I would guess they are no longer active. That is a real shame as this album has a lot to offer and is well worth seeking out.
May 2014

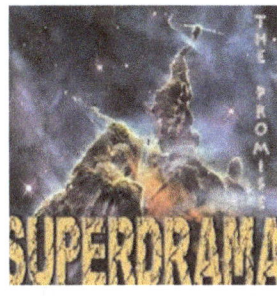

SUPERDRAMA
THE PROMISE
When I came across this CD I was immediately intrigued as although this is a debut release, it has been released in the form of a hardback book, containing an extensive booklet and the CD as a digipak. Now, apart from the English lyrics the whole thing is in German, so it is somewhat lost on me, but it did show that someone somewhere thinks a lot of these guys. Superdrama was formed in 2004 by Robert Gozon (vocals, keyboards) and Robert Stein-Holzman (drums), and was initially known as Noble Effort. After a few line-up changes Thomas Klarmann (bass, flute) from Argos became involved, as did guitarist Michael Hahn, and the line-up is now completed by Thilo Braud on organ.

In many ways this is classic neo-prog, but with leanings towards Seventies bands such as Gentle Giant. Strangely enough, the band they remind me most of is the much-missed Grace who I was lucky enough to see in concert multiple times in the Nineties (and whose album 'The Poet, The Piper and The Fool' should be in everyone's collection), as although musically they are quite different there is a definite similarity in the way they structure the material and also in the vocal attack. The more I play this the more I enjoy it, as it is such a fun album to listen to and contains many of the elements so beloved of progheads such as intricate songs, strong musicianship, wonderful interplay and a feeling that these guys really mean it. They contain the humour of Gentle Giant as well as some of the off-beat tempos and staccato sounds, yet temper this with some fine rocking guitar.

This really is a delight from the first note to the last, and I can only hope we don't have to wait ten years for the next album as that would be criminal. This is an incredibly strong debut, one I highly recommend!
Jun 2014

SYNAETHESIA
SYNAETHESIA
As soon as I saw this band had released their debut on GEP I was excited to hear what they are about. The label may not have released many different artists over the years but given that their roster has included acts such as Jadis, Threshold and Big Big Train, as well as of course the mighty IQ, then my excitement is fully justified. Then I realized that it had been produced by none other than Mike Holmes himself, so I became even more intrigued. Add to that the fact that the opening song is some 22 minutes long and all the signs were pointing in the right direction. This band has been put together by a young unknown keyboard player, Adam Warne, who also wrote all the songs and sang them, which only added to the interest.

I felt there was no way that I could possibly be disappointed by this, and boy was I right. Slightly more Crossover than Neo, this is an album that is immediate and for me hearkens right back to the Nineties when the UK scene was exploding with incredible bands and great albums. This has pretty much all one could wish for from a progressive rock album: it turns and twists, allowing everyone to take the spotlight when the time is right, and always driving forward. Although Adam is a keyboard player this is not an album that is overtly dominated by keyboards but is incredibly well balanced and allows the twin guitars to shine and dominate when the time is right. He also has a Steven Wilson approach to vocals, and there is clarity and emotion in all he does in that arena, shining above the music with real passion and vitality. There have been some standout debuts in the last six months or so (Mice on Stilts and Perfect Beings for example) and this is yet another. Their links with IQ have already seen them benefit in terms of gigs, but they must stand on their own right and with this album they definitely do it. No doubt this is going to feature in many end of the year lists, it is that good.
May 2014

SYNAPTIK
JUSTIFY & REASON

Since forming in 2012 from the ashes of such bands as Fifth Season, Inner Sanctum, and Twisted Autumn Darkness, the primary concern of Norwich, England's SynaptiK has been musical intensity. They definitely have a knack for fusing technical sophistication with traditional metal sonorities such as blast beats; powerful riffs; and screaming, Priest-styled melodic vocals. In March of 2016, SynaptiK recorded their sophomore album with Meyrick de la Fuente at Floodgate Studios in London, and this is what I am now listening to. I never heard their 2014 debut 'The Mechanisms of Consequence', but now I am seriously wondering what I was missing out on. This is a truly stunning album, bringing together influences from bands as diverse as Queensrÿche, Nevermore, Threshold, Evergrey and even Protest The Hero!

It is heavy, it is progressive, it is intense and wonderfully compelling. John Knight is a great singer, Kev Jackson and Pete Loades tie up the rhythm section, and provide a platform for Ian Knight and Jack Murton to riff as one or drop in Maiden-esque duets when the timing is right. It is the sheer tightness of this album that makes such a difference – they know what they are doing, trust each other implicitly, and deliver a high-octane result every time. This is easily one of the most important progressive metal albums I have come across for a while.
May 2017

SYNCAGE
UNLIKE HERE

Syncage are a four-piece band based around the song writing talents of vocalist and guitarist Matteo Nicolin, and this is a modern concept album, with jazz, fusion, and metal influences as well as classic prog styles to create an energetic, youthful mix. To further move this away from the norm there is a large use of a string quartet, as well as guest musicians adding additional textures on trumpet and vibes. The album was co-produced by noted Italian engineer Mike3rd (Tony Levin, Benny Greb, Pat Mastelotto) and mastered in California by Ronan Chris Murphy (King Crimson, Steve Morse, Terry Bozzio). In many ways this is classic progressive rock, bringing together multiple forms and styles, but is also refreshing and new. Strangely, the band I find myself most reminded of is classic Tull, but that is far more to do with the approach than the actual sound. At times there is large use of acoustic guitars, others electric, while although there can be a lead violin or trumpet there is also heavy use of the string quartet which provides yet another style again. It can be simplistic, at others incredibly grandiose, but there is always a sense of both space and direction which makes this a wonderful album to listen to, as the listener is taken on musical journey that is always interesting, never knowing what is coming around the next bend. Yet another essential release from BEM.
May 2017

t
FRAGMENTROPY

This 2015 album was the fifth from multi-instrumentalist Thomas Thielen under that name, and as always, he provided all the music, lyrics, vocals, performances and arrangements (he did let someone else master it). Although there are seven separate songs, they are arranged into three chapters entitled 'Anisotropic Dances', 'The Politics of Entropy' and 'The Art Of Double Binding', and as always this never comes across as the work of a solo musician but rather of a band that is very tight and organised. Thomas likes to mess with a listener, going off on tangents, repeating melodies, only to twist and turn into new directions, providing harmonies and then throwing vocal stylings into the mix.

I normally enjoy his work, but there is something about this album I found difficult to really fall in love with. Yes, it's very clever, incredibly well-played and produced, but is it something that I would listen to for pleasure and enjoyment? The answer to that just must be "no": I recognise how much work has gone into it, but this isn't an album I can get excited about at all. I know many others will disagree with me, and I have seen plenty of reviews claiming this as a masterpiece, but it's not for me.
Apr 2017

t
EPISTROPHOBIA

Having not exactly been a raving fan about Thomas Thielen's 2015 album, I wasn't looking forward to listening to his latest work, but whereas last time I was on the wrong side of being impressed, this time nothing could be further from the truth. There is something about the soundscapes, the music, the songs that this time hit the nail every single time. I found myself thinking of King Crimson, Peter Gabriel, Geoff Mann, Muse, Marillion, Radiohead and a whole host of others, and listening to this intently I wanted to know where the journey was going to take me, as from one second to the next I just couldn't be sure what was coming.

It is an incredible piece of work, draining in its sheer intensity and inventiveness, and it is almost impossible to realise this is the work of just one man. Whereas the last album suffered from a lack of outside point of reference to provide control and restraint, this album is only possible with just one person who has the musical vision, skill and tenacity to see it through to the end. This is modern progressive music that has no thoughts as to whether it is commercial and is all the better for it. In many ways it is challenging, as there are so many diversions from the main musical path, yet for all the chaos and confusion there are also large elements of musical clarity where it soars and shines, all the more so for the contrast. It is a stunning album, nothing more or less.
Apr 2017

TAKE ME FAR AWAY
CONTEMPLATION OF INFINITY
Here we have yet another Russian progressive rock band who were unknown to me until I received this debut album which was released towards the end of 2016. This is a four-piece with two guitars, bass, and drums, and for the most part they play psychedelic-influenced hard rock with progressive tendencies. Where they really shine though is when the two guests (who provide viola and keyboards respectively) are more to the fore. When that happens, the music takes on a new life and vitality, and is infinitely more interesting than when it is the two guitarists crunching out riffs and using some distortion pedals. Overall, this is a good album, but not great, and the guys need to give some serious thought as to how they move forward with the next one.
Sep 2017

TAYLOR'S UNIVERSE
EVIDENCE
So here we have the second album from 2013 for Robin (guitars, keyboards, bass, flute, percussion), and he has been joined again by Karsten Vogel (sax, clarinet), Klaus Thrane (drums) and Louise Nipper (gentle vocals on one number). But he has also brought into the band for the first time both Claus Bøhling (guitars) and Thomas Thor Viderø Ulstrup (synthesizer). I have long since learned that Robin has an immensely broad musical palette, and I should never really be surprised at what I hear, but yet again I find myself nodding sagely and wondering just how he does it. What we have here is an album that in many ways is more restrained and immediate that many of his works, just four songs giving us 44 minutes of music. The gentle keyboards provide the foundation for Claus and Karsten to let loose when they feel the need. Such is Claus's control and feel I did some searching on the web to discover a bit more about him, and was not surprised to find that he has been around for a large number of years, most notably in the power trio Hurdy Gurdy at the end of the Sixties (Donovan wrote the song "Hurdy Gurdy Man" for them, but after a disagreement on how it should sound he released it himself). He is fluid and dynamic, with plenty of attack and pace while also knowing how to be restrained and emotional.

There is a lot of space within this album, and a feeling of timelessness as the listener gets taken away to a different world where there is nothing but the music. The only thing wrong with the album is that it is too short! The more I played it the more I enjoyed it, and though there are some elements of Oldfield, the guitar especially takes it to a different level. 31 albums down, and Robin shows no sign at all of slowing, I just wonder what the next one will be like as this is one of his very best.
Jan 2014

TAYLOR'S UNIVERSE
ACROSS THE UNIVERSE

Robin is one of the most prolific artists I have come across, normally working under one of three different guises, and for this release he has put together a special line-up of the band. The album itself contains a selection of highlights from the later repertoire of Taylor's Universe – here in altered 2015 versions: rearranged, partly re-recorded, remixed and remastered. No room for Karsten Vogel or Carsten Sindvald, both of whom have been important members in the past, but he has instead again relied on Jakob Mygind to provide dynamic saxophone and has brought in two more guitarists to add weight to the sound, in the form of famed Danish musician John Sund and Frank Carvalho (from Etcetera), neither of whom have recorded with him in the past. Thomas Thor Viderø Ulstrup is again providing synths, while Klaus Thrane is still here on drums, and Louise Nipper and Jan Fischer provide some wordless vocals.

Robin, as always, is at the very centre, providing whatever musical textures and nuances that are required, working as the conductor and organiser to ensure everything is focussed and finessed to perfection. With as much in common with jazz thinking as it does with progressive rock, Robin continues to operate at a very high level indeed, creating music that is thought provoking and intense while staying accessible and dynamic. As with all his releases, this won't be for everyone, but those who appreciate this type of music will find a great deal here to enjoy.
Jan 2017

TAYLOR'S UNIVERSE
FROM SCRATCH

This is one of two releases by Taylor's Universe in 2015, but in many ways, this is the direct follow-on from 2013's 'Evidence' in that the main core of the band stayed the same, with Karsten Vogel (sax, clarinet), Claus Bøhling (guitars), Thomas Thor Viderø Ulstrup (MiniMoog), Robin Taylor (guitars, keyboards, bass, flute, percussion) and Klaus Thrane (drums). There were also some guests involved this time, including saxophonist Jakob Mygind (who appeared on the other TU release of 2015, 'Across The Universe') and long-time collaborator Carsten Sindvald (also sax). There isn't much in the way of guitar from Robin himself on this album, rather he defers to others while ensuring the music is going exactly the way he wants it to.

Robin brings in the right people for the right job, so a song may just feature him and Claus, while another has Karsten on bass clarinet, Jakob on soprano sax and Carsten on baritone as well as Finn, Thomas, Robin and Klaus to provide a meaty complex sound. The use of a MiniMoog as the main keyboards provides a distinct style to the overall sound, which as always is complex and constructed in such a way that the tangents always make complete musical sense. Three different singers provide the wordless vocals, but many of the songs are completely instrumental, and when the voices are used

it is always for an effect – never the main driving part of the piece. It is relaxing, it is interesting, it is melodic and can be challenging, yet as with all of Robin's releases one is all the richer for having heard it. Yet another great release to add to his canon.
Jan 2017

TAYLOR'S UNIVERSE
ALMOST PERFECTED
Looking at my CD shelves I can see nearly thirty albums recorded by Robin Taylor in one or other of his projects, and after a break of a couple of years, he is back with the latest from Taylor's Universe. The concept behind this was quite simple, take some old tunes and then re-arrange them with the current line-up in mind, and re-record them. Given that some of the current musicians had never heard the originals they were bound to give them a different interpretation, and the result is an album quite unlike many of Robin's other works. Robin tends to often approach music from a jazz viewpoint, taking it to more extremes with Taylor's Free Universe, but what strikes the listener with this album is just how melodic and progressive sounding it is. Yes, there are jazz elements here and there, as well as RIO, but this is fluid, melodic and complex yet always retaining a simplicity within its structure.

There are only four songs on the album, with a total length of forty-six minutes, but one is never sure exactly what is going to happen on the musical journey. "Mean Attack" starts with gentle percussion, held-down chords and a quiet gentility, which is smashed to pieces at about one minute twenty before it resumes again. Jakob Mygind again provides a sterling performance on various saxophones, while the guitars of John Sund and Robin cut through dynamically. For sheer listening pleasure this must be one of my favourite albums from the Danish master, it's great to have him back!
Dec 2017

IL TEMPIO DELLE CLESSIDRE
ALIENATURA
This is the second album by Il Tempio Delle Clessidre, following on from their debut in 2010. Since then, they have gained a new singer, but I haven't heard the previous album so can't comment as to what impact he has had to the sound. What I do know, is that I am going to have to go back and search out the debut as yet again this is a superb release from Black Widow. At just under an hour long, this brings together orchestration and harmony in a way that is reminiscent of the early Seventies Italian Prog Scene, along with early Genesis, but somehow brought up to date with some driving guitar although the mellotron is never too far away. As well as the main lead male vocal, their keyboard player Eliza also has a fine voice which allows the band to totally change the scene when they wish to.

The album commences with the sound of wind and gentle acoustic guitar and percussion before moving into a much more Oriental feel, which is at musical odds with what follows but somehow sets the scene very nicely indeed. 'Alienatura' is a word that the band have invented themselves to describe the intersection of the words alien and nature. This is very much a complete piece of work, again hearkening back to the early Seventies, where the album art is very much part of the complete picture. Here Nature is depicted ripping a curtain and invading the homes and villages while the lyrics tell how we often forget our bond with nature. So, a complete piece of work, and even though it is hard for the non-Italian speaker to understand the full concept without notes, there is so much going on that this is a sheer delight from start to end. If you enjoy classic prog, whatever the form or language, then this is something you ought to seek out.
Jan 2014

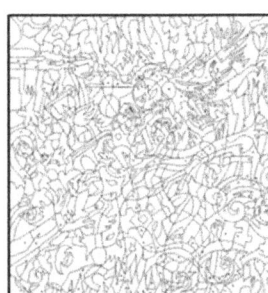

IL TEMPIO DELLE CLESSIDRE
IL-LŪDĔRE
I was quite a fan of this Italian progressive rock band's previous album, 'AlieNatura', which was released in 2013: this was their second release, but the first with singer Francesco Ciapic. Again, there has been a change in membership between albums, as drummer Paolo Tixi has been replaced by Mattias Olsson (Änglagård, White Willow, Necromonkey), while Anna Holmgren (also of Änglagård) adds her delicate flute to one number. This is a progressive rock album that is dominated by the vocals, and to my ears works incredibly well. Musically this has a lot in common with the early Seventies progressive rock and hard rock scene, and the use of a strong singer in the hard rock style certainly provides this music with some additional edge, which is sadly often missing from the progressive scene.

Too many bands seem to forget the "rock" section of "progressive rock", and concentrate too much on keyboards and delicacy, but here ITDC are using plenty of dynamics, with light and shade emphasising both areas. But these guys are still first and foremost a progressive band, it's just that they are refusing to be bound by what many feel is the sort of music which should be coming out of the RPI scene. I really enjoy Francesco's singing style, as his vocals carry emotion and although he can sing higher when he wishes to, he generally stays in the lower registers, and this allows emotion to really shine through.

My one regret is that I don't understand Italian, so have no idea at all what he is singing about but feel that if this had been in English then it would have diminished it somewhat. Yet again this is an incredibly strong release from Black Widow, and well worth investigating.
Jun 2017

COLIN TENCH PROJECT
HAIR IN A G STRING
The first solo album from Colin was released in 2016, with the full title of 'Hair In A G

String (Unfinished But Sweet)'. Colin and I are both originally from the UK, but he went North while I ended up as far South as I could. He first contacted me some five years ago, asking me to review an album by Corvus Stone, and even stayed in touch when I didn't enjoy it as much as I might have! He has worked on different things through the years, building up a strong set of contacts who admired him as a guitarist, and who were readily to hand when he started working on this album.

There are well in excess of 20 other musicians involved, while Colin himself provides acoustic and electric guitars, piano, synthesizer, drum programming and percussion. Musically this is all over the place, combining progressive rock with classical, pop, rock, and lots more. Colin is as happy double-tracking on acoustic guitar as he is providing Jeff Beck-style searing solos. He has always been a bit of a magpie, bringing in bits and pieces from his travels and discoveries, and his album is a microcosm of all that. Incredibly inventive, it is packed full of differing styles, so it always feels fresh, inviting, and something that really needs to be listened to. The very first time I played this I was sat quietly, with a wonderful glass of Pinot Gris, and a book I was looking forward to reading. But the book stayed by my side unopened as it just isn't possible to concentrate on the plot and follow this album at the same time. A mix of instrumentals and songs, this really is a very special album indeed, and one that all lovers of fine music would do well to investigate.
Jan 2018

COLIN TENCH PROJECT
MINOR MASTERPIECE
Just before Christmas I got my act together and sent my Christmas note to all the record labels, PR companies and musicians I am involved with. One of the first responses I had was from Colin, and we swapped emails over the next couple of days – me taking the piss out of him being so cold, and him responding to my comments about the wonderful summer we were having by saying "Now I must go out and drive about in the snow a bit. Hotness is for losers! Ha ha". The last email he sent me, received here on Christmas morning, was signed off "Colin from the North". It was an incredible shock to hear that only four days later he had passed away from natural causes, and to be honest I still can't believe it. Here I am listening to his brand-new album, and I have no way of telling him just how much I enjoyed it, or how much more complete I feel it is than his debut. That it feels much more like a band, and the reduction in personnel has had a major positive impact, that the contribution from Peter Jones (Tiger Moth Tales, Camel, Red Bazar) is immense, or that I can totally see why he was so proud to tell me that Joe Vitale (Joe Walsh, Barnstorm, CSN) was a full member of the band because he believed in it so much, or that his guitar-playing is the best I have heard from him, and his use of acoustic guitars at the relevant times make a huge difference.

I can't tell him any of that, nor that his mix of so many different styles, as his brain

moved from one place to another, is so typically him. I also can't work out if I have enjoyed this album so much because I wanted his final album to be worthwhile and memorable, or if it is my emotions that are mixed up with it that have caused me to hear more than is already there. I hope and believe that it is the former, but music is always subjective as opposed to objective, no matter how hard we work at it, so who is to say? You owe it to yourselves, and to the memory of someone who I have never heard a bad word said about, to give it a try. Kevin from the South.
Jan 2018

THANK YOU SCIENTIST
THE PERILS OF TIME TRAVEL
This New Jersey act are new to me, and I only came across them because I was asked by someone at work what I thought of them. Being unable to answer I took the only course of action possible, and immediately tried to find out more. 'The Perils of Time Travel' was their debut release, a thirty-minute-long EP they released in 2011. Even before the music starts one realizes that here is a band that are somewhat out of left field. While a septet isn't really that unusual in music, the instrumentation being portrayed by some of the line-up certainly is. Sal Marrano (vocals), Tom Monda (fretted and fretless guitar), Greg Colacino (acoustic and electric bass) and Odin Alvarez (drums) can be said in some way to be the "normal" side of the band. They are joined by Russ Lynch (violin and viola), Ellis Jasenovic (tenor and soprano sax) and Andrew Digrius (trumpet, flugelhorn, and synth). Even discounting that the much-maligned flugelhorn hasn't seen many rock outings outside of Jethro Tull or Gryphon, it is certainly unusual to find any band combining strings with brass, and little in the way of keyboards.

What is even more interesting is just how commercial they sound, certainly not what one would expect from a line-up like this. They mix Coheed and Cambria with a gentler version of Protest The Hero and manage to make djent, jazz, pop and prog sound as if they were destined to be together. Yes, they can go off into tangents when they wish to, and Tom is an amazing guitarist, but it is the sheer joy from the music that makes one keep going back for more. Somehow it manages to be inventive, fresh and new, yet stays accessible and soon the listener wonders how they managed to live their musical lives without ever coming across these guys before. Some of these songs could even make it onto rock radio, what on earth is going on?

It is rare to discover a band truly formed and with strong direction on their very first release. What on earth could an album be like?
Jun 2017

THANK YOU SCIENTIST
MAPS OF NON-EXISTENT PLACES
Just one short year after the debut EP, and the band were back with a full-length album of all-new material. The line-up was the same as before, and they had even managed to lift

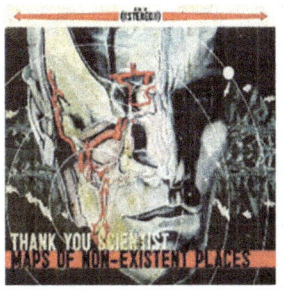
their music a notch, as the listener is dragged straight in with the acapella opening: from there on it just gets even more intense and exciting. It is rare to hear music this complex and invigorating which is also incredibly commercial. They mix rock and metal with prog, jazz and fusion, not bothering to worry about whether the music fits within any particular genre and not only breaking through preconceived boundaries but smashing them to pieces. This is progressive rock in its very truest sense, with every note and nuance having its place. They combine together far tighter than any band of this size should ever be able to do, and if you don't believe me then listen to the complex introduction of "Feed The Horses": that the song then becomes a Seventies funky pop classic before moving into something else just proves the point.

Sal somehow manages to always stay in control, no matter what is going on around him, and his style certainly adds to the overt commerciality of some of the material. But how can it be commercial when a brass section is playing delicately, someone is ripping a violin to pieces, and there is also a metal band at full pelt? None of this makes sense unless you are listening to the album, then nothing else matters. In some ways this reminds me of Spock's Beard, not in the way that the music is constructed, but that they are daring to do something different. While the music is heavily arranged, it has to be with this many musicians involved, somehow it is still fresh and exciting. This isn't music designed to smother, but instead is a living, breathing force to be reckoned with. If crossover progressive rock, in its purest form, is what you wish for, then Thank You Scientist are a band you need to discover immediately, if not sooner.
Jun 2017

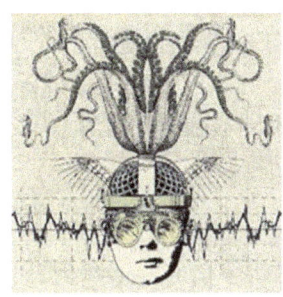
THANK YOU SCIENTIST
STRANGER HEADS PREVAIL
It took until 2016 for the next album, during which time they gained a new bassist and violinist, but even though some personnel had changed they stayed true to what they had been producing on their previous works. They even started this one with an a capella introduction as they had with the last. Again we are being treated to a band that want to mix so many different styles and musical influences that it is superfluous to even mention them, but when Coheed and Cambria lay down next to Frank Zappa who is cosying up to Mars Volta, then one knows that one is in the presence of something quite special indeed. It is fresh, it is exciting, it is invigorating, and most of all it is just great fun to listen to!

This is not a prog band that wants to copy Genesis, King Crimson, VDGG or Yes, but instead want to get out there and make a name for themselves performing the music they wish, and no matter what everyone else may think of it. Interestingly, the vast majority of progheads who have come across their music think they are amazing, so how come they aren't more well-known? Certainly, they had missed me by totally, of which the only

advantage I can think of is that now I know about them I have a few hours' worth of music to discover instead of just one album. That they can mix this complexity and intricacy in a way that makes it so easy to listen to is an art in itself, and something that very few bands ever manage. Full of light and shade, dynamics aplenty, this is an incredibly exciting album and one I could listen to all day. Each time I play it I make more discoveries, with each musician being an integral part to the musical whole. If, like me, this amazing band had passed you by, then now is the time to discover some of the most interesting music you will find in the current prog scene.
Jun 2017

THIEVES' KITCHEN
THE CLOCKWORK UNIVERSE
Whilst the core line-up of Amy Darby (vocals), Phil Mercy (guitars) and Thomas Johnson (keyboards, ex-Änglagård) were still here from the previous album, this 2015 album saw a few changes in the guests. Anna Holmgren (flute, Änglagård) and Paul Mallyon (drums, ex-Sanguine Hum) have now been joined by Johan Brand (bass, Änglagård), and this time there is no trumpet or cello. Although this is a Thieves Kitchen album, it means that of the six involved, half of them recorded the 2012 Änglagård album 'Viljans Öga'. I have heard all of the TK albums, but it was 2008's 'The Water Road' where they made a significant musical leap, which is where Thomas joined the band. 2013's 'One For Sorrow, One For Joy" saw a continuation of that, so what would the 2015 release bring?

The one word that shines throughout this album is quite simple, "confidence". Here are a group of musicians who have been working together in one form or another for quite a few years now (Anna was involved as long ago as 'The Water Road' with Amy, Phil and Thomas), and they know what they want to achieve and trust each other implicitly. This is all about producing complex progressive music, but always allowing Amy to shine with strong clear vocals. She is at the forefront of everything they are doing, with everyone else combining to provide a suitable backdrop. This could mean acoustic guitars, or classic organ sounds, complex drumming, striking repetitive bass or clear flute. This is progressive music that can be incredibly complex, or simple almost to an extreme, melodic, or discordant, languid or rapid, whatever is the right setting for the arrangement. They can be King Crimson, or Gentle Giant, Renaissance or Änglagård, but first and foremost they will always be Thieves' Kitchen. This is the type of music which got me interested in progressive rock in the first place: I want to hear music that is complex and complicated, where the mind and ears wonder where they are going to be taken to next on a journey of musical adventure and exploration. At the same time, I want it to make total musical sense, so I don't get lost along the way but feel I am being taken on a circuitous route to ensure I don't miss any of the wonders that are available. This is yet another stunning album from Thieves' Kitchen, and I can't believe that it has taken me so long to write about it. But I know they are currently recording the next one, so hopefully there will be even more to hear soon.
Apr 2017

THINKING PLAGUE
IN THIS LIFE

Reissued as a remastered edition in 2015, 'In This Life' is not merely a fascinating album of extraordinary rock-based songs. It is a landmark recording in the life of one of America's most distinctive bands and in the international spread of Rock In Opposition-style sophisticated post-rock. Recorded in 1988-89 by Denver-based Thinking Plague, one of the most esteemed and longstanding American avant-progressive ensembles, 'In This Life' marked Thinking Plague's stylistic coming-of-age. The band had recorded two earlier albums in the years since its 1982 co-founding by Mike Johnson and Bob Drake: those early works brought Thinking Plague national "underground" acclaim. But the line-up responsible for 'In This Life', with Mike Johnson handling composition and Susanne Lewis supplying lyrics and vocals, proved to be the early group's ideal creative brew. It was originally released on Recommended Records (ReR), the London-based label run by Chris Cutler, founder of the Rock In Opposition movement and member of renowned band Henry Cow. One track on the album featured a guest appearance by Fred Frith, the legendary Henry Cow/Art Bears guitarist. It became ReR's first-ever release on the then-radically new format of CD - a format that simplified the disc's international distribution.

Even now, all these years on from when it was originally released, this is in many ways quite a frightening and disturbing album, almost as if Art Zoyd have gone to another level and then brought in a female singer who is totally at odds with what else is going on musically behind her. This was never meant to be an album that was easy to listen to, and with its discordant melodies and other worldliness, is one that will repel far more people than would ever listen to it. It is off key, it is controlled, it is anarchic, yet for me is also deeply compelling. It isn't an album that I will ever play a great deal, but I find myself drawn back to it time and again. This isn't music for a large audience on a bright sunny day, but is to be enjoyed in the night, when nothing else will suffice. RIO doesn't get much more inventive and important as this.
Mar 2017

THINKING PLAGUE
HOPING AGAINST HOPE

Fast forward to 2017, and Thinking Plague show no sign at all of compromising their ideals. Mike Johnson is the only person who has been there throughout, but he is steering this ship on a very clear path. The line-up now is Mike (guitar, samples, midi instruments), Mark Harris (soprano and alto saxes, B-flat standard and bass clarinets, flute), Dave Willey: (bass, drums, accordion), Elaine di Falco (voice, accordion, piano), Robin Chestnut (drums, percussion) and Bill Pohl (guitar). Now, I have come across Bill quite a few times previously, having reviewed his solo album 'Solid Earth' back in 1994, plus some other of his bands since then such as The Underground Railroad, so I was intrigued to see his involvement. He has always been a fine guitarist with a passion for music that can be somewhat different and difficult to listen to, and here is being allowed to give that full rein.

In many ways, this is a more melodic and easier album to listen to than some of their others, but that isn't to say they have moved away from their core purpose of RIO, just that it has a slightly different flavour. There are times when the woodwind instruments take the lead, repeating motifs, but this just allows the guitars to break in and out of the song with extremely quick runs. Elaine doesn't have the same natural other worldliness displayed by Susanne on the classic 'In This Life' but fits in perfectly with this adjusted style of music.

Thinking Plague may have changed somewhat in the intervening thirty years between these two albums, but hasn't everyone? But they are still true to their roots, and this could never be any other band. Exciting and enthralling, there really is no-one else quite like them. They will only ever appeal to a select few, but those few will be greatly enriched by hearing this.
Mar 2017

THE THIRTEENTH SUN
STARDUST
Although this Transylvanian outfit self-released their debut EP as long ago as 2012, this is their debut album, which was recorded under the watchful eyes and ears of Edmond Karban (Negură Bunget, Dordeduh) last year (Edmond also provided some guest vocals). In many ways this is a progressive album, but it is also incredibly atmospheric, bringing in elements that certainly wouldn't sound out of place on an album by either Negură Bunget or Rakoth. At times it is almost black metal, others quite psychedelic, and yet others quite definitely progressive, so there is a lot going on. But it never gets too much for the listener and is yet another album that is compelling with plenty of depth.

Radu, who also provides lead guitars, has a wonderful clear and emotional voice with virtually no accent, and this also makes the album incredibly easy to listen to. The melodic English vocals sometimes work seamlessly with the music, while at others float effortlessly above so it falls away to become a backdrop to something quite special. It may have taken five years for the band to move from an EP to an album, but let's hope we don't have to wait as long for the next release, as this is incredibly enjoyable.
May 2017

STEVE THORNE
ISLAND OF THE IMBECILES
When Steve released his debut album on GEP back in 2005 I was immediately struck not only by the music but also by the artwork. So much so that I visited the website of artist Danny Flynn and purchased two framed prints, including that of 'Emotional Creatures

The Progressive Underground Vol 5

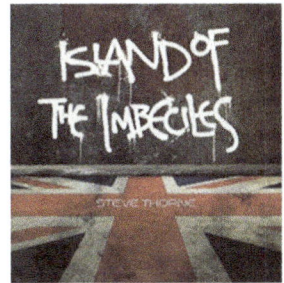

Part One' (which is inspired by "Squonk"), and they are still on my walls today. All my other music prints or framed albums are in my study, but these are in other places in the house, so Steve has had quite an impact on me. Tony Levin and Nick D'Virgilio were on that debut album, and they are still here on this his latest, joined by solo artist Robin Armstrong and well-known British musician James McLaren. Steve plays all other instruments; indeed, some tracks are genuine solo efforts!

This is true crossover prog, highly influenced by the likes of Jadis and the more pastoral side of IQ (Paul Cook, Martin Orford and Gary Chandler all played on the debut as well). Steve has a wonderfully clear vocal style, is a strong songwriter, and I find myself at a loss to explain why he isn't more well-known as an artist. As I write this there isn't a single review written for this 2016 album on ProgArchives, yet his music is always of the highest quality and he is able to get some of the very finest musicians to work with him, so is highly regarded in the scene even if the wider progsphere is yet to uncover his work. This is his fifth studio album in eleven years, so he's been working hard.

Lyrically, this is hard hitting and passionate, a mixture of political comment, opinion and a lamentation on the current state of modern life, and its effect on people both spiritually and physically. They are honest, sincere and he also provides brutal social comment, and when combined with the music and the complex yet simple nature of the songs one has to wonder why this hasn't been more widely received. Definitely worthy of further investigation.
Feb 2018

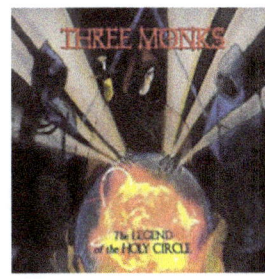

THREE MONKS
THE LEGEND OF THE HOLY CIRCLE
The first time I played this I had a huge smile on my face, and the more I played it the bigger it got. Three Monks are comprised of Paolo Lazzeri (pipe organ), Maurizio Bozzi (bass) and Roberto Bichi (drums) and together they are channelling bombastic Wakeman with some of the finer elements of Emerson. The use of a pipe organ throughout definitely provides an additional element of power and majesty, almost Wagnerian in its concept. When I started listening to it, I was listening for similarities between this and ELP/Wakeman, but while this has obviously been influenced by the darker side of those outfits, this is very much a band in its own right. Both Keith and Rick have employed pipe organs (and synthesised versions of the same) to great effect throughout their career; and when I saw The Nice some years ago at the Royal Festival Hall the show commenced with Keith playing that establishment's organ (with plenty of the stops pulled out), so there are bound to be some similarities, but Paolo doesn't use any other keyboards at all and Maurizio and Roberto are here in a supporting role. There are no vocals, and no overt flashiness from anyone, just a concentration on producing the best neo-Gothic Romantic progressive classical rock they can.

This is very much a band, all pulling together in the same direction, showing just how powerful a pipe organ can be in the hands of someone who really knows what he is doing. Apparently, Paolo is heavily influenced by the music of composer Julius Reubke (1824-1858), as well as his love of progressive rock, but that is yet another composer I have never heard of so can't say if it comes through into the album. What I do know is this is an incredible example of keyboard based progressive rock, and fans of this style need to seek this out.
Jan 2014

THRESHOLD
FOR THE JOURNEY
2014 saw Threshold return with their tenth studio album, their second since Damian Wilson had returned on vocals for the third time. The previous album, 2012's 'March of Progress' had been one of the finest in their canon, so perhaps it isn't surprising that this one isn't quite in the same league. The songs are powerful, the vocals spot on, but there isn't quite the same spark and vitality as there had been previously. It is still a great album, and one that is head and shoulders above most of those dwelling in the progressive metal arena, but I did find myself wondering if all was well within the camp. I don't believe that Threshold could ever release a bad album, or even an average one, as they are just too good for that both collectively and individually, but I realised that although I was enjoying it immensely while it was playing, I wasn't overly keen about pressing repeat when it finished, which says a great deal for me. Were the band just marking time waiting for the next stage? Only time will tell.
Sep 2017

THRESHOLD
EUROPEAN JOURNEY
2015 saw the fifth live album from Threshold, but strangely enough this is the first one to feature Damian on vocals as the others had all been released during one of his breaks from the band. It was the first one in nine years, and with two recent studio albums behind them it made sense for this to be released when it was. As would be expected with the live set it concentrated on the most recent studio albums, with nine of the fifteen songs coming from the last two, but perhaps what is somewhat surprising is that there were far less songs that one might have expected from the earlier period of the band. I would have loved to have heard more songs, well any songs, from 'Wounded Land', the debut that shot them to stardom all those years ago. Okay, I was lucky enough to see them a few times in the Nineties, but that was some time ago now, and given this was Damian's first live recording with the band surely there could have been room for "Sanity's End" or "Paradox"?

But to be honest, it's always going to be hard to pick a setlist to please everyone with such a history behind them, so let's concentrate instead on what we do have. Johanne James has been sat at the back for a good many years now, and I firmly believe that in many ways he is one of the most under-rated and overlooked drummers in the scene. He knows when to be powering and driving, and when to take a step back, and his relationship with bassist Steve Anderson is second to none. I still find it strange that Nick Midson is not there anymore, given the way Karl Groom and he used to seem locked as one, yet Pete Morten is far more than just a stand-in, while keyboard player Richard West knows exactly what is required to move the music away from pure over the top metal. Then there is Damian. Mr. Wilson is one of the finest rock singers of his generation, and I still believe Iron Maiden made the wrong call when they chose Blaze Bayley above him when they both auditioned to replace Bruce. He sings like an angel, and his power and range are incredible.

The new songs fit well with the slightly older ones, and it is interesting to hear Damian take on numbers originally recorded by a different singer. Highlight for me is "Long Way Home", from 2001's 'Hypothetical' when it was sung by Mac, but while Damian does a good job it is the power of the band behind him that really makes this shine. To my ears this is a strong album, but 2004's 'Critical Energy' takes some beating when it comes to the ultimate in live Threshold albums.
Sep 2017

THRESHOLD
LEGENDS OF THE SHIRES

It was something of a shock to fans of the band when it was announced they had parted ways with their singer Damian Wilson, for the third time. Also, Richard and Karl decided they wanted to take the band musically back to more of where they used to be in the Nineties, which led them to asking what Glynn Morgan was doing? Glynn sang on 'Psychedelicatessen' in 1994, as well as the ensuing live album, but had also been involved in bits and pieces with the guys through the years. A decision was also made to just have one guitarist and reduce to a five-piece, so the line-up was Glynn (vocals), Richard (keyboards, backing vocals), Karl (guitar, backing vocals), Johanne (drums, backing vocals) and Steve (bass, backing vocals). But that wasn't all, as the guys also invited original bassist Jon Jeary in to provide vocals on one song. Jon was in the band for many years, and I always felt his vocals in the live environment were incredibly important to the overall sound, so it is wonderful to see him involved again, even if it is just for a cameo.

With these changes made, great artwork and a double CD, the guys knew this had to be an epic release, as anything less than that would be seen to be a failure. So it's probably just as well that they have released their most varied and dynamic album for years, possibly their finest yet. This album has far more depth and breadth than we have heard recently, with Richard to the fore, and much more melody and straight progressive tendencies backed up by strong guitars as opposed to crunching riffs that have the edge removed as has sometimes been the case in the past.

This is well thought out and constructed music and shows that although they still inhabit the more metallic end of the prog metal spectrum than bands such as Dream Theater, they still know exactly how to satisfy the progheads. Moving back to a more progressive style, and changing singers, is obviously a risk but it has paid off with this album making the Top #5 of the UK Rock Charts, and entering Sweden, Germany and Switzerland in the Top 15, and getting to #31 in Austria. Threshold have taken a breath, decided how they wanted to move forward and grabbed it with both hands. They are touring in November and December across Europe and the UK, ending at the 02 Islington Academy, and that will be a tour not to miss. Now all I need to do is convince Karl he ought to come down here. This is an absolutely essential indispensable album.
Sep 2017

TICKET TO THE MOON
AE SENSE OF LIFE
Ticket to the Moon are from Basel, Switzerland, and were formed in 2003 by Daniel Gosteli (drums, vocals, percussion) and Andrea Portapia (guitars, vocals). The band went through several changes until Guillaume Carbonneau (bass) and Matthias Zwick (keyboards) joined in 2007, and this was the line-up that delivered 'Dilemma On Earth' in 2012. 'Ae Sense of Life' is their second album, self-released in 2015. Their PR company describes their sound is a blend of atmospheric rock with strong metal influences, producing modern, melodic and powerful progressive music influenced by the likes of Enchant, Ayreon and Dream Theater. They may well indeed have been influenced by them, but that doesn't mean that they are remotely in the same league as any of the above. Musically this doesn't gel as it should, and jars as it moves from one area to another as there is a real lack of continuity. There are times when they capture an almost Meshuggah or System of a Down feeling to what they are doing, and in my mind that is the sort of style they should be concentrating on, as they have talent in that area. But the main thing against this album is the quality of the vocals, which simply aren't strong enough. If these guys are ever going to make serious inroads into the progressive scene, then they need to undertake more work on the arrangements and get themselves a decent singer.
Feb 2018

TIGER MOTH TALES
THE DEPTHS OF WINTER
Multi-instrumentalist (and Camel live keyboard player) Peter Jones is back with his third album under the name Tiger Moth Tales, and this time he has brought in some friends to assist him on a couple of songs, but for most of the time it is just Peter. Mind you, a very special mention must be made of Luke Machin's incredibly fluid solo on "Winter Maker", one of three songs that break the ten-minute barrier. The album isn't a concept album per se, more a thematic collection of wintery

concepts, and stories that take place in the winter season. There are a number of different themes explored, including winter folk tales and characters such as the Ojibwe wind spirit, Biboon, the Viking legends of Baldr, Loki and Frigga, and the death of English folklore hero, Robin Hood. As with previous Tiger Moth Tales albums, this new collection of works includes a broad range of musical feelings and emotions, from dark themes such as a grim fight for survival in "Winter Maker", and the terrible scenes described in "Exposure", based on the Wilfred Owen poem of the same name, to the warmer feelgood tracks such as the joyous and exuberant "Sleigh Ride" and the closing track "Hygge".

Unlike many multi-instrumentalists Peter has a strong voice, and writes to his strengths, so the songs always feel emotional. There are definite nods to Hackett, both solo and also in his time with Genesis, and there were times when I found myself wondering if a particular song might fit on 'Wind & Wuthering', such is the quality. There is only one downside to me with this release, and that is the "drums". Peter really needs to invest in a live drummer as opposed to a machine, as it drags the music down, and with a quality person behind the kit it would assist in taking this to the next level. As it stands, it is still an essential release, and I am very much looking forward to the next one.
Feb 2018

TNNE
WONDERLAND
Three years on from 'The Clock That Went Backwards', Luxembourg's TNNE (which as the band was seen as a continuation on from No Name, was called TNNE for The No Name Experience) are back with the second album under that banner, or sixth studio album overall. There has been a major change in the line-up, with Claudio Cordero coming on board, who of course has been guitarist with the mighty Cast for more than ten years. That he has had a major impact on the band is never in doubt, with his more metallic guitar riffs and solos definitely enhancing their neo prog credentials. The PR company likens them to RPWL and IQ, and while I do struggle a little with this, I can understand why those comments have been made although TNNE are far heavier, without ever moving into the prog metal genre.

Alex Rukavina on keyboards is an excellent foil to Claudio, while both drummer Giles Wagner and bassist Michel Casadei della Chiesa are far more in your face and driving melodies than is usual, creating a quite different dynamic. The first time I played the album I discovered I was smiling all the way through, and my feelings towards it have only warmed. In many ways, it does hearken back to the Nineties, yet also feels incredibly current and with a powerful production it becomes an album that is surely at the vanguard of the current neo prog scene. Highly recommended, as with soaring vocals from Patrick Keifer, melodies and counter melodies, complexity and simplicity, layers and space, this is a prog album to savour.
Dec 2017

The Progressive Underground Vol 5

TOHPATI ETHNOMISSION
MATA HATI
Tohpati Ario Hutomo (a.k.a. Bontot) is probably best known for his twenty-year tenure in the incredible simakDialog, but he launched his project Ethnomission back in 2010 with 'Save The Planet', and at long last he has brought the band back for a second venture. He of course provides all the guitars, and is joined by Demas Narawangsa (drums), Indro Hardjodikoro (bass), Endang Ramdan (kendang – a type of two-headed drum used in Gamelan ensembles) and Diki Suwarjiki (suling – a bamboo ring flute, also used in Gamelan music). If that wasn't enough, they are all joined on the opening track by the Czech Symphony Orchestra, conducted by Michaela Ruzickova, which certainly adds a different feel to the overall piece. With the instrumentation being used, it would be easy to imagine this is a hard to listen to (to Western ears) romp through traditional Indonesian music, but that is a long way from reality. Tohpati is a guitarist with an incredibly clear sound, and while he is often at the core of what is taking place, he knows just when it is time to step to one side and let others take over. Indro is a revelation, with some stunning bass lines, and one can imagine Tohpati there with a huge smile on his face as he lets his bandmate take centre stage. There is a lot of Indonesian musical references and styles, of course, but this is fusion at its very truest, bringing together not only jazz and melody but also Asia and the West in a way which is seamless, marvellous, and entrancing. There is only one thing to be done with an album as good as this. When you shake yourself back into the real world after the fifty-two minutes have flown by, have a good stretch, settle back, and put it on again.
Mar 2017

TOLERANCE
WHEN TIME STOPS
I must confess and say I don't know that many bands from Venezuela, but apparently these guys have been around for some ten years and have now produced their debut, which has been made available through Musea. I think the only question now is will we have to wait another ten for the next one? I certainly hope not! The band is made up of Ricardo Figueroa (vocals), Carlos Cabrices (guitar), Ricardo Nunez (drums), and Antonio Ramirez (keyboards), (other instruments are provided by guests). Now, musically they come across very much in the realm of Dream Theater, but when one looks a little more deeply at their history possibly that isn't too surprising as they have similar backgrounds, in that the three musicians are all professionally trained. Rodrigo N attended "Ars Nova School of Music", a Berklee oriented school where he got his musical degree, Antonio attended Los Teques Musical Conservatory for two years while Carlos attended Simon Bolivar Musical Conservatory to study classical guitar and then attended I.U.D.E.M, a Venezuelan musical college where he got his musical degree and majored in composition.

Ricardo F needs to be at the very top of his game to cope with this, but he knows how to cut a dashing James LaBrie vocal, with great range and power, and he has no problem hitting the heights that have been set by those around him. But what really makes this stand out for me is that not only are these guys great performers who can be as complex and complicated as any in the genre, they also know how to write songs that are immediate and controlled. Of the eight songs on offer, only two are nine minutes long, so no drawn-out epics here, although they are obviously more than capable of doing them if they wished. They are quite staccato in much of their playing, which gives a real edge to the overall sound, and they are incredibly tight, with everyone really hitting the marks. I was a little surprised to see they don't have a permanent bassist, as they often allow that instrument to take the main role (there is some beautiful fretless bass on "Beware of the Birds" for example) when the need is there and don't keep it hidden in the background.

Overall, this is a stunning debut, and if you enjoy complex prog metal then you can't afford to let this one pass you by.
Apr 2014

KALIN TONEV
MACHINE YEARS

Kalin is a "new" musician to me, but he has been involved in the progressive scene in his native Bulgaria for some years, both in bands and by running a regular radio show. What we have here is an instrumental album, with Kalin providing keyboards and drum programming, and then he has been joined by three different guitarists. But it must be said that this doesn't sound like a solo project, but much more like a band. Kalin relishes in a filthy keyboard sound, providing chords and passages that wouldn't sound out of place on a Keith Emerson album, if Keith was in his darkest and foulest mood as opposed to his honky-tonk sideshows. The best way I can think of putting it, is that if Chris Squire played keyboards instead of bass, then he would have a sound like this.

Although there is a darkness to this album, it is complemented by plenty of light and brightness and is full of invention and dynamics. There are very little "Look at me and see how quickly I can play" moments, but rather this is an incredibly well-arranged album where there are times that he links into the guitar as if it is Jon Lord and Ritchie Blackmore, or Ken Hensley and Mick Box. This isn't a keyboard solo release, but a progressive rock album with plenty of guts and balls, where the lead instrument is often (but not always) the keyboards. Now I've heard this it has got me wondering what his "real" band albums are like, and when we're going to get the next solo release. But for now, I'll just keep playing and enjoying the wonderful album that is 'Machine Years'.
May 2017

LA TORRE DELL ALCHMISTA
NEO
Don't let the album title provide any confusion: this is not a neo prog album, but instead is a high class RPI release that has been heavily influenced by PFM and most especially Seventies ELP. Although they do have a guest guitarist who makes the odd appearance, for the most part this is a band with a highly complex rhythm section, an amazing keyboard player, and a wonderful singer. There is only one thing wrong with this album, and that is it is only fifty minutes long! I could play this all day, probably every day. When music is as good as this, with musicians as highly skilled as these, then it is always a delight from start to end. Melodies and counter melodies, traditional style keyboard sounds, fretless bass, incredibly deft touches on beautiful piano, a wise use of guests (the sax, when it is employed, works incredibly well). This is just so good it is hard to know where to start.

I am amazed this album didn't make a much bigger splash when it was released in 2007, and I firmly believe that the title probably had quite a lot to do with it, as it may well have put off some people who otherwise would have investigated it. This was their second studio release, and as this had taken six years from the debut, hopefully now it is ten years since this came out there may be another in the works (certainly that is implied, hopefully, from their Facebook site). If you enjoy regressive progressive rock, taking you back to the heady days of the Seventies, then this is something that needs to be investigated. There is space, there is light and shade, there are dynamics and elements of real grace. I can't rate this too highly.
Jan 2017

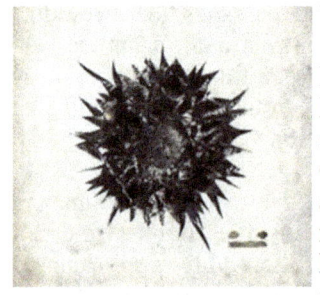
TOXIC SMILE
7
I have learned to have high expectations of releases on Progressive Promotion, and this digipak has yet again set the standard very high indeed. This is the seventh release by German band Toxic Smile but is the first time I have come across them, looks as if I am going to have search out their old releases now as if they are anything like this then I need to hear them! The core of the band has been together since 2000, although they have been through a few drummers in that time, while Marek Arnold (keyboards, sax) and Uwe Reinholz (guitars) started playing together as students in 1996. What makes this band so interesting for me is the sheer diversity of music they are playing, happily moving through the progressive spectrum from light to heavy, simple to complex, yet always maintaining a strong melody line.

Most people would classify them as prog metal, and that is probably the best single sub-genre to fit them into, but there are times when they are clearly Crossover, at others the Neo influence comes in while jazz is never too far behind either. Yes, they can crunch out some strong syncopated rhythms when they want to, but they know how important it is to balance this with a keyboard solo or drop into a piano-led section. I'm not sure how they

would be able reproduce this in the live environment as Marek is often playing multiple parts using different keyboard sounds at the same time, yet it is only when listening hard that one realizes just how much he is contributing as the ear is naturally drawn to the bombast of the guitars, bass and drums. Robert Brenner provides some great bass touches here and there that really lift the overall sound and performance, while singer Larry B. has a wonderfully melodic voice. This is a wonderfully accessible metallic prog album with loads of influences, with the only real moan that at seven songs and just forty-seven minutes long it is just too short!
Apr 2014

TREM DO FUTURO
TREM DO FUTURO

The progressive rock band Trem Do Futuro (Train Of The Future) was formed in 1981 in Ceará, a state located in the north-eastern region of Brazil. Given that this is an area better known for its deep folk roots and rhythms, it perhaps isn't too surprising that it took some fourteen years for the band to build enough momentum to release their first album! The self-titled 'Trem Do Futuro' was released through the Progressive Rock Worldwide label in 1995. Since then, it has been unavailable, and has now been released digitally for the first time, by Progshine Records, who keep unearthing gems from Brazil. It is obvious the band were heavily influenced by both the British and Italian progressive scenes, while flautist Ulisses Germano had obviously been playing very close attention to Ian Anderson. His phrasing, and the use of clear sounds at certain points combined with a rougher much harder approach at others, intervening at just the tight time, is one of the highlights of this album. But the band never sound like Tull, as their symphonic approach, combined with some folk influences, is quite different indeed.

The lyrics are sung in Portuguese, but even without knowing the language this is an album that can be enjoyed immensely and on the very first time of playing. The band are content to move between direct rock and acoustic styles, but they are let down at times with the quality of the production, and I'm still not totally convinced about singer Paulo Rossglow. It could be argued that he is singing with lots of emotion, but he doesn't always hit the notes as true as he should. It doesn't sound like an album of the Nineties to me (apart from the odd keyboard sound), as this feels much more like a long-lost album from the Seventies as it feels genuinely of that period, as opposed to attempting to recreate something that had gone before. But, given that the band took fourteen years to release the debut album that may well have something to do with it as they did start playing together back in 1981.

Overall this is an interesting album, and all power to Progshine for making it available again after so long.
Oct 2017

TREM DO FUTURO
O TEMPO

It may have taken the band fourteen years to release their debut, but they took only twelve to come up with their second. If possible, this one is even more drenched in the Seventies than the debut, and here Paulo's vocals come across as being packed full of emotion. I found that when he was singing, I kept thinking of the mighty Roger Chapman, as he is very much in the same style and manner. Musically this is complex symphonic prog, but although it was released on CD by Masque Records at the time (and now being made available by Progshine Records for the first time since then), I do wonder if the band provided the label with a finished tape as there are instances when the production is somewhat lacking, and instances when they should have re-recorded a passage. Not surprisingly, given the time between the two recordings, there had been a few line-up changes, but possibly the most interesting was Ulisses was still there on flute, they had also added Sidarta Guimarães on violin. It is rare to find both woodwind and strings in the same setting, but here it works very well indeed.

The band are at their best when they throw caution to the wind and indulge in rapid repeated passages where everyone is following the same melody. It is at places like this that their musicianship and understanding of the genre really shines. They are still mixing acoustic and rock, and with a Hammond Organ often coming into play, this certainly doesn't sound like an album recorded this century. There is more complexity and depth than with the original, with a wider use of instruments, including some very pleasant piano. Although it has some faults, this is far more complete than the debut, and is certainly worthy of further investigation.
Oct 2017

TREM DO FUTURO
TR3S

So, back with their third album in 2015, the band had again made some changes in personnel, one of which being the loss of some of the founder members, including flautist Ulisses, although there is uncredited flute and saxophone on the album. Violinist Sidarta Guimarães was still there, and for the first time it felt as if the band had jumped forward in time as although this still contains Seventies influences, it no longer feels as if it was recorded during that decade. It also feels less British, and more Italian, while the production is also much better and even the artwork has been brought more up to date. This was a self-release at the time, and again it has now been made available by Progshine. Three albums in more than thirty years of existence certainly doesn't sound like very many but given they come from an area of Brazil where this music is rarely played, let alone recorded, perhaps it isn't surprising.

The opening song, "Viajantes Do Tempo" is one of the longest at more than eight minutes, but contains some passages that feel muddied, as if the arrangements weren't

totally thought through properly, and this is something that unfortunately does happen at various places during the album. The result is something that feels brighter and more modern than before, but also doesn't have the musicality of the others, which means that the listener starts looking for faults and flaws instead of sitting back and letting the music wash over them. Of the three, this is the one I enjoyed least, and would still point to 'O Tempo' as being the album to start with.
Oct 2017

TRIOXYDE
HEY CARLOS
Over the last few years, I have been playing a great deal of golden age of jazz, pre-war blues, and generally increasing my musical repertoire. I knew this album was dedicated to Carlos Santana, so perhaps I shouldn't have been surprised that it was jazz rock with the lead guitar often taking the melody lines (this is instrumental), but I wasn't quite ready for the huge number of blues and early Seventies influences that was also involved. I first played this in the car on a beautiful February summer's evening, and I was blown away by what I was hearing, as it was a perfect accompaniment to the vista I was seeing through my windscreen.

This is classic, and class, early Seventies jazz rock with almost as many stylings being borrowed from Peter Green's Fleetwood Mac as it is from Carlos himself. John McLaughlin can also be heard if you pay close attention, but this is not the dramatic speedy runs one sometimes gets from fusion, but a band playing close attention to the placement and spacing of each note and the impact being driven from all of this. Drummer Charles Beauregard is a jazz man at heart, and can go from rim shots to complex rolls, or moving around the kit or dancing on the cymbals, whatever is the right way to provide the desired emphasis. Michel Mergaerts has a wonderfully warm and delicate approach to bass, so that while he can bang it in with the guitar, he is often found playing a beautiful counter melody that adds a depth which allows the lead musicians to shine.

These are Dostaler William who not only provides piano, but some wonderfully dated organ sounds, and J-F Girard on guitar. These two are normally the ones at the front, although they do allow the others to come through when the time is right, and the production provides clear space between the two of them. There is little in the way of over-dubbing, so the sound is always clear and feels pure. Is it a perfect album? Well, it is hard to say anything is ever really perfect, but this is close. Damn close.

Over the years I have heard many of the releases from the great Canadian label Unicorn, and this is easily one of their very best. This is for those who want to hear great music taking influences from the best of jazz and the best of blues to produce something that is quite special indeed.
Feb 2017

The Progressive Underground Vol 5

TROJAN HORSE
FUKUSHIMA SURFER BOYS
This is my first introduction to Trojan Horse, and I must confess that it took me a while to understand what was going on. This is true progressive music, refusing to conform to just about anything, and has very little in common with much of the modern progressive scene. Mind you, even though I would point to Krautrock in general and Can in particular as being an influence, along with the iconic Art Zoyd, they don't have anything in common with much of the past either. They have also found room for guests Jimi Goodwin (Doves), Kavus Torabi (Knifeworld/Gong/Guapo/Cardiacs) and Pete Trewavas (Marillion), but don't waste your time trying to work out who is providing what as this music just doesn't work this way.

When music is as "out there" as this, it does take time for it all to make sense, even for a hardened proghead such as myself, but it is more than worth the effort. Just when I think I've got them worked out they disappear off onto another tangent and I must reset my mind and settle down again. I can imagine Robert Fripp listening to this and smiling, as there are times when they take even some of his work to an area he has yet to investigate, while I am sure Frank Zappa would have enjoyed this as well. This sheer refusal to confirm to any preconceived norms is bound to restrict their fanbase, but if quantity of people buying music was an indicator of worth then we would all be listening to the likes of Justin Bieber. This won't be for all progheads, but for those who have more discerning tastes will find much here to enjoy.
Jan 2017

TUCANA
TUCANA
Swedish proggers Tucana describe themselves as a baroque progressive band, and they been around for some considerable time but only released their debut at the end of 2012. Comprising Jonas Nitz (piano, string arrangements, backing vocals), Mikael Larsson (guitars), Jari Katila (drums), Niklas Birgersson (vocals), and Johnny Rosengren (bass) they describe the album itself as taking he listener on a journey in a Rock opera/Musical way by mixing progressive rock with classical orchestral arrangements on the (sometimes) heavier side. Certainly, there is a lot going on, but I'm not sure I would call this baroque, as it just doesn't have that feel for me, and is far purer symphonic in nature. But this is definitely more to the progressive side than, say, Nightwish who get to this style by coming from metal whereas Tucana are coming from prog. The music is extremely fluid, and they have added in certain instruments just for short passages (such as flute during "The Needle of Ended Days" where it adds to the overall feel).

The only real way of describing this album is as being majestic, as there is something about the sound that is extremely large and symphonic, as if it was being performed in a

large hall instead of a tiny studio somewhere. Mikael is an incredibly fluid guitarist and knows when to really let rip and increase the note density in a fashion not too dissimilar to Malmsteen, but he also knows when to show restraint and keep it much more under control so that others can shine. All in all, this is a very powerful symphonic prog album that uses large orchestral elements to tie in with the metallic to make something well worth investigating.
Apr 2014

TWELFTH NIGHT
SKAN DEMOS/FIRST TAPE ALBUM
If ever there was an underground progressive rock band who should have really made the big time, then surely it must be Twelfth Night. Through many different factors, not all of their own making, they released just four full-length studio albums during their career, along with a couple of live albums plus some long-deleted and not available cassettes. However, due to the increased interest in the prog scene in general, and TN in particular, there have been quite a few compilations and live archive releases released under the watchful eye of Brian Devoil, and there has even been a reunion and some gigs! But what I am playing now is another of the Archive releases, and one of incredible importance to fans as it contains the very first demo from the band, the legendary 'SKAN' recordings when the band were just a trio, plus two songs from, the 'First Tape' album which was released later the same year (1979) when Rick had joined on keyboards.

Listening to these songs makes one realize just what incredible musicians these guys were, and also what a huge influence they must have been on Ozric Tentacles as "Fur Helene II" could easily have come from those guys. The songs themselves, albeit recorded in a studio, were actually 'live' with little in the way of overdubs and were normally first or second take. Andy is an incredible guitarist, while Clive was never content just to provide solid backing and wanted to be in on the melody which left Brian at the back trying to hold everything together and ensuring they all kept on track. The sound is really good, especially considering this was an unsigned band recording some 35 years ago, and certainly doesn't sound dated. But this is an album that while not exactly the one I would recommend as an introduction to the band (their best studio album is 'Fact and Fiction', live is 'Live and Let Live') it is something that even those who don't know the band will enjoy as the swirling complex musical motifs move in the air to create something that is incredibly beguiling, compelling, and entrancing. If you are a fan of the band, you will recognise sections of songs that later on became parts of others and having two versions of "Sequences" is always a good thing. I must confess that each time I hear the early instrumental versions I still 'hear' Geoff singing over the top. To take such a monumental instrumental number (one version here is nearly eighteen minutes long) and add lyrics to it in a way that makes it seem that it was always meant to be heard that way is an incredible achievement. I have been a fan of the band for years but had not heard these versions until now and it is wonderful to have them available once again.
Jan 2014

UKOG
VAAYA AND THE SEA
UKOG, or The National Orchestra Of The United Kingdom Of Goats to give them their full name, are a heavy alternative progressive rock quartet from Bolzano, Italy. The members prefer to remain anonymous and use costumes and pseudonyms so all we are sure of is that the band comprises 'The Admiral' (guitars, vocals), 'The Coachman' (bass, background vocals), 'The Seer' (drums) and 'The Insane' (electronics). Now, one might imagine that the music they are providing is highly experimental and almost unlistenable, but in reality, what we have here is an album of incredible depth and emotion that is accessible the very first time it is played and just keeps growing on the listener each time after that.

They are bringing together elements of Porcupine Tree, Mars Volta, Radiohead, Muse, Pink Floyd and so many more to create a soundscape that is powerful and hard hitting, yet also with a depth and delicacy so that it seems the musical notes may shatter like a pane of glass if treated too roughly. There are time changes, staccato moves to break up the serenity, strident guitars to take over from the keyboards, but always there is a continuity and direction that keeps the music moving forward. Always moving forward, progressing towards the goal. This, their full-length debut album, came out towards the end of 2012 so let's hope that they will soon return with another as this is superb.
Mar 2014

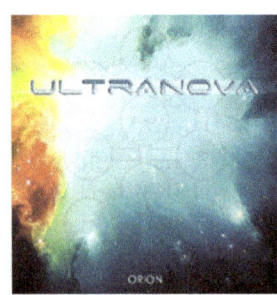

ULTRANOVA
ORION
Ultranova is a Brazilian progressive rock group formed by Thiago Albuquerque (piano/synth), Daniel Leite (electric guitar), Príamo Brandão (bass) and Henrique Penna (drums). The idea was to create a band with a unique sonority, as their own identity, without departing from the style to which they were identified in artists like Emerson, Lake & Palmer, King Crimson, Yes and Pink Floyd. They began to stand out in 2012, and from then on, the band started to perform at festivals and events sharing stages with renowned Brazilian artists such as Hermeto Pascoal, Egberto Gismonti and Violeta de Outono. Rock Symphony released their debut album, 'Orion', in Brazil and it was then picked up by Musea for European release while Progshine Records have made it available digitally.

This is instrumental progressive rock, with a great deal of interplay between Thiago and Daniel. Starting with a number that is almost ten minutes in length is brave for anyone, especially if they are an instrumental act, but I found that I was soon intrigued in what was going on, as the interaction between guitar and keyboards is interesting. There are times when they do let everything slow down somewhat, and if ever there was a risk of the listener's attention wandering then it is during these periods, but when they keep things at a slightly higher tempo, they are exciting and vibrant. There is just one number where it all falls apart, and that is "Salinas" where for some reason the guys move into slow Seventies-style fusion of the type that can only ever be background noise. But thankfully it is just the one song and the title track, which is more than thirteen minutes in length, more than makes up for it.

I will be interested to see what happens with the band from here on in, as being picked up for distribution by Musea should see them gaining a lot of publicity. I would certainly like to hear more.
Oct 2017

UNCREATED LIGHT
WHOM SHOULD I BLAME?
Artem Mokry (guitars, keyboards, writing, arrangements) and Helen 'Eldiva' Musienko (vocals) formed Uncreated Light in 2008, following on from their previous band New Land. Here the line-up is completed by Ilia Mamikin (bass) and Viktor Bilan (drums), and the Ukrainians released this their debut album in 2009. The ten songs are sung in Russian, with four of them then repeated as English versions. Stylistically this is mid-period Nightwish, with Helen's vocals being very much in the style of Tarja Turunen, but the main difference between the two bands is down to the quality of the songs. The musicianship is good, and the arrangements generally okay, but there is just nothing here to really grab the listener. Songs in a foreign language are not an issue for me, and those in their native tongue seem to work better than those that have been Anglicized, but I found my attention drifting, even with the occasional power riffs. It is symphonic metal with extremely operatic vocals, but it just doesn't seem to have any soul or depth, and there are times when it seems singular as opposed to multi-layered.

I normally really enjoy this style of music, but this never really lifts out of second gear and perhaps it isn't surprising that as of yet there hasn't been a follow-up.
May 2014

UNIVERSAL TOTEM ORCHESTRA
MATHEMATICAL MOTHER
This band was originally formed as an offshoot of Runaway Totem, which probably goes some way to explaining why they released their debut in 1999, their follow-up in 2008, and this their third in 2016. They are often described as Zeuhl within the prog world, but I'm not convinced myself that the term has a great deal of merit outside of Magma, so let's instead keep this simple. However one wants to classify this album, or whatever sub-genre one wants to put it in, it can all be said in one little word, "beautiful". Whether it is the soaring classical vocals, the perfect piano accompaniment, the amazing bass, or the move between jazz, fusion, funk, classical, Arabian, and progressive styles, it really is the only word that matters. This is a delicate

album with instrumental passages that are dynamic and powerful, with vocals that can be strident or fragile, with everything always working together in perfect harmony. Some of the guitar on opener "Terra Cava" is sublime, and it shows that even proggers can shred when they wish to, it's just that they often don't feel the need. At fourteen minutes long, this is an epic song in so many ways, not just in length, but in the sheer complexity and the way all the passages make sense individually and come together to create a whole that is breathtaking both in its complexity and melody.

'Mathematical Mother' is a very special album, one that is incredibly complex and intricate, yet also very easy to listen to, and totally enjoyable the very first time it is played. Let's hope we don't have to wait quite so long for the next one.
Jun 2017

UNWRITTEN PAGES
NOAH
Apparently, this originally started life as a story-based project back in 2005 by Frederic Epe (vocals, keyboards), but over time it became a musical collaboration between Frederic and Michel Epe (guitars) with Glenn (production, guitars). To create the science fiction concept album they wanted, they brought in others such as Damian Wilson (Threshold, Ayreon), Karl Groom (Threshold), Davy Mickers (Stream of Passion, Ayreon) and Alejandro Millán (Hello Madness, Stream of Passion) who joined the project to bring the story to life. Swedish designer Mattias Norén, created the artwork that appears in the booklet with the lyrics. But, while this 2010 album has been hailed as a major success by some, I'm not one of them.

It is doubtful that I will ever criticise an album that involves Karl and Damian as I am such a fan of both their works, but what lets this down is not the performance but the quality of the songs. This is prog metal, but it is disjointed in just so many ways. A good project album will feel either like a band, or a rock theatre production, yet this one falls between the two camps and comes across as disjointed and just way too over the top. It is too layered, too over produced, just too much altogether! There are bits that grab the attention, but for the most part it is about wondering how much longer this has to go, and whether now might be a time to switch to something else.

It's not awful, it's not bad, but I can't bring myself to say that it is anything more than good at best, and when looking at some of the people involved it just goes to show that the basis of any album must be the quality of the songs. If the foundation is shaky, then the structure is never going to be sound and stable. The only real positive about this is that now I've written about it I don't have to play it again, and it is doubtful I will.
Feb 2017

VALDEZ
THIS
Whichever way you look at it, Valdez are a super-group formed by some of the finest of the progressive scene. The singer/guitarist is none other than Simon Godfrey (Tinyfish, Shineback and solo artist) who emigrated to the States in 2014, bassist/singer Tom Hyatt was of course in the much-missed Echolyn, while keyboard player/singer Joe Cardillo is from Cold Blue Electric and drummer Scott Miller (Stone Jack Baller) completes the band. If that wasn't enough, Echolyn's Brett Kull produced it as well as providing additional guitar and vocals. Tom and Simon met by chance at a comedy club in Philly and got on so well they decided to jam the following evening at an open mic night. The duo was an instant hit with the crowd and as they left the stage, they agreed to form a band that would go on to become Valdez.

It is almost as if Tinyfish have joined forces with Echolyn, and in many ways I guess they have. For many of us following the scene in the Nineties, Echolyn was one of the most important prog bands to come out of America, with 'As The World' making a huge impact on everyone. Simon first made his presence felt with his brother in Freefall, but it was some years later that Tinyfish came to everyone's attention, with two incredibly well-received albums, and now here we have Simon and Tom working together in this new entity. This may also be the first time that Tom is back working with Brett in more than twenty years, given that Tom didn't re-join Echolyn when they reformed in 2000.

So, enough history, what about the album? Well, it's a masterpiece of course. The worry when well-known musicians get together is that they rest on their laurels and rely on their reputations to get them through, but here the guys left their egos at the door and instead have concentrated on as wonderful a piece of crossover poptastic progressive rock as one could ever wish to hear. To say this is a joy to listen to is to understate it immensely, and Simon in particular is a revelation. I don't think I've quite heard everything he has released, but I've certainly heard most of it, and based on that I can say it is easily the best thing he has ever been involved with. It oozes class, has hooks aplenty, loads of space and room to breathe, and is just awesome.

I refuse to pick a favourite, as whatever song I am listening to is the best, whether it is the melodramatic or bouncy and vibrant, there seems to be nothing these guys can't excel at. It really is an album that is packed full of songs, no over the top soloing or unnecessary note density here, it is all about what is best for the music as a collective whole. And I love it (in case you hadn't guessed). Truly essential.
May 2017

VANGOUGH
WARPAINT
I can't remember how we first got in touch, but singer/guitarist Clay Withrow and I have been in contact since the time of their stunning debut 'Manikin Parade' some eight years ago, and I have been fortunate enough to hear all their albums, of which this new release

is the fifth. The first thing I noticed is that the rabbit is back, having been on the front of their third album 'Kingdom of Ruin', and the EP 'Acoustic Scars' (where he was joined with the raven from the debut). But here he seems to be way more menacing, ready for the battle that is coming as suggested by the album title. Vangough are quite a rarity in the prog field, in that firstly they are a prog metal band without a keyboard player, but also, they are a trio. Now, that's not too uncommon in some ways, as often a trio will double up on instruments in the studio, but while Clay may have put a few guitars on the same track, all we are getting are drums (Kyle Haws), bass (Jeren Martins), guitar and vocals. Before I get into the music I must also comment on the production, which is superb. There is real separation in the music, and songs such as "The Suffering" just blow away the listener with the move from gentle acoustic notes that have been plucked and gently fade to hard riffing. It is also great to be able to clearly hear the bass and drums, and the impact they are having on the song structures. This isn't a wall of mud turned up loud, this is finesse played with skill and care.

They have been cutting their teeth in the live environment, and it comes through on this album as it is easy to imagine all these songs moving well onto a stage. After a raucous performance at the annual ProgPower USA music festival in 2014, they set out on their first North American tour with Pain of Salvation and the following year with Fates Warning. The learnings they have taken from these tours have been invaluable, and (nearly) forgives them the four years it took from 'Between the Madness' to this one. Here we have a prog metal band with technical influences that aren't afraid to shift tack quite abruptly within a song, and to be punishingly heavy when it is required or quieter and more reflective as the mood takes them.

I have been playing this album a lot since I first had the opportunity to hear it, and although I've never been a fan of a rock band fading out a song (as on the aforementioned "The Suffering"), it does lead into the very different "Gravity" which goes from gentle into a Muse-inspired belter, so I think I'll forgive them. I gave their debut five stars as I was so incredibly impressed, and now is the time to do the same again. Awesome.
Mar 2017

VISIONS PROJECT
VISIONS PROJECT
Formed in 2012 by keyboardist Oleg Polyanskiy and guitarist Dmitry Zhinkin, the Ukrainian band Visions Project have delivered one of the most diverse albums I have ever come across. Keyboard player Oleg Polyanskiy had a vision of creating an album that features a variety of styles, from classical and jazz fusion all the way through to progressive metal and in many ways he has succeeded. Guitarist Dmitry Zhinkin bought into the whole concept, and he wrote approximately half of the album, so it is very much a joint effort. They started recording in 2010, but due to

geography the album took three years to complete as Oleg lives in Doha (Qatar), Dmitry in Moscow (Russia), bassist Shirhan Agabeyli in Kiev (Ukraine), while the drummers Vadim Samosyuk, Sergey Balalaev and singer Vlad Volovikov in Kharkov (Ukraine).

They are all session musicians, and this definitely comes through in the performance as some of the pieces are just stunning, such as the incredible guitar solo which is "Prelude". But, although in many ways this album is a great success in that it achieved exactly what Oleg wanted with a real diversity of sounds and styles, that is also its' greatest weakness. On their own, many of the pieces (especially the instrumentals) are just wonderful, but when put into a whole album it becomes a series of disconnected pieces that could almost be by different bands as opposed to something that I would believe is by a single entity. It is almost too clever for itself, and the result was something that I could never really get inside of, there is too little continuity for me to want to play this repeatedly. That is a real shame, as there are some wonderful performances on here, but the complete result is something that for me misses the mark.
Apr 2014

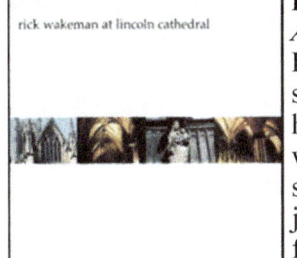

RICK WAKEMAN
AT LINCOLN CATHEDRAL
It is safe to say I am a fan of Rick Wakeman and listen to his solo albums far more than I do of any of the bands or projects he has been involved with during his long career. Of course, even with his solo works there are many different versions, and I have seen him play live with a full-on rock band as well as seeing him just sat at a grand piano. This is far closer to the latter than the former, as in 2001 he was given the opportunity to spend a day at Lincoln Cathedral playing their organ, and this is the result. The music was written specifically for the instrument itself, and apparently "is based around a combination of fixed notation and improvisation fuelled by pure emotion".

For anyone who was brought up in a traditional church as I was, there is just something about the sound and power of a pipe organ which is quite awe-inspiring. This is a long way removed from his New Age series of albums yet is also very different from much of his canon as well, as he has brought into this quite a hymnal approach to the music, more Handel, than Mozart or Ravel. This isn't an album that is going to appeal to many progheads, but for someone like me who was raised listening to religious organ and piano music, then this is wonderful. Rick isn't a master of this type of instrument, and I can hear him struggling at times, especially when he trying to bring the pedals to bear, but that adds to the joy of this for me.

I can see Rick in my mind, with his eyes closed, at one with the music he is performing, and this is an album to which I will often be returning.
Mar 2017

The Progressive Underground Vol 5

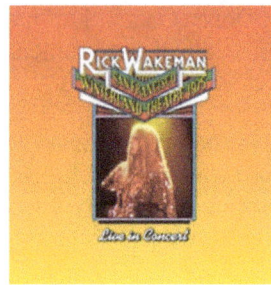

RICK WAKEMAN
WINTERLAND BALLROOM 1975

Apparently, I have 97 Rick Wakeman solo albums according to iTunes, which means I'm still missing some, and that doesn't include his work with other artists and bands! Yes, it's safe to say I'm a fan. I also have multiple DVDs and books of his, and it is a serious regret of mine that I have only seen him in concert twice, once on the 'Out There' tour and once on a solo piano tour. Now, most people are aware that just a few days before the 'Out There' tour Rick's singer, Damian Wilson, decided that he couldn't do the gig anymore, but instead of abandoning the shows Rick instead contacted his old mate Ashley Holt, and with a rejigged set list the tour was saved.

Heading all the way back now to 11th February 1975, and this CD captures Ashley also singing his heart out for Rick, but here it was at a concert in San Francisco, following on from Rick's three massive albums 'Journey', 'King Arthur' and 'Henry'. This was recorded and broadcast as a radio show, and it is obvious there has been no cleaning up at all, as there are a few duff notes here and there. Also, it must be realised that there was no expectation of making this commercially available so there are times when the sound is dated, and I noticed an audible hiss at some points. But, and it is a huge "but", the concert itself is quite astounding.

With both trumpet and trombone in the band, it gives the music a very different feel, as does the use of percussion as well as drums. This means there are times when "real" instruments are used where Rick usually plays the sounds on keyboards, which allows him to go off on piano or another musical tangent. There is strong use of acoustic guitar as well as electric, and this really does feel like a band as opposed a keyboard player and session musicians.

Is this an album that I would recommend to someone trying to discover Rick for the first time? To be honest no, there are better live albums around, and certainly better studio releases. But in terms of historical context and Rick's overall biography this album is fascinating and is one that any fan needs to have in their collection. With sleeve notes by Gonzo's own Jon Downes, this is a CD to which I will often be returning.
Oct 2017

RICK WAKEMAN
MADE IN CUBA

Fast forward some thirty years from the San Francisco show, and Rick found himself in Cuba, having been invited to Havana for a series of concerts by the Ministry of Culture, the Cuban Music Institute and the Swiss foundation, "Association Friends of Cuba". A very different line-up now, with an additional keyboard player and no brass or extra percussion, but Ashley was there again! Of all the singers that have been used by Rick, he is the one that most will associate for his incredible work on so many classic albums, and for me I always think of 'Journey To The Centre of the Earth' and not only is it difficult to imagine anyone else singing it, but it is also hard to imagine Rick playing a show with Ashley without featuring at least part of it. So it is here, with the first CD commencing with a 24-minute version, showing that Ashley has lost none of his power.

I soon found myself relaxing into the album, pouring myself just a little more NZ wine (we are certainly blessed with both the quantity and quality of our vineyards), closing my eyes and letting myself drift along with the music. There is a selection of songs from throughout his career, but of course with Ashley on board there are quite a few from the Seventies. Again, Rick allows his musicians to have some fun and there are some quite extended passages where he takes a real backseat. I get the impression that there must have been a request from someone important that they play "Starship Trooper" (followed by Steve Howe's "Würm"), as although Ashely does his best it is well outside his range and it is interesting, if not always exactly as it should be.

Strangely the show finishes with a tape playing part of "Out There", which must have been as it was the most recent studio release at the time of the gig. But if a nearly two hour long double CD isn't enough, there is also a DVD in this triple disc set. The complete set is available, which has been filmed with multiple cameras in very high quality, and there is also a really interesting documentary showing some of the behind the scenes with Rick talking about his experiences and how the gigs came about.

This is an indispensable set for anyone who loves Rick's music.
Oct 2017

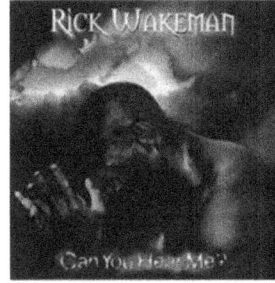

RICK WAKEMAN
CAN YOU HEAR ME?
'Can You Hear Me' was released in 1996 and was one of a series of Christian albums from Rick. The album itself contains some recordings that had appeared previously, although now with additional instrumentation and choir, as well as some new songs. "Hymn of Hope" was originally called "The Battle Hymn" and appeared on 1991's 'Softsword', and it had additional guitars and keyboards added in 1992 and it then showed up on 1992's 'Prayers' before the guitars were replaced and a choir added, and here makes its third appearance! The album featured a few Wakeman regulars such as David Paton and Fraser Thorneycroft-Smith, while Chrissie Hammond provides the vocals, but sadly Tony Fernandez wasn't utilised for some reason, so the drumming is programmed, and it shows.

Although this isn't classic Wakeman, the use of Chrissie and the English Chamber Choir was quite inspired. While some numbers are reflective, they still contain more dominance and direction than the 'Aspirant' series, and Chrissie shows that while many think of her a straight rock singer she can easily handle those of a more religious and almost hymn-like nature. This is a Christian album, and one can imagine many of these songs being

well suited to a church or cathedral setting. It doesn't really fit into either his more progressive or more rocky ventures, as that wasn't the intention, and for me this is solid, and one that I am pleased I have heard and to have on the shelf, but whether I will return to it often is another matter altogether as this just isn't my style.
Dec 2017

RICK WAKEMAN
CHRISTMAS VARIATIONS

Having already released an album of variations on hymns, it was suggested to Rick that he record variations on Christmas carols. Originally, he deferred, but finally relented and the end result is an album of variations on ten classic carols. When I say "classic" I mean exactly that, as everyone in the Western world will recognise these, and even sing along (even if it is just inside their head). I have long felt that Rick is often at his very best when he allows himself to go deep inside the music and let his hands do the talking through his piano, and that is definitely the case here. It's not all piano-led, there are plenty of synths as well, but they tend to be played as if Rick was still sat at a harpsichord or piano.

The only word to truly describe this album is "beautiful", and at this time of year I can't imagine a more tranquil and wonderful way of getting into the Christmas spirit. This isn't an album that will be played in shops with all the plastic razzmatazz where they attempt to persuade everyone that the true spirit of Christmas is how much you spend on gifts, but rather is a contemplative approach to the season. There has been a great deal of thought and care put into these variations, and I can "see" Rick with his eyes closed (as normal) falling deeper and deeper into the music, taking the simplicity and giving it more meaning and love. If I have to suffer carols at Christmas, then truly this is the only way to do it.
Dec 2017

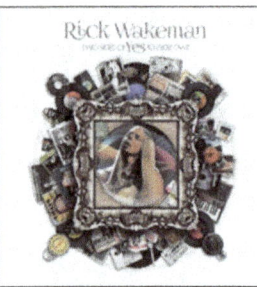

RICK WAKEMAN
TWO SIDES OF YES

Originally released as two separate volumes in 2001 and 2002, 2016 saw a reissue of both sets as a double CD set (missing only a 'bonus' video which was originally on Volume 1). The reason it is indicated as "Two Sides" is not for the number of discs, but rather there are two totally different approaches to the music contained within. Some of the interpretations feature just Rick on piano, while others feature Alan Thomson on bass and long-time collaborator Tony Fernandez on drums. Now, I have been a fan of both Wakeman and Yes for well over forty years and have managed to see both in concert twice, although unfortunately not on the same stage at the same time. To me this is a lost opportunity, in that the band versions don't always add a great deal to the original, and sometimes are less. The first time I played Rick's version of "Going For The

One" I straight afterwards went to the original and played them back-to-back, with Rick's sadly lacking in comparison.

But they are pleasant enough even if they're not essential, but the piano pieces are a revelation. Here classic numbers have been stripped, and then provided with totally new arrangements yet still staying true to the original. These are superb, and if these two discs were comprised solely of Rick providing piano variations of classic Yes numbers that this would be essential. As it stands, it is interesting to those like me who have followed both careers with interest for longer than they would really like to admit, but not as important as it could be.
Dec 2017

WALFAD
AB OVO
WALFAD (short for We Are Looking For A Drummer) was founded by singer/ guitarist Wojciech Ciuraj in 2011, and this is their debut album, recorded in 2013. Apparently, it is a concept album, but given it is performed entirely in Polish the theme is somewhat lost on me, but it concerns a young man growing up in Silesia who comes to believe that even in an industrial landscape something special can emerge. Overall, this is a very pleasant piece of work, with some nice basslines behind the main guitar that definitely adds to the overall feel. But the downside is that it is just that, pleasant. There is nothing here that really excites me, and the effect is somewhat muted as if the band wanted to play their version of neo-prog very safely indeed and not take any risks. But without excitement and drama this album comes across as being quite one-dimensional, which is a shame as they obviously know what they are doing, but they need to inject some more contrast into the music and not take such a singular path. There have been some very good Polish bands over the years, but these guys are going to have to take a serious step up to be considered in the same terms as Collage or Riverside.
Jun 2014

DEAN WATSON
SUM OF PARTS
One day I was reading through some of the threads on ProgArchives and came across one where someone called Dean Watson was asking if anyone would be prepared to review his new album? So, I popped over to his artist page on the site and was intrigued to see that here was a multi-instrumentalist I hadn't heard of, and this was his fourth album. The others had received good reviews, so I thought I'd give it a try and got in touch. A short while later I was playing the album and was again trying to comprehend how an artist with this amount of talent had passed me by, and why on earth were people with no musical ability superstars when artists such as Dean had

received virtually no recognition? Anyway, Dean provided all the instruments on the album, and moves between providing the lead on keyboards and guitar, whatever is right for the moment. Some of the keyboard sounds give this a late Seventies feel, and I am sure Allan Holdsworth has been an inspiration in the guitar stakes, with some wonderful fusion and glistening runs. That he is adept with different instruments is never in doubt, and this allows him to bounce ideas as he moves through different sounds and styles, with jazz fusion and progressive rock coming together in a beautiful whole. This is a light and uplifting album that I enjoyed immensely, so guess that means I have some research to do on his back catalogue. I look forward to it.
June 2017

WET RABBIT
OF CLOCKS AND CLOUDS
Wet Rabbit is the project name of Hungarian multi-instrumentalist Zoltan Sostai, and on this concept album he provides the vocals, guitar, drums and synthesisers while Kinga Szabo provides some piano parts. The album is apparently loosely based on ideas about indeterminism, fallibilism and open thinking developed by Austrian-British philosopher Karl Popper. It is especially dedicated to the future artificially intelligent being based on Popper's work on human understanding. Musically this appears to be an attempt to combine Eighties style electronica with progressive rock and pop. It is incredibly dated in the sounds being used, with synths that are more in common with The Human League and OMD than Vangelis or Jean Michel Jarre. There are also issues with the vocals, which aren't strong enough to take on the lead. The result is an album that really doesn't have a great deal going for, it, and will probably not find favour in any of the camps he is trying to bring together.
Feb 2018

WHALEPHANT
KAMMA
One of the joys of being involved in the progressive scene for more than twenty-five years, is that I am often contacted and asked if I would like to review an album by a band I have never heard of. As I am always open to new experiences (how else would you know how delicious snails can be?), I inveterately say yes. So, this is how I came across Whalephant, yet another progressive band hailing from Russia. I can remember when coming across a Russian progressive act was quite a rare event, especially pre-internet, but these days the scene seems to be exploding over there, and what I find particularly of great interest is the way they often refuse to conform to what many people view as "progressive", both in terms of the music they play and the instruments they use to do it. I had a look at their website but given it's all in Russian it may as well be Greek as I don't understand it, but it is possible to stream the album, watch some videos and also look at their official press photos, which show a seven-

person line-up. According to Bandcamp, it is Nickolay Inshakoff (composer, sound producer, violin, keyboards and synthesizers), Ilia Yartsev (clarinet, synthesizers), Veronika Chagrina (guitars), Dmitry Sokolov (bass), Anna Kuryachaya (drums), Ekaterina Bakanova (vocals), Elizaveta Yartseva (violins, violas), Aleksey Zlenko (cello), Ivan Shcherbakov (didgeridoo) and Ivan Kalugin (vocals) (I know that's more than seven, but what can I say?). Yes, there is quite a mix of things going on in there. There is also a statement from the band that reads "We hope that everyone will find himself and his story in it, notice allusions and reminders inside the track and the album. Do not look for religious or political overtones - they are not there. Listen with your heart. Immerse yourself in the soundtrack to your dreams and thoughts. Take a walk with us on your own mind".

In many ways I find myself being reminded of Roz Vitalis and given how highly I think of them that certainly isn't a bad thing, as they bring the kitchen sink into their style of eclectic progressive rock. Another band that springs to mind is iamthemorning, yet another Russian act that are refusing to conform to any pre-conceived ideas. Whalephant have long instrumental passages, but also have some beautiful accent free female vocals, and musically the band melds and flows so that the instruments and even the number of those playing them can vary immensely from song to song. This is very much an album for the listener to lose themselves inside and is one which is all the better for being concentrated on by using headphones. Yet another wonderful debut album, from a band that need discovering and heard by a much wider audience. Why not stream the album yourself and give them a try?
May 2017

WHEN MARY
7SUMMERS7WINTERS
When Mary came into being after Trude Eidtang (vocals, synthesizer, percussion) left White Willow and joined forces with Christian Paulsen (guitars, programming, synthesizer), wanting to create music inspired by Kate Bush, Björk and Peter Gabriel. I didn't read the press release until after I had been listening to the album, and already had those three artists in mind to put into the review so wasn't surprised when I read it in black and white. Although this was released in 2013, I have only just come across it, which is a shame as there is a great deal here to enjoy. Musically it is mostly electronic, with small amounts of guitar, and all the focus being on the vocals. There is a great deal of reverb within the album, the result being something that is incredibly atmospheric, and Trude's vocals just bring the listener into a wonderful world. The more I played this the more I liked it (apart from the bloody drum machine – I hate those so much!), but the song that took me totally by surprise was John Denver's "Annie's Song". The original must be known by just about anyone my age, as it was all over the place in the Seventies, but here it has been slowed down and stripped back and taken to a totally different place. This album is only 33 minutes long but is well worth investigating.
Feb 2018

WHEN MARY
TAINTED
It took four years for Trude and Christian to come back with their second album, and again most of the album is just the two of them, although they have used some additional musicians and singers on a couple of the songs. The album is inspired by the classic tale of Faust, the man who drives himself to damnation in his search for true enlightenment. It is shaped like a German Song Cycle and draws inspiration from the Franz Schubert song "Gretchen am Spinnrade", in which he portrays the mental and emotional turmoil of one of the characters. It is both more electronic and heavier than the debut album, with a darkness in place of the lightness.

Trude is also often singing in a more standard rock style, with "Soothing Stitches" being a case in point. This is almost commercial and would find a happy place on the radio (apart from the drum machine, which has still yet to be taken out and shot). There is a gothic element, as the guys bring together classical, art pop and trip hop among others. In many ways this is an easier album to listen to than the debut, one that is much easier to get inside, and possibly that is why I didn't enjoy this quite as much as the debut. I would much rather they had followed their own path instead of conforming to be more like others.
Feb 2018

WHITEWATER
UNIVERSAL MEDIUM
Whitewater was formed in 2013 by Stuart Stephens and Paul Powell. Stuart is singer, guitarist, and keyboard player, while Paul handles a complex range of percussion as well as drum programming. Stuart has been an avid progressive rock fan for as long as he can remember, and states he formed Whitewater to combine the sounds of classic prog bands like Pink Floyd and Supertramp with a more contemporary ambient aesthetic more akin to Orbital or The Future Sound of London. They aim to combine traditional prog influences and the ambient sensibilities of more modern acts, a spirit of experimentation with a distinctive signature musical landscape. This is their third album, where they collaborate with fellow BEM alumnus Mike Kershaw who co-wrote and sang on two songs.

Overall the album is more relaxed and quieter than what I would normally listen to, but there is a definite feeling of direction, and with far more substance than just some ambient meanderings. There were times when I found myself thinking more of Tangerine Dream than a modern outfit, but with keyboard sounds that far more up to date, often with a tripping sensibility that can be best described as being a very laid-back Ozric Tentacles. The production is very strong indeed, and there is a real sense of space and silence being used as an additional instrument. There are so many gaps between the layers of the arrangements that one could almost walk straight through the cords binding it all together without touching a thread.

It feels quite simplistic and repetitive at times, but that is just part of the overall plan to drag the listener in, with stark electronic keyboards against a very warm bass. In many ways, this is the perfect end to a long day with a glass of your favourite spirit close to hand.
Jan 2017

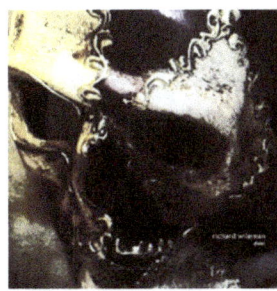

RICHARD WILEMAN
GHOST
And so, Richard is commencing on a new musical journey. I think I first came across his music about 25 years ago, when he was the driving force behind Lives & Times. In turn that became Karda Estra, and now here he is releasing an EP under his own name for the very first time. No room for the haunting vocals of Ileesha, but instead we have Richard providing vocals himself on the title cut. This is the furthest removed from KE of all the songs, as it really is a song, as opposed to an almost orchestral soundscape. But, even on the others, especially "Chaos Theme For Clarinet" we can hear Richard is taking a different approach, as although he has worked with Amy Fry in the past, here she has provided a far jazzier style to her clarinet than she has in the past.

Just four songs, with a total playing length of twelve minutes, it will be interesting to see what else he releases in this style, as it is an interesting progression from where he has been in the past, although with his use of acoustic guitar and arrangements it is still something that will appeal to fans of his other works.
Nov 2017

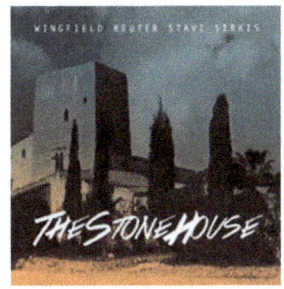

WINGFIELD REUTER STAVI SIRKUS
THE STONE HOUSE
This is one of those real rarities in modern music, an album that was recorded live in the studio with no overdubs and completely improvised, with no rehearsals or agreement beforehand as to where the direction was going to take them. Mark Wingfield (Jane Chapman; solo artist, and one half of the long-running guitar duo, with acoustic maestro, Kevin Kastning) on guitar, and Germany's Markus Reuter (Stick Men; The Crimson ProjeKct; Centrozoon) on touch guitar, they take the limits of their instruments and then just keep going. There are times when it is hard to realise that the sounds are coming from guitars as they are taken into brand new areas of tonal adventures.

On this journey they are accompanied by bassist Yaron Stavi (David Gilmour, Phil Manzanera, Robert Wyatt, Richard Galliano) and drummer Asaf Sirkis (Tim Garland, Mark Wingfield, Nicolas Meier), and of all four musicians it was to Asaf that I found my

concentration drawn most frequently. His deft touch on cymbals, and his use of different drums and approaches, often turned the soundscapes of Mark and Markus into the background for him to play against. Yaron keeps the overall sound warm and comforting, removing the sterility that is coming from the guitars. Fully impovised music is rarely as compelling or interesting as this, as the quartet don't feel the need to be flashy all the time but often just play and hold notes so that the tune can easily reach a logical conclusion. It is more New Age than jazz, more Brian Eno than John McLaughlin, although there are some feelings of fusion in what they do. This is yet another incredibly important release from Moonjune and Leo, and I look forward to their next endeavours with great interest.
Mar 2017

WINGFIELD REUTER SIRKIS
LIGHTHOUSE
Recorded during the same sessions that resulted in the release of the highly critically acclaimed 'Stone House', 'Lighthouse' again finds guitarist Mark Wingfield working with Markus Reuter (touch guitars) and Asaf Sirkis on drums. However, this time they worked as a trio, with no room for bassist Yaron Stavi who appeared on the first album. Recorded in a single day, what we have here are three musicians, all at the very top of their game, who are challenging the preconceived ideas of music, and bouncing off each other in what must have been an incredibly frenetic and inspiring environment.

Markus most often plays the role of lynch pin, holding the music into some semblance of constraint, while Mark rolls into multiple musical tangents as his fingers and mind wanders, finding their way through the maze of their mind, and then there is Asaf. The man is a multi-jointed octopus, who hands and legs obviously do not belong to the same body, and I was intrigued to discover just how many times my attention was being drawn from what many would think was the lead instrument and was instead marvelling at the complexity and many different styles he was bringing to the party.

This is jazz, it is fusion, it is progressive in its very truest sense, and is totally off the wall. This won't be for everyone, but to my mind and ears there is something incredibly special about this album, where the three of them are improvising both against and with each other, taking their instruments to the limit of musicality. A stunning release.
Feb 2018

WINTER
ACROSS THE CIRCLE'S EDGE
In 1987, Winter came together as a band in Newtownards, Co. Down, with Johnny Lennie (vocals & lyrics), Rab Beggs (electric/acoustic guitars), Phil Murray (keyboards/additional vocals), Rick Loyer (bass guitar) and John Murphy (drums/percussion). They released this EP on vinyl on their own label in 1990, but what may not be known by

many is that it was always just intended to be a demo (because of that there are occasional little timing issues or blips in one or two places) and the idea was that by using this they would be able to secure a recording deal and then record a complete album. During 1991, having not secured a recording deal, the band decided to attempt a tour of Holland rather than record new material. Murray and Murphy felt the band should concentrate on writing and recording more songs as the best means of securing a deal, so they decided to leave. Rab Beggs did tour with Winter in Holland but left after a few gigs and later formed rock groups Mr. Jinx and Native Sun with Phil Murray.

Loyer and Lennie formed a new version of the band in London and the EP was remastered and released on CD by SI Music, and to this day is still something I play regularly. Then, one day when I was perusing the web, I discovered Phil Murray had added keyboard parts that were missing from the original recording and was making the EP available again. Of course, I was soon in touch, and I am now listening to the 'new' version. I must confess and say it is almost impossible for me to write anything constructive about this. I saw the later line-up in concert three times, and right from the first I was blown away by the sheer onstage presence of Johnny combined with some of the most wonderful and powerful neo-prog I ever had the pleasure to witness. "Toybox" is one of the greatest prog epics never to have been heard by many, and I wish for the day when someone discovers this lost gem and restores it to its rightful place as one of the top in the prog canon. I know this so very well indeed, that initially I found Phil's keyboards quite jarring as they weren't what I was used to, but the more I played this the more I fell in love with what he had done to the music. Bear in mind he hasn't added anything, but rather has replaced something that was missing from something that was never expected to be the finished article.

Many of the 'lost' bands of the Nineties have had their music reissued on CD, and I can only hope that the same fate befalls Winter as to my mind they were a band that had incredible potential and really should have been known by many more progheads. Maybe Phil would consider getting this pressed alongside the tracks that appeared on singles and tapes (it was the Nineties after all), or maybe adding some live recordings? Sheer quality from start to finish.
Jun 2014

WINTERSUN
THE FOREST SEASONS
Founded back in 2004 by front man Jari Mäenpää, Finnish epic metallers Wintersun released their highly acclaimed debut album the same year. The band took the listener to a Nordic land filled with both, soaring and frosty guitar lines and relentless drums played by Kai Hahto. Eight years later, their second 'Time I' was also greeted with high praise, and they were soon touring with Korpiklaani, Eluveitie, and Fleshgod Apocalypse amongst others.

It hasn't taken them quite so long to come back with the third album, only five years this time, and here they invite the listener to embark on a musical journey through a mystical forest with just four songs, but a total running time of 54 minutes.

The first track of this new sonic adventure, "Awaken From The Dark Slumber (Spring)", begins with a mysterious, dreamy melody, accompanied by subdued forest animal sounds. With driving guitars and pounding drums, the song snakes through an unstoppable 15-minute course. Massive choirs, beautiful and furious Asian-influenced guitar and orchestral sounds come together in this monumental opening track and let the listener experience the awakening of the forest. Second up is "The Forest That Weeps (Summer)", which also starts with a calm and gloomy acoustic intro until you get woken up by haunting low guitars, continuing the previous lead melody. Even more tiny sonic details rise up all around and lead through the harsh verses to the track's majestic clean vocal choruses, followed by a heavily grooving and increasing instrumental interlude. In the end, after reaching its pinnacle in the form of the final chorus including an even more massive choir, "The Forest That Weeps (Summer)" abruptly returns to its original theme and fades away slowly...

Silence is reigning... A foreboding wind is drawing near... "Eternal Darkness (Autumn)", the third track, catches you by surprise and keeps what its title promises with its black metallic elements - devastating blast beats and harsh vocals await! The threatening orchestral sounds evoke the depressive and sad atmosphere that captures the listener and then leaves you behind with a soundscape filled with melancholic melodies until the song comes to a relentless and ominous end, recapturing its brutal beginning. Traditional folkish tunes lead into the most emotional, saddest, and concluding part of the album, "Loneliness (Winter)".

Complex, magical, full of beauty and hidden depths, this is a journey that in many ways is epic yet at others passes by incredibly quickly. This is a superb piece of work, one that is going to make many people sit up and take notice. Indeed, when compared to recent albums by both Korpiklaani and Eluveitie, both bands who are more well-known than Wintersun, I know which one I would much rather listen to. This is epic, nothing less.
Sep 2017

WOBBLER
FROM SILENCE TO SOMEWHERE
Mellotrons, how do I love thee, let me count the ways, one, one thousand, two, one thousand, three, one thousand. I can't help it; the first time I played this I got an image of Roger Rabbit in my mind, and it won't get out! But, instead of a fluffy white rabbit in a film where Bob Hoskins was cruelly denied an Oscar, what we have here is the Norwegian quintet back with their fourth studio album. To say this album is making waves in the prog scene is something of an understatement: as I write this, after 138 ratings this is the top ranked album from 2017 according to ProgArchives, and by a country mile the top ranked Norwegian progressive album of all time. So, critically it's not doing too

bad at all!

The one thing I can't really make my mind up on with this is whether I should say in the review if the album belongs from 1971 or 1972: part of me is having an argument with the rest to say that it could be as late as 1973 but I'm ignoring that at present. This is classic retro prog as they say, in that not only has it take the influences of bands such as Genesis, ELP and Yes but have decided that there is no need at all to move any further and can stay quite happily there and expand on the themes, musical motifs and styles. At this point, progressive rock truly becomes a genre and style, as opposed to music that is challenging boundaries and creating something which is different and exciting. This is where I have another discussion with myself in that part of me gets annoyed that a band is attempting to move music back forty-five years, but the rest of me says "who cares when it is this damn good?!". Maybe I should start taking tablets… Anyway, there is no denying that this is an amazing album in many ways. If you are the type of discerning proghead who bemoans the demise of flares and sitting cross-legged at gigs while partaking of various illegal and legal substances, then this is for you. To be honest, this is something that progheads simply can't ignore as pretty much all will love it to one degree or another, as it really is quite special. Did I mention the Mellotrons?
Jan 2017

WOLFSPRING
WOLFSPRING
Having previously reviewed the second album from the side project of Nemo singer/guitarist JP Louveton, here we go back to 2010 and the debut where JP provided guitar, bass and vocals and was joined by Julian Clemens (vocals), Guillaum Fontaine (keys) and Ludo Moro-Sibilot (drums), all of who also played on the follow-up, 2013's 'Who's Gonna Save The World?' As with their later album, here is a progressive band that are at times very metallic, more so than the prog metal tag would normally suggest. But there are also times when they have a very Porcupine Tree feel to the music, and this combined with strong musicianship and some great songs makes this an album I fell in love with this the very first time I played it and the more I listened the more I got from it.

JP is always going to be associated with the mighty Nemo, and rightfully so, but this band feels much more than just a side-project, and when he riffs out on "Carpathian Wolves" I can feel the fun he is having by being able to play plenty of power chords and just blasting it out. This song in particular has a real Seventies groove, and I just want to keep turning it up. In fact, it's hard to type when I'm bouncing around as much as I do when listening to this, like the rest of the album it makes me smile, and isn't that what music is about? Enjoyment?

Having been playing this so much recently I am going to have to rediscover the latest album, then drop JP a line and ask when the next one is coming out! Superb.
May 2014

THE WOOD DEMONS
THE LOST DOMAIN

This is the debut five-track mini-album from London-based band The Wood Demons, and very pleasant it is too. They have tagged the music as rock, acid-folk, prog, prog rock, psychedelia, psychedelic, psychedelic folk, space rock, space-rock and symphonic prog, so as one can see, there is a lot going on here. Musically this is going back to the late Sixties, with influences from the likes of Pink Floyd, Jefferson Airplane, The Beatles and The Byrds before bringing in some Camel and Curved Air, while also having room for some neo-prog from the Nineties. The use of violin is a nice touch, and the harmony vocals are both a strength and a weakness.

Back before the days of digital releases, this is the type of album I would have expected to have been sent to me as a demo tape. Musically it is interesting, with some nice songs, but perhaps not always performed quite as well as it could be (although bassist John Silver has a very nice touch indeed, which makes a considerable positive difference), with vocals that do suffer from time to time. But I still have in my collection the very first demo from Big Big Train and look where they are now. It will be interesting to see what happens next with these guys, as this is at least pleasant, if not essential.
Feb 2018

WORLD TRADE
UNIFY

Lead vocalist and main songwriter, Billy Sherwood has been a fixture of the L.A. studio and recording scene since the mid-80's. Billy's talents range from producing a Grammy-nominated album for Paul Rodgers to being the current bass player of Yes, handpicked by Chris Squire to replace him before his untimely death. He also recently joined up with Asia as a replacement for John Wetton after his passing for their current US tour with Journey. Guy Allison (keyboards) and Bruce Gowdy (guitars), a pair of musicians also known for being behind the awesome melodic rock band Unruly Child, and drummer Mark T. Williams (son of famed composer John Williams and brother of Toto singer Joseph) round out the line-up.

This is band that is going to generate a great deal of column inches just because of who is involved in the recording, but part of me does wonder how much press this would receive if it was by some unknowns. That the harmony vocals and musicianship are of the first order is never in doubt, but I was left feeling this is far too one-dimensional for me. There is a feeling that there is something missing, almost as if the music has been performed with no passion or soul. Heavily influenced by '90125'-era Yes, sadly this isn't in the same league. I am sure that there will be many out there who disagree with me, but this is too clever for its own good and while I can appreciate all the skills that went into it, there are many other albums I would much rather play.
Oct 2017

ROBERT WYATT
'68

Just four songs, a fraction over 45 minutes long, comprise this release, which is a complete set of Robert Wyatt's solo recordings made in the US in late 1968. Until reappearing last year, the demo for "Rivmic Melodies" (all 18 minutes of it), an extended sequence of song fragments destined to form the first side of the second album by Soft Machine, was presumed lost forever while the shorter song on the same acetate, "Chelsa", wasn't even known to exist! Wyatt recorded these songs during some down time during and after Soft Machine's second American tour with the Jimi Hendrix Experience. He multi-tracked the recording, playing piano and organ as well as drumming and singing, and even some bass - although Hendrix himself provided the bass for "Slow Walkin' Talk".

There is something incredibly fragile about these recordings, with Wyatt alone in the studio setting the scene for what the Softs were going to be doing in forthcoming years. It is quite hard to judge this music on its' own merits, given its importance historically, but fortunately this is something that every Softs/Matching Mole/Wyatt (and even Hendrix) fan will want to have not because it was going to form the basis for so much musical experimentation, but because it is so damned good. There is a depth and quality to this music that belies the fact that these songs were recorded on acetate 45 years ago. They have been cleaned up incredibly well and I am sure they sound better now than when they were first heard all those years ago. Robert's piano work is strident, structured and fluid yet also staccato, while his drumming is an incredibly important part of the overall sound. His vocals are delicate, emotional, fraught and another sound to be utilized. To me "Rivmic Melodies" is a stunning piece of work, with the repeated high notes taking the song into another area altogether.

This has been made available on CD with a 16-page booklet, and as seems fitting it is also available on limited edition vinyl (with the same information on an insert). Released with Robert's approval and full co-operation, this is essential stuff.
Jan 2014

XBRAY
RUPTURE

Thierry Sportouche of Acid Dragon recently sent me this CD, and I then discovered just how hard it can be to find out any information about an album when Google believes that I was searching for "X-ray" and "Rapture". But I refused to give up, and on searching the CD cover guessed that 'Xbray' was the artist name for Thierry Exbrayat, who I then managed to stalk on Facebook. He was a bit surprised to be contacted by someone from New Zealand asking about a French language, small release, CD from 2012 but kindly provided me with some background.

Thierry is a guitarist and vocalist who has been in many bands, probably the most well-known of which was the trio Ph7, who released 'Commissaire Magret' in 2011. After 20 years of concerts and fun together, bassist Manu Defaÿ had to leave France for work, and the band decided to take a break. It was only when this happened that Thierry wondered if he could write material on his own without his companions. So, he started working without having any idea of whether it would ever be released, but just knew it was something he needed to do. One day he was talking to Jean Pierre Louveton of Nemo (Thierry and Jean Pierre live in the same region and have been friends for a long time) about what he had been doing, and after hearing a few songs, Jean Pierre invited Thierry to record, mix and release an album. Thierry asked Jean Pierre to help him with vocal melodies, and additional guitars, while Manu returned to provide bass while other friends assisted to complete the sessions. After the album was released, they were asked to play some gigs, which they undertook with JPL again assisting, but the band was never expected to be a full-time project and soon folded. These days Thierry is again making music with Jamel of Ph7, with two new musicians in Bêta Bloqués. He no longer provides vocals, just guitar, and loves it!

So, there's the story behind the album, but what about the album itself? Released as a digipak, with a small booklet containing all the lyrics, it does feel as if it is a project as opposed to a band, but there are some fine moments on here. "Disjointed" is the only song with English lyrics, but what makes this stand out are not the words per se, but the dynamics of the song which is a powerful neo prog number with some great guitar interplay. "Enciélé" is a very different number, both in phrasing and approach, slow and delicate, and somehow very French. What I really like about this album are the number of different styles from pop rock through to neo prog, but first and foremost these are songs, and good ones at that. No room for egos, it's all about what is right for the moment.

The album is still available from the record label, and it's a pretty safe bet that none of your friends will own a copy, so why not stand out from the crowd? Thierry later returned the favour of JP, and appeared on a couple of his solo albums, all of which are also available from the label.
Jun 2017

X-PANDA
REFLECTIONS
Formed in 2009 in Tartu, Estonia, this 2016 album follows on from their 2011 debut 'Flight of Fancy', which made such an impact that it was nominated for album of the year in the metal category of the Estonian Music Awards. Musically this is progressive metal, but they're not just another Dream Theater clone, bringing in elements of Porcupine Tree, Muse and others into something that is a strange yet enjoyable mix of many different styles. They are not content to stay firmly within the boundaries of what many feel is progressive metal, but instead move and flow, bringing in different styles. They have even used a full orchestra (the Tartu University Symphony Orchestra and a choir (E STuudio Youth Choir), I mean, what on earth is going on?

There have been a few bands who attempted to bring together a rock band and "real" orchestra with mixed results, but here the guys have worked with arrangers who are totally in tune with what they are trying to achieve, and the result is seamless, so the band and orchestra are one, not two different entities being forced together in unholy matrimony. Tamar Nugis has a vocal style which sounds as if it belongs on a stage as opposed to in a band, but the music works perfectly with him as frontman. There are some great passages within the songs, such as the fretless bass solo during "Denial" which takes us into the fluid guitar solo, it is so different to what has gone before and what has yet to come that it is refreshing to the ear.

Overall, this is quite some album, and if the band were operating in the UK or the States, I am convinced we would be hearing a great deal more about them. As it is, this is a stunning album and I look forward to the next one with great interest.
Dec 2017

RYAN YARD
THE NATURE OF SOLITUDE
This is the latest album from Ryan Yard, who is a member of Robert Reed's Sanctuary live band, so perhaps it is to be expected that like Robert's solo material this is heavily influenced by Mike Oldfield. Containing just two long tracks (plus an edit that has been mixed by Rob Reed), the album was recorded using just an iPad and a variety of apps (and a keyboard, of course), with Justin Towell guesting on guitar. Keeping with the Oldfield relationship, it was mastered by none other than Tom Newman, which undoubtedly has also assisted in capturing an Oldfield sound to proceedings.

Ryan was determined to create an organic album in a digital age, so every note was played by hand, often without a click track. He also embraced the mistakes, timing issues and noises that would normally be erased from history, to show this is real music, even if it wasn't created in how many would view the traditional sense. The result is an album which flows and is far more direct than albums which would normally be considered ambient or New Age, while also having feet firmly in those camps, more so than the progressive. It is music to relax to, creating a feeling of being at one with the world, and letting the stresses of the day just slip away. Highly recommended for those who enjoy this style of music, I certainly did.
Feb 2018

YETI RAIN
STARS FALL DARKLY
Back in the Nineties I was lucky enough to hear some albums by the American progressive band Kopecky and was always incredibly impressed by their musicianship. They were somewhat unusual in that they were a trio of brothers, with William on bass, keys and sitar, Joe on guitar and Paul on drums. I hadn't heard anything from them since

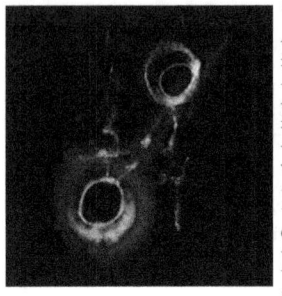'Blood' in 2006, but now I know William has been busy on other projects, and this is the fourth album from Yeti Rain. Like Kopecky this is a trio, and William is playing bass, but at that point all similarities end. Originally a duo with William and Roger Ebner (saxophones, synthesizer, flute), they became a trio with the addition of Craig Walkner on percussion in time for the last album, 'III' which came out in 2010. Having not heard any of the others I can't say if 'Stars Fall Darkly' is of similar ilk, but I do know I can say with some confidence that this is a Marmite album. You are either going to love it or hate it, there is not going to be any middle ground.

This is a progressive album in its' truest sense, throwing loads of things into the melting pot and seeing what comes out at the other end. That being said, there is also a great deal in common with avant-garde jazz and black metal, and it is only those who can say they have truly catholic tastes in music who will be interested in this, but for those who are, you are in for a real treat. William is a wonderful bassist, here playing mostly a fretless with wonderful depth and warmth, but while he uses the harmonics that can provide, he also has it set so he doesn't play notes as much as move tectonic plates around with his fingers. That Craig manages to make sense of this by providing a strong percussive backbone just shows how much understanding there is between the two musicians, as they move together and allow each other to fully express themselves. Then we have Roger, who is obviously schooled in free form jazz as he goes off on tangents and uses the melodies provided by William and the rhythms provided by Craig to create something that is often off worldly and more than just musical notes.

There is an incredible depth of emotion and passion with this music, and it is something which is all encompassing that takes the listener to a different place where nothing else exists except the music. I felt I was being taken down into a deep dark cave with the music resonating all around me, no light and no direction apart from the all-encompassing sound. There are times when one or other of the musicians doesn't play, which again drives the feeling into a new dimension, and this is a piece of art where the listener gets more from it each time it is played.

Music that has improvisation at its' very core will only ever be accessible to a select few, but if you are one of these then this is something you need to investigate further as it is rare indeed that music containing this much presence and power is released. If one imagines that most pop music is plastic and disposable, then this instead is like a piece of rich deep swamp kauri (if you're not a kiwi you'll need to look up this analogy), aged and powerful with hidden depths. A truly wonderful album.
Jun 2014

ZERO TIMES EVERYTHING
SONIC CINEMA
My initial reaction when first playing this was that it reminded me somewhat of 'My Life In the Bush of Ghosts' in terms of style, and I was therefore pleased to see the band

reference that seminal work as a major influence on what they are trying to achieve. The band is a trio of Richard Sylvarnes (Kaoss Pads, loops, synths, rhythms, guitars, vocals), Pietro Russino (guitars, loops, violin) and Tony Geballe (guitars, synths, loops), and they initially met at Robert Fripp's Guitar Craft Seminars at Claymont Court, and from there a group to provide live music for Richard Sylvarnes' film "The Last Words of Dutch Schultz". The band themselves describe the music as "Avant-garde post-industrial pre-cambrian pan-ethnic serial noise proto-punk neocortex music. It lives at the intersection of "My Life in the Bush of Ghosts" and Autechre, mixing glitchcore, ambient, and progressive rock." So, there you have it. Add into the mix plenty of King Crimson influences, passages of spoken texts; either through a disembodied heroine's chant from a 1930's gangster film or robot voices reciting Marxist texts, then one can understand why the album has been titled as it has.

There is a darkness to this, as if one is living in a surreal Mickey Spillane movie at night, and of course it is raining, and one feels under threat. There is an aura of danger, as this music creates a soundscape that is incredibly visual in its approach. There is a lot to take in, and is best played when there is nothing else happening, as it needs firm concentration to get the best from it. But there is one number on the album I did find quite jarring, "Schizoid", where a young girl speaks the lyrics to "21st Century Schizoid Man" against a totally different musical backing. I believe I understand what they are trying to achieve, as this is piece is incredibly fraught and passionate, but I and many others know these lyrics so well that it just doesn't have the impact it should, and for me is a distraction. Overall, this is yet another intriguing album from 7D Media that is worth investigation.
Apr 2017

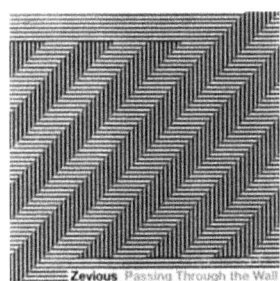

ZEVIOUS
PASSING THROUGH THE WALL
The trio of guitarist Mike Eber, drummer Jeff Eber, and bassist Johnny DeBlase started in 2006 as a 'normal' jazz group before commencing their own very different fusion journey. They brought in loads of influences from other musical styles such as progressive (King Crimson being an obvious band they have been paying attention to) and technical metal as well as moving more into improvisational to create something that is fusion in its very truest sense, and also truly progressive. There are also weird time signatures, and drum rhythms and patterns that point towards Meshuggah as another influence: showing yet again that although these guys are jazz, they are very much pushing the boundaries of both it and progressive rock.

This is their third album, and I am going to have to dig out the other two as well, as these guys can play: I mean, they can really play. I don't think they would know what to do with a straight 4/4-time signature and verse/chorus number if it hit them over the head with a baseball bat. Although Mike is often the lead 'voice' that is only to be expected, but his cousin Jeff isn't afraid to try to dominate proceedings, and the same goes for Johnny as well. But, somehow all three of them manage to keep their own creative reins in check just enough so we get an incredibly complex montage of music as opposed to everyone powering in over the top.

There are some amazing fusion albums coming out at present, but this is one of those vying to be at the very top of the heap. It is challenging at times, but incredibly welcoming at others, and if you want your music to be complicated and moving in different directions yet somehow always making sense then this is for you.
Jan 2014

Interviews

Robert Berry, Jul 2018

The working relationship between legendary keyboard player Keith Emerson and singer and multi-instrumentalist Robert Berry started in 1987. The plan was to form a more melodic, song-oriented band (compared to ELP), which would allow Emerson, Berry and Palmer to follow in the footsteps of the success that Asia and GTR were enjoying in that period. The result of the collaboration was 3, and the album '... To The Power of Three', which was released in 1988. The first single, "Talkin' 'Bout" reached #9 on the Billboard Magazine charts and the band toured the US to support the album.

Fast forward many years, and Robert began speaking to Keith about finally releasing a follow-up, and there was an exchange of musical ideas and song collaborations. After Keith passed away, Robert was left with Keith Emerson's final musical ideas, and from old cassette tapes, keyboard parts written over the phone, to long discussions about style, the framework of the album was set and ready to be produced. After several months of grieving and contemplation about what to do with these co-written songs and musical fragments from Emerson, Robert decided to resume work on the material that was created and craft a record that would ultimately be a fitting tribute to Keith Emerson's musical legacy and at the same time re-energize and update the musical style started with '3' some 30 years ago. The result is the forthcoming release by 3.2, 'The Rules Have Changed', due out mid-August.

I purchased the original album as soon as it was released, 30 years ago, and have always enjoyed it. After the demise of the band, I came across Robert's work here and there, and when I heard there was a new album coming out, I jumped at the opportunity of catching up with him for a chat.

Who or what first got you interested in music and what were your inspirations?
My first recollection of being fascinated by music was when I was quite young. My dad had a big band, and my mom was the singer. They played music like Frank Sinatra or Benny Goodman and there was lots of sax and trumpet around the house. Somewhere in an old 1/4 tape there is a recording of my dad saying, "get that kid out of here". He had made the mistake of giving his 4-year-old son the drummer's old snare drum. Just a side note, I still have that drum and used it on many of my early recordings before 1985. With their band always rehearsing in the living room I got the music bug fairly easy. The song on the new album "Powerful Man" is about that kind of influence. I'll talk about that a little later,

I had eight years of classical piano lessons and two years of jazz piano lessons. I didn't like to practice my piano so my dad asked the teacher if she would teach me some boogie woogie songs. Well, she was not too happy about that, but my dad owned the piano store where she taught, so she had no choice I suppose. The boogie woogie could go on for hours, but practicing the classical stuff rarely came through unless my mom stayed on me. And she did. Since my parents had the piano store and my teacher was their prize teacher, I had to be her prize student. I was entered into countless music teacher recitals where they show off their best student to all the other music teachers. I don't believe I was her best student though. The problem was that you couldn't play the boogie woogie pieces at these things, strictly very difficult music from the classical composers: I knew them all. I look at that music now and can't believe that I played it at such a young age. I wish these days I could just sit down and whip out a Beethoven or Bach piece. Again, this is for later but with the new album I had to get my piano playing back up to that standard.

When I was 12, two guys that were seniors in high school (17, 18 years old) came into my dad's music store. They had heard I could play and thought they'd get free music equipment if they had this little kid with the dad that had the well-known music store son in their band. I joined up, they didn't get free equipment, but I got a head start playing some classic older rock and roll that gave me a great foundation for what was to come.

How did Hush come about?
I had been in a few bands during high school. Some decent bands with some very good players for young guys. But nobody had started as young as me and I seem to be a little ahead of the curve. I was majoring in music in college and playing in a nightclub at night with a fake ID so that I could buy a new BMW: it had been on the top of my list for a few years. The drummer in that band, Mike Dimock, also had a dad that owned a music store. In fact, I taught piano there and sold Fender guitars and amps for him while I was in high school. I knew their family well and Mike and I had really hit it off. After a year or so of playing the night clubs, a local booking agent called me and said he had an idea, he wanted to put myself and Mike with two other guys and put together sort of a local super group. It sounded like a cool idea, so we met, liked each other, and started to rehearse for the next two weeks before a big showcase for booking that was coming up. We had ten minutes to fill. The idea was to segue six or seven songs together, playing a verse and chorus of each, so that we could showcase more of what we would be playing for the listeners. No band had done this before, and at that showcase we got all the gigs.

The buyers were local high school and college bookers, and they loved what we had brought to the show. By the way, I had got my dad to contact a big importer of English musical equipment to the US and find out how I could get a Mellotron. Yes, it was the first time a local audience was exposed to real violins, choirs, and flutes. We were a force to be reckoned with, LOL. The only bad thing was that the newly named Hush had only learned a verse and a chorus of six or seven songs, we didn't have time to learn the whole song for this showcase. So now we had 20 or 30 gigs starting in about a month and we needed to have two hours of music ready to go. It was a great way to start a new band. Years later my band 3 kind of started in the same way, we had two songs to present to record companies and that was it. We got signed immediately by Geffen and had a short lead time to get them a full album.

How did you first meet Keith Emerson?
I had met Carl Palmer about a year earlier, it had been recommended he listened to my cassette tape by John Kalodner at Geffen Records, Asia's label. We tried for six months to start a band with a few different people, but nothing seemed to click. My manager, Brian Lane, called me one day and said that he wanted me to meet Steve Howe. Steve Hackett had left GTR, and they needed a songwriter and guitar/keyboard player. I thought it sounded really interesting, so I met Steve at his home. We hit it off really well with the song writing and as friends. He is quite a talented guy if you didn't know. LOL Oh, I thought you probably did. I spent the better half of the year writing and rehearsing with GTR but had difficulty with their singer. I told Brian that I was willing to give up my solo career and my possible new band where I'd be singing with Carl Palmer, for GTR if I could at least sing one song on each album. I thought that was the deal, but the singer was having nothing to do with that. In fact, even when I sang harmony or background parts of some type he would come out and double me live right there on my mic.

I decided this wasn't a good fit for me, so I left GTR and had planned on heading home from London. Brian Lane called me the day before I was to leave and said that Keith Emerson would like to have lunch. I was a little shocked, I had just backed out of my first big break and was a little unhappy about my decision. I accepted the invite of course but was quite nervous about meeting him. I had spent time with several big names before but this guy, the king of the keyboards, the Jimi Hendrix of the keyboard players? We met for lunch and right away he made me very comfortable. Such an easy going, fun, warm personality. I thought I was meeting some mad scientist or some computer programmer type that didn't speak the kind of English us common folk speak. But he was the exact opposite. We hit it right off and spoke of plans to possibly start a new band. At the end of what was about a two-hour lunch he said he only had one thing he wanted to ask me. I thought uh oh, what could it be? Maybe he wanted to own all the songs? He wanted to be the singer? LOL funny if you ever heard him sing - but no he simply said, "would you mind playing a few ELP songs if we go on tour?" I told him I'd be honoured and said I would never expect him to leave behind such a legacy. I saw another part of his personality right there, he looked at me with those caring eyes of his and said "really?" I didn't get it then, but years later as we spent time writing, recording, and touring I realized that Greg had made things very difficult when it came to control. I on the other hand am a team player and want the team to all benefit equally. He was pleased as we parted that day. Then came the first trip out to his house in Sussex with Carl driving. To say I was excited, well I don't think I have to explain to any of your readers how I felt. It's hard to put into words anyway.

ELP broke up in 1979, reforming as Emerson Lake & Powell in 1985 and releasing that album in 1986, but two years later it was 3 who were together and releasing an album. How did that all happen?

3 got together in the middle of 1987, we wrote and recorded a few demos. After sending them to Geffen we went in and did a video to the song "8 Miles High" we had been working on. Brian had hired a video crew for a thousand pounds to spend two hours with us. His only instructions were to make the video look like the movie 'Close Encounters'. Not sure what he really meant, but the crew took it to mean lots of lights blurring out the camera when they were shooting past us. It was genius to me. That video looked so energetic and had the feel of what we would become on stage, a much less formatted band than ELP was. We had our parts that were written in stone, but there was room to jam and expand in a different way every night. That came across in "8 Miles High" before we had ever stepped on a stage together.

There was a lot of damage left behind by Emerson, Lake & Powell financially: they played arenas and rarely sold out, so they lost money. As much as I loved the album and loved Cozy's playing, it just wasn't the draw without Carl. 3 decided to start as a new band would start, bring this new album to the fans in small venues and we played something like 1000 to 5000 seaters. Sold out, fans seeing Emerson, Palmer, and the new guy 'Yank' up close and personal. Never before or never again would that be possible, it was truly a great experience. We also made a profit and didn't create any loss for anybody involved in our tour and business. Keith owed so much money from the Emerson, Lake & Powell disaster that he thought he didn't make any money with 3, but that was so untrue. 3 paid off his debt so he was free of their past. Just to show you how well we actually did, I built a house in a very nice area of Silicon Valley and paid cash. Not that the band was about money, it wasn't. We were about starting their career in a new way and mine in a first launch.

We had hoped for longevity and of course a hit record. We got the hit record with "Talkin' Bout", #9 on the Billboard charts which brought us new fans. By the time it rose to the Top 10 we were seeing younger people coming to the shows: the Ritz in New York had quite a few young girls in the audience. They wanted to hear that new band that they had heard on the radio, but then there were the die-hard ELP fans who wanted to hear ELP material. They wanted nothing to do with this new guy that wasn't Greg Lake. This began to take its toll on Keith, and he would get quite a few fans telling him that they hated that he was playing on more pop rock songs, and they hated the female background singers. In fact, one guy wrote him a letter that it was embarrassing for Keith to be doing that. He left his phone number on the letter and Keith called him; he was sensitive that way. All this criticism led to 3 breaking up after just a year and a half of working together. Right when we knew who, what, and how we should do a follow album up Keith was done with it. I would find that in later years that fan criticism really held a spell over him,

Were you simply asked to step aside so Lake could return?

I explained a little bit about that in the previous answer but let me just say this - Keith and Carl had always told me to be myself. Do not do what you think the fans want or what Greg would have done, just be you. There is nothing more empowering than two of the greatest musicians in our lifetime wanting me to be me. They had also had their fair share of problems with Greg. Don't get me wrong, I only met Greg once and we got along great. I am a fan of his voice, his playing, and that special thing that made him great enough to take John Wetton's place for one show in Japan: the job he did with that was amazing. But as far as ELP was concerned, he wanted the power and made most of the money. He wrote the hit songs, and the writer gets the publishing dollars and therefore lots of times seems to have a bigger say so. I think Keith especially felt slighted by that. After all, who in the band was the only one of a kind? From 3 on, the ELP reunions were about money. Of course, now remember that this is my point of view, but I did remain friends with Keith and Carl, and you can read between the lines during certain conversations how they felt.

3 was very high profile, yet from there you appeared to take a step into the shadows as it were. Was that a conscious decision, and if so, why?
This is a very interesting point of view for me. It made me think about all the other musicians I love that seem to disappear for a while. What happens with me is a book of its own. I had many songs I had written with Steve Howe, I had many songs I had written with Keith and Carl, and I had songs during that period that I had written for other purposes. One day I was working in my studio with Andy Latimer from the band Camel and he asked me about all this material, and asked what I was going to do with it, to which I said "nothing". Those bands are gone for me. He told me he thought I should put it out, fans would love it, and it was just laying around anyway. I thought about it and decided to take his advice. I put out 'Pilgrimage to a Point' mail order from my studio and it sold like hotcakes, I couldn't believe it. Not high profile, but honest and rewarding. Then in the mid 1990's I got asked to play with Sammy Hagar as he was having problems with Van Halen and needed a bass player for his solo gigs. This was a great time in my life, Sam is a dynamo to say the least. It was the hardest rock as in Hard Rock that I had ever done. I found myself enjoying that edginess, so I wrote an album I called 'Takin' it Back'. To me it was time to take back my career and I wanted to move forward. I signed with a company in Germany that went bankrupt about three months after my album was out, strike out for me.

In 2004 another opportunity came up, I got asked to join the band, Ambrosia. I was thrilled, one of my favourite bands. The perfect blend of progressive and pop. I got to sing songs like "Life Beyond LA", progressive, and "Biggest Part of Me", beautifully crafted blue eyed soul pop. I spent two years trying to get them to do a new album. I had a studio, two of the other guys had studios, and I couldn't get them to budge. I had written a few songs that I thought were good for that band, and Joe Puerta the bass player had a few that were really good already, but I just couldn't get them to move on it. I learned something very important during my time with them. Their material was so demanding to sing, that when we toured, I would constantly gargle with Listerine so that I wouldn't get sick. For the first nine months I was doing great. But as time went on my voice got rougher and rougher. By the time I gave them notice that I was going to leave, I was struggling with some of the high notes vocally. What had happened, and what I didn't realize, was that the alcohol in the Listerine was stripping my vocal cords. Just like the way alcohol dries out a wound when you put it on your skin, it dried out my vocal cords. I didn't realize this until six months or so later when I was a little under the weather for a gig I was doing, so I drank lots of water. All of a sudden, I realized I was singing better than I had in years. The show I would do locally was a sort of greatest hits of my career, so I'd play "Talkin' Bout'" and I'd also play "Biggest Part of Me", both very demanding, and they were flying out of my mouth with ease. I did a little research and found out what I had done to myself by gargling the Listerine. So, we move up to around 2008 and I get a call from Greg Kihn, his bass player Steve Wight had a stroke and he needed someone to fill his shoes. From then on, I've been touring and writing songs with Greg. He's a very prolific guy and lots of fun to work with. The music is very simple, and it was a challenge to wrap my head around at first. But we put out an album last year that got very high marks from all the reviewers and Greg Kihn fans. So, to answer your question - LOL, I have been busy trying to stay in front of an audience but sometimes things don't go as planned. I have a song on the new album that Keith and I wrote called "What You're Dreaming Now". It's about moving forward. That my motto - 'today was a good day, now what can I accomplish tomorrow'. You can't let disappointments or failures stop you.

I have come across your some of your work with different musicians over the years.
I have been blessed with the gift of creativity. I am never at a loss for a lyric, a musical section, or for that matter a complete song. One of the great joys I have is working down at my studio Soundtek. Five days a week, when I'm not on the road, I work with mostly unknown singer/songwriters that are at my studio to record their most important work. That song that came out of them, that is unique to their life that will live on forever in their families. They don't have to be famous; they don't even have to have a completed thought or arrangement; I am there to do the parts that they don't have. Be it lyrics, chords, arrangements, or just playing the instruments to complete their vision. I do from 100 to 300 songs a year for clients like that. Sometimes I have bands like the Celtic rock band Tempest in the studio and I am mostly producing, I have done twelve albums for them over the years. I love every bit of my musical life. Nobody is too small or too big, it's all just music to me. Imagine if Keith and Carl would not have given me that same opportunity, you would not be talking to me now.

Why 3.2, and why now?
Why now is a loaded question, as for 28 years Keith had wanted to leave 3 behind. He would always say how much fun we had, but never really talk about the music, the criticism was hard on him. But then a record company wanted to put out the 3 'Live in Boston' performance. It was really just a pay check for Keith at the time, so he signed the deal. I was very excited that there was enough interest in 3, that 28 years later a new album would come out. Not really thinking about it again, Keith received the CD in the mail. He was home alone one evening, enjoying a glass of wine as he's been known to do, so he decided to put on the CD. He listened to the whole thing and immediately called me. His voice sounded so excited. He said "Robert, we were really a good band. No really a good band." I couldn't believe my ears. I had always thought that but never thought he'd give it another chance, and there it was. The open door to my 28-year dream. After we spoke about how much fun we had had and how the spark on stage with

the jamming was just the best time ever I broke the question. I said that a record company had been bugging me for years to do a follow up album, but I knew he wasn't interested. I said "What about now Keith? Any chance you'd consider working with me to do one more great album?" He gave it a mild "yes" and that was enough for me. I called the record company and asked if they were still interested, they were. I called Keith back; we discussed the ideal parameters for such an album and the record company agreed to every detail. Keith was amazed at their deal, the advance involved, and the interest being so high. He was ready to start so we did.

How much of the material was originally developed at the time of the first 3 album?
Only one of the songs came from the original 1986 or 87 cassette tape. There were also some linking sections for new songs and some solo chord sections I used from that cassette. The rest was written from new digital files Keith had sent me, and lengthy phone conversations where we both had our digital pianos going and would play back and forth: I would record my version of what he was playing on the other end of the line. A lot of times he would say "no, no, you're missing a note there" or "that chord needs the 9th with the ..." That was fun. He was creating and teaching me his ideas at the same time, as I would consistently miss a little subtlety that was Emerson-esque. I had about 20% of his parts already done and played by him on the album.

Was the original plan for you and Keith to work on the new release together?
This was to be the follow up 3 album, there was only the idea that we were to continue where we left off. We had talked to Carl, and he was committed to his own band, so that was not a consideration. Our actual choice for the album was Simon Phillips, but we weren't going to even talk to him until we had got together at Soundtek and recorded the basic parts of the newer songs.

Keith and I lived fairly close to each other, while Carl was always on the road. To be honest with you, and maybe a little snobby, I had been disappointed in the efforts of ELP since 3. I didn't hear that fiery playing, those amazing arrangements, or the greatest songs. 'In the Hot Seat' wasn't too bad, but after that I just didn't feel that they were playing up to their potential. It wasn't that they weren't capable, I believe it was just the spark of creativity was not gelling after all these years. I also didn't care for the Keith Emerson Band stuff. To get the most out of Keith I believe you have to either be a keyboard player and speak his language, or just piss him off so much that he brings all that energy to the playing, LOL. That was referring to the way it sounded to me that he and Greg had worked at times. Again, just my point of view and not based on me being there at the time.

What's next?
I do have some more pieces on that cassette tape, and I have lots of music in those digital files he sent me. But my heart is with this album. There will never be another phone conversation, a goofy joke, a happy day, a stressful day, an idea that is burning to get out that includes a very brilliant, lovely man with a heart of gold on the other end of the phone. This was my last chance to work with my friend, the bandmate of my greatest success, and to complete a 30-year dream. This is the only time this could ever happen.

Will a band be put together to tour?
From the beginning, Frontiers wanted us to do a few live shows. Keith was not keen on this as his arm had been bothering him and he was trying to wind down the live performance. We had the exclusive right to choose if and what we did live, so my idea was just to let it sit until we saw how the album had done. He would consider it if he felt like it, which was good enough for me. Now of course that can't happen where Keith is involved. But I must say that the response to the album has been so wonderful that I am trying to work on a tour now. I had no idea that so many fans of progressive music would discover this album and take it to heart for exactly the reason it was done. A follow up that gets what 3 should have been, right. Fans have embraced it, and that has sparked my interest in taking it on the road. Hopefully there will be an extensive tour early next year. That is what I am dreaming now to coin a phrase!

What will the next piece of work be from Robert Berry?
In all honesty, I am feeling like the 3.2 tour may be something that keeps me on the road a lot and working more progressive concerts and productions. It's funny to say, I think it's time as I've been waiting for this for 30 years but —it's time!

As I said earlier, I am in the studio every day that I'm not on tour with Greg or playing somewhere solo. In November/December of every year, my holiday band December People gets together, and we do shows for different charities. December People is Gary Pihl, guitarist from the band Boston, David Lauser, drummer for Sammy Hagar, Dave Meed, keyboardist for The Tubes, Jack Foster from the Jack Foster band, and me. It is a special brand of holiday songs you have to hear to believe. You can check out the website if you enjoy rock Christmas music, but you've never heard something like these versions.

Throughout all this I will be enjoying studio clients from 13 years old to 70 doing what they have always wanted to do - record their original songs. I love it and it also keeps me finely tuned for when that song pops into my head or just some idea to spring off of.

I appreciate you helping to spread the word on 3.2. It has been a labour of love and I am very proud of the final product. I finished it exactly the way Keith and I had set the outline. We spent three months preparing for what we hoped would be a rekindling of a fun time, a very creative time, and a very successful time. Yes, I know that critics like to say it wasn't, but I would say a Top 10 hit and a successful tour launched a very successful friendship that lasted almost 30 years. I hope you hear that when you listen to 'The Rules Have Changed'.

Steve Bonino, Oct 2018

With the release of Steve's new album, 'Stargazer', now seemed a great opportunity to have a catch-up, and discover a little more about his past and what the new album is all about.

What was it like growing up in a house with a professional singer and a professional

actress for parents?
My mom and dad met in NYC while my dad was on tour as a professional crooner. She was dancing at the time. They had me and both moved to Italy for a brief time then broke up. My mom returned to NYC and raised me alone, so I never actually lived with my dad except as a new-born. My mom worked very hard to raise me alone for which I am eternally grateful, she always encouraged me to be what I wanted to be. I got to spend a few summers with my dad, which I enjoyed very much. He always showered love and beautiful Italian clothes on me as well as teaching me all the Italian curse words which made him incredibly proud of me and gave my mom no shortage of heartburn. He passed a few years ago and I am so grateful for the time I was able to spend with him.

What are your earliest musical memories, and what/who directly influenced you to start playing and singing yourself?
I remember sitting on the floor in front of the couch watching The Beatles on The Ed Sullivan Show like it was yesterday. I was floored by their performance and charisma (and all the girls in love with them) and knew then and there that I had to be a musician. I remember the first album I purchased was 'Cheap Thrills' by Janis Joplin and the Holding Company. What a voice she had, and I loved the band's performance as well. Through my early years I grew up on The Mamas & The Papas, The Monkees, The Turtles, Jimi Hendrix, Tomita, Cream, Joni Mitchell, Crosby, Stills, Nash and Young, Mountain, Led Zeppelin, Black Sabbath (and too many others to name) and of course the prog gods and early fusion; Weather Report, Miles Davis, Jean Luc Ponty, Mahavishnu Orchestra and Return To Forever. Truly inspiring music.

How did you get the gig with the NBC TV series: "The Kids From C.A.P.E.R.", how old were you when you started on that?
I was friends with an actor/musician named Craig Wasson. He auditioned for and got the role of P.T. on the show, but I believe he turned it down at his agents' behest. He suggested I read for the role to the show's producers (thank you again, Craig) and the rest is history. It was 1975 when the process started, so I was 18.

Do you view yourself as a musician who acts, an actor who plays, or an all-round entertainer, and why?
I am solely a musician now. I acted for a decade from approximately 1973 to 1983. It was always my objective and desire to be a musician, but I was side-tracked accidently into being an actor. My mom was an actress in NYC, and I was in tow as she was auditioning for a commercial. I was being a rambunctious young man, jumping up and down on the couch in the waiting room. The director for another commercial in one of the adjoining rooms walked outside his audition room and saw me bouncing up and down uncontrollably. It just so happened he was casting a commercial about a kid jumping uncontrollably in a car. He asked me if I wanted to audition, and I agreed. I got the part. I was allowed to work on a Screen Actors Guild waiver, but it opened the door for me to join the union and be a professional actor should I be cast again which did happen a bit later. My mom was influential in me being an actor for my brief acting period. I did enjoy the experience and learned quite a bit about character motivation which I believe has served me well in song writing. The grind of auditions, wrangling with agents and hard luck took its toll and I stopped acting in the early 80's.

How did you first come across Peter Matuchniak, as you have worked together a great deal?

Peter worked for Mazda in Orange County, CA as a programmer along with the guitarist in my cover band, Steve Fazio. I first met Peter when he came to see our cover band, The Trip perform and that started our musical relationship. I must say that my musical experiences with Peter have been nothing but joyous. He is a true gentleman and major talent. I must also say that the real reason I work with him is because he brews a mean cup of coffee. (Just kidding, sort of).

You have recorded both under your own name and as part of groups. Can you describe their styles to people who may not have heard them?

I am currently working in a number of bands:

Bomber Goggles:
Peter Matuchniak, guitar and vocals
Vance Gloster, keyboards and vocals
Steve Bonino, bass and vocals
Jimmy Keegan, guest drummer
Style: Progressive rock with a touch of jazz and pop influence.

Children Of The Moon:
Pascale Elia, vocals
Jimmy Keegan, drums, percussion, keyboards and vocals
Steve Bonino, bass, guitar, keyboards and vocals
Style: Pop rock with folk, prog and art rock influences.

Zabocus:
Ted Zahn, guitar, keyboards, bass and drum programming
Steve Bonino, bass, guitar, keyboards and drum programming
Style: Americana with folk, pop and rock influences

The Steve Bonino Project:

Recording band:
Steve Bonino, bass, vocals, guitar, keyboards and drum programming
Böhn: Guitar
Bingo Brown: Drums

Live band:
Steve Bonino, bass and vocals
Jimmy Keegan, drums and vocals
Peter Matuchniak. Guitar and vocals
Jonathan Sindelman, keyboards and vocals
Seth Romano: Guitar, keyboards, percussion and vocals
Style: Progressive rock with pop, jazz, classical and AOR influences.

Your last release prior to this was Bomber Goggles' 'Gyreland', which was yourself, Peter, Vance Gloster and guest Jimmy Keegan – how did that come about?
Peter was debating whether to work on a follow up to Gekko Projekts' wonderful 'Reya Of Titan' release or to try something new, something new was decided and he and Vance invited me to join as bassist co-songwriter in this new venture which was a blast to write and record. We did it the old-fashioned way, facing each other in a rehearsal room throwing out ideas. I've always loved that process.

As with your most recent release, 'Stargazer', it is a concept album – what interests you about this art form?
Ever since I heard 'Tommy' by The Who I've been a big fan of the genre. I always wanted to try working on a concept of my own but never quite had a story that fuelled the fire. Zabocus is currently completing the third album in a trilogy titled 'Trouble Town' based on the death and rebirth of an American town. Bomber Goggles continued my learning curve of following a story line from inception to conclusion with the album 'Gyreland'. I followed this up with my own concept album inspired by my dear friend, Linda Kay. She originally designed what was to become the Stargazer album cover for the Children Of The Moon debut. It wasn't chosen for that release, but the cover stayed in my mind. One day I sat down to write the title track 'Stargazer', inspired by the cover. My mind began to put together a story in which Stargazer, the hero, travels to Alpha Centauri to carry on the human race after we hit the point of no return due to neglect here on Earth. The songs came together rather quickly once the idea came.

Why have you released this under the name 'The Steve Bonino Project'?
I was on the phone with Nick Katona, the owner of Melodic Revolution Records. As we were discussing details for the release of 'Stargazer' I mentioned that I'd read, in general, that bands were more popular than solo artists. He suggested I release the album as 'The Steve Bonino Project' as opposed to being a Steve Bonino solo release. I agreed that was a good idea. Besides, I like working in a band context as I've grown up being in bands.

Who plays on the album?
Two of my neighbourhood musician friends helped me out. Böhn has played guitar for years and offered to play some parts on the album which I gladly agreed to. It was pretty much the same for drummer, Bingo Brown who used his electronic kit to record some drum parts for the album.

What is the story behind 'Stargazer'?
In the not-too-distant future, man's neglect has brought the Earth to the point of no return. Our hero, Stargazer works for the Hubble Space Station and is a leader in the scientific community. A starship named 'Phoenix' has been constructed to take a select group of people with enough genetic diversity to carry on the human race on the planet Proxima b in the Alpha Centauri galaxy. Stargazer is chosen. He and his fellow passengers make the most terrifying and hopeful voyage in mankind's history to their new world.

The Stargazer saga will carry on in Stargazer 2 and 3 whose story lines are inspired by Linda Kay. I will not divulge too much information at this point, but I do believe the entire story would make a good sci fi movie. Certainly one I would enjoy seeing. She and I are discussing writing a book as well. Large ambitions that I hope will come to fruition. I'm certainly loving the journey, wherever it leads.

Which science fiction authors do you believe influenced you most, and why?
I love the superhero mythos. To this day I dream I have the ability to do exceptional things. I gravitate to those stories, such as the Quizat Haderach in Frank Herbert's 'Dune'. Of course, Arthur C. Clarke's 'A Space Odyssey' was an influence on a generation and helped me fall in love with space. I loved 'The Martian Chronicles' by Ray Bradbury. I'm sure it inspired the humans fleeing to another planet to save the human race story line I borrowed for 'Stargazer'. George Orwell's '1984' and Ray Bradbury's 'Fahrenheit 451' are brilliant and symptomatic of the human traits and desires too many of us possess that can lead to making 'Stargazer' a reality. I am also a tremendous fan of the dark works of Stephen King, H.P. Lovecraft and Edgar Allan Poe.

What do you believe has musically influenced you most with this?
I am a hodge podge of influences. I don't know where my Beatles intersects with my Bach, where my Who morphs into Mahavishnu, where my Rundgren meets Joni Mitchell. It's all a beautiful mess in there and I just see what comes out. I have been enjoying revisiting the albums of the prog gods; Yes, Gentle Giant, Genesis, Pink Floyd, Jethro Tull, ELP, King Crimson, etc. as well as enjoying the newer generation; Steven Wilson/Porcupine Tree, Spock's Beard, Snarky Puppy, Frost, The Neal Morse Band, Big Big Train, etc. I do not know which of these influenced me most, but it is in there somewhere.

What is next?
I'm already halfway finished with 'Stargazer 2' which carries the story on to life on Proxima b and an amazing, life altering discovery on the planet. My objective is to release it April 2019. Ted Zahn and I have the final instalment in the Zabocus 'Trouble Town' trilogy titled 'Dream Machine' scheduled for release in 2019 as well. I am writing songs for the second Children Of The Moon album and I know Peter and Vance are planning Bomber Goggles' second album as well. Whew, maybe I actually need to become a superhero to get all this done. My superpower could be: Not Needing Sleep.

Mark Healy, Hibernal, Feb 2017

It was in July 2013 that I first came across Hibernal, when I received a message through ProgArchives saying that someone called Mark had read some of my reviews and wondered if I was interested in his debut release under that name? As I have always endeavoured to increase my musical awareness I said "Yes", and in due course a Bandcamp code was sent to me and I downloaded the album, called 'The Machine'. Instead of starting with music, this commenced with spoken words and sound effects, and within the first minute I was enthralled, and the real world had fallen away: I was already deep inside the world of Hibernal. This is not a concept album in the normal sense, neither is it a story with some music in the background, rather this is a genuinely new and exciting art form where music and actors combine to create a short film for your ears.

Fast forward to 2017 and Hibernal has released their fourth album, 'The Dark of The City', so now seemed the right time to sit back and have a chat.

What inspires you musically?
In terms of music, I pick up inspiration from all over the place. I first took up guitar because I wanted to play Tool songs, so Adam Jones has obviously been very influential in my song writing. I'm also a huge fan of stoner rock bands like Kyuss and Monster Magnet. In terms of more contemporary Prog, I like Karnivool and Porcupine Tree, and I especially love the way Steven Wilson constructs his longer tracks like "Arriving Somewhere". That's the kind of song that takes you on a journey as a listener, which is what I try to do with my own albums. The stuff I write for Hibernal tends to gravitate toward atmospherics and soundscapes, so I also take inspiration from post rock bands like Hammock and Cloudkicker as well.

I was also into lots of industrial music in the 90's, with bands like Ministry, Front Line Assembly, NIN and KMFDM constantly blaring from my car stereo. I had a pretty decent mullet at the time, and I undoubtedly looked cool hooning around in my beat-up Toyota Corolla. With industrial, I loved the blend of harsh guitars, electronic elements, and vocal sampling. In fact, the prototype Hibernal song I developed back in 2012 used vocal samples to create a very rudimentary kind of narrative, but I found that searching for the right samples was very time consuming and ultimately limited the scope of what I could do. That's when I came up with the idea of using my own story, told via voice actors, rather than samples from other sources.

What inspires you in literature?
Some of my favourite authors include Arthur C. Clarke, Neal Stephenson, Stephen King and George RR Martin. Clarke and Stephenson are both masters of detail; they create such vivid realities with their writing that it feels like you are reading documented accounts of things that happened. I've learned in my own writing that filling the world with detail certainly lends authenticity to the experience for the reader, so I plan my speculative universes for months in advance before putting pen to paper. Or fingers to keyboard as it is these days.

Oddly enough, my writing has also been inspired by music many times. One example is the short story that formed the basis for the album 'The Machine'. This entire story came to me one night driving in my car listening to Pink Floyd's "Welcome to the Machine". I still remember the throbbing bassline at the start of the track inspiring the notion of the 'sickly heartbeat' heard by the narrator when he first confronts the device in the bowels of the Machine Co. building. It was a freaky, scary, and awesome experience, the kind of thing only great music can evoke. This is what I try to emulate with Hibernal.

Are you a writer who can play music, or a musician who can write books?
I'm a writer who plays a bit of music on the side! In fact, I'm a bit of a bedroom guitarist to be honest. I took up guitar late in life and never had lessons. I'm more of a storyteller and someone who creates moods and atmospheres, and luckily for me that's a good

skillset for a project like Hibernal. I play to my strengths and don't try to be something I'm not. I think that understanding your limitations is a huge part of being successful as an artist, and I certainly know mine!

What made you decide on this type of art form?
I had been wanting to put a band together for several years. I wrote about fifty songs (lyrics and music) over the course of three or four years and tried to recruit band members, but there was no chemistry with the people I was jamming with.

My singing is total garbage, so doing the album solo was out of the question. I considered arranging the songs as instrumentals, but in truth I wanted to do something that was more compelling, and which allowed me to captivate the listener (which I didn't think I could do with music alone).

As I mentioned above, I messed around with using samples from movies in my songs to heighten the experience and I was immediately struck by the power of those simple additions, I got some chills happening for sure. However, apart from the time-consuming nature of finding samples, I was worried about the legality of 'stealing' them from movies, so I scrapped the idea.

At that point I was ready to give it all up, as it seemed as though I was out of options. Then I remembered the short story I'd written a decade before called 'Welcome to the Machine'. It had been selected to appear in an anthology with some big-name authors - all very exciting for a young author like me - but after working on edits for months, the anthology was cancelled at the last minute, and nothing was published. (This also caused me to give up writing in disgust at the time, since it all seemed like a big waste of time).

But those chills, man. I wanted to experience that creative buzz again. I kept messing around with the format, and soon realised that I could adapt the story into a simple, condensed script and set it to the music I'd written, and that would allow me to make a concept album with narration instead of song lyrics. To be honest, the idea was a bit ridiculous - combining a spoken word piece with instrumentals - but when I started to play around with it, I had a lot of fun. I told myself that it would be a good exercise in writing, recording, mixing, and mastering an album, so I kept going with it. I matched songs I'd written with different scenes from the script and composed more music from scratch where nothing fit.

The decision to hire professional voice talent wasn't an easy one. When I checked it out, I found it to be quite expensive, but I decided that if I was going to make the album and put my name on it, I'd do it with the highest production values possible. I released 'The Machine' on Bandcamp and told a few friends about it, looking for feedback on the audio quality and any other general thoughts. I waited, and waited, and there was deafening silence. I could almost picture them sitting there scratching their heads as they tried to figure out what the hell I'd created. It was about that time I went searching for a very large hole to crawl into.

I was too embarrassed to send the album out to any bloggers or reviewers because I thought they'd find it ridiculous. Then, about a week after release, complete strangers started to pay money for the album even though it was listed for free on Bandcamp. They messaged me wanting to know if I was going to make more albums. It was only at that point I realised Hibernal might have some appeal for a small fan base. So, Hibernal wasn't something I planned, but rather something that came about through experimentation and trial and error.

You've released instrumental versions of the first three albums – do you personally prefer these or the ones containing the stories?
I've only ever made the instrumental albums for the fans. (I have awesome fans, by the way, so it was the least I could do.) Initially I had no interest in doing the instrumentals at all, but I finally caved after receiving so many requests from fans for the 'narration-free' versions. I've never written a song with the intention of it ending up as an instrumental, even the songs I wrote in the early days before Hibernal had accompanying lyrics. I do enjoy listening to instrumentals by other artists, but when it comes to my own creations, I seem to have a driving need for a theme to be included in there somewhere.

The future per Hibernal is bleak, and not a lot of room for humanity. Do you see each of the albums as different facets of the same future, or are they alternative realities?
Guilty as charged, I do write some bleak stuff! I have always used art as a kind of catharsis, dealing with my fears by writing them down in the form of a story. 'The Machine' is a perfect example. When I wrote it, I was at the point in my career where I was beginning to worry that I was spending too much time at work. Then, bam! This story falls out of my head about a man who surrenders every part of himself to his job. Coincidence? Probably not!

'After the Winter' - while ostensibly about nuclear war, synthetics, and the end of the world - is just a story about a man struggling for self-acceptance. Almost all my stories are just tools for examining the things we all grapple with in our day-to-day lives.

In terms of continuity, the albums could be loosely considered to be set in the same universe, especially the first three. When I wrote 'The Dark of the City', however, I considered it to be a clean slate, because I didn't want to have to conform to previous timelines and events. There are still some commonalities between the stories simply because I tend to revisit certain themes, and if you connect enough dots, you could say that it's still the same universe, but it's not necessarily something I've done intentionally.

Have you ever felt that you ought to go back to any of the stories and provide a sequel?
I get asked to do sequels a LOT. I had people asking me to write sequels right from the first album. I suppose the reason I haven't is because I view the albums as an exploration of a single idea, and once that's done, I'm ready to move on to another idea. Plus, I don't like treading over old ground. I try to make each album sound and feel different from the last, and I'm not sure I could effectively do that with continuing storylines and characters.

Having said that, I wouldn't completely close the door on the concept of an album sequel. If I came up with a killer idea for a continuing storyline that was fresh and interesting, I would go ahead with it.

Each of the stories is compelling and complete yet it is incredibly hard to write a short story that is complete in every way – how do approach this?
Writing a story for an album is very challenging. In fact, at times it's a total pain.

First, I set myself a limit of 2500 words. If it blows out more than that, the ratio of narration to music gets too high and it starts to feel like an audiobook with a bit of music on the side. So, within that very small amount of real estate there's many tasks that need to be accomplished: describe the world and the setting; create character arcs; have plot and resolution; tackle themes that lie at the core of the story.

That's a lot to do in a short amount of time. For that reason, I rely on archetypes quite heavily. For example, in an early draft of 'Replacements', the main character Artimus was working in a spare parts store and explaining the social structure of the world through people who came into the store, as well as revealing his own backstory, but it took me six tracks to get to the plot. It just wouldn't have worked on an album because I'd have lost the interest of the listener by that point. So, I ditched that setup in favour of an introductory track that gave a brief outline, followed by a whole bunch of cyberpunk tropes - synthetics, rain, shuttles flying overhead, and the overall film noir mood. That saved me spending 2000 words establishing the world, and instead allowed me to get straight into the plot.

Likewise, there's no time to create complex characters. The version of Artimus that ends up in the final script has very little backstory. He's a loner who restlessly wanders the streets looking for meaning. That's it. And I think that works well because it creates a sense of mystery about him. The audience is given a few crumbs about his outlook on the world and his motivations, and the rest is a blank canvas for them to fill in.

I think I cranked out close to fifty drafts of 'Replacements' over a three-month period before I got something that ticked all the boxes that need to be ticked. It's an iterative process and it just takes a lot of time and patience to find the right balance.

What comes first, the story or the music?
For the first album, I developed the story and the music separately, thinking the two would never end up together. After the idea for Hibernal hit me, I adapted the 6500-word short story into a 2500-word script and broke it up into eleven scenes. Then I went through the catalogue of songs I'd written looking to see if any of them fit the mood for each individual scene. Lucky, some of them did. I had to write an additional 20% of new music for the scenes I couldn't match.

After that first album, I had a better idea of what I was doing, and I developed the script and the music together. I would come up with a story idea in my head and write some music that I thought might accompany it, and once I had a few decent songs together I would flesh out the script and start the drafting process. It was a lot more organic. On the first album, most of the narration and dialog happen between the sections of music, often between songs in short segues. On the subsequent albums, it's far more integrated, with narration and dialog happening during songs, almost like lyrics. It was a conscious choice to compose music that could more effectively accommodate the story in a more fluid fashion.

Why change to a female first person in TDotC?
I must give credit to my collaborator Rowan Salt for this one. I had originally written the script with a male in the lead role, and it was his idea to try it the other way around. As Rowan suggested, there's an interesting dynamic when the female partner is in control. Also, I already had Faleena Hopkins (from previous Hibernal productions) lined up to appear on the album, and we wanted to give her a larger role and really 'stretch her wings' so to speak. She didn't disappoint.

Another reason why I jumped at the idea was because it was another way to differentiate TDotC from previous albums. As I said earlier, I like each album to have its own feel. For TDotC, I shortened the length of the album considerably and wrote the script in present tense, which is something I hadn't done before. Making the lead character a female was another great way to give the album a unique feel in the Hibernal catalogue.

What's next?
I'm currently putting the finishing touches on the instrumental version of 'The Dark of the City', that one should be coming to an internet near you some time in the next few weeks. After that, I'm going to spend some time concentrating on my writing. I plan to publish at least three more novels this year as I continue my march toward world domination.

After that, things get a bit nebulous. I'll confess that I haven't written a single track for another Hibernal album, and although I've tinkered with a few scripts, I haven't come up with anything I'm happy with. I've also toyed with the idea of creating a podcast that features one story over five or ten episodes - like a radio play type deal - but I don't think that will happen.

Most likely I'll blow the cobwebs off my guitar at some point soon and see what comes out. Whether that's a Hibernal album or something else, I don't know. I'll just see where the creative juices take me.

I strongly believe that Mark has released some of the most compelling albums I have heard over the last four years. They should come with a government health warning as it is just not advisable to drive when playing these; reality disappears and the bleak science fiction world of the future and the stories of those involved are the only things that matter.

Ben Morley, Mice On Stilts, Dec 2016

What are your first musical memories and what inspired you to start writing and performing your own music?
When I was 13, I was put into a foster home due to a rough home environment, and my foster parents had a son who was into a lot of jazz and metal. He tried to get me into to jazz stuff, but I really identified with the metal at that age. The album he gave me that I believe formed the platform from where I explored music was 'Lateralus' by Tool. I was

really attracted to how challenging it was to listen to, in the sense that there was a lot to figure out. That was just me being a nerd at 13, I guess. I must have listened to it every day for about six years (no exaggeration), and I remember feeling disconnected from everything else when I listened to it. It was just me and them. Up until that point I'd never had an experience like that: I was totally addicted to music from that moment on.

What were you doing prior to MOS?
When I was eighteen, I went to the UK for six months and kinda over did it on using certain... shall we say, herbs. Turns out that when I got home, I had a 'drug induced psychosis' and I was unable to work as I was sleeping all day and awake all night and couldn't control my emotions. It was a horrible time and as I needed to do something I got back into guitar and started writing a bunch of techy metal riffs. I discovered some guys through the internet and started a totally instrumental band called Gate. We were influenced by Meshuggah, Isis, Neurosis and Devin Townsend and used lots of long riffs that didn't repeat. Eventually I felt that Gate wasn't satisfying enough for me and what I wanted to do. I've always been attracted to the darker, more melancholy, stuff but I couldn't find that in the metal that we were playing.

After Gate I had a break for a couple of years, but a lot of dark shit took place during that time that led me to form another band. Shortly after I decided on starting the band, I was trying to come up with some kind of idea of exactly what we would look like, and the name was literally the first thing in my head after a really vivid dream one night. I've my own meaning behind the name, which came later, and I see it as an analogy for justice in a strange way.

MOS have a very unusual line-up, with sound effects and both violin and brass, how did this come about?
When I first had the idea of starting this band it was originally meant to be a four piece with cello, guitar, violin, and piano. That was all well and good until I met Rob (drummer). We had a jam with him, and he never stopped turning up, so from then on it was a process of finding the right people, which probably took over a year. We took an open-minded approach where we didn't say no to anything until we started to find the right sounds through trial and error. A few people quit the band in the first year, as it wasn't really their thing. Hence why we saw many faces up until that point.

How would you describe each member of MOS? What other bands have they been involved with, and what do they bring to the mix?
Rob Sanders - Drums (In Company, Ben Prestige Band)
This man embodies none of the stereotypes of a drummer. He shows up on time, carts all our gear around without asking anything in return and doesn't play wanky drum solos at sound check. Rob and I have recently started exploring the mountains and volcanoes around Auckland. Love this man.

Joseph Jujnovich - Vocal Effects (Coconut Porn Company)
I was on a bus to the north shore when I got chatting to Joseph, who I had met once before in a sex shop (but that's an entirely different story). He was one of those guys that I had seen around town for a few years, but for some reason had never really engaged

with. I think in terms of what he adds to this band is really the bones of it, aside from Rob. I really like music that is unsettling as it makes me feel alive. Joseph is somehow capable of giving our songs an eeriness to it that has, at points, kept me awake at night.

Tim Burrows - Bass / Production (Outrun the Buffalo, Scatterbrain)
Tim and I met a church when were about 14 years old, and through a mutual love of Led Zeppelin we became best of mates. In fact, we were living together when this whole thing was starting. He is also responsible for recording and mixing everything we do and I'm proud to have him as a friend. He quit his day job to produce music full time, and he is actually doing it.

Calvin Davidson - Synth / Sax (Outrun the Buffalo, Scatterbrain)
We also met at church when we were 13 or 14. Calvin and Tim used to play in Scatterbrain, and then Outrun The Buffalo. Although he doesn't play much guitar in MOS, he is one of the best guitar players I've ever seen play. The addition of the synth has been interesting, as I didn't think it was going to work as well as it has. Used sparingly, understated.

Aaron Longville - Sax / Trumpet
We met at house party where he was walking around with a saxophone playing jazz. Aaron is 'the horns guy' and plays about 5 different types. He is also a very insightful person that has a lot of wisdom to offer.

Brendan Zwaan - Piano (Shepherds of Cassini, Emberglow)
I first met Brendan through his band Shepherds of Cassini (which by the way, if you like prog metal, you are in for a treat as they play incredible music and are one of my favourite kiwi bands, hands down). He plays guitar in Shepherds, and I had no idea he

played piano, but when we advertised for a new pianist, his name kept coming up. A few people separately mentioned to me that we should at least talk to him. I can only describe him as a total musical genius.

Sam Hennessy –Viola
When we were three weeks away from our first tour in early 2013, our violin player ditched us – I'm not sure it was his thing. So, Joseph and I desperately emailed just about anyone we could to find a replacement. As I recall, I even spoke to the violin player in Shepherds of Cassini. We must have reached out to about 20 players with no luck at all. However, Sam had just put an incredible article on the internet about a local Christian music festival that we had both attended years before. I read it and felt the need to email him to say thank you. We got chatting, and when I found out that he played a viola I instantly invited him on this tour with us. I just love how liquid life can be sometimes, when everything just falls into the place it needs to be in. Sam is a wonderful human being with a lot to share.

Just thinking about these people has made me realize how much I love these guys.

For those who have yet to hear the EP, please talk through each song and what it means both musically and lyrically.
It is strongly centred on loss, and I thought that it would be cool to use the imagery around drowning to convey that.
SYDS SOCKS - This is the homage to Mr Barrett.
BINOCULAR BATH - Single.
A MOSS OCEAN - The song with the feelings
VULNERABLE VADER - Coming to the end of the journey now. This one is a snapshot of a depressing few weeks I had a few years ago. It also has the most violent moment on this recording, but if I'm being honest, it really is just us trying to rip off Kayo Dot.
TUATARA LAWN - Much to my surprise this became the most listened to song from the whole EP. It's just over 12 minutes long, so it's the longest by a mile and is the 'prog' song.

Many have described your music as "crossover progressive", but you call yourselves "Acoustic Doom". How did that tag come about?
The doom thing was actually something that happened on a live on-air interview. We were on 'Freak the Sheep', which is a local music show run by Silke on 95BFM here in Auckland. She has been so, so, lovely to us since we met her in 2012 and she asked me what our genre was. Tim was behind me filming (he wasn't in the band at this stage), and he just whispered in my ear 'doom folk bro'. It kind of stuck, I say it stuck, what I mean is we just call ourselves doom folk. Everyone else just thinks we're dickheads.

In terms of how we sound, I'm not sure I'm the best person to ask because I still genuinely believe we make sad pop music. We use many instruments, and across one recorded song there could be as many as thirteen throughout the whole thing, so I guess you could say it's quite layered. Emotionally I'd like to think it's rather draining, that's my perspective anyway but I'm not sure about the listener. 'An Ocean Held Me' is about drowning in the sea, but somehow it all being ok in the end. This is my outlet, it's where I currently place any feelings I struggle with. Dynamically we go from a solo piano to full blown apocalyptic bulldozer (that's Steve Von Till's phrase), and we're still trying to figure out everything in between. How do we sound? I'm not sure.

Catharsis? Oh wait.... Doom

Were you surprised as just how well this has been received in the prog world outside of NZ, and what has been the highlight to date?
It has honestly been the biggest surprise of all, as at no point did we ever try to write progressive rock. It is a real honour to be included within that genre. I listen to a decent amount of prog anyway, but this band wasn't meant to be that at all! My highlight of everything so far is still just playing in this band with these people and being allowed to continue doing this. I've some great friends that I love very much and many of them I wouldn't have met if I hadn't had started Mice. Getting that email from Daniel (Gallifrey from ProgArchives) was important to me. A few months after we had released the EP, he sent me an email to tell me how much he loved the recording. Kev, you coming out to that Kings Arms show also blew me away. Releasing vinyl was another one. Recording a choir for the new album. A few weeks ago, we supported Yes at the Aotea Centre, which was unreal!

How is the new album going?
It is very, very, very, close to completion. All my parts are done but there are still some horns to be recorded. We need to start thinking about how we are releasing it etc., but hopefully it will be early to mid-next year. It still doesn't have a track listing although the songs are 95% recorded. Here are details of three of the songs that will feature.

FUNERAL - Last year one of my close friends he wasn't having the best of times, and we were really worried about him. On one occasion I had to go and pick him up, take all his meds away from him and offer him a mattress on my floor for a few nights until he felt safe, and this song is about him and the possible reality that he might not be here. It's directed at him, although it could be about anyone. Look after yourself, the people you love and those who are currently strangers. Musically this is our heaviest. It has the quietest moment in all our songs and then over ten minutes it builds to the loudest.

HOROEKA HAUNTING - I used to suffer from something called 'Night Terrors', which are nightmares so horrific that it affects you on a mental, emotional, and psychical level. For me, what that looked like was waking up screaming (which is the first line of this song). Most of the time when I awoke, not only was I filled with a genuine sense of fear but would often be hallucinating as well. The worst one I ever had, I woke up on the floor and there were bats flying around my ceiling. This song is essentially about that and musically it is very slow and sludgy.

AND WE SAW HIS NEEDS THROUGH THE CASKET - Last year I came across an article on Wikipedia while surfing the web one night called 'DEATH OF KELLY THOMAS' which is about a 37-year-old homeless man who suffered from schizophrenia for most of his life and was beaten to death by police officers in Fullerton, California three years ago. There is raw footage on the Internet captured by local CCTV, and after reading through the article a few times made myself watch the video. In it you can clearly see three men in uniform saddle up to Kelly and pick on him, threaten him and eventually let loose on him and it's incredibly horrific to watch. Kelly calls out for his dad 31 times, and these guys were supposed to be looking out for him! To add to this, all three of them got off their charges. It made me so angry inside, and I couldn't stop thinking about this poor man and what he suffered through for absolutely no reason at all. "AND WE SAW HIS NEEDS THROUGH THE CASKET" is my song for Kelly. It features a choir, comprised of our friends, all incredible singers and they sound beautiful.

So, what's next for MOS after the album?
Playing shows outside of NZ is what I really want to focus on for us next, and I am keen to tour through Europe, which would be a dream come true for me.

Aroha nui

The Progressive Underground Vol 5

Live Reviews

Yes, Mice On Stilts
ASB Theatre, Auckland, 10/11/14

Earlier this year Yes announced they would be playing Auckland at the beginning of a tour. To say that I was stunned is something of an understatement, as when they played here two years ago it was the first time they had ever played New Zealand in their history! That night was a special night for all those who went, not just because it was the first time new singer Jon Davidson played with the band.

So, like many others, I purchased the tickets as soon as they went on sale and waited for

the night with bated breath. Then a week before the gig it was announced they had decided that they were going to have a support band, and it was going to be none other than Mice On Stilts! To say the band and label were excited about this is something of an understatement, as although the band have been gaining a significant amount of international acclaim for their debut it has been hard going in New Zealand itself and this would be easily their biggest gig to date when they could get in front of a really appreciative crowd.

Finally, Monday night came around, and I headed into the city to meet up with Triple A Records label head honcho TeMatera Smith at their office, and to sample a local ale or two. We then headed down to the venue and bumped into MOS singer Ben on his way out – he was incredibly pumped and kept saying that he couldn't believe he had seen

Steve Howe walking around during their soundcheck! TeMatera and I felt another small libation was in order, and then we went into the venue to settle into our seats. We were both pleased to see that many of the audience had also decided to check out the support band, but I must wonder how many questioned what was going on when eight people came onto the stage! With two brass musicians, a violinist and someone providing sound effects combined with melancholy and drama, Mice On Stilts are unlike any other progressive band you have ever come across. They only had time for four songs, so started with "Binocular Bath" from the debut, which allowed them to settle some nerves and really get into it. Two new songs followed, "Funeral" (which is awesome) and "Khandallah" before closing with "Tuatara Lawn", which is possibly one of the most emotive songs ever performed and ended with Ben knelt on the stage coaxing the last notes out of the band. Were they perfect? No, and the sound mix also left something to be desired (especially THAT trumpet introduction), but they made a lot of friends, most of whom had never realised that in Auckland they had a quite stunning progressive rock band all their own. The fact they sold out of CDs at the merch stand, as well as selling some vinyl, just goes to show the impression they made.

It wasn't long to wait until the main attraction came to the stage. Now, I bought the tickets as soon as I knew that Yes were coming and hadn't realised that tonight was going to be a very special event indeed. So, on they come, and without saying anything moved straight into "Close To The Edge". They were incredibly tight, and Jon has come of age since I saw them last. I always enjoyed his work with Glass Hammer and knew what he was capable of, and he now seems to accept he is a member of one of the finest bands ever to grace a stage whereas last time he still seemed very much in awe. There is no awkwardness, just total confidence. A few technical issues with Steve's steel guitar were soon sorted and he again showed why he totally stole the show when he was here before. The other guys are important, of course, but it is Steve that really provides Yes with that melodic bite.

After "Close To The Edge" they went straight into "And You And I", and it was only at that point that I realised that they were playing the complete album straight through and I was just stunned as I never expected to see/hear that – I mean, that album came out in 1972! It was only when the album was completed that Chris spoke to us and reminded us that this was only their second time in NZ but they were very much enjoying being there. He then started talking about the new album, which I must confess to have still not purchased yet – I keep meaning to, but rarely have I seen an album so universally disliked. So, I expected a 'normal' gig from this point but instead we were treated to just two songs, back-to-back, from 'Heaven & Earth'. They were okay to be honest but did seem very different to what had gone before.

Then, at the end of that Steve took over on the microphone and said that before 'Close To The Edge' they had recorded another album, and before my brain could comprehend what was being said, they had gone into "Roundabout". I turned to TeMatera and said, "They're going to play the whole of 'Fragile'!", the response was "You're kidding!" I wasn't, and they did. I was blown away – here was a band that I had followed for some forty years playing two of the most important albums ever released, one after the other! The performance was faultless, and with just a small video screen at the rear showing images of the band, and some pretty basic lighting, this was all about the music. Jon was having a ball, singing epic after epic, and while Geoff Downes is certainly no Rick Wakeman, he more than held his own throughout. All too soon the album was finished, and so were the band. There was rapturous applause, and although the guys were bowing and leaving us, we all knew they would be back, they had to be.

They didn't keep us waiting too long and returned with "All Good People". This was the only time where there was a musical issue during the whole night, as Jon appeared to get lost at one point, but Steve and Chris soon got everything back on track. Given what we had heard before I did feel that the choice of "Owner Of A Lonely Heart" as the closer to be somewhat strange, but really that was just being picky.

It was a hell of a night, as yet again they were starting a tour in NZ, and I can only hope they come back here again. But even if they don't, I can say I have heard them play two of the most important progressive albums of all time in the same night, something I never thought would happen. Mice On Stilts were there to show that progressive bands certainly come in many different guises, and while musically they are very different to Yes, they appeal to the same market and possibly this could be the start of them being appreciated more in their own country. All in all, this was an experience to savour and reflect on – incredible.

Steve Hackett
Auckland Town Hall, July 28th, 2017

Now, as my children will tell you, I'm really old – although I do sometimes wish I was a little older. I missed most of the progressive bands of the Seventies due to a combination of my age and geography, Devon never was a hotbed of the live scene. But at the tender age of 17 I managed to see Genesis in concert as they undertook a small halls tour, but this wasn't for any of their amazing Seventies' albums but was for 'Duke', by which time the band had of course been reduced to Phil, Mike and Tony plus Chester and Darryl. Most Genesis fans seem to fall into either the Gabriel camp or the Collins camp, but I would like to tender another option for consideration, namely that the "real" Genesis was the line-ups that included one Stephen Richard Hackett.

In the nineties the stars aligned, and I finally saw the man himself in concert at a tiny village hall in Whitchurch. The landlord of the local pub was a proghead and he had managed to convince some of the underground bands such as Galahad, Freewill and Pendragon to play at the hall opposite the Red Lion. Then, amazingly, he convinced Steve it would be a great place for a warm-up for the next British tour. I made sure I was in the hall for the soundcheck, and soon realized that instead of playing a few bits and pieces to ensure the gear was working, Steve and the band were instead playing everything. So I saw the full set in the afternoon, and then again that night! Awesome.

Fast forward a few years and I moved from the UK to NZ, which immediately improved my quality of life, but also curtailed my gig going. For those of you who know little about the country apart from the all-powerful All Blacks, then here's some context: the land mass of NZ is a little larger than that of the UK and comprises two main islands plus many smaller ones. The population is a little more than 4.5 million, with more than a quarter of that situated in and around Auckland. I live close to the third largest city, Christchurch on South Island, which has a population of approx. 450,000. So, when it comes to the number of people who live here there are very few, so it isn't really profitable for bands to come over, although many are now either starting or ending tours here so that they can either brush off the cobwebs or stay for a holiday. So, when a band comes then it is a matter of grabbing the opportunity, and when Steve announced he was coming to NZ for the very first time it was a case of buying both concert and airplane tickets as there was no way I was going to miss out on this.

Auckland Town Hall is not a venue that many bands play, and it was my first time there for a gig. With the huge organ as a backdrop, and just a few lights on the stage and a small amount hung in the air, it was obvious tonight was going to be all about the music. No support band either, but that was okay, as tonight was going to feature two quite different musical legacies, an introduction of Hackett material to warm us up for the main event, Genesis. Tonight's line-up was one that will be recognizable to fans of Steve. On bass, pedals, guitars and backing vocals was Nick Beggs (Kajagoogoo, Iona), drums and lead vocals was Gary O'Toole, keyboards was Roger King, while Rob Townsend provided the kitchen sink (flute, sax, keyboards, pedals, percussion, vocals). Centre stage was the man himself, on guitar and vocals, and of course they kicked the evening's festivities off with "Every Day". Given how long these guys have played together it was no surprise that they were incredibly tight, and while Rob disappeared at times when his skills weren't required, it was amazing to hear just how strong these guys were and how the blend of voices was wonderful.

Steve apologized for having taken 67 years to get to New Zealand (I seem to recall Chris Squire making the same type of comment and then they returned a couple of years later, so I live in hope that Steve will be back). We were then treated to some newer songs from Steve's canon, until he ended the section with a blistering totally over the top version of "Shadow of the Hierophant". Then it was time to introduce singer Nad Sylvan (Agents of Mercy), and the guys kicked it up a gear with "Squonk". The reaction from the crowd was immediate, as here was the music they had come to hear. Genesis may be no more, and there are arguments as to who has had the best solo career of all of them (in terms of musical quality Hackett beats the rest hands down), but the music lives on in the hearts and minds of many. It was obvious that Nad was having issues, and that he was struggling to hit all the notes, something rather unexpected given his reputation, but it is a long way to come in an air pressurised tin can, and this was the first night of the tour.

During "Dancing With The Moonlit Knight" I honestly felt the band were getting ready to move into "Clocks" but that was not the case. Instead, Gary took the lead for "Fly On The Windshield", which turned into something far heavier than I could ever have imagined – the man is awesome, and I am going to search out more bands he has been involved with, as he is really quite exceptional. There aren't many drummers who can fill in for Collins and seem totally at home. "Firth of Fifth" had people clapping along and got the band their first standing ovation of the night, something that was then repeated at the end of each subsequent number. "Musical Box" was turned into something even more magical than before with the addition of saxophone, but all too soon it was time for the final number of the night. By now Nad's problems had resolved themselves, but that didn't really matter as every person there was singing for him "Walking across the sitting room, I turn the television off...."

More than two hours had flown by, and of course it couldn't end there, and the band came back on for a steaming version of "Los Endos". The guy next to me was upset that they hadn't played "I Know What I Like", but with classics such as "Eleventh Earl of Mar" and "Carpet Crawlers" being aired I walked away a very happy punter indeed. Will Steve and the guys come back to the land of the long white cloud? I have no idea, but I can only hope. This was one of the best gigs I have ever attended, with no stage trickery, just a few lights, great musicians performing classic songs. Maybe next time he can come back and play no Genesis material at all, but highlights of his solo career, now that would be a gig to fly up for all over again.

The Progressive Underground Vol 5

Kev Rowland

Kev Rowland is a self-confessed music addict, who has never really been the same since he heard 'Sabbath Bloody Sabbath' in 1975. In the Eighties he spent quite a ridiculous amount of money on all things related to Jethro Tull and was asked by David Rees to write a piece on Carmen (the band including John Glascock, not the opera) for the Tull fanzine 'A New Day'. This simple request was life-changing, although neither realised it at the time.

Kev discovered he enjoyed writing about music and submitted reviews for the inaugural Mensa RockSIG newsletter, before becoming secretary himself in 1990. Over the next 16 years, the newsletter gained a name, and he put out more than 80 issues, many of them doubles, in excess of 11,000 pages. When he moved to New Zealand in 2006, he retired from the music scene, but was pulled back in, initially kicking and screaming until he accepted his fate. These days he can be found contributing to many magazines and websites, and somehow is still writing more than 250,000 words a year.

When he isn't listening to music, writing about music, or thinking about music, then he can be found on his lifestyle block with his wonderful wife Sara, and their 6 dogs, 5 cats, chickens, sheep, lambs, bees and cattle. Oh, apparently, he has a day job as well.

Online:
http://www.progarchives.com/Collaborators.asp?id=5626

The Progressive Underground Vol 5

Kev Rowland's previous collections of his progressive rock reviews and interviews written between 1991 and 2013 are essential for all lovers of the genre, but don't just take our word for it.

A book that will be quickly referred to as "a bible".
Daryl Easlea, Record Collector

His writing is informative, intelligent, and generous... As Brian Appleton would put it, thank you Kev for your contribution.
Rychard Carrington, Rock n Reel

It is unvarnished and unencumbered by any expectations of PR; the reviews are clearly done for no other reason than love of the genre.
DE, Prog Magazine

This is best treated as a kind of guide to the neo-progressive genre... progressive rock has never really died, it just went from the mainstream to the underground.
Artur Chachlowski, MLWZ

All I can say is if you are a true proghead this book should be in your library of progressive rock literature. Because it's a great work. A book to be considered of superior or lasting artistic merit.
Henri Strik, Background Magazine

Chronic well-crafted, short and mostly written in order to develop the subject with ease... I believe that many current columnists should emulate the writing of Mr. Rowland.
Fred, ProfilProg

All four volumes are essentially icings on a huge, delicious prog cake and should be an integral part in every prog-lovers' cabinet.
Jan Buddenberg, DPRP.net

I continue to find these books extremely enjoyable and consider Kev a role model. "Read on" Kev indicates in his introduction. I fully concur.
Paul Rijkens, iO Pages

The Progressive Underground Vol 5

Robert Newton Calvert: Born 9 March 1945, Died 14 August 1988 after suffering a heart attack. Contributed poetry, lyrics and vocals to legendary space rock band Hawkwind intermittently on five of their most critically acclaimed albums, including Space Ritual (1973), Quark, Strangeness & Charm (1977) and Hawklords (1978). He also recorded a number of solo albums in the mid 1970s. CENTIGRADE 232 was Robert Calvert's first collection of poems.

Hype 'And now, for all you speeding street smarties out there, the one you've all been waiting for, the one that'll pierce your laid back ears, decoke your sinuses, cut clean thru the schlock rock, MOR/crossover, techno flash mind mush. It's the new Number One with a bullet ... with a bullet ... It's Tom, Supernova, Mahler with a pan galactic biggie ...' And the Hype goes on. And on. Hype, an amphetamine hit of a story by Hawkwind collaborator Robert Calvert. Who's been there and made it back again. The debriefing session starts here.

Rick Wakeman is the world's most unusual rock star, a genius who has pushed back the barriers of electronic rock. He has had some of the world's top orchestras perform his music, has owned eight Rolls Royces at one time, and has broken all the rules of composing and horrified his tutors at the Royal College of Music. Yet he has delighted his millions of fans. This frank book, authorised by Wakeman himself, tells the moving tale of his larger than life career.

The Progressive Underground Vol 5

 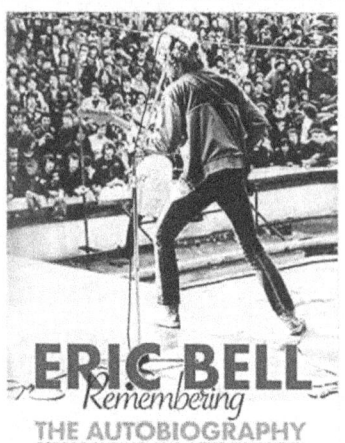

Who or what was Robin Hood? Brian Allan shows that the truth is very different from what tradition tells us. Was he a fearless fighter for truth and justice who robbed the rich to help the poor and oppressed, or was he simply an outlaw who robbed anyone who crossed his path and kept the proceeds for himself: or was something else entirely

Discover that the Robin Hood myth, complete with characters like the Merry Men, the wicked Sherriff of Nottingham and the beautiful Maid Marian, finds an exact match in tales from ancient India and beyond. Also discover that there was more than one Robin Hood and the origins of this character lie hidden deep within the legends of magical beings like 'Herne the Hunter', 'Jack o' the Woods' and the 'Green Man'. Even the title 'Robin Hood' was not a name, it was a definition and originally meant something entirely different. This book reveals that the legend of Robin Hood is exactly that, a legend, but designed to show that good always triumphs over evil, something that still resonates in the public imagination.

Porcupine Tree is an enigma. How do you categorise them?

Over 14 issues of *Voyage35*, I tried to seek out and define them. Just as I thought we, the fans, had it nailed, then Steven Wilson promptly changed styles or threw us a curveball. Unfortunately for some, the changes were too drastic and had moved too far from the origins of the band (or Steven's highly acclaimed bedroom tapes), whilst others, particularly from the US, embraced the new style.

Having seen Voyage35's selling for some quite exorbitant sums on E bay recently I thought it time to revisit the pages of the Fanzines and consolidate those articles that formed the essence of each issue.

Eric Robin Bell (born 3 September 1947 in Belfast, Northern Ireland) is a Northern Irish rock and blues musician, best known as a founding member and the original guitarist of the rock group Thin Lizzy from 1969 to 1973. After his time in Thin Lizzy, he briefly fronted his own group before joining The Noel Redding Band in the mid 1970s. He has since released several solo albums and performs regularly with a blues based trio, the Eric Bell Band.

The Progressive Underground Vol 5

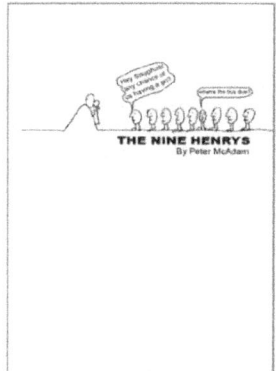

There are nine Henrys, purported to be the world's first cloned cartoon character. They live in a strange lo fi domestic surrealist world peopled by talking rock buns and elephants on wobbly stilts.

They mooch around in their minimalist universe suffering from an existential crisis with some genetically modified humour thrown in.

Marty Wilde on Terry Dene: "Whatever happened to Terry becomes a great deal more comprehensible as you read of the callous way in which he was treated by people who should have known better many of whom, frankly, will never know better of the sad little shadows of the past who eased themselves into Terry's life, took everything they could get and, when it seemed that all was lost, quietly left him … Dan Wooding's book tells it all."

Rick Wakeman: "There have always been certain 'careers' that have fascinated the public, newspapers, and the media in general. Such include musicians, actors, sportsmen, police, and not surprisingly, the people who give the police their employment: The criminal. For the man in the street, all these careers have one thing in common: they are seemingly beyond both his reach and, in many cases, understanding and as such, his only association can be through the media of newspapers or television. The police, however, will always require the services of the grass, the squealer, the snitch, (call him what you will), in order to assist in their investigations and arrests; and amazingly, this is the area that seldom gets written about."

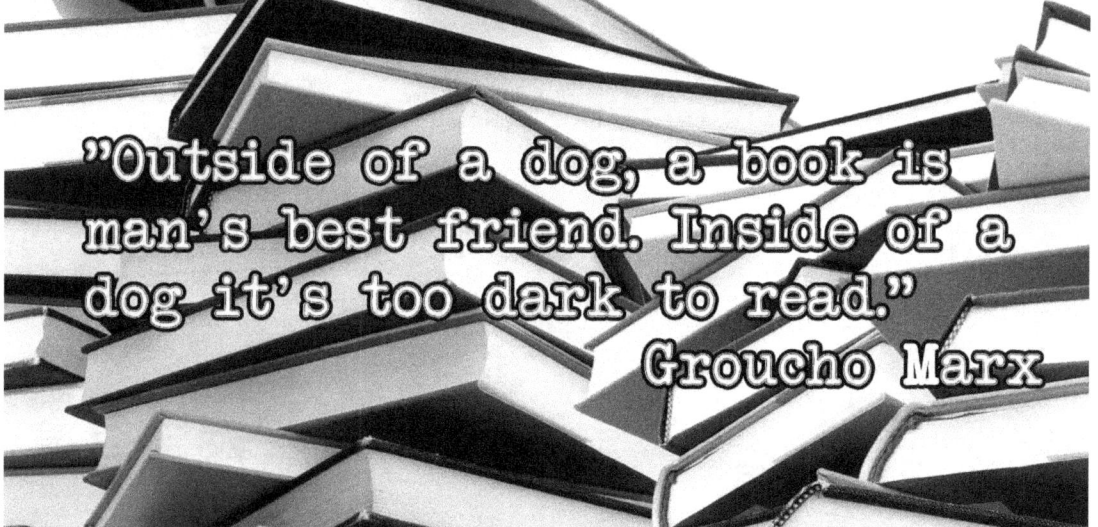

"Outside of a dog, a book is man's best friend. Inside of a dog it's too dark to read." Groucho Marx

The Progressive Underground Vol 5

THE COMPLETE OZ

OZ was an underground alternative magazine. First published in Sydney, Australia, in 1963, a second version appeared in London, England from 1967 and is better known.

The original Australian OZ took the form of a satirical magazine published between 1963 and 1969, while the British incarnation was a "psychedelic hippy" magazine which appeared from 1967 to 1973. Strongly identified as part of the underground press, it was the subject of two celebrated obscenity trials, one in Australia in 1964 and the other in the United Kingdom in 1971. On both occasions the magazine's editors were acquitted on appeal after initially being found guilty and sentenced to harsh jail terms. An earlier, 1963 obscenity charge was dealt with expeditiously when, upon the advice of a solicitor, the three editors pleaded guilty. The central editor throughout the magazine's life in both Australia and Britain was Richard Neville. Co editors of the Sydney version were Richard Walsh and Martin Sharp. Co editors of the London version were Jim Anderson and, later, Felix Dennis.

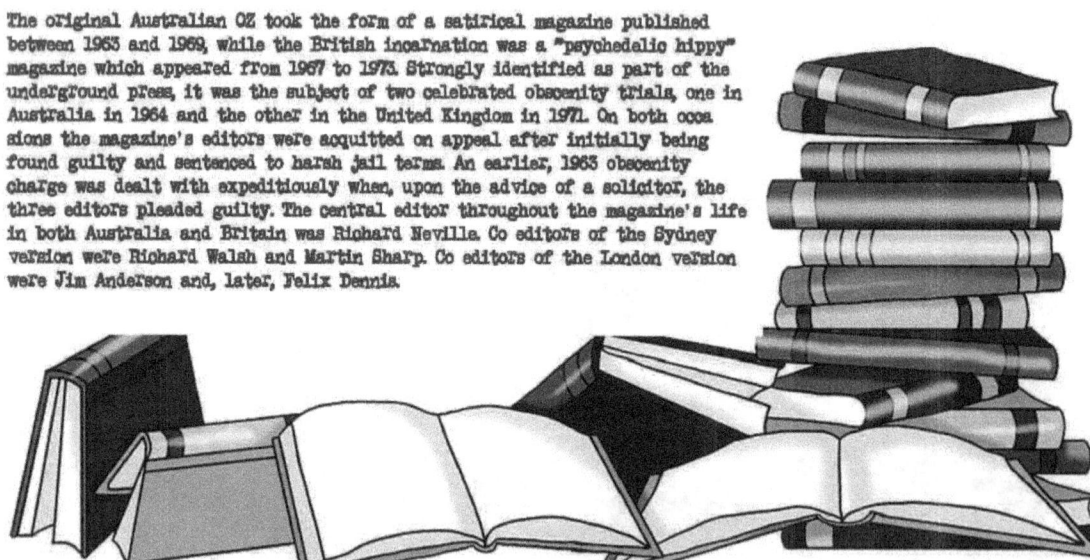

The Progressive Underground Vol 5

Bill Harkleroad joined Captain Beefheart's Magic Band at a time when they were changing from a straight ahead blues band into something completely different. Through the vision of Don Van Vliet (Captain Beefheart) they created a new form of music which many at the time considered atonal and difficult, but which over the years has continued to exert a powerful influence. Beefheart rechristened Harkleroad as Zoot Horn Rollo, and they embarked on recording one of the classic rock albums of all time Trout Mask Replica - a work of unequalled daring and inventiveness.

Politics, paganism and .... Vlad the Impaler. Selected stories from CJ Stone from 2003 to the present. Meet Ivor Coles, a British Tommy killed in action in September 1915, lost, and then found again. Visit Mothers Club in Erdington, the best psychedelic music club in the UK in the '60s. Celebrate Robin Hood's Day and find out what a huckle duckle is. Travel to Stonehenge at the Summer Solstice and carouse with the hippies. Find out what a Ranter is, and why CJ Stone thinks that he's one. Take LSD with Dr Lilly, the psychedelic scientist. Meet a headless soldier or the ghost of Elvis Presley in Gabalfa, Cardiff. Journey to Whitstable, to New York, to Malta and to Transylvania, and to many other places, real and imagined, political and spiritual, transcendent and mundane. As The Independent says, Chris is "The best guide to the underground since Charon ferried dead souls across the Styx."

OF PISCO AND PERU is a 'Fear and Loathing in Lima' meets 'Heart of Darkness' gonzo travelogue.

On the advice of his booze addled life coach, ne'er do well Doug ghosts his job and heads to Peru, where he meets Auntie M, a singing tour guide who's everything he's not. As the odd couple traverse the beaches, Andes and byways, Doug's South American dream lurches into a New World nightmare, and that's when things take a turn towards the insane.

How about this for a author's summary: ndy Duke has been writing gonzo from the get go, contributing articles in the virtual sphere for Gonzo Today, GoGonzo Journal, and Bad Literature, Inc. When he's not scribbling on his computer, you can be sure he's traveling, exploring, and searching for that perfect Pisco sour. Cheers

"The person, be it gentleman or lady, who has not pleasure in a good novel, must be intolerably stupid."

— Jane Austen

www.ingramcontent.com/pod-product-compliance
Lightning Source LLC
Chambersburg PA
CBHW082035230426
43670CB00016B/2662